HELLHOUND ON HIS TRAIL

HELLHOUND ON HIS TRAIL

. . . .

The Stalking of Martin Luther King Jr.

and the International Hunt for His Assassin

HAMPTON SIDES

Doubleday   *New York   London   Toronto   Sydney   Auckland*

DD

DOUBLEDAY

Copyright © 2010 by Hampton Sides

All rights reserved. Published in the United States by Doubleday,
a division of Random House, Inc., New York, and in Canada by
Random of Canada Limited, Toronto.

www.doubleday.com

Photo credits: Title page, Henry Groskinsky/Getty Images;
page 1, © Bettmann/CORBIS; page 11, AP/Wide World Photos;
page 385, © Bettmann/CORBIS

Book design by Maria Carella

Library of Congress Cataloging-in-Publication Data
Sides, Hampton.
   Hellhound on his trail : the stalking of Martin Luther King Jr. and the
international hunt for his assassin / Hampton Sides.—1st ed.
      p. cm.
   Includes bibliographical references.
   1. King, Martin Luther, Jr., 1929–1968—Assassination.   2. Ray,
James Earl, 1928–1998.   I. Title.
E185.97.K5S534 2009
364.152'4092—dc22   2009043659

ISBN 978-0-385-52392-9

PRINTED IN THE UNITED STATES OF AMERICA

10   9   8   7   6   5   4   3   2   1

First Edition

For McCall, Graham, and Griffin

The future looks bright

Discrimination is a hellhound that gnaws
at Negroes in every waking moment of their lives.

MARTIN LUTHER KING JR. (1967)

And the days keep on worrying me
There's a hellhound on my trail.

ROBERT JOHNSON (1937)

CONTENTS

I was just a kid when it happened—six years old, living in a rambling brick house on Cherry Road close by the Southern Railway. My father worked for the Memphis law firm that represented King when he came to town on behalf of the garbage workers, and I remember my dad rushing home that night, pouring a screwdriver or three, and talking with alarm about what had happened and what it meant for the city and the nation and the world. I remember the curfew, the wail of sirens, a line of soldiers with fixed bayonets. I remember seeing tanks for the first time. Mainly, I recall the fear in the adult voices coming over the radio and television—the undertow of panic, as it seemed to everyone that our city was ripping apart.

Four days after the assassination, Coretta Scott King arrived in Memphis, wearing her widow's veil, and led the peaceful march her husband could not lead. For several miles, tens of thousands of mourners threaded through the somber downtown streets to city hall. Enveloped in the beautiful sadness, no one breathed a word. There was no shouting or picketing, not even a song. The only sound was leather on pavement.

All writers sooner or later go back to the place where they came from. With this book, I wanted to go back to the *pivotal moment* in the place where I came from. In April 1968, a killer rode into a city I know and love. He set himself up with a high-powered rifle a few blocks from the Mississippi River and took aim at history. The shock waves still emanate from room 306 at the Lorraine Motel, and continue to register across the globe. The Lorraine has become an international shrine, visited by the likes of the Dalai Lama and Nelson Mandela and the boys from U2—a holy place. People come from all over the world to stand on the balcony where King stood, squinting in the humidity, surveying the sight lines of fate. They try to imagine what really happened, and what larger plots might have been stirring in the shadows.

The first writer I ever met, the great Memphis historian Shelby Foote, once said of his Civil War trilogy that he had "employed the novelist's methods without his license," and that's a good rule of thumb for what I've attempted here. Though I've tried to make the narrative as fluidly readable as possible, this is a work of nonfiction. Every scene is supported by the historical record. Every physical and atmospheric detail arises from factual evidence. And every conversation is reconstructed from documents. I've consulted congressional testimony, newspaper accounts, oral histories, memoirs, court proceedings, autopsy reports, archival news footage, crime scene photographs, and official reports filed by the Memphis authorities, the FBI, the U.S. Justice Department, the Royal Canadian Mounted Police, and Scotland Yard. Along the way, I've conducted scores of personal interviews and traveled tens of thousands of miles—from Puerto Vallarta to London, from St. Louis to Lisbon. Readers who are curious about how I constructed the narrative will find my sources cited in copious detail in the notes and bibliography.

As for King's assassin, I've let his story speak for itself. Whether witlessly, incidentally, or on purpose, he left behind a massive body of evidence. Much of my account of his worldwide travels comes from his own words. The rest comes from the record. The killer left his fingerprints, both literal and figurative, over everything.

HAMPTON SIDES, SANTA FE, NEW MEXICO

HELLHOUND ON HIS TRAIL

PROLOGUE

#416-J

. . . .

THE PRISON BAKERS sweated in the glare of the ovens, making bread for the hungry men of the honor farm. Since dawn, they'd prepared more than sixty loaves, and now the kitchen was redolent with the tang of yeast as the fresh bread cooled on the racks before slicing. A guard, armed but not very vigilant, patrolled the galley perimeter.

One of the bakers on this bright Sunday morning was Prisoner #00416-J, a slender, fair-skinned man in his late thirties whose raven hair was flecked with gray at the sideburns. Beneath a flour-dusted apron, he wore his standard-issue garb—a green cotton shirt and matching pants with a bright identifying stripe down the outseam. Convicted of armed robbery in 1960, 416-J had served seven years inside the Missouri State Penitentiary at Jefferson City; before that, he'd put in four grim years in Leavenworth for stealing—and fraudulently cashing—several thousand dollars' worth of postal money orders. He'd spent most of his adult life behind the bars of one jail or another and had become a stir-wise creature, canny to the ways of prison survival.

More than two thousand inmates were crammed inside "Jeff City," this vast Gothic bastille, which, upon its founding in 1836, was the first U.S. prison west of the Mississippi. Over the decades, it had developed a reputation as a school for rogues—and as one of America's most violent prisons. In 1954, a team of corrections experts described riot-prone Jeff City this way: "Square foot for square foot, it is the bloodiest forty-seven acres in America." Yet the prison complex was set in a lazy, almost bucolic part of the Midwest. Beyond the limestone walls, tugboats churned through the Missouri River, and Vs of geese honked in the haze along the flyway toward summer haunts. Freight trains could often be heard singing out their whistle sighs as they clacked and heaved on the old tracks that ran beside the river.

At Jeff City, 416-J had spent a lot of time looking out over that countryside, dreaming of how to get himself there. He'd become an old hand in the bakery; he had done kitchen work for years and never made any trouble—in fact he scarcely drew any attention to himself at all. Most prison officials didn't know his name and could barely recall his face—to them he was just another inmate with a number. One Jeff City warden described him as "penny ante." A corrections commissioner put it slightly more bluntly: "He was just a *nothing* here."

A state psychiatrist had examined 416-J the year before and had found that though he wasn't outright crazy, he was "an interesting and rather complicated individual—a sociopathic personality who is severely neurotic." He was intelligent enough, with an IQ of 106, slightly above average. But the psychiatrist noted that the prisoner suffered from "undue anxiety" and "obsessive compulsive concerns" about his physical health. He was a thoroughgoing hypochondriac, always complaining of maladies and poring over medical books. He imagined he had heart palpitations and suffered from some strange malformation of his cranium. He often could be seen with a stopwatch in hand, checking his own pulse. His stomach bothered him, necessitating that he eat bland foods. He took Librium for his nerves and various painkillers for his nearly incessant headaches, but the doctor thought he should have more attention.

"It is felt that he is in need of psychiatric help," the state shrink observed in closing. "He is becoming increasingly concerned about himself." This evaluation could have been used to describe a lot of prisoners in Jeff City—maybe hundreds of them—so the corrections officers paid little attention to the psychiatrist's report.

■

IF THE GUARDS had been watching him closely during the past few weeks of April 1967, they would have observed that 416-J was behaving strangely. He had been plowing through travel books about Mexico and checked out an English-Spanish dictionary from the prison library. He experimented with making his skin darker by applying a walnut dye. He drank considerable quantities of mineral oil (one of the many odd health remedies he swore by) and stayed up far into the night, his mind racing with ideas.

Often as not, those ideas were fueled by amphetamines, which by whatever name—speed, bennies, splash, spaniels—were rife inside the walls of Jeff City. He usually took the drug in pill or powder form, but he also shot up with needles, and he was known among the prison population as a "merchant" in the amphetamine trade. "When he was using," said one inmate who'd known him for years, "he would lay down in his cell and he would think. He would say how it made his mind clear up. He would go all the way back until he was six or seven years old. Or, he might go over a job and see the mistakes he had made."

Lately, 416-J had been practicing yoga in his cell, or at least something that *looked* like yoga. He would curl himself in a tiny ball and hold the position for hours, straining to crunch his body into the tightest possible space. This human pretzeling might have looked odd to a guard walking the cell block, but then 416-J was always doing push-ups and calisthenics, always grunting and walking on his hands and carrying on in there.

But there was something else: just the day before, on April 22, 416-J had received a guest down in the visitation room. This was highly unusual—he was a loner who seemed to have no family or friends on the outside. The prison grapevine had it that the visitor was his brother from St. Louis, but 416-J would not talk about it to anyone.

At around eight o'clock this morning, he was allowed to leave his cell and head up to the kitchen. He toted a small sack of toiletries, which drew no one's attention, since culinary employees like him were allowed to shower and shave in the kitchen bathroom. He took the elevator up to the bakery, arriving well before the start of his eleven o'clock shift. He proceeded to cook—and devour—a rather astonishing quantity of eggs: one dozen.

Then 416-J slipped into the break room, ostensibly to wash up. Inside his sack were a small mirror, a comb, a razor with several extra blades, a bar of soap, and twenty candy bars. There was also a Channel Master pocket transistor radio that he'd bought from the prison canteen two days earlier. As required by Jeff City rules, the number 00416, in tiny print, was permanently etched on the side of the radio's housing. In his shoes, pressing uncomfortably into the soles of his feet, were two wads of cash totaling nearly three hundred dollars.

Somewhere in the break room, several days earlier, 416-J had hidden a clean white shirt, and a pair of prison pants that he had dyed black with stencil ink, taking special care to cover up the telltale stripe down the side. Quickly, he removed his prison garb, then slipped on the black pants and white shirt. He put his prison uniform *back on*, so that he now wore two layers of clothing.

Next, 416-J took the elevator down to the loading dock area, where a hinged metal box had been partially loaded with fresh bread for the honor farm. The box—four feet by three feet by three feet—was easily large enough for a man to climb inside. And that's exactly what the prisoner did. He crushed several layers of the warm soft bread as he eased himself into the box, and then curled into a tight fetal ball.

At this point he must have had an accomplice—or several accomplices—because a false bottom, punctured with tiny holes for ventilation, was placed on top of him. And then, above that, several more layers of bread were loaded into the box until it was filled. The hinged lid was closed tight. Then the box was dollied outside and placed near the lip of the loading dock.

A few minutes later, a freight truck pulled up. Two inmates hoisted the bread crate into the bed of the truck, which was enclosed with a canopy on three sides but open in the rear. When the prisoners waved the truck on, the driver pulled out from the loading area and approached the security tunnel. An officer came out and inspected the vehicle for a stowaway. He checked the undercarriage and the engine. Then he climbed up into the truck bed to examine the cargo.

The prisoner, hot and clammy inside his tight berth, breathed uneasily in the doughy fumes as someone above him opened the lid of the bread box. The guard thumped and shook the container a bit but saw to his satisfaction that the loaves were stacked all the way to the top. The prisoner must have sighed in relief as he heard the box lid swing shut.

Stepping back from the truck, the guard nodded his okay. The gate clicked open and the driver roared on, bound for the honor farm.

■

THAT SAME MORNING, at precisely the moment 416-J was making his escape, a politician whom the prisoner greatly admired sat a thousand miles away in an NBC television studio. Facing questions from the moderator, Lawrence Spivak of *Meet the Press*, this controversial figure announced to the country that he was considering running for the White House. His name was George C. Wallace, the former governor of Alabama who had stunned the nation a few years earlier by standing in the schoolhouse door at the University of Alabama to prevent integration.

The forty-seven-year-old George Wallace was a firebrand who typically pranced and fulminated and played to the audience with his energetically arching beetled brows; it was sometimes said that he could strut while sitting. On this morning, however, Wallace tried to project an air of presidential sophistication and calm. He wore a crisp suit, modulated his voice, and kept his stage theatrics to a minimum. His usual oil slick of hair seemed to shine just a little less greasily. He was not a racist, Wallace wanted to assure the nation, and his campaign was not predicated on a "backlash against anybody of color."

However, he added, "There *is* a backlash against big government in this country." He looked deep into the camera, his bituminous eyes lit up for the millions of Americans who were waking across the heartland.

"This is a movement of the people," he said, "and it doesn't make any difference whether the leading politicians endorse it or not." His campaign would focus on the "average man in the street . . . this man in the textile mill, this man in the steel mill, the barber, the beautician, the policeman on the beat, the little businessman. They are the ones. Those are the mass of people that are going to support a change on the domestic scene in this country."

Then, with a faint snarl, Wallace squinted at the camera and said: "If the politicians get in the way of this movement, a lot of them are going to get run over."

■

Once outside the walls of Jeff City, 416-J crawled out of the box, trampling and mashing the bread as he wriggled himself free. The bread was so ruined that when it arrived at its destination, the farmhands gave it all to the chickens. Standing in the truck bed under the covered canopy, the prisoner stripped out of his uniform and stuffed the old green prison clothes in his sack. Having peeled down to his dyed black pants and white shirt, he now looked passably like a civilian. The truck crossed over the river and was now moving along at nearly fifty miles an hour, too fast for him to make a safe exit. But when the driver slowed for a few seconds at the graveled entrance to the farm, the prisoner leaped out of the back. The truck chuffed on—the driver hadn't seen him in his mirror.

Now 416-J walked hurriedly down to the river's edge. He made for an old junkyard near the bridge and hid in the weeds among the rusted husks of abandoned cars, keeping his ears tuned all day for the sound of men on horseback or the yelping of bloodhounds. Every so often he turned on his little transistor radio for bulletins announcing his escape. So far, so good: the newscasts mentioned nothing, although soon the Missouri Corrections Department would put out a "Wanted" notice with a modest reward of fifty dollars for his recapture.

Once darkness descended, he crossed back over the river and began walking west along the railroad tracks toward Kansas City—which was a ruse, for he had no intention of going to Kansas City. The prison officials knew he had family in St. Louis (about a hundred miles due east), and they would naturally suspect that he'd head in that direction. By walking west toward Kansas, he hoped he could buy some time.

So for six days he clomped west along the railroad tracks, eating his stash of candy bars, drinking water from the occasional spring, and lighting campfires with matches he stole from an old trailer. "I looked at the stars a lot," he said later. "I hadn't seen them for quite a while." One night a couple of railroad crewmen startled him as he warmed himself by the fire. He told them he'd been hunting along the river and had gotten drenched. They seemed to buy his story and left him alone. But then another night he saw state troopers patrolling the rural road that paralleled the tracks, and he was sure they were on his scent.

By the sixth day, however, he began to sense that the heat was off. He kept listening to his radio and was surprised that the newscasts made no mention of his escape. Somewhere along the way, he found a file or some other suitable tool and tried to rub away his prison number—00416—from the housing of the radio.

On the sixth night, he saw a little store in the distance, its lights gleaming invitingly. Not wanting to look like a desperado, he cleaned himself as best he could and shambled inside. He bought sandwiches and some beer—the first real food he'd had since the enormous mess of eggs he'd fixed for himself in the prison bakery.

He was ravenous, footsore, and irritable from a fugitive week of tense nerves relieved by little sleep. But now, as he ate his sandwiches, he might have allowed himself a smirk of satisfaction. *A bread box!* He had to savor it, had to congratulate the classic beauty of the feat. Jeff City was an impossible joint to break out of—that's what he'd always heard, that's what most of its denizens believed. In the institutional memory of the place, there had only been three known escapes—and they had all failed.

He'd been stuck inside Jeff City's sad gray ramparts for seven years, and he had another eighteen hanging over him. While there, he'd organized his life around the goal of escape—it was the central idea that had focused and sustained him. He'd scrimped and schemed in the shadows of a deliberate and tenacious obscurity. He'd perfected a kind of anti-identity, so that no one would notice him when he was there—or miss him when he was gone.

That night, 416-J called his brother and arranged a rendezvous spot. Then he hopped an eastbound freight train. Feeling what must have been some mixture of anxiety and delight, he rolled past the Jeff City prison complex. How many jittery nights had he lain awake in his prison cell, listening to the whistle of locomotives running over these same tracks that now gave him flight?

Sprung from Jeff City's walls, he let his mind begin to churn with thoughts of other jobs, other projects of greater complexity and ambition. But now he was heading home, in the direction of St. Louis.

BOOK ONE

IN THE CITY OF THE KINGS

. . . .

When I took up the cross I recognized its meaning . . . The cross is something that you bear and ultimately that you die on.

MARTIN LUTHER KING JR. (1967)

IN EARLY MAY 1967, three hundred miles downstream from St. Louis, the citizens of Memphis stood along the cobblestoned banks, enjoying the musky coolness of the river. Seventy-five thousand people, dressed to be seen, waited in the twilight. They'd come from all the secret krewes— from the Mystic Society of the Memphi, from Osiris and RaMet and Sphinx. They'd come from all the clubs—Chickasaw, University, Colonial, Hunt and Polo, the Memphis Country Club—and from the garden societies. The good families, the old families, in their finest James Davis clothes, bourbon flasks in hand, assembled for the start of the South's Greatest Party.

The brown Mississippi, wide with northern snowmelt, was a confusion of crosscurrents and boils. In the main channel, whole trees could be seen shooting downstream. A mile across the river lay the floodplain of Arkansas, a world of chiggers and alligator gars and water moccasins that lived in swampy oxbow lakes. On the long sandbars, feral pigs ran among graveyards of driftwood and rotten cypress stumps.

But in the clearings beyond these wild margins were hundreds and hundreds of miles of cotton fields. Cotton as far as the eye could see, row after perfect row. *Gossypium hirsutum.* White gold, mined from the world's richest alluvium.

Memphis was built on the spot where the Spanish explorer Hernando de Soto, in 1541, became the first European to lay eyes on the Mississippi River. The city was founded 278 years later by Andrew Jackson and a group of his investor cronies, and named for the ancient Egyptian capital near the Giza pyramids. Memphis didn't really take off, however, until the dense hardwood forests along the river began to be cleared in the mid-nineteenth century, finally making farmable the flat, rich floodplain known as the Mississippi Delta. As the country slid toward Civil War, Memphis became the capital of a region that was constructing a last frenzied iteration of Southern planter society. If the Delta came late to cotton, it came to it with a vengeance, and with all the defiant desperation of someone following a wounded creed.

Cotton had grown along the Nile near the original Memphis, and cotton was what modern Memphis had come to celebrate on this fine humid evening of May 10, 1967. In the fields of Arkansas, and down in nearby Mississippi, the little darlings had already begun to push through the dirt, the crop dusters were preparing to rain down their chemicals, and the old true cycle was in the offing. Now it was time for Memphians to pay homage and to bless another season in cotton's splendid realm.

The thirty-third annual Cotton Carnival, Memphis's answer to Mardi Gras, was about to begin. Later in the week, there would be luncheons, trade shows, and charity balls. A beauty contest would declare the fairest Maid of Cotton. Many thousands would visit the giant midway and attend parades with elaborate floats, some of them spun from cotton, depicting the gone-but-not-forgotten Old South and the treachery of the long-snouted boll weevil. All week there would be parties on the rooftop of the Peabody Hotel, where mallard ducks lived in a scaled-down mansion when they weren't marching down a red carpet to splash around in the lobby fountain.

Tonight was the high pageant that kicked off the whole week—the majestic arrival of the King and Queen, sitting upon their thrones with their sequined court all around them, on a great glittery barge that was scheduled to nudge into the Memphis harbor shortly after sunset. It was a celebration not only of cotton but also of the peculiarly settled life that thrived on it—the life of dove hunts and pig roasts and debutante balls, the genteel agrarian world that could still be found in the fertile realms surrounding Memphis.

Cotton, cotton everywhere. Crane operators, hoisting dozens of five-hundred-pound cotton bales, had constructed colossal arches that spanned the downtown streets. All attendees were urged to wear cotton, and they did: party girls in crinoline dresses, dandies in seersucker suits, children in starched oxford cloth. People even ate cotton candy while they waited with the crowds for the Royal Barge to arrive.

Representatives from all echelons of the Delta cotton world had joined the masses on the river—the factors, the classers, the ginners, the brokers, the seed sellers, the plantation owners, the compress owners, the board members of the Cotton Exchange, the loan officers from the Union Planters Bank, the chemical engineers who'd learned how to tease out the plant's oils and secret compounds for every industrial purpose Mammon could devise.

Cotton's presence, and cotton's past, could be felt everywhere along the shadowed waterfront. Behind the cheering crowds, high on the magnolia-lined bluff once occupied by Chickasaw Indians, sat Confederate Park, with its bronze statue of Jefferson Davis, who'd made his home in Memphis after the Civil War. A block from the park was the place on Adams Avenue where Nathan Bedford Forrest once operated a giant slave market, said to be the South's largest, that boasted "the best selected assortment of field hands, house servants, and mechanics . . . with fresh supplies of likely Young Negroes."

Running lengthwise along the same bluff lay Front Street, cotton's main drag. In the upstairs classing rooms, sharp-eyed savants still graded cotton samples by pure intuition under north-facing skylights—judging according to quaint industry distinctions like "strict low middling" or "strict good ordinary." Memphis remained one of the largest cotton markets in the world, with massive fortunes made and lost and made again. Many of the names were legends—Dunavant, Cook, Turley, Hohenberg, Allenberg—high rollers in a vaguely druidic enterprise. In October, during harvest time, the skies above Front Street still swirled with snows of lint.

Cotton cotton cotton. Memphis couldn't get enough of it. Cotton was still king. It would always be king.

■

IN TRUTH, THOUGH no one wanted to talk about it on that roistering night in 1967, the old world of Delta cotton was in serious trouble. Life on the plantations had changed so fast it was hardly recognizable. Soybeans had made inroads as the new mono-crop of choice. Polyester had encroached upon the American wardrobe. Massive mechanized cotton pickers, along with new soups of pesticides and herbicides, had rendered largely obsolete the life of the Delta sharecropper. Thus demoted by petrochemicals and machines, many thousands of black field hands and their families steadily left the plantations over the decades and came to Memphis—the nearest city, and the only American city of any size named after an African capital.

Other than mule skinning or chopping cotton, though, most Delta field hands had little in the way of marketable skills when they came to the city. Some found success playing the blues on Beale Street—the central thoroughfare of black Memphis. But most settled into low-end jobs that merely recapitulated the racial and socioeconomic hierarchy they'd known on the plantations. Many became maids, janitors, waiters, yardmen, cooks, stevedores. Some had no choice but to take the lowest-end job of all: they reported to the Public Works Department and became garbagemen.

At least they'd come to a city with a history that was rich and gothic and weird. Memphis, this city of 600,000 people wedged in the southwestern crotch of Tennessee, had always had a touch of madness but also a prodigious and sometimes profane sense of humor. It was a town known for its outlandish characters and half-demented geniuses: wrestlers, riverboat captains, inventors, gamblers, snake-oil salesmen, musicians high on some peculiar native vibe that could be felt but whose existence could not be proved. For 150 years, all the pain and pathos of the river seemed to wash up on the cobblestoned banks. In 1878, the city was nearly completely destroyed by a yellow fever epidemic, but the Metropolis of the American Nile had recovered, madder and stranger and more full of brawling ambition than ever. Memphis, as one writer famously put it, "was built on a bluff and run on the same principle."

It was a city that, since its very inception, had been perched on the racial fault line. The first mayor, Marcus Brutus Winchester, created a major scandal by falling for, and eventually marrying, a "woman of color." One of the area's most fascinating citizens in the late 1820s, a Scottish-born utopian named Fanny Wright, created an experimental commune of slaves whom she sought to educate and bring into full citizenship. Several generations later, Memphis gave the world Ida B. Wells, an early titan of the civil rights movement, a woman of profound courage who, in the 1890s, repeatedly risked assassination with eloquent protests against lynching. Then there was the ever-cryptic Mr. Forrest, who quit his slave mart and took up a sword in the Civil War, becoming one of the most wickedly brilliant generals in American history. After the war he returned to Memphis, where, after briefly serving as the first Grand Wizard of the Ku Klux Klan, he apparently experienced an epiphany—renouncing the Klan with seeming genuineness and calling for racial reconciliation shortly before his death.

But music was the city's greatest gift and particular genius: the blues of W. C. Handy's Beale Street, the soul of Stax Records, and a certain interracial sound stew that a redneck wizard named Sam Phillips cooked up in a tiny studio on Union Avenue, less than a hundred yards from where Forrest lay buried. At its essence, the music of Memphis was about the fecund intermingling of black and white. Elvis Presley, coaxed and prodded by Phillips, found a way to transmute the raw sound of Beale Street into something that would resonate across the world. The stars, white and black, who had passed through the studios and nightclubs of Memphis were as numerous as they were legendary: not just Elvis, but Rufus Thomas, Johnny Cash, B. B. King, Albert King, Carl Perkins, Ike Turner, Jerry Lee Lewis, Carla Thomas, Isaac Hayes, Roy Orbison, Muddy Waters, Howlin' Wolf, Otis Redding, John Lee Hooker, Memphis Minnie, Memphis Slim. The phantom-like Robert Johnson, perhaps the greatest of the Delta bluesmen, lived in and around Memphis much of his short, tragic life. It could be argued that over the decades, Memphis's musical ferment had done more to integrate the country than a hundred pieces of legislation.

In a way, cotton was at the center of the ferment, for cotton had spawned the blues, and cotton had built the city that gave the blues its first wider expression. But there was no mistaking the fact that most black folks in Memphis were good and done with cotton, and they hated most everything about the hairy prickly shrub that had so long enslaved them. Certainly not many black people were to be found on the banks of the river on that May night in 1967, awaiting the arrival of the Royal Barge.

■

THE SKIES OVER Arkansas ripened to a final brilliant red before closing into darkness. It seemed as though the sun had literally buried itself in cotton fields. An orchestra played strains of Vivaldi, and the heavens crackled with fireworks.

Then, from under the bridge, the dazzling vessel slipped into view, with the crowds gasping in wonder. At first it was just a burst of bright light, a diaphanous vision floating out on the currents. As it drew nearer to the harbor, the ravishing details began to emerge. The barge was the size of a football field, with a giant art deco cotton boll rising over the sparkling set. Egyptian motifs were woven into the decorations—pyramids, sphinxes, hieroglyphics: the Old South meets the land of the pharaohs.

Seated on their thrones high up in the towering boll were King Joseph and Queen Blanche, 1967's monarchs, wearing their crowns, holding their scepters. As always, they'd been chosen in secret, by some obscure protocol known only to the Mystic Society of the Memphi. As always, he was an older man, a business potentate, while she was a nubile paragon of Southern pulchritude, college aged and presumably a virgin. They were blindingly white people, in blindingly white clothes, sitting high in their resplendent perch. In unison, they cupped their gloved hands and gave the crowds tiny swiveling waves, as if to say, *Here we are! . . . There you are! . . . We're all here!*

More than a hundred people made up the royal court, all posed together on the barge like the largest wedding party ever assembled. There were the duchesses, the counts, the pages, the princesses and their tuxedoed escorts. There were the young girls, who curtsied with labored formality and attended the train of Her Majesty's gown. There were the weevils, the masked green jesters whose identities were unknown. On one side of the Royal Barge stood the Ladies of the Realm—belles from plantation towns all over the Mississippi Delta. On the other side were the Ladies-in-Waiting—belles from the city, from good families, and of marriageable age.

The court moved about the barge in a carefully choreographed promenade. Everyone was smiling, bowing, waving, beaming. "Don't get wise with me," the king warned, "or I'll have you all beheaded." When the music reached a fever pitch, King Joseph and Queen Blanche rose and took a bow. All along the bluff, the seventy-five thousand loyal subjects erupted in thunderous cheers: Hail, King Cotton and His Queen!

Then, in a swirl of lights, the court began to parade off the stage, and off the barge, and onto the old cobblestones, the royals closely guarded by uniformed young men dressed as Confederate colonels. Like Peabody ducks, the revelers strutted down a long red carpet to a waiting convoy of Cadillac convertibles and were whisked away to the first parties of the season.

2 ▪ GOING FOR BROKE

SIX MONTHS LATER, in November 1967, Martin Luther King Jr. found himself in Frogmore, in the swampy Low Country of South Carolina not far from Hilton Head, where his civil rights organization, the Southern Christian Leadership Conference, was having its annual conclave. King had decided to use the retreat as a platform to announce a bold new direction for the SCLC. With nearly a hundred staffers, board members, and volunteers in attendance, he would unveil an ambitious turn in the organization's focus. It would be controversial, radical, revolutionary in scope.

King had decided that late next spring—the spring of 1968—he would return to the Washington Mall, the site of his triumphant "I have a dream" speech. Only this time, he envisioned something much more confrontational than an afternoon of soaring oratory. Instead, he would bring an army of poor people from all around the country—not just African-Americans, but indigents from various Indian tribes, whites from Appalachia, Chicanos, Puerto Ricans, Eskimos, Pacific islanders from the U.S. territories. They would camp out on the Mall for weeks, living in a vast shantytown at the foot of the monuments. They would paralyze the city. They would tie up traffic. They would hold daily sit-ins in the halls of government. They would occupy the nation's capital and refuse to leave until their demands were met. It would be an act of civil disobedience on a scale never witnessed before. The only precedent that King could come up with was the Bonus Marchers, the World War I veterans who descended on Washington in the summer of 1932 to claim their promised benefits.

King had been moving in this direction for years, but his thinking had really crystallized over the summer, after the horrific riots in Detroit and Newark led him to believe that America—its structures and its practices, its very *idea*—was in serious trouble. "For years," he said, "I labored with reforming the existing institutions of society, a little change here, a little change there. Now I feel quite differently. I think you've got to have a reconstruction of the entire society, a revolution of values."

America, he believed, was now a sick society in need of "radical moral surgery." It had become arrogant, selfish, more interested in things than in people. Washington was moving forward with its disastrous war in Southeast Asia while pursuing Cold War policies that seemed to be taking the world to the brink of nuclear annihilation. "My own government," he said, has become "the greatest purveyor of violence in the world today."

The specter of mass riots was a symptom of a larger disease within the body politic, he said. Consumed by Vietnam, the space race, and other expensive military-industrial projects, the government was unwilling to confront the appalling conditions in the ghettos of America. This lack of compassion was shortsighted, he felt, for if something wasn't done immediately, there would be more riots next summer—much more destructive riots. King genuinely feared the country might slip into a race war that would lead, ultimately, to a right-wing takeover and a kind of fascist police state.

Some of the root problems had to do with capitalism itself, he argued. For years, King had been accused of being a secret Communist, which was flatly untrue, but for several years he *had* been moving toward advocating a form of democratic socialism similar to that practiced in Scandinavia (a notion inspired in part by his 1964 visit to Sweden and Norway to collect his Nobel Peace Prize). "The good and just society," he said, "is neither the thesis of capitalism nor the antithesis of communism, but a socially conscious democracy which reconciles the truths of individualism *and* collectivism."

King's vision for a poor people's descent on Washington had grown out of months of soul-searching, and a summer he spent living in a tenement in one of Chicago's worst slums. He'd been thinking closely and intensely about poverty—its origins, solutions, and effects. He viewed the new campaign as an alternative to riots, a last chance for nonviolence. His Poor People's Army would demand that the government initiate a kind of Marshall Plan to attack poverty in America—programs for mass job creation, health care, better schools, and a guaranteed minimum income for every person in the land.

He realized this was much more radical than anything he had ever attempted before; it would be a tough sell at any time, but especially in wartime. He understood that the project he was undertaking lacked the logistical and moral clarity of the old days of the civil rights movement, when the evils seemed so manifest, and when the nation seemed more easily swayed by his ferocious eloquence. Instead of asking for something that was already guaranteed in the Constitution, he was now asking the country to dig deep into its coffers to solve one of humanity's most ancient and intractable problems. "It didn't cost the nation one penny to integrate lunch counters," King said. "It didn't cost the nation one penny to guarantee the right to vote. But now, we are dealing with issues that cannot be solved without the nation spending billions of dollars—and undergoing a radical redistribution of economic power."

Nonetheless, King insisted that the SCLC forge ahead with the campaign, this epic *camp-in*. "I'm on fire about this thing," he told his staff in Frogmore. "We've got to go for broke this time."

■

MOST OF KING's aides were *not* "on fire" with the idea, however. They thought the Poor People's Campaign sounded quixotic from the start—and worse, that it reflected their leader's troubled state of mind.

By the fall of 1967, Martin Luther King had become stressed to the breaking point. At age thirty-eight, he had been doing civil rights work, nonstop, for twelve years. His life was not his own. His punishing schedule, his late nights and endless traveling—what his aides called his

"War on Sleep"—had taken a toll. He was smoking and drinking too much, gaining weight, downing sleeping pills that seemed to have no effect. He received death threats almost daily. His marriage was crumbling. His criticism of the Vietnam War had lost him nearly all his key allies in Washington. Increasingly, he was viewed as a once-great leader past his prime.

Certainly he was no longer welcome at the White House. Martin Luther King and Lyndon Johnson had made history together—collaborating on the passage of the landmark Civil Rights Act of 1964 and Voting Rights Act of 1965—but now Johnson wouldn't even talk to King. The president viewed him as a traitor, once calling him "that nigger preacher."

Though still widely revered, King had slipped in stature, even among his own people. That year, for the first time in a decade, King didn't make the Gallup Poll's "Ten Most Popular Americans" list. His base of support had been slowly eroding for several years. In 1965, when he showed up in Los Angeles during the Watts riots, black folks *booed* him on the streets. His vision of nonviolent protest was losing purchase in the ghettos. Many young people called him "Da Lawd" and dismissed him as an out-of-touch Southern preacher, square and behind the times. The black-power movement, led by young radicals like Stokely Carmichael and H. Rap Brown, was in the ascendancy. King seemed in constant danger of being outflanked.

At times he thought about quitting the movement altogether. Why should he keep going? He'd done and suffered enough. Ever since 1955, when he reluctantly agreed to become the spokesman of the Montgomery bus boycott, history had seized him and wouldn't let go. His bravery was staggering. He'd been jailed eighteen times. His house had been fire-bombed. He'd been stabbed by a deranged black woman, punched in the face by a Nazi, and struck in the head with a rock. He'd marched all over the country, in the face of tear gas, police dogs, cattle prods, and water cannons. No one knew how many times he'd been burned in effigy. And everywhere he went, the FBI was on his tail, watching, listening.

Sometimes he dreamed about following a simpler life as a full-time pastor, or an academic, or an author. Other times he talked about taking a vow of poverty, giving up his few belongings, and spending a year abroad. At the very least, he knew he should go on a brief sabbatical, get away from the movement and collect his thoughts. "I'm tired of all this traveling I have to do," he told his church congregation in Atlanta. "I'm killing myself and killing my health. I'm *tired* now." Living under the daily threat of death, he said, "I feel discouraged every now and then and feel my work's in vain. But then the Holy Spirit revives my soul again."

■

IN THE END, King couldn't extricate himself if he tried. The movement was, literally, his life. He had no choice but to take the struggle to its next logical phase.

As he saw it, the central issue had shifted from the purely racial to the economic. King likened the situation to a lifelong prisoner who is released from jail after the warden discovers that the man was falsely accused all along. "Go ahead, you're free now," the jailer says. But the prisoner has no job skills, no prospects, and the jailer doesn't think to give him money for the bus fare into town.

The Poor People's Campaign, then, would address the lengthened shadow of slavery, the *economic* shadow. King prevailed over his skeptical staff. The SCLC would devote the intervening months to organizing the great campaign.

King returned home to Atlanta buoyed by his decision at Frogmore. On December 4, he gave a press conference. "The Southern Christian Leadership Conference will lead waves of the nation's poor and disinherited to Washington next spring," he announced to a somewhat perplexed national media. "We don't know what will happen," he said. "They may try to run us out. They did it with the Bonus Marchers years ago, you remember."

King was the first to admit that his plan was risky. But *not* to act, he said, "represents moral irresponsibility. We were told when we went into Birmingham that Congress wouldn't move. We were told the same thing when we went to Selma. We have found throughout our experience that timid supplication for justice will not solve the problem. We have got to confront the power structure massively."

He was anxious to get started on what would be the most sweeping project of his career. "This," he said, "is a kind of last, desperate demand for the nation to respond to nonviolence."

ON AN EMPTY beach outside of Puerto Vallarta, brushed by the sibilance of Colima palms, Eric Galt aimed his camera at the young Mexican woman stretched across the sand. Fussing with his new Polaroid 220 Land camera, he tried to find the right plays of light, tried to frame a shot like the ones he'd seen in the pinup magazines.

It was a warm tropical day in November 1967. Through his viewfinder, Galt could see the waves tunneling in from the Pacific. At his back, the foothills climbed steeply toward a jungle of orchids and bromeliads, its canopy swarming with parrots.

The monsoon season had ended, and the atmosphere had taken on a new crispness, so that Galt could see across the Bahía de Banderas, the second-largest bay in North America, to the shaggy headlands of Punta de Mita far to the north. Along the great scallop of shoreline were scores of secret beaches like this one, some of them reachable only by boat, hidden places where tourists could linger all day and fry like wild Calibans in the sun.

The beach that Galt had found was so secluded that his model, a local girl named Manuela Medrano, had little cause to feel self-conscious;

save for the ubiquitous fishing *pangas* bobbing in the distance, the photographer and his subject had the place all to themselves.

At one point, Galt told Manuela to climb behind the wheel of his Mustang, put her feet on the dashboard, and hike up her skirt. She giggled and smiled, but she was happy to oblige him, and he began to photograph her from different angles. Such exhibitionism was nothing out of the ordinary for her; though she was only twenty-three years old, Manuela had long worked in a brothel called the Casa Susana—Puerto Vallarta's largest—where she was considered one of the marquee attractions.

Galt played with the instant camera some more, coaching Manuela on her poses. He'd snap a shot, remove the exposed film, and watch the image resolve before his eyes.

A pale, nervous man in his late thirties with a lanky build, Galt knew nothing about the art or business of photography, but he was eager to learn. For some time, he'd been toying with the idea of getting into the porn industry, X-rated films as well as girlie magazines. It was one of several business schemes swimming in his head. He imagined that one day he would manage a stable of talent, with publishing connections, distribution connections, connections to buy off the law. He was ambitious and willing to work hard. He knew that if he ever hoped to become a player, he would first have to master all his new equipment.

Through a mail-order catalog, he had recently bought a Kodak Super 8 movie camera, a Kodak Dual projector and splicing machine, a twenty-foot remote-control cable, and various accessories. He also looked into purchasing sound stripers, a sound projector, and an automatic cine printer to run off copies of the films he eventually hoped to make. He read *Modern Photography* magazine. He procured sex manuals and sex toys. He studied the smut magazines to learn what looks were selling and noted that publishers particularly liked to have pictures set in exotic foreign locales—like secluded beaches in the tropics.

But when Galt examined his Polaroids of Manuela, he was cross with himself. The images didn't grab him; they were flat and uninteresting. Perhaps he was beginning to fear he had no talent behind the camera. Manuela could see the frustration on his face. Visibly upset, he took the Polaroids and tore them all up.

∎

Eric Starvo Galt had ridden into Puerto Vallarta on Highway 200 three weeks earlier. On that afternoon—Thursday, October 19—he checked in to the Hotel Rio at the end of the cobblestoned main drag and just a block from the beach. The Rio was a modest but respectable enough place with white stucco walls, iron-lace balustrades, and a roof of Spanish tiles. For about four bucks a night, he secured a second-floor room that overlooked the river Cuale, where fishermen would string nets across the brackish water and fry their catch in the shade of the rubber trees that lined the musky banks.

The hotel management didn't know what to make of this mysterious new guest. Galt was a fidgety gringo who wore shades and mumbled when he spoke. His two-door Mustang hardtop was a 1966 model with mud-splattered whitewall tires and Alabama license plates. Galt told the front desk he was a "publisher's assistant," but he told others around town that he was a writer on vacation. He kept a manual typewriter in his room, and he sometimes stayed up late at night pecking away at the keys while listening to a pocket transistor radio.

Galt found the scenery around Puerto Vallarta "idyllic" and soon grew so fond of the life there that he considered settling down permanently. Before coming to Puerto Vallarta, he had spent most of 1967 on the move—St. Louis, Chicago, Toronto, Montreal, then Birmingham, Alabama. He wasted a few days in Acapulco but found that he hated the place—it was overdeveloped and touristy, he thought, and "everybody there wanted money, money, money." Puerto Vallarta, on the other hand, was still a ragged paradise—bathwater ocean, blood orange sunsets, wild lagoons prowled by crocodiles. Frigate birds and pelicans flapped in the skies. Humpback whales, having migrated here to breed in warm waters, could sometimes be seen spouting in the bay. The steep hillsides flickered with butterflies, and every morning a thousand roosters announced the day. The people around P.V. seemed poor but happy, living outside, eating outside, sleeping on rooftop pallets beneath the stars. Everything about the place was relaxed, especially the dress code, which succinctly boiled down to a popular local aphorism: "Men, wear pants. Women, look beautiful."

Not long after he arrived in Puerto Vallarta, Galt began a regular nocturnal routine of visiting the cathouses. There was one particularly cheap place where a customer could climb a ladder to a stack of cubicles, each occupied by a prostitute. He'd dive into one of these little matchboxes and have a quick-and-dirty for a few pesos, with the moans of the other lovemakers seeping through the paper-thin walls. It resulted in a kind of erotic feedback loop: each noisy couple going at it, while simultaneously hearing all the other noisy couples, created an exquisite cacophony that Galt found titillating.

Later Galt began frequenting the slightly classier Casa Susana. In the downstairs receiving room, which also served as a bar and cantina, the whores sat on metal chairs lined along the dingy walls. Small translucent lizards clung to the ceiling and cheeped in the shadows between their mosquitoey meals. A grinning bartender with atrocious teeth kept the booze flowing while customers sat around tables or danced to Broadway tunes playing on a decrepit jukebox. Rustic, easygoing, a bit down-at-the-heels, Casa Susana was a community gathering place of sorts; lots of locals went there just for the spectacle, and it was not uncommon for squealing children, or even squealing pigs, to scamper through the downstairs rooms.

Something about Manuela Aguirre Medrano caught Galt's eye. She was slightly plump, but she was young, with a broad smile and dreamer's eyes the color of rich chocolate. She introduced herself as Irma—her professional name, it turned out, lifted from the French stage show *Irma la Douce*, which Billy Wilder had recently turned into a Hollywood film starring a chartreuse-stockinged young Shirley MacLaine as a popular Paris prostitute.

Galt took Manuela upstairs and had his way with her for the equivalent of about eight dollars. He returned a few nights later and requested her again. Gradually they struck up a friendship. Galt would sit with her through the night at a table in the Casa Susana cantina, drinking screwdrivers. Manuela spoke almost no English, and he almost no Spanish, so they whiled away the hours with caveman gestures and awkward smiles.

Sometimes they would go out together during the day and drive around Puerto Vallarta in his Mustang, fishtailing on the muddy roads. Having grown up in a town with only a few relics and sputtering jalopies, a town where most men drove only burros, Manuela had never seen such a fancy car, let alone ridden in one, and she felt like a queen as he squired her about the *ciudad*.

On several occasions they drove the twelve miles down to the beach at the little village of Mismaloya, where four years earlier John Huston had filmed *The Night of the Iguana*. Eric and Manuela liked to sit and drink cervezas under a palm tree in a secluded cove not far from the *Iguana* set, which was still largely intact. The great bay was spread before them, and in the foreground dolphins could often be seen playing around a chain of three cave-riddled rock islands, known as Los Arcos.

Huston's movie—"One man . . . three women . . . one night," went the desperate poster tagline—starred Richard Burton as a defrocked priest and Ava Gardner as the randy owner of a cheap seaside hotel not unlike the one where Galt was staying. During the filming, dozens of paparazzi descended on Puerto Vallarta to cover the combustible mix of personalities, including the playwright Tennessee Williams (on whose play the film was based), yet the world media were primarily interested in the torrid affair that Burton was then pursuing with Elizabeth Taylor. Although both were married to other people at the time, Burton invited Taylor down to Puerto Vallarta to be with him during the filming. He ensconced her in a house across the street from his and then built a pink "love bridge" to connect the two residences.

Their romance was considered such an international *scandale* that even Vatican officials weighed in, accusing Taylor of "erotic vagrancy." *Iguana*'s box-office success, combined with its accompaniment of behind-the-scenes press, cemented Puerto Vallarta's reputation as a place of louche living and sultry intrigue—and got the first wave of gringos coming.

In 1966, the writer Ken Kesey, on the lam from the FBI after faking his own suicide following a series of drug busts, had come to hide out in Puerto Vallarta and its shaggy environs. Now, a year later, Eric Galt was part of the exodus. He'd first read about Puerto Vallarta in one of the many magazine articles that covered the making of Huston's movie. During his nearly monthlong stay in Mexico, he lived an expatriate life of sloth and debauchery quite true to the spirit of Huston's film. In between his drinks and his whoring, he was (or was pretending to be) an author, a journalist, a photographer, a filmmaker; he was developing a kind of recombinant personality, sifting and sampling the lifestyles he'd read and heard about.

Like the doomed iguana in the story, Galt appeared to be a creature who'd come to the end of his rope. Manuela found him strange. He complained of headaches, stomach problems, and other maladies. He was introverted, distracted, perpetually tired. He rarely tipped and never laughed. He was paranoid of the cops, always looking over his shoulder. Under the seat of his car, he carried a loaded Liberty Chief .38 snub-nosed revolver, which he called his "equalizer." He claimed to have served twenty years in the U.S. Army. He made trips into the hills from time to time, apparently to buy marijuana.

For someone who hung out in grimy whorehouses, he was a surprisingly meticulous dresser and a person of tidy habits. He took lunch nearly every day at 3:00 p.m. at the same place, the Discotheque Café, where he always ordered the same thing—a hamburger and a Pepsi. Galt was keen on learning Spanish and toted an English-Spanish phrase book nearly everywhere he went. He was equally keen on learning the steps of local Mexican dances; though Manuela tried to teach him what she knew, his clumsy feet never got the hang of it.

Yet for all his oddities, Galt was nice to her, Manuela had to admit. They walked the Malecón together, soaking up the colorful street life— the Day of the Dead curios, the vendors selling mangoes on a stick, the weird beaded figurines of the peyote-loving Huichol Indians who lived back in the Sierra Madre. Several times, when he'd been drinking, he asked Manuela to marry him (she politely refused). He even went out and looked at a piece of property to buy—a local man proposed to barter his land for Galt's Mustang. "I seriously considered the trade," Galt later said. "Mexico's an earthy place. I got to like Puerto Vallarta so much, I was thinking I could throw up a lean-to and retire."

■

ONE EVENING AT the Casa Susana, Manuela Medrano glimpsed another side of Eric Galt that gave her pause. He entered the cantina around nine that night—a Monday—and took a seat next to her at a table, as was their usual routine. They sat and drank and tried to listen to the jukebox, but a few tables over, six American revelers were making a racket—apparently, they'd just come in off a yacht. Two of them were white, and four were black.

One of the African-Americans, who was drunk, stumbled as he brushed by Galt's table, perhaps en route to the bathroom, and he reflexively reached out and touched Manuela's arm to break his fall. Galt suddenly tensed and leaned into Manuela, blurting out something about "niggers." She had never known him to blow his stack like this. "He said many insulting things—son of a bitch and other names," she recalled, although the language barrier made it difficult for her to understand most of what he was saying. He suddenly rose, stormed over to the table, and yelled an insult to the offending black man. There was a standoff, with hot stares and macho posturing, but then Galt came back and sat down.

Yet that was not the end of it. As the jukebox played on, Galt continued to sulk. In a few minutes, the black man wandered over and tried to make peace, but Galt muttered yet another insult. Then he rose again from the table and this time went outside to the parking lot. A few minutes later he returned.

"Where did you go?" Manuela asked.

"Feel my pocket," he replied, with a furtive look.

She ran her hand over his pocket and realized he had a gun, the same revolver he carried under the seat of his Mustang.

Apparently unaware of this latest development, the party of Americans soon got up and left the cantina: they were prudently calling it a night. Then Galt started for the door in pursuit. "I'm going to kill them," Manuela thought he said.

She managed to intervene, somehow communicating to him that the police would be dropping by soon for their usual ten o'clock visit. It would be foolish for him to cause trouble with these men now—foolish for him, and foolish for the whole operation at Casa Susana. Her argument carried weight—Galt had always seemed deeply fearful of any sort of run-in with the police—and he finally began to simmer down. It was unclear, in the end, whether Galt's fierce reaction to the black patron at Casa Susana grew from racial prejudice or simply from the fact that a strange man had touched what passed for his woman. But Manuela had never seen Galt like this before. The whole fracas made her extremely uncomfortable—and leery of his mercurial moods.

Yet in his sloppier moments of drunkenness, he kept proposing to Manuela, and she kept on refusing. Among other things, she knew that he was sleeping with other women—or, rather, seeing other whores. One night when she rebuffed his proposal a final time, Galt pulled his .38 revolver on her and threatened to kill her.

■

GALT DID NOT linger long in Puerto Vallarta. Predictably, his relationship with Manuela fizzled, and for a week or so in early November he took up with another young local woman, named Elisa, who worked as a cigarette girl and photographer's aide at the Posada Vallarta. They went out to nightclubs and slept together at the Hotel Las Glorias.

Galt's main interest in Elisa was her knowledge of photography. He wanted to soak up everything she'd learned from her day job. Much as he had done with Manuela, he took Elisa out to secluded beaches, and they'd kill the afternoons taking Polaroids. On one occasion, using the remote cable he had purchased, he straddled Elisa and photographed the two of them in a pornographic pose. Other times, he would take mug shots of himself. He seemed obsessed with the contours of his own face. He had a mirror, and he would stare at himself for minutes at a time, grimacing at certain features he didn't like—his prominent and slightly bulbous nose, his jug ears. He said he wanted to have "a face that no one can describe."

Galt told Elisa he was heading to purchase marijuana in Yelapa, a nearby fishing village without electricity or roads that was accessible only by boat. A few American expats had set up there, living the simple life with the locals in open thatch *palapas*, and hippies went in search of the strong weed that was said to grow in the jungles hanging over the town. Before Galt took off on his errand, he gave Elisa forty-eight dollars to rent a little love-nest apartment for them, but instead she took the money and bolted for Guadalajara. She left him a note with the bartender of the Posada Vallarta—a Dear John letter, basically—in which she pleaded with him to forgive her.

Galt had been resoundingly jilted, and it was enough to sour him on Puerto Vallarta for good. "I couldn't accomplish anything further in Mexico in the way of securing permanent residency," he rationalized. "I don't believe you can live in Mexico. They don't have no middle class, see, you are either on top or on the bottom, and I think it would be difficult to accustom yourself to living on the bottom because there is all types of ailments and things."

A week later, probably on November 16, Eric Galt carefully stuffed the inner tube of his spare tire with some of Jalisco's finest cannabis. He packed up his Mustang and headed out of town. Soon he was on Highway 15, aiming north, in the direction of Tijuana.

DURING THE LATE fall and early winter of 1967, Martin Luther King pressed forward with his ambitious plans to lead his Poor People's Army to Washington the following summer. One person who was most assuredly keeping a close eye on King's proposed demonstration was J. Edgar Hoover, the seventy-two-year-old director of the Federal Bureau of Investigation. Hoover was born and raised in the District of Columbia and had spent his entire professional life there, serving under nine presidents. A devout Presbyterian who once dreamed of being a minister, Hoover had long ago appointed himself a guardian of the capital's morals. The director saw the prospect of an army of indigent subversives encamped on the Mall not only as a threat to the Republic but also as a Vandal attack on his native city.

Sitting at his desk in his inner sanctum on the third floor of the gray granite Justice Department building, with his mother's black Bible always parked at his elbow, America's number-one G-man had read the FBI reports about the new SCLC project with increasing alarm. What was King really up to? he worried. Was this the start of a full-scale black revolution? Were the Soviets behind the scheme? Most important, how could the burrhead be stopped?

Burrhead—that was one of his many names for King, the man on whom he had fixed a nearly pathological hatred ever since the civil rights leader first emerged on the national scene in 1955. Hoover's FBI had been waging a protracted yet so far unsuccessful campaign designed (as various FBI memos colorfully put it) to "see this scoundrel exposed," to "take him off his pedestal," and to "neutralize him" as a force in American life. In a private communication earlier in 1967, Hoover told President Johnson: "Based on King's recent activities and public utterances, it is clear that he is an instrument in the hands of subversive forces seeking to undermine our nation."

Although J. Edgar Hoover was still utterly in control of the FBI, he was in his waning years, a liver-spotted and somewhat fusty caricature of himself. He had developed a paunch, his eyes were baggy, and his chin had become an odd-looking knob of ruddy flesh. He suffered from hypertension and other ailments. He still dressed as dandily as ever, in sharp pin-striped suits with color-coordinated handkerchiefs and ties, but he had lost some of his boldness of step. He had developed weird phobias about germs, about flies, about the slightest breach in the yolk of his morning poached egg. His speech seemed curiously dated now; he peppered his tirades with Depression-era phrases that gave some of his younger agents pause, phrases like "criminal scum" and "moral rats" and "alien filth." He was fond of saying that his enemies were afflicted with "mental halitosis."

By the late 1960s, Hoover was a living anachronism, dwelling in a rigid world of his own making. Art Buchwald joked that he was "a mythical person first thought up by the *Reader's Digest*." As always, Hoover wielded his blue pen with grumpy exactitude. As always, he composed his Rabble-Rouser Index and other lists of dangerous radicals, real or imagined. He still took his regular "non-vacations" (the press was told that even when he was away from Washington, the director never stopped working) to shuffleboard palaces in Miami Beach or to hotels of faded glory near the horse tracks at Del Mar or Saratoga Springs, where he always booked adjoining suites with his lifelong friend and second-in-command, Clyde Tolson. Hoover's confirmed bachelorhood, combined with his curiously matrimonial relationship with Tolson, had led to widespread speculation. And to endless jokes, like this one from Truman

Capote: "Are you familiar with the term 'killer fruit'? It's a certain kind of queer who has Freon refrigerating his bloodstream. Like Hadrian, or J. Edgar Hoover."

■

HOOVER'S FBI HAD become a curiously self-reinforcing enterprise. The six thousand agents spread across the country were expected to ape the director's views, mimic his style, and anticipate his needs. "You must understand," one special agent in charge wrote to a colleague, "that you're working for a crazy maniac and that our duty is to find out what he wants and to create the world that he believes in." Once, when Hoover broke out his blue pen and scrawled angrily over a memo, "Watch the borders," agents scurried to the Mexican and Canadian borders to ascertain what Hoover meant—only to learn that the boss was merely concerned with the width of that particular memo's margins.

Hoover's FBI office was a reliquary of former times. There was John Dillinger's death mask on the wall. There was the cozy arrangement of feminine-looking overstuffed chairs, the dainty teacups and other pieces of china handed down from his dear departed mother, his trophy sailfish displayed over the door. There was his steadfast secretary, Helen Gandy, working away in the adjoining room. She took his calls, paid his bills, checked in his laundry, arranged for the gardener to visit his house, and handled every imaginable piece of minutiae, just as she had done for forty-nine uninterrupted years.

If Hoover was a throwback, he still had a powerful political currency—and a job security perhaps unmatched in Washington. He had become director of what was then the Bureau of Investigation in 1924, when he was twenty-nine years old. As the FBI's first and only director, he sat at the center of a world he had practically invented. The nomenclature, the clerical voice, the dress code, the penchant for acronyms and quasi-military structures—it was all his. At every inauguration since that of Calvin Coolidge, Hoover had been there, unbudging and apparently unfireable. He was a man who possessed a "terrible patience," it was said. The veteran Washington hand Hugh Sidey, writing in *Life*, noted the countless times he'd attended inaugural parades or funeral corteges or moments of national celebration, only to look up and see Hoover standing on his office balcony, "high and distant and quiet, watching with his misty kingdom behind him, going on from President to President, and decade to decade."

Through all those years, Hoover brought an air of professionalism and scientific rigor to police work. He had overseen the adoption of every imaginable advance in the craft of criminology—from centralized fingerprinting and a state-of-the-art ballistics-firing facility to a system-atized method of bureau reporting and note taking. The FBI Crime Lab, the Public Enemies list, America's Most Wanted, the widespread use of fiber and handwriting analysis—all of it came about during Hoover's long tenure. With good reason, the journalist Jack Anderson wrote that Hoover had "transformed the FBI from a collection of hacks, misfits, and courthouse hangers-on into one of the world's most effective and formi-dable law enforcement organizations."

Late in the second decade of the twentieth century, the young Hoover had made himself Washington's first expert on the perils of anar-chism and Communism, and since then every subversive, or alleged sub-versive, had passed within his sights. He'd led the notorious Palmer Raids on suspected radicals. He'd hounded Marcus Garvey. He'd arrested and deported Emma Goldman. During the Depression, the bureau became virtually synonymous with solving high-profile crimes. Hoover's agents had caught Machine Gun Kelly, had caught and killed John Dillinger, had caught the Lindbergh baby murder suspect, Bruno Hauptmann. In the Cold War, G-men had helped snag Alger Hiss and Ethel and Julius Rosenberg.

Over the years Hoover had developed files on countless public fig-ures, collecting every morsel of compromising gossip and lore. Frank Sinatra, Harry Truman, Eleanor Roosevelt, Charles Lindbergh, Helen Keller—Hoover, it seemed, had kept his eyes on everyone. John F. Kennedy had tried to get rid of Hoover but feared, with good reason, that the resourceful director had too much dirt on him. The president's brother Robert, who as attorney general had nominally been Hoover's boss, called the director "dangerous and rather a psycho . . . I think he's senile and rather frightening."

After JFK was assassinated, Lyndon Johnson also briefly consid-ered letting Hoover go, but then saw the light, reportedly saying: "I'd rather have him inside the tent pissing out than outside pissing in." On January 1, 1965, when Hoover reached the mandatory retirement age of seventy, Johnson waived the requirement and kept him on as director indefinitely. "J. Edgar Hoover," the president declared in a ceremony, "is a hero to millions of decent citizens, and an anathema to evil men. Under his guiding hand, the FBI has become the greatest investigative body in history."

Hoover, Johnson later rhapsodized, "is a pillar of strength in a city of weak men."

■

HOOVER HAD BEEN obsessed with Martin Luther King Jr. for at least a decade. Throughout most of the 1960s, Hoover had been carrying on a semipublic feud with King and the SCLC. The FBI director openly called King "the most notorious liar in the country." When *Time* proclaimed King its "Man of the Year" of 1963, Hoover indignantly scrawled on a memo, "They had to dig deep in the garbage to come up with that one." In 1964, after the news broke that King had been awarded the Nobel Peace Prize—the youngest recipient in history—Hoover groused that the only award King deserved was the "top alley cat prize." When King visited with Pope Paul VI at Vatican City, Hoover was beside himself. "I am amazed," he scribbled over a news clip, "that the Pope gave an audience to such a degenerate."

Hoover had been convinced early in King's career that the civil rights leader was a tool of the Soviets, and in late 1963 he persuaded Attorney General Robert Kennedy to authorize the use of wiretaps and other surveillance to ferret out King's supposed Communist ties. Years of focused investigation and countless man-hours of surveillance failed to bear out Hoover's suspicion, however. The best evidence the FBI was able to dig up was that one of King's legal advisers, a liberal Jewish attorney from New York named Stanley Levison, had in his youth been briefly associated with the Communist Party but that he had, by all accounts, severed his ties years ago.

Hoover's agents also learned that a man affiliated with the American Communist Party who shared King's blood type had answered a public call and apparently donated blood to King in 1958 when he was stabbed during his book signing in Harlem; for a time FBI memos made much of the fact that Commie blood was thus literally coursing through King's veins.

Yet this was the sum total of the investigatory fruit gleaned from Hoover's many expensive years of watching and Red-baiting King. Martin Luther King Jr. was not a Communist, had never been one, and had no ties to China or the Soviets. The massive FBI effort spent chasing this will-o'-the-wisp was a profligate waste of public dollars. As King once put it, "There are as many Communists in the freedom movement as there are Eskimos in Florida."

All those years of spying on the civil rights leader did produce other kinds of intelligence, however—intelligence that Hoover found equally tantalizing. King, the FBI discovered, had a weakness for women. His agents found out about his several mistresses and discovered that beautiful young ladies had a way of throwing themselves at him as he moved about the country, advances the civil rights leader did little to discourage. Not only that, Hoover was shocked to learn, King used raunchy language when he talked about sex, he smoked and drank and partied into the small hours, and he told off-color jokes. The FBI had taped a garbled recording of King in a hotel in Washington supposedly having intercourse and using rather profane language during the act.

Hoover was appalled and at the same time titillated by what he read, calling King "a tom cat with obsessive degenerate sexual urges." One FBI official wrote that Hoover, when studying King's surveillance reports, would "narrow his eyes and purse his lips." The straitlaced Hoover "saw extramarital sex as evidence of moral degeneracy—an opinion that many Americans still shared in the 1960s, before Hollywood taught that promiscuity was ennobling."

Robert Kennedy, no stranger to sexual high jinks, said that "if the country knew what we know about King's goings-on, he'd be finished." Hoover certainly tried to share his growing King dossier with the nation; his FBI subordinates regularly leaked salacious details to the press, to members of Congress, to President Johnson, and even to diplomats overseas. But the media never took the bait, and the charges never stuck.

For Hoover, this was a source of powerful frustration. "I don't understand why we are unable to get the true facts before the public," he wrote in one memo. "We can't even get our accomplishments published. We are never taking the aggressive."

Yet finally, the FBI *did* take the aggressive. An FBI official, believed to have been the head of intelligence operations, William C. Sullivan, sent King an anonymous package that contained a kind of "greatest hits" compendium tape of the FBI's most lurid recordings, accompanied by a hateful note urging King to commit suicide. "King, look into your heart," the note began. "You are no clergyman and you know it . . . you are a colossal fraud and an evil, vicious one at that. King, like all frauds your end is approaching. You could have been our greatest leader. But you are done. Your 'honorary' degrees, your Nobel Prize (what a grim farce) and other awards will not save you. King, I repeat you are done. The American public . . . will know you for what you are—an evil, abnormal beast. King, there is only one thing left for you to do. You know what it is . . . There is but one way out for you. You better take it before your filthy, abnormal fraudulent self is bared to the nation."

What made this package all the more disturbing for King was that Coretta opened it. Yet the note with its accompanying tape—most of which was inaudible anyway—failed to produce the desired effect. If anything, it strengthened King's marriage and his resolve to carry on in the face of what he and Coretta both now realized was a full-scale FBI effort to ruin him.

"They are out to break me," he said to a friend. "[But] what I do is only between me and my God." King, in his own way, was determined to fight back. "Hoover is old and getting senile," he said, "and should be hit from all sides."

5 ■ DIXIE WEST

THROUGH EARLY WINTER of 1967, Martin Luther King was increasingly troubled by a new political development: an age-old nemesis was running for president—and enjoying an astonishing surge in popularity.

As a candidate for the self-styled American Independent Party, George C. Wallace had been traveling around the country almost as frenetically as King had, drumming up his blue-collar base from coast to coast. The nation's best reporters and political phrasemakers had a field day covering the Alabama demagogue's outrageous but unfailingly colorful appearances. Wallace was the Cicero of the Cabdriver, it was said. He was so full of bile that if he "bit himself he would die of blood poisoning." He was, said Marshall Frady, "the surly orphan of American politics . . . the grim joker in the deck, whose nightrider candidacy [is] a rough approximation of the potential for an American fascism."

People loved his bumptious sense of humor, the rockabilly growl in his voice, the way he shook his fist in defiance when he really got worked up. Wallace, a former Golden Gloves boxer, was battling forces no one else seemed to have the gumption to take on. At rallies around the country, he had a litany of phrases that he used over and over, lines calculated to get a lusty guffaw out of the crowds. When he won the White House,

Wallace said, he was going to take all those "bearded beatnik bureau-crats" and hurl them and their briefcases into the Potomac. He railed against "liberal sob sisters" and "bleeding-heart sociologists." Wallace liked to say that whenever disturbances like the Watts riots swept the streets of America's cities, you could count on "pointy-headed intellectu-als to explain it away, whining that the poor rioters didn't get any water-melon to eat when they were 10 years old."

Though he was careful to moderate his most incendiary racial rhet-oric, Wallace continued to preach states' rights and the separation of the races and said the recent gains of the civil rights movement should be overturned. At friendlier venues he went so far as to argue that blacks should not be able to serve on juries, noting that "the nigra would still be in Africa in the brush if the white people of this country had not raised their standards." He called the civil rights legislation that President Johnson had pushed through Congress "an assassin's knife stuck in the back of liberty."

"Let 'em call me a racist," he told a reporter in Cleveland. "It don't make any difference. Whole heap of folks in this country feel the same way I do. Race is what's gonna win this thing for me."

■

FROM THE START of his governorship, George Wallace had made white supremacy—sometimes cloaked in the more respectable veil of states' rights, but usually not—the centerpiece of his platform. In his 1962 inaugural speech, delivered in Montgomery on the gold star marking the spot where Jefferson Davis was sworn in as president of the Confederacy, Wallace gave a stem-winder that was written by the speechwriter Asa Carter, a well-known Klansman and anti-Semite. "In the name of the greatest people that have ever trod this earth," Wallace said, "I draw the line in the dust and toss the gauntlet before the feet of tyranny, and I say: Segregation now, segregation tomorrow, segregation forever!"

If those words put Wallace on the national radar screen, his actions at the University of Alabama a few months later placed him on a historic collision course with the federal government. On June 11, 1963, flanked by state troopers, Wallace physically prevented two black students from entering an auditorium at the University of Alabama to register for classes. His "stand in the schoolhouse door" did not work, of course—two federal marshals dispatched by the Kennedy Justice Department immediately ordered him to stand down. But in the process Wallace had made himself the civil rights movement's most vocal and visible bogeyman.

Throughout the 1960s, Wallace had repeatedly focused his ire on one figure: Martin Luther King Jr.—in no small part because King had scored his sweetest victories in Wallace's home state. Wallace had called the Nobel laureate everything but the Antichrist, but in an odd way Wallace needed King, for the governor understood that great political struggles can exist in the abstract for only so long before cooking down to the personal.

Certainly Wallace's slights and epithets cannot be faulted for their lack of energy or brio. He called King "a communist agitator," "a phony," and "a fraud, marching and going to jail and all that, and just living high on the hog." He once said that King spent most of his time "riding around in big Cadillacs smoking expensive cigars" and competing with other black ministers to see "who could go to bed with the most nigra women." And yet, to Wallace's outrage and consternation, the federal government had consistently sided with King. Leaders in Washington, the governor said, "now want us to surrender the state to him and his group of pro-Communists."

On numerous occasions, King had lobbed invectives of his own. In a 1963 interview with Dan Rather, King called Wallace "perhaps the most dangerous racist in America today . . . I am not sure that he believes all the poison he preaches, but he is artful enough to convince others that he does." When segregationist thugs bombed Birmingham's Sixteenth Street Baptist Church in September 1963, killing four girls attending Sunday school, King sent the governor a withering telegram that all but accused him of the murder, saying "the blood of our little children is on your hands." Two years later, when King marched from Selma to Montgomery and gave a triumphant oration outside the Alabama state capitol, he aimed his message right at the governor's office. Segregation was now on its deathbed, King pronounced; the only thing uncertain about it was "how costly Wallace will make the funeral."

Still, through all his entanglements with Wallace during the 1960s, King had to confess a perverse admiration for his talents on the stump.

"He has just four [speeches]," King once said of the governor, "but he works on them and hones them, so that they are all little minor classics."

Now, incredibly, this neo-Confederate was running for president—a development that King found immensely troubling. King remarked to a television reporter that he thought Wallace's candidacy "will only strengthen the forces of reaction in the country and incite bigotry, hatred, and even violence. I think it will arouse many evil forces in our nation."

Even so, Wallace's bid was already starting to show a vitality that America had not seen in an independent candidate since Teddy Roosevelt's Bull Moose campaign of 1912. Pundits were projecting that even though he had no hope of winning, Wallace could potentially spoil the 1968 election, forcing the House of Representatives to decide the president for the first time since 1825. National polls indicated that his appeal was steadily climbing, from 9 to 12 to 14 percent of the American electorate. "In both the North and South," declared *Life* magazine, "Wallace appears to be tapping a powerful underground stream of discontent."

■

IN THE FALL of 1967, California became the heart of Wallace's fight for the presidency. In November, he began an intense effort to get his name on the state's unusually restrictive ballot for the June primaries. California election law required a new candidate from any unregistered party to gather sixty-six thousand signatures. It was probably the most onerous ballot requirement in the country, but Wallace's advisers felt that California, as the nation's most populous and influential state, represented the first crucial test of his nascent campaign.

So Wallace moved most of his staff to Los Angeles, and hundreds of devoted volunteers from Alabama soon followed him. In newly opened American Independent Party offices across California, drawling armies of phone workers, fresh from Mobile and Tuscaloosa and Birmingham, clogged the lines with their solicitation calls. Working in an extracurricular capacity, Alabama legislators, commissioners, clerks, and other government employees made the trek out to the West Coast to moonlight for the cause. Meanwhile, Wallace himself crisscrossed California, speaking at hundreds of rallies and fund-raisers, guarded by swaggering hosses who were usually out-of-uniform Alabama state troopers.

The Bear Flag State, it seemed, had become Dixie West. "The capital of Alabama is *not* Los Angeles," one *Wall Street Journal* political reporter noted, "but it might as well be."

What made the Montgomery decampment to Los Angeles all the more surreal was that "Governor" Wallace was not the duly constituted governor of Alabama. Because of a strict anti-succession statute, Wallace had been forced to step down, despite immense popularity, when his first gubernatorial term ended in 1966. He resented this brusque termination of his tenure, for he felt he needed political viability in Alabama as a base from which to pursue his national ambitions. Then, in a moment of craftiness, he realized that nothing in the Alabama statutes prevented *his wife* from running for governor.

So, in 1967, First Lady Lurleen Wallace, a perfectly put-together, and widely beloved, traditional Southern woman with scarcely any interest in political life, ascended to the state's highest office—on paper, at least. George Wallace became officially known as the "First Gentleman of Alabama," but few people in Montgomery labored under any misunderstandings about who was actually running the state's affairs. It was an unorthodox arrangement, to say the least, but Alabama voters had to hand it to their ever-resourceful governor for installing his own surrogate—and for pulling off what would later be called one of the most brazen acts of "political ventriloquism" in American history.

Lurleen Wallace occasionally ventured out to California to campaign with her husband, but she was quite ill and unable to exert herself. She had recently been diagnosed with colon cancer, had undergone an operation to remove an egg-sized malignancy, and was receiving cobalt treatments at a hospital in Texas. She was slowly, surely withering away. Her doctors believed she had only a few months to live.

George Wallace, in a fugue state of campaigning, carefully hid the seriousness of her illness from both his Alabama and his California publics—and kept to the hustings.

ERIC GALT CLUTCHED his diploma and posed for the photographer. It was "commencement day" at the International School of Bartending on Sunset Boulevard. Galt, wearing a borrowed bow tie and a black tuxedo jacket, stood in a softly lit room that was a mock-up of a cocktail lounge, with minimalist modern furniture and plush wall-to-wall carpeting that muffled the steady clinking of tumblers and collins glasses behind the test bar.

It was here, under the direction of a primly mustachioed man named Tomas Reyes Lau, that Galt and his fellow pupils had learned the mixologist's trade, assaying the chemical mysteries of Rusty Nails, mai tais, Harvey Wallbangers, sloe gin fizzes, and Singapore slings. Over the six-week course, which cost Galt $220 in cash, he had mastered the recipes of more than 112 cocktails.

Mr. Lau, an unctuous, precise man with a Latin American accent, was impressed with Galt and thought he had promise in the business. "A nice fellow, very intelligent, quiet and reserved," Lau judged him. "He had the ability to develop this type of service." Galt told people around the school that he had worked as a "culinary" on a Mississippi River steamboat, but that now he said he wanted to settle down—and, one day, open up a tavern in Los Angeles.

Lau had already succeeded in finding him a bartending job, but to Lau's surprise Galt turned it down. He planned to go out of town soon, he told Lau. "I have to leave to see my brother," Galt said. "What good would it do for me to work only two or three weeks? I'll wait till I get back, then I can take a permanent job." He said his brother ran a tavern somewhere in Missouri.

Now the cameraman was poised to snap the picture. Galt stood next to Lau, who fairly beamed with pride at his new graduate. Galt stared anxiously at the lens and concentrated on the photographer's movements. Though he had made failing attempts at proficiency *behind* a camera, and had almost obsessively taken Polaroid mug shots of himself while in Puerto Vallarta, he hated being photographed by others, hated the whole tedious ritual—the pointless lingering, the sense of momentary entrapment, the knowledge that his image would reside in another's hands.

Galt's posture grew rigid. He fidgeted, tightened his lips, and cocked his head slightly. Then he did something strange: at the last possible moment, Galt closed his eyes and kept them mashed shut until he was sure the portrait was taken.

■

IF ERIC GALT had enjoyed an interlude of carefree freedom while slumming in Puerto Vallarta, he had known something deeper and more fulfilling these past few months in Los Angeles. He'd arrived in L.A. on November 19 and soon found himself drawn to the city's restless energy. He eventually made a home at the St. Francis Hotel on Hollywood Boulevard, in a drab room that cost eighty-five dollars a month. There was a bar downstairs on the ground floor of the blond brick building, a smoky little joint called the Sultan Room, where he liked to while away the nights watching prizefights on the TV set or shooting pool on an old scuffed table while nursing sixty-cent drinks. When he got bored, he'd head out on the town, nosing his Mustang through the freeway traffic, listening to country-and-western songs on his car's push-button radio—he particularly liked Johnny Cash. He took comfort in knowing that if he ran into trouble, he still had his loaded "equalizer" hidden under the seat.

Over the past few months Galt had enjoyed his share of the considerable good life that Southern California had to offer single men of appetites in the go-go days of the late 1960s—self-realization, alternative lifestyles, transcendence, casual sex, drugs. He had a fast car with a V-8 engine and a hot red interior—the windows affixed with Mexican "Turista" stickers that seemed to advertise his wide-ranging prowls. He had some money to spend, money apparently derived from various robberies and smuggling schemes, and from the sale of the marijuana he'd brought back from Mexico. He had girls on those nights when he wanted them— "exotic dancers" he met at clubs along Hollywood Boulevard. It's likely that he had amphetamines, which he liked to use to sharpen his thoughts as he burned through the lonely nights.

At his hotel, he would turn on his Channel Master transistor radio and burrow into books—he was a fan of detective thrillers and Ian Fleming's James Bond. There, he would read far into the night, as a fizzly neon sign outside his hotel window shot his room—403—with shards of tangerine light. He was intensely, almost desperately focused on improving himself, as though he were running out of time to make something stick. He wanted to do something purposeful with his life and find some kind of happiness. He still nursed dreams of getting into the porn business— while in L.A. he bought sex manuals and a set of Japanese chrome handcuffs and even corresponded with a local club for swingers—but that idea had foundered a bit since leaving Puerto Vallarta. Instead, he enrolled in a correspondence locksmithing course offered by a company in New Jersey, for he was seized with the notion of becoming a first-rate thief, a safecracker, a moonlight yegg. He took dance lessons, read self-help books, and even consulted a cosmetic surgeon to see about making a few small repairs. Now he'd "graduated" from bartending school.

It was, for Eric Galt, a time of branching out, of creative and eclectic if somewhat frantic growth. He was like an empty vessel for all the trends of the zeitgeist. He tried on different lives for himself, fresh looks and new styles. He began to think about moving permanently to a foreign country—New Zealand, perhaps, or someplace in South America or southern Africa. He talked vaguely about starting an orphanage for neglected children—child abuse being his soft spot, the one subject that consistently aroused in him noticeable stirrings of empathy. Other times he dreamed of working in the merchant marine or using his newfound bartending skills to open up a pub in Ireland. Here in the bright forgiving anonymity of L.A., in the early spring of 1968, Eric Galt thought he could do just about anything.

And what a boomtime it was to be in L.A.—this twitchy young metropolis of starlets and jet-setters, webbed with highways, exploding with myriad fads, its multiple skylines sprouting new stalagmites of mirrored glass, its hectic airport presided over by a futuristic tower that looked like a flying saucer on four legs. Lew Alcindor was perfecting his skyhook for UCLA, while Elgin Baylor and Jerry West were riding high with the Lakers. The Doors' third studio album, *Waiting for the Sun*, was deep in gestation. Rosey Grier had just finished his last season with the Rams, as part of the "Fearsome Foursome," perhaps the greatest defensive line in football history. Popular TV shows coming out of Los Angeles included *Laugh-In*, *Gunsmoke*, *Star Trek*, and *The Beverly Hillbillies*. While Galt was gaining proficiency with a shaker and a shot glass, a new movie hit theaters that perfectly captured the country's restive, contrarian mood. It was called *The Graduate*.

■

ERIC STARVO GALT was forty years old, clean in his appearance, his skin smooth and clear but of an almost fish-belly wanness—whatever tan he had acquired on the beaches of Puerto Vallarta had long since faded. He lived on aspirin, and complained of headaches, insomnia, and nameless concerns. His heart raced, and he felt odd pains in his chest. Though a recent eye test revealed that he had twenty-twenty vision, he sometimes worried that he was going blind. He was constantly adjusting his medications, refining his regimes of self-maintenance. He took One A Day vitamins and various supplements. If he was a bit scrawny, he kept his muscles lean and tough with regular calisthenics and weight lifting—he'd recently bought himself a set of barbells.

Though Galt dressed cheaply, he dressed with neatness and exactitude. He buffed his fake-alligator loafers to a fine polish. He made sure his tailored suit was crisp and sharp and took his clothes every Saturday afternoon to the Home Service Laundry on Hollywood Boulevard, just down the street from his hotel.

In like fashion, Galt fussed with his grooming and was no stranger to a mirror. He kept his face clean shaven, his nails trim, his charcoal hair combed straight back and oiled with Brylcreem, so that it gave off a petroleum sheen in the light. His tidiness and hygiene were a source of special pride; though he frequented the sorriest flophouses and dives, and felt at home among the most unsavory characters, he took satisfaction in knowing that, in his way, he'd risen above the filth around him.

For all his preening, Galt lacked confidence about his looks; he seemed an oddly skittish man, awkward around people and hard to pin in a conversation. He gave off the appearance of a hustler preoccupied with sub-rosa enterprises he did not wish to divulge. Most people took the cue and left him alone.

Those who did speak with him found him hard to understand, for he blurted out words in unrhythmic spates and monosyllables, mumbling softly, his lips cramped in an uncomfortable-looking construction, as though his mouth were full of sharp rocks. He spoke in a drawl that was hard to place; it was the drawl of rural Illinois, along the Mississippi River valley, where he had grown up during the Depression in a succession of impoverished towns. It was the drawl of St. Louis, the city he and his family had lived in and out of—the city that, in his drifter's way, Galt considered home.

Galt was willing to spend good money on certain prescribed things—like dance lessons and bartending school or his portable Zenith television—but at heart he was a cheapskate. He darned his own clothes, sewed buttons on his fraying shirts, drank horse-piss beer, lived in prideful squalor, rarely tipped in restaurants, and prowled drugstores for bargain-basement sales on toiletry items. If he dined out, he usually ordered greasy hamburgers at drive-ins, but more often he ate in his room, subsisting on crackers, canned food, and powdered soups that he warmed in a mug with an electric immersion heater. "He was tight as a tick," said one acquaintance; his expenses amounted to scarcely more than five dollars a day.

Galt was equally stingy with his words and thoughts. His emotional life was a mystery. He rarely gestured and almost never laughed. He liked to leave people guessing and once described his personal motto as "Never let the left hand know what the right is doing." He once said, in the manner of a boast, that he had not cried since he was twelve years old.

His sexual relationships were fleeting and superficial. Women, he had said, were to use and forget. He'd never married, and he'd never been in love—indeed, he hated the word "love." "I don't think that a man sits around talking about love and so on. It sounds sort of odd to me. Women—they'll break down and cry and all that stuff." As he had in Puerto Vallarta, Galt frequented hookers, and according to one acquaintance his preferred mode of pleasure was "to get his knob polished." His life seemed devoid of romance. "You can't trust anyone too far, especially the women type," Galt later wrote. "No woman has ever thought much of me—and anyways, marrying would have interfered with my travels."

Those who conversed with Galt often came away with the unsettling realization that he had revealed nothing of pinpointable substance—and that he rarely returned a gaze. An introduction to Eric Galt was an unsatisfying affair—his handshake was limp and unresponsive. Blinking rapidly, Galt would turn his head and look downward or sideways, so that even close up it was hard to appraise the man. Like a squid, he seemed to throw up clouds of obscuring ink, hoping to screen himself from scrutiny and keep others guessing who he was and where he stood.

Students at the National Dance Studio, where Galt took rumba and cha-cha lessons for several months, quickly noticed his mysterious reticence. The school, on Pacific Avenue in Long Beach, was a melancholy place where lonely hearts came to meet under the net of easy intimacy that close dancing threw over strangers. Galt, however, would not interact with the other students, and refused to join in the fun. He was grimly determined to learn his moves; he said he might soon relocate to a Hispanic country. "I find myself attracted to the Latins," he said. "They're easygoing. They're not too bothered by rules and regulations." But, he said, "it helps socially if you know a little something about the Latin dances." He did in fact memorize the steps, but he was stiff and ungraceful. He got the mechanics of the rumba, but none of its soul.

Galt was especially self-conscious around his female partners and would not allow himself to succumb to their harmless flirtations. He would just shiver bashfully in their arms and look down.

"He was shy," one instructor said. "One time I talked with him for an hour and tried to break him down. When the conversation got personal, he became quiet." Rod Arvidson, the manager of the National Dance Studio, concurred: "He was the withdrawn type, the type that often *needs* to learn to dance."

Nearly everything about Eric Galt seemed bland and retiring, the details of his appearance falling somewhere in the statistical middle: average height, average weight, average build, average age. The cumulative effect of all these milquetoast qualities made him strangely forgettable.

If one lingered and studied him awhile, though, certain attributes began to reveal themselves, like previously unnoticed images rising in the chemicals of a darkroom sink. There was the crooked grin on his face, which, though subtle, was a nearly permanent feature—a smirk that curled with irony and seemed to suggest he knew something he would never tell. There was the tiny dimple on his chin, the touch of gray in his sideburns, the thick cross-hatching of dark hair on his forearms, and a small scar in the center of his forehead. There was his lumbering, slough-footed gait, the stride of a much older man, punctuated by a faint limp. There, too, were the rabbity little tics: the way he constantly tugged on his left ear, the weak nervous giggle, the compulsive habit he had of shuttling his glass of vodka—back and forth, back and forth—on the lacquered wood of the bar.

And so most people who met Eric Starvo Galt, if they noticed him at all, came to regard him as an oddity: a null set of stewing ambition, wiry and watchful, seemingly paranoid—and emphatically alone.

■

FOR SOME TIME since his arrival in Los Angeles, Eric Galt had been paying visits to a clinical psychologist named Dr. Mark O. Freeman. Their first appointment was on the late afternoon of Monday, November 27, 1967, and Galt, sharply dressed as usual, walked into Freeman's Beverly Hills office at around five o'clock. Dr. Freeman wrote in his daybook that his new patient hoped to "overcome his shyness, gain social confidence, and learn self-hypnosis so he could relax, sleep and remember things better."

They began to talk, and Dr. Freeman got a sense of the man. Galt naïvely seemed to believe that hypnosis was a form of communication expressed directly eye to eye, through some mysterious medium of thought rays. "He had the old power idea of hypnotism," Freeman said. "He actually thought you could go around looking people in the eye and hypnotize them and make them do whatever you wanted them to do."

Galt placed great value on the touted health benefits of hypnosis—and especially hoped to learn how to put himself under. All told, he met with Dr. Freeman on six occasions, throughout the months of November and December 1967. Dr. Freeman later said that Galt "made a favorable impression" on him. The sessions were productive, he thought, and the two men got along well.

"He was a good pupil," Freeman said. "This fellow really wanted to improve his mind. He had a bent for reading. He didn't fight hypnosis. I'd show him how to go under, and pretty soon he'd be lying on the couch on his back and start talking. I taught him eye fixation, bodily relaxation, how to open himself to suggestion. I gave him a lot of positive feelings of competence." While Freeman said that Galt confessed to no "deep dark secrets," he did note that in at least one of their sessions together, Galt disclosed a "deep antipathy to negroes."

Then, for reasons not known, Galt severed his relationship with Freeman, saying only that the psychologist "didn't know nothing about hypnosis." He canceled his last appointment with Freeman, telling him that his brother had found a job for him as a merchant seaman in New Orleans. Freeman never heard from Eric S. Galt again.

IF MARTIN LUTHER KING had a committed enemy in J. Edgar Hoover, he had an equally staunch ally working in the same Justice Department building: the attorney general of the United States, Ramsey Clark. Ambitious, idealistic, a Marine with both a master's and a JD from the University of Chicago, the forty-year-old Clark was a tall, slender man with smoldering eyes and a full head of black hair. Clark had long admired King. He regarded the civil rights leader as "a moral crusader, a unifying force, a persuasive voice demanding social justice, and an apostle of perhaps the most important lesson a mass society can learn—change through nonviolence."

As the nation's highest law-enforcement official, Clark had long feared the possibility that someone might kill King. For years, his office had tried to keep abreast of every alleged plot and rumored bounty on King's head. Two years earlier, Clark, then an assistant attorney general, had traveled to Alabama to monitor the Selma-to-Montgomery march and personally scouted sections of the route for likely places where an assassin might hide. He had a strong premonition that King might be shot in Selma, a premonition based on hard evidence: the FBI had identified more than twelve hundred violent racist white males, many with felony convictions for racial offenses, who reportedly planned to converge on Selma. Worried about the threats, Clark sought out King during the march and found him in a tent by the side of the road, sound asleep.

"Here we all were biting our nails," Clark recalled, "and he was just sleeping like a baby. The man knew no fear—he literally walked in the valley of the shadow of death. I came to respect that."

Born in Texas in 1927, Clark was the son of Tom Clark, a prominent Dallas lawyer who had himself served as attorney general (in the Truman administration) and who had recently retired as a Supreme Court justice. As a fair-haired prince of Washington, young Ramsey had grown up in a house filled with government insiders, diplomats, judges, and bureaucrats. When his father was AG, Ramsey used to toddle down the halls of the FBI and was even allowed to sit in J. Edgar Hoover's office.

The FBI director still viewed Clark as a little kid and patronized him to extremes. Hoover took a dim view of Clark's squishy liberal politics and his egghead notions about the root causes of crime. Hoover believed Clark was soft on Communism, soft on civil unrest, soft on law and order. Clark was the sort of man who, in his frequent writings on crime, was not the least bit bashful about writing sentences like this: "We must create a reverence for life and seek gentleness, tolerance and a concern for others." Troubled by the rise of what he regarded as an American police state that increasingly relied on electronic technology to spy on its own citizens, Clark argued that "a humane and generous concern for each individual will do more to soothe and humanize our savage hearts than any police power that man can devise."

These were the sorts of sentiments that made Hoover sick to his stomach.

Even though Clark was, technically speaking, his boss, Hoover freely telegraphed his disdain for his younger superior down through the FBI ranks. He had a variety of nicknames for the attorney general. He called him "the Jellyfish." He called him "the Bull Butterfly" and "the Marshmallow." He said Clark was the worst head of Justice he'd ever seen. He even suspected the nation's top law-enforcement official might be a hippie. He once visited Clark's house and was appalled to find Mrs. Clark barefoot in her own kitchen. "What kind of person is *that*?" Hoover later groused to a reporter.

Clark, for his part, kept wisely discreet on the subject of Hoover. "I describe our relationship as cordial and he describes it as correct," Clark had been quoted a few months earlier. Off the record, however, he believed Hoover's bureau had become too "ideological" and too obsessed with finding Communists under every rock. Most important, he felt, the FBI was compromised "by the excessive domination of a single person and his self-centered concern for his reputation."

Clark knew all about Hoover's fixation on Martin Luther King. He *had* to know: Hoover's FBI kept coming to him with requests to wiretap and bug King's office, residence, and hotel rooms, and in every case Clark denied the request. The attorney general believed electronic surveillance could be used only in matters where national security was demonstrably threatened. "Surreptitiousness is contagious," Clark argued. "If you invade privacy with a bug, why not break and enter? A free society cannot endure where such police tactics are permitted. Tomorrow *you* may be the victim." The practice of bugging and wiretapping, he said, was "more than a mere dirty business—it tinkers with the foundations of personal integrity."

With subversives of King's caliber, however, Hoover saw no point in such constitutional niceties. As an object of Hoover's wrath, King represented the perfect trifecta, Clark realized. "Hoover had three fairly obvious prejudices," Clark told Hoover's biographer Curt Gentry. "He was a racist, he upheld traditional sexual values, and he resented acts of civil disobedience—and King offended on every count."

On the subject of King and nearly every other issue, Hoover and Clark failed to see eye to eye. Their worldviews were diametrically opposed, and their dysfunctional relationship was strained all the more by the simple administrative fact that Hoover *had* to deal with Clark's office on a daily basis. To handle that noxious task, the director nearly always relied on a trusted surrogate named DeLoach.

■

CARTHA D. DELOACH (everybody called him Deke) held the august position of assistant to the director, which made him third in command at the FBI. He was officially in charge of the FBI's General and

Special Investigative divisions, as well as Domestic Intelligence and Crime Records. His real job, however, was to divine, down to microscopically fine tolerances, the boss's cryptic and ever-changing whims. He was good at it—so good, in fact, that many insiders considered DeLoach the likely successor to Hoover should the director die or step down.

DeLoach didn't relish his role as Hoover's liaison to Ramsey Clark. He hated being put in this delicate position between two powerful men—"wobbling on the tightrope," he called it. In truth, DeLoach had no great love for Clark either, but he thought Hoover went too far sometimes, that he treated Ramsey Clark "like a small child."

A tall Irish Catholic from the little town of Claxton, Georgia, Deke DeLoach had hooded eyes, a pink jowly face, and sandy hair oiled back into the tamest possible suggestion of a pompadour. Forty-eight years old, he'd labored for twenty-six years in the FBI, serving as a special agent and gradually working his way up in field offices as varied as Cleveland and Norfolk. A power broker within the American Legion, DeLoach was an accomplished consigliere and Washington company man, someone adept at navigating the vast rivers of memos Hoover's FBI released each day.

In fact, DeLoach practically *spoke* in FBI memo-ese, in a rounded, sonorous, slightly officious drone that said everything and nothing but somehow reassured people. Among his various responsibilities, DeLoach was Hoover's liaison to the White House, and he had so successfully installed himself there that President Johnson effectively let him set up a second office in the West Wing. One reporter called DeLoach the FBI's "Dutch uncle." Graced with the politesse Hoover lacked, he could be charming in a guarded, superficial way, yet his temperament could turn on a dime, and he'd lash out with the full institutional fury of the agency he represented. One did not want to get crosswise with Deke DeLoach.

Although DeLoach loyally defended the director and daily did his bidding, he had to concede that Hoover was "a man of monstrous ego," as he later put it. He was "crotchety, dictatorial, at times petulant, and somewhat past his prime." Like MacArthur during the occupation of Japan, DeLoach said, Hoover had made himself "a demigod." In his presence, "you were not so much an individual personality as a cog in the vast machinery of the universe he'd created. You existed at his whim, and if he chose to, he could snap his fingers and you'd disappear."

DeLoach had been watching Hoover's "intense animosity" toward King for years. And not only watched: the assistant director had played a direct role in many of the COINTELPRO activities (as the FBI called its various counterintelligence campaigns) against King. DeLoach seemed nearly as shocked by King's sexual escapades as Hoover. "Such behavior," DeLoach later wrote, "seemed incongruous in a leader who claimed his authority as a man of God. So extravagant was his promiscuity that some who knew about it questioned his sincerity in professing basic Christian beliefs and in using the black church as the home base of his movement."

Yet DeLoach thought the FBI feud with the civil rights leader had gone too far—he described Hoover's anger as growing "like the biblical mustard seed, from a small kernel into a huge living thing that cast an enormous shadow across the landscape." At the very least, he thought, the bureau's war against King was "a public relations disaster of the first order" that would "haunt the FBI for years to come."

■

IN LATE 1967, as more reports came filtering into the FBI about the planned Poor People's Campaign, Hoover began to chomp at the bit for better intelligence. He wanted new wiretaps placed on the SCLC head-quarters in Atlanta. A memo was circulated throughout the FBI hierarchy, discussing the merits of installing taps. "We need this installation," the memo said, "to obtain racial intelligence information concerning their plans . . . so that appropriate countermeasures can be taken to protect the internal security of the United States."

By late December 1967, a formal request for legal authorization to install telephone wiretaps had reached Deke DeLoach's desk. As usual, it would be his odious task to serve as a buffer between Hoover's FBI and the attorney general. He, for one, was not optimistic about Clark's re-sponse. "A.G. will not approve," he predicted in a memo, "but believe we should go on record."

On January 2, 1968, the formal request was sent to Clark seeking his legal approval to tap the SCLC offices in Atlanta. "We [must] keep apprised of the strategy and plans of this group," the request argued.

"Massive demonstrations could trigger riots which might spread across the Nation."

But just as DeLoach guessed, Clark rejected the request out of hand. "There has not been an adequate demonstration of a direct threat to the national security," Clark replied. The attorney general did leave the door slightly ajar for future discussion, however. "Should further evidence be secured of such a threat," he wrote, "or should re-evaluation be desired, please resubmit."

WHILE ERIC GALT was living in Los Angeles, one other passion, aside from rumba dancing, bartending, and hypnotism, absorbed much of his time and imagination: he became infatuated with the Wallace campaign.

Ever since Wallace announced his intention to run for the White House, Galt had followed the candidate with quickening interest. In November 1967, shortly after he arrived in Los Angeles from Puerto Vallarta, Eric Galt volunteered at Wallace headquarters in North Hollywood and did what he could to help the campaign gather the required sixty-six thousand signatures for the primary ballot.

For a time, he came to view Wallace activism as his primary occupation. When he applied for a telephone line, Galt told a representative of the phone company that he needed to expedite the installation schedule because he was "a campaign worker for George Wallace" and thus depended upon phone service for his job. He became an American Independent Party evangelist—trolling taverns, buttonholing strangers on the street, and beseeching everyone he knew to go down to Wallace headquarters.

The grunts who volunteered for the Wallace campaign in Los Angeles were an odd assortment of mavericks, xenophobes, drifters, seekers, ultra-right-wingers, hard-core racists, libertarian dreamers—and out-right lunatics. As a largely improvisational enterprise, the Wallace move-ment had to rely on the energies of eccentric foot soldiers who seemed to come out of the woodwork and could not be properly canvassed—if organizers were disposed to canvass them at all. One of the head Wallace coordinators admitted that the lion's share of the work in California was being done by what he described as "half-wits" and "kooks." As the biog-rapher Dan Carter put it in his excellent life of Wallace, *The Politics of Rage*, "Several recruits, who recounted grim warnings of Communist conspiracies and the dangers of water fluoridation, seemed more like mental outpatients than political activists."

An unmistakable paramilitary streak ran through the ranks. In one telling anecdote, Carter reports that Tom Turnipseed, a Wallace cam-paign staffer, flew in from Birmingham to meet with one of the Los An-geles district coordinators and was surprised to hear the man boast that he was going out "on maneuvers" over the weekend. When Turnipseed inquired if he was in the National Guard, the gung-ho coordinator replied, "Naw, we got our own group," and then led Turnipseed out to his car to show him the small arsenal of weapons in his trunk—including a machine gun and two bazookas. Alarmed, Turnipseed asked him what he and his "group" were arming themselves *against*. The man, thinking the answer rather obvious, said, "The Rockefeller interests—you know, the Trilateral Commission."

These were the kinds of people Eric Galt found himself working with in late 1967, and though he did not fraternize with them much, he seemed to fit right in with this loose confederacy of misfits. As a volun-teer, Galt almost certainly attended some of the Wallace rallies held around Los Angeles. Held in strip mall parking lots, Elks halls, or county fairgrounds, these homespun entertainments were heavily at-tended by longshoremen and factory workers and truck drivers, many of them the children of Okies who had moved to California during the years of the dust bowl. They were God-fearing, hardworking folk, Wal-lace liked to say, people who "love country music and come into fierce contact with life."

One of the largest and most successful of these political hoedowns was held at a stock car track at the edge of Burbank, less than a twenty-minute drive from where Galt lived. A gospel group warmed up the venue, and then, as Wallace arrived in a motorcade, the emcee, a bourbon-swilling actor named Chill Wills, whipped the audience into a howling frenzy. When Wallace took the stage, the volatile crowd erupted in rowdy cheers, shoving, and fistfights.

Wallace seemed to draw strength from the restiveness in the air. "He has a bugle voice of venom," a commentator from the *New Republic* wrote, "and a gut knowledge of the prejudices of his audience." A *Newsweek* correspondent covering the Wallace rallies, noting "the heat, the rebel yells, the flags waving," and the legions of "psychologically threadbare" supporters, declared that Wallace "speaks to the unease everyone senses in America."

■

To THE CORE of his angry soul, Eric Galt identified with Wallace's rants against big government, his championing of the workingman, his jeremiads on the spread of Communism. He even identified with the governor's Alabama roots—Galt had lived for a brief time in Birming-ham in 1967, and his Mustang still bore Alabama plates, which sported the state nickname, HEART OF DIXIE.

What Galt found most appealing about Wallace, though, was the governor's stance as an unapologetic segregationist. Wallace's rhetoric powerfully articulated Galt's own smoldering prejudices. Although Galt was not politically sophisticated, he was a newspaper reader and some-thing of a radio and television news junkie. His politics were composed of many inchoate gripes and grievances. On most topics he might best be described as a reactionary—he was, for example, drawn to the positions of the John Birch Society, to which he wrote letters, though never for-mally joined.

By late 1967, Galt had begun to gravitate toward stark positions on racial politics. He became intrigued by Ian Smith's white supremacist regime in Rhodesia. In Puerto Vallarta he had bought a copy of *U.S. News & World Report* in which he found an advertisement soliciting im-migrants for Rhodesia. The idea appealed to him so much that on De-cember 28, 1967, he wrote to the American–Southern Africa Council in Washington, D.C., to inquire about relocating to Salisbury.

"My reason for writing is that I am considering immigrating to Rhodesia," Galt said in his letter, noting that representatives from the John Birch Society had referred him to the council. "I would appreciate any information you could give me." Not only did Galt hope to gain citizenship in Rhodesia; he was such an ardent believer in the cause of white rule and racial apartheid that he planned, as he later put it, to "serve two or three years in one of them mercenary armies" in southern Africa. While living in Los Angeles, he wrote to the president of the California chapter of the Friends of Rhodesia—an organization dedicated to improving relations with the United States—raising still more questions about immigration and inquiring about how he might subscribe to a pro–Ian Smith journal titled *Rhodesian Commentary*.

Galt was apparently also an occasional reader of the *Thunderbolt*, a hate rag published out of Birmingham by the virulently segregationist National States Rights Party. Galt was enamored of the party chairman, a flamboyant, outrageous race baiter named Jesse Benjamin Stoner. Born at the foot of Tennessee's Lookout Mountain, a Klansman since his teens, J. B. Stoner believed, literally, that Anglo-Saxons were God's chosen people. Among his more memorable statements, Stoner called Hitler "too moderate," referred to blacks as "an extension of the ape family," and said that "being a Jew should be a crime punishable by death." Lyndon Johnson, Stoner said, "was the biggest nigger lover in the United States."

All of this wasn't just talk: J. B. Stoner was a lawyer who had successfully defended Klansmen and was suspected by the FBI of direct involvement in at least a dozen bombings of synagogues and black churches throughout the South (in fact, he would be convicted years later of conspiracy in a Birmingham church-bombing case). The chief of the Atlanta police said about Stoner in 1964: "Invariably the bastard is in the general area when a bomb goes off."

A confirmed bachelor who had a speech impediment and walked with a limp from childhood polio, Stoner was given to wearing polka-dot bow ties and displaying the banner of the National States Rights Party—a Nazi thunderbolt, adapted from Hitler's Waffen-SS, emblazoned on the Confederate battle flag. According to the historian Dan Carter, a distinct strain of homoerotic camp ran through the NSRP membership. At least one party stalwart, an archly effeminate organizer known as

Captain X, wore jodhpurs and jackboots with stiletto heels; on at least one occasion in 1964 an undercover Birmingham Police Department detective observed Captain X sashaying about the party's headquarters, heavily made up in mascara and rouge—and smacking a riding crop.

The *Thunderbolt*, the National States Rights Party's monthly newsletter with a circulation of about forty thousand die-hard readers, railed with predictable regularity against King and called Wallace's presidential campaign "the last chance for the white voter." Among other things, the *Thunderbolt* called for the execution of Supreme Court justices and advocated the mass expulsion of all American blacks to Africa. Galt apparently loved reading Stoner's screeds in the *Thunderbolt* and repeated his trademark zingers: like Stoner, Galt took to calling King "Martin Luther Coon," and even pasted the racist sobriquet on the back of a console television he kept in his room in Los Angeles.

■

HAVING LONG MARINATED in this genre of hate literature, Galt's prejudices sometimes took on an edge of violence in Los Angeles. One night in December, Galt was having a drink at a dive called the Rabbit's Foot Club at 5623 Hollywood Boulevard, where girls danced in nightly floor shows. It was, according to one journalist who went there, "a murky, jukebox-riven hole in the wall for lonely people with modest means." A regular at the Rabbit's Foot for weeks, Galt usually drank alone, but lately he had been "preaching Wallace for President" to anyone who'd listen, according to the bartender James Morison. Another regular at the Rabbit's Foot remembered Galt as "a moody fellow from Alabama" who drank vodka and preferred the stool closest to the door. He told people he was a businessman, and that he'd just come back from Mexico after spending a few years running a bar down there. For added credibility, he'd toss out a few expressions in Spanish.

On this particular night in December, a young woman named Pat Goodsell—reportedly one of the floor-show dancers—was sitting next to Galt at the Rabbit's Foot bar, engaged in harmless conversation with several other regulars about the state of the world, when the subject turned to the Deep South after someone noticed the Alabama tags on Galt's Mustang outside. "I don't understand the way you treat Negroes,"

Pat Goodsell said to Galt. She only ribbed him at first, but when he dug in and tried to defend Wallace's home state, she pressed the matter. "Why don't you give them their rights?" she asked.

At this, Galt grew incensed, and the others in the bar could feel the tension rising. It was a side of this seeming wallflower they'd never seen before. He said to Goodsell, "What do you know about it—you ever been to Alabama?"

Suddenly Galt sprang from his stool, clutched Goodsell by the hand, and yanked her off *her* stool. It almost seemed as though he were spoiling for a fistfight.

Then he started berating her, his voice rising to a queer, high register. "Well," he shouted, "since you love coloreds so much, I'll just take you right on over to Watts and drop you off down there. We'll see how much you like it!"

When he stormed out of the Rabbit's Foot, two men followed him from the bar, one black and one white. Outside, they picked a fight— "they jumped me," Galt later put it—and wrested his suit coat and watch from him. "To get away from them," Galt said, "I picked up a brick and hit the nigger in the head."

Galt sprinted to his car with the intention of grabbing his Liberty Chief .38 revolver under the seat, but only then did he realize the real trouble he was in: the Mustang was locked and his keys were in his stolen coat, as was his wallet, which contained his Alabama driver's license and about sixty bucks. Although his apartment wasn't far away, he didn't dare head home, for fear that his two attackers would return and steal his car. So he spent the whole night crouching in the shadows of the Rabbit's Foot, holding vigil over the Mustang.

In the morning he found a locksmith who made a new key. (Although he was taking a locksmithing correspondence course, his skills were not yet up to snuff.) Then Galt placed a long-distance call to the authorities at the motor vehicle division in Alabama and, for a nominal fee, arranged for a new license to be sent to him in Los Angeles, marked "General Delivery."

"DID YOU GET them?" Martin Luther King asked his wife over the telephone from his office. "Did you get the flowers?"

It was wintertime, and King was about to go away on one of his many trips. Coretta Scott King, his wife of fifteen years, was recuperating from a recent hysterectomy after a tumor was discovered in her abdomen. Knowing that she felt tender and vulnerable, he was moved to send her flowers, through an Atlanta florist delivery service. The gift arrived at the King home, a modest split-level at 234 Sunset, nestled among red clay hills in the Vine City section of Atlanta, not far from King's alma mater, Morehouse. The house was sparsely furnished, with a few heirloom pieces and a portrait of Gandhi on the wall.

The flowers were carnations, a shock of deep red. "They're very beautiful," Coretta said. "And they're . . . *artificial.*"

Over the years, King had given Coretta flowers countless times, but never fake ones. She was not miffed or insulted by the choice—merely puzzled. "Why?" she asked.

There was a long pause. Then King said, "I wanted to give you something that would last. Something you could always keep."

Coretta thought that her husband was "a guilt-ridden man." He felt unqualified in his role as a symbol, as the representative of black America. "He never felt he was adequate to his position," she wrote. King often said he was "mystified" by his own career, from the moment he was catapulted onto the world stage as one of the architects of the Montgomery campaign against segregated seating on city buses. But in recent years the movement had truly consumed him, taken him far from his wife and family, and left him feeling more regretful than ever. He was married to the movement. "Tonight I have taken a vow," King once told an SCLC audience. "I, Martin Luther King, take thee, nonviolence, to be my wedded wife."

That winter, just after Christmas, he sat Coretta down and confessed to her about one of his several mistresses—the most important one, the one he had grown closest to. She was an alumna of Fisk University in Nashville, a dignified lady who now lived in Los Angeles and was married to a prominent black dentist. The affair had lasted for years, and King made no promises that it was over. King did not tell her about the other women in his life—the mistress in Louisville, the one in Atlanta, and other women of lesser consequence. In his sermons, he hinted at his failings with increasing frequency. "Each of us is two selves," he once told his congregation. The "great burden of life is to always try to keep that higher self in command."

His confession must have devastated Coretta, and yet she must have suspected something for a long time. They'd been growing apart for years, and the tensions were palpable. "That poor man was so harassed at home," said one SCLC member. "Had the man lived, the marriage wouldn't have survived. Coretta King was most certainly a widow long before Dr. King died."

King's affairs and escapades were only one source of their marital stress. Coretta was unhappy in her role as a traditional housewife, stuck at home with their four children while her husband lived in the international spotlight. She rarely got to use her considerable gifts—as a singer and speaker—for the good of the movement. The fact was King wanted her at home. He was a traditionalist, some might say a chauvinist, but he also feared what would happen to the children if they were both killed. "Martin had, all through his life, an ambivalent attitude toward the role of women," Coretta later said. "On the one hand, he believed that women are just as intelligent and capable as men and that they should hold positions of authority and influence . . . But when it came to his own situation, he thought in terms of his wife being a homemaker and a mother for his children. He was very definite that he would expect whoever he married to be home waiting for him."

Like most married couples, they argued about money. When they met at Boston University in the early 1950s, King was a bit of a dandy—he lived in a swell apartment, drove a nice car, wore immaculate clothes. Now King was all but an ascetic. His salary as co-pastor of Ebenezer Baptist Church was only six thousand dollars a year, and he drew no stipend from the SCLC. Much to Coretta's chagrin, he donated nearly all his other income to the movement—his speaking fees, his grants, even his fifty-four thousand dollars from the Nobel Prize. They almost never went out together and rarely took vacations. Through most of their married life they'd lived in a small rented house, had no servants, and drove only one car. The place on Sunset was a recent acquisition, and it was very basic indeed. "There was nothing fashionable about his neighborhood," Andrew Young said. "It was all but a slum." Coretta was irritated that King had not set aside money for an education fund for their children. He hadn't even written a will. "I won't have any money to leave behind," King said in a sermon at Ebenezer Baptist. "I won't have the fine and luxurious things to leave behind. I just want to leave a committed life behind."

King once said that his weaknesses "are not in the area of coveting wealth. My wife knows this well. In fact, she feels that I overdo it." He knew that Coretta would have liked some of the finer things of life—and that, too, was a source of abiding guilt.

Ever since King struck upon the Poor People's Campaign, Coretta noticed a change in her husband, a frantic urgency, as he flew about the country. "We had a sense of fate closing in," she later wrote. "It seemed almost as if there were great forces driving him. He worked as if it was to be his final assignment."

In those last months, she often recalled how her husband had reacted to the news, in 1963, of President Kennedy's assassination. He stared at the television screen and said, matter-of-factly, "This is what will happen to me." Coretta said nothing in reply. She had no words of solace for him. She did not say, "It won't happen to you." Even then, she felt he was right.

"It was a painfully agonizing silence," she later wrote. "I moved closer to him and gripped his hand in mine."

IN THE FIRST weeks of December, Eric Galt became acquainted with a young woman named Marie Tomaso, a cocktail waitress at the Sultan Room, the bar on the ground floor of his hotel. She was an olive-skinned, dark-eyed woman from New Orleans who had a Rubenesque figure and wore a striking black wig. Some nights she worked as an "exotic dancer" at a club nearby on Hollywood Boulevard.

Marie Tomaso thought Galt seemed completely out of place in the Sultan Room. He wore a nice dark suit and kept to himself, hardly speaking a word. She noticed that his skin had an unhealthy pallor, "like he didn't get out too often." He told her he'd lived in Guadalajara for six years and had operated a bar down there. They became friends, and one night he drove her home, where she introduced him to her cousin, a go-go dancer named Rita Stein. The three began to hang out together.

Rita Stein was a young mother whose life had recently been plunged into emotional turmoil; she had left her eight-year-old twin girls in New Orleans with her mom, but apparently a child services official there had threatened to place them in a foster home. Now Rita desperately needed to fetch her children—but she had no car and no money and could not easily break away from her job as a dancer. Eventually,

Rita and Marie prevailed upon Galt. He told them he'd be glad to help. He had a soft spot for kids in trouble—and needed to attend to some "business" in New Orleans, anyway. Besides, he could use a break from Los Angeles.

Rita introduced Galt to her brother, Charlie Stein, who lived around the corner from the St. Francis Hotel on Franklin Avenue. At Rita's urging, Charlie had volunteered to join Galt on the road trip and help out with the driving.

Charles Stein was a deeply eccentric man—perhaps even stranger than Galt. A convicted pimp and drug dealer, and a dedicated chess fiend, Stein believed himself to be a psychic healer. He talked to trees and other life-forms, and practiced odd remedies: he swore he had once healed Marie of an arthritis flare-up by removing her panties and then burying them in the backyard. Stein also believed in flying saucers; he liked to drive out to Yucca Valley on weekends and scan the skies for UFOs.

Although Stein and Galt were the same age, they could not have contrasted more starkly in appearance: Stein was a disheveled, balding moose of a man, weighing more than 240 pounds. He had a biblical black beard and wore beads and sandals. He was a hippie, basically—a decidedly far-out version of the breed. His mother, who lived in New Orleans, described him as "crazy but harmless."

Galt was suspicious of Charlie Stein. When Rita first suggested her brother as a traveling companion, Galt thought he smelled a rat and told Rita and Marie, in a blind rage, "I got a gun—if this is a setup, I'll kill him."

Charlie Stein didn't think much of Galt, either. He thought Galt wore "an excessive amount" of hair cream. From the moment they met, the psychic picked up powerful "anti-vibrations." But Stein wanted to help his sister Rita reunite with his little nieces, and he was looking forward to revisiting the Big Easy, his old hometown, where, among other things, he had once been a bouncer at a French Quarter strip joint.

So it was decided: on December 15, this spectacularly odd couple packed up the Mustang and prepared to embark on a chivalric errand to Louisiana to collect two distressed waifs in time for Christmas. Before leaving, Galt had one stipulation: he wanted Charlie, Marie, and Rita to accompany him to the American Independent Party headquarters on Lankershim Boulevard in North Hollywood and sign their names on the

"Wallace for President" petition. Galt was stone-cold serious about this: he would *not* drive to New Orleans unless the three signed their names. They found it a highly weird eleventh-hour demand—particularly since they had no interest whatsoever in George Wallace—but they gave in and lent their names to the cause. "I figured he was getting paid for votes," Charlie later said, noting that Galt seemed quite familiar with the Wallace headquarters and "knew his way around the place."

When Charlie Stein signed the petition, the registrar at the counter, a sweet elderly lady named Charlotte Rivett, thanked him and said, "God bless you for registering for Mr. Wallace."

Stein darted his eyes at her and said, "What's God got to do with it?"

Now that Rita, Marie, and Charlie had met their end of the bargain, Galt was keen to go. He dropped off Rita and Marie straightaway, and Charlie threw his stuff in the trunk of the Mustang, next to Galt's blue leatherette suitcase and a Kodak camera box. That afternoon Eric Galt and Charlie Stein headed east through the traffic snarls of Los Angeles.

■

THEY RODE ALL night through the desert and into the following day, trading off whenever one driver grew tired. They passed through Yuma, Tucson, Las Cruces, and El Paso and bored deep into the mesquite country of Texas. Sometimes when Galt was sleeping in the passenger seat, he said, "Charlie would nudge me awake and exclaim that a flying saucer had just passed the car." They made a few pit stops for hamburgers—Galt always ordered his with "everything on 'em." On two different occasions along the way, Galt got out of the car and called someone—he didn't say whom—from pay phones. Stein assumed it was someone he planned to meet in New Orleans.

They didn't talk much during their cross-country marathon, but Galt did mention at one point that he had served in the Army and that he was now living off money he'd gotten from selling a bar he owned somewhere in Mexico. Galt liked to drive with the wheel in one hand and a beer in the other. They got to talking about George Wallace and "coloreds" at one point. Galt told Stein that his Alabama license plates made it dangerous to pass through black neighborhoods in L.A. "Once," he said, "they threw tomatoes at me!" Throughout the drive, Stein kept getting more "anti-vibrations" from his traveling companion. He was sure Galt had "a mental block."

"He was a cat on a mission," Stein later said. "He was acting a part. He never talked much—you couldn't get near him."

"What did you say your last name was?" Stein once asked during the drive.

"It's Galt," he replied peevishly. "Eric Starvo Galt. *Galt!*" For once, he enunciated, as though he wanted to make absolutely sure Stein heard what he said. Stein thought he protested too much, that something sounded phony about the name and the exaggerated firmness with which he stated it.

After passing through San Antonio and then Houston, they pulled in to New Orleans on December 17. Charlie Stein stayed at his mother's place, but Galt checked in to the Provincial Hotel, on Chartres Street in the French Quarter. He signed the register "Eric S. Galt, of Birmingham." Galt didn't tell Stein what he planned to do—"just some business," is all he'd allow—though he did say at one point that he planned to meet some guy with an Italian-sounding surname. Galt also said he'd be hanging out on Canal Street at Le Bunny Lounge, a local dive.

A mere thirty-six hours after arriving in New Orleans, however, he was ready to leave. On the morning of December 19, he picked up Charlie and the eight-year-old twins, Kim and Cheryl, along with some clothes and a few toys—including a miniature blackboard. Then they drove straight back to Los Angeles. Aside from gas, food, and bathroom breaks, they stopped only once—for a snowball fight in Texas. Kim and Cheryl, who rode in the backseat, hated the country music Galt played on the radio—and were annoyed by the way he hummed along. To them, he sounded like "a train whistle."

This highly dysfunctional party of Joads arrived in Los Angeles on December 21, a Thursday. Galt and Stein delivered the girls to their mother just in time for Christmas. Galt spent the next few days holed up in the St. Francis Hotel. There wasn't much else to do—even the Wallace campaign was winding down for the holidays. Wallace himself had returned to Montgomery, where his wife, the real governor, now lay bedridden and dying.

On Christmas Day, Galt kept to his room, reading and basking in the orange light thrown by the neon sign outside his window. "You ought to know that Christmas is for family people," he later wrote. "It don't mean anything to a loner like me. It's just another day and another night to go to a bar or sit in your room and look at the paper and drink a beer or two and maybe switch on the TV."

For New Year's, Galt decided to head out to Las Vegas and have a look around—he drove by himself and slept in the Mustang. "I didn't do any gambling," he said. "I just drove up there and looked around and watched people poking money into slot machines."

When he returned to Los Angeles, the newspapers were full of good news: the Wallace project in California had been a resounding success. The American Independent Party had met its deadline and announced on January 2, 1968, that it had gathered more than a hundred thousand signatures, nearly twice the required number. Pundits were dumbfounded by the Wallace phenomenon. The triumph of the petition drive was, according to one political scientist, "a nearly impossible feat."

"The experts said it couldn't be done," Wallace proclaimed to roaring crowds in Los Angeles. "This points out again that, really, the experts insofar as politics are concerned are the people themselves. If you can get on the ballot in California, you can get on the ballot of any state in the union!"

Eric Galt could begin the New Year with the satisfaction of knowing that he had done his small part to put George Wallace's name on the official ballot for the California presidential primary in June.

■

A FEW DAYS later, January 4, 1968, Galt went to see another L.A. hypnotist, the Reverend Xavier von Koss, at his office at 16010 Crenshaw Boulevard. Koss was a practitioner of good reputation in Los Angeles and the president of the International Society of Hypnosis. Galt consulted with Koss for an hour and discussed his desire to undergo treatment. But to Galt's irritation, Koss pressed him with larger questions. "What are your goals in life?" Koss asked him.

Galt tried to answer him as narrowly as possible. "I'm thinking about taking a course in bartending," he said.

"But why are you interested in hypnotism?"

Galt said he thought hypnosis would improve his memory and make him more efficient in carrying out mental tasks. "Somewhere," he said, "I saw where a person under the influence of hypnotism can solve problems in thirty seconds that would take an ordinary person thirty *minutes*."

Koss could sense that there was more to Galt's interest in hypnosis than merely mind fortification. Koss thought he was a lost soul, someone searching for some kind of validation—and a way to fit into society. "All persons, like myself, who work in the profession of mind power can readily discern the main motivational drive of any person," Koss later said. "Galt belongs to the *recognition* type. He desires recognition from his group. He yearns to feel that he is somebody. The desire for recognition for him is superior to sex, superior to money, superior to self-preservation."

Koss advised Galt that in order to reach a better and more meaningful life, he had to see in his mind's eye what he wanted to achieve—a statement that Galt seemed to agree with vigorously. He recommended three books for Galt to read—*Psycho-Cybernetics*, by Dr. Maxwell Maltz; *Self-hypnotism: The Technique and Its Use in Daily Living*, by Leslie LeCron; and *How to Cash In On Your Hidden Memory Power*, by William Hersey. Galt was grateful—he jotted down the titles and would later buy every one of them.

Yet books alone would not accomplish much, Koss cautioned. He began to tell Galt about all the hard work that lay before him if he truly wanted to improve his station in life. Koss said, "You must complete your course in bar-tending, you must work hard, you must go to night school, you must construct a settled-down life."

It was all too much for Galt, and he began to retreat from the conversation. "I lost him," Koss said. "I could feel a wall rising between us. His mind moved far away from what I was saying to him."

Still, Galt said he was interested in undergoing hypnosis, and the Reverend Xavier von Koss was willing to oblige. He began a series of tests to ascertain whether Galt would be a good candidate. Quickly, however, he detected "a very strong subconscious resistance" to his procedures. "He could not cooperate," Koss said. "This is always the case when a person fears that under hypnosis he may reveal something he wishes to conceal."

FEBRUARY 1, 1968, was a rainy day, the skies leaden and dull. On Colonial Road in East Memphis, the spindly dogwood branches clawed at the cold air. A loud orange sanitation truck, crammed full with the day's refuse, grumbled down the street, past the ranch-style houses, past the fake chalets and pseudo Tudors, where the prim yards of dormant grass were marred only by truant magnolia leaves, brown and lusterless, clattering in the wind.

At the wheel of the big truck was a man named Willie Crain, the crew chief. Two workers rode in the back, taking shelter in the maw of its compacting mechanism to escape the pecking rain. They were Robert Walker, twenty-nine, and Echol Cole, thirty-five, two men who were new to sanitation work, toiling at the bottom of the department's pay scale, still learning the ropes. They made less than a hundred dollars a week, and because the city regarded them as "unclassified laborers," they had no benefits, no pension, no overtime, no grievance procedure, no insurance, no uniforms, and, especially noteworthy on this day, no raincoats.

The "tub-toters" of the Public Works Department were little better off than sharecroppers in the Delta, which is where they and their families originally hailed from. In some ways they still lived the lives of field hands; in effect, the plantation had moved to the city. They wore thread-bare hand-me-downs left on the curbs by well-meaning families. They grew accustomed to home owners who called them "boy." They mastered a kind of shuffling gait, neither fast nor slow, neither proud nor servile, a gait that drew no attention to itself. All week long, they quietly haunted the neighborhoods of Memphis, faceless and uncomplaining, a caste of untouchables. They called themselves the walking buzzards.

The truck Walker and Cole rode in—a fumy, clanking behemoth known as a wiener barrel—was an antiquated model that the Department of Public Works had introduced ten years earlier. It had an enormous hydraulic ram activated by a button on the outside of the vehicle. Though the city was in the process of phasing it out of the fleet, six wiener barrels still worked the Memphis streets. These trucks were known to be dangerous, even lethal: in 1964, two garbage workers were killed when a defective compactor caused a truck to flip over. The faulty trucks were one of a host of reasons the Memphis sanitation workers had been trying to organize a union and—if necessary—go on strike.

Having completed their rounds, Crain, Walker, and Cole were happy to be heading toward the dump on Shelby Drive—and then, finally, home. They were cold and footsore, as they usually were by day's end, from lugging heavy tubs across suburban lawns for ten hours straight. The idea of *wheeled* bins had apparently not occurred to the Memphis Sanitation Department. Nor were home owners in those days expected to meet the collection crews halfway by hauling their own crap to the curb. So, like all walking buzzards across the city, Walker and Cole had to march up the long driveways to back doors and carports, clicking privacy gates and entering backyards—sometimes to the snarl of dogs. There they transferred the people's garbage to their tubs while also collecting tree cuttings, piles of leaves, dead animals, discarded clothes, busted furniture, or anything else the residents wanted taken away.

Now, as Crain, Cole, and Walker headed for the dump, their clothes were drenched in rain and encrusted with the juice that had dripped from the tubs all day. It was the usual slop of their profession—bacon drippings, clotted milk, chicken blood, souring gravies from the kitchens of East Memphis mingled with the tannic swill from old leaves. Plastic bags were not yet widely in use—no Ziploc or Hefty, no drawstrings or cinch ties to keep the sloshy messes contained. So the ooze accumulated on their clothes like a malodorous rime, and the city provided no showers or laundry for sanitation workers to clean themselves up at the end of the day. The men grew somewhat inured to it, but when they got home, they usually stripped down at the door: their wives couldn't stand the stench.

■

AT 4:20 THAT afternoon, a white woman was standing in her kitchen, looking out the window at Colonial Road. She heard something strange—a grinding sound, a shout, a scream. She rushed out the front door and looked in horror at the scene unfolding before her.

Willie Crain's big wiener-barrel truck had stopped outside. Some kind of struggle was taking place. The two workers, Walker and Cole, had been standing in the back of the truck, but they were in trouble now. The wires to the compacting motor had shorted out, and something had tripped the mechanism. A shovel wedged in the wrong place, perhaps, or lightning in the area—something had caused an electrical malfunction.

Now the hydraulic ram was turning, grinding, squeezing, groaning. Crain slammed on the brakes, hopped out of the truck, and raced back to the safety switch. He mashed it and mashed it, but the ram inside would not stop.

Logy in their heavy, wet clothing, Walker and Cole tried to escape as soon as they heard the compactor motor turn on, but the hydraulic ram must have caught some stray fold or sleeve—and now began to pull them in. One of them seemed to break free, but at the last moment the machine found him again.

The screams were terrible as the compactor squeezed and ground them up inside. Crain frantically mashed the button. He could hear a terrible snapping inside—the crunch of human bone and sinew. The motor moaned on and on.

The horrified home owner, who witnessed only the second worker's death, talked to reporters. "He was standing there on the end of the truck, and the machine was moving," she said. "His body went in first and his legs were hanging out. Suddenly it looked like that big thing just swallowed him whole."

■

THE STORY OF the fatal accident scarcely made news in the Memphis paper the next morning. There was just a small item in the *Commercial Appeal*—a drab announcement with all the emotion of a bankruptcy notice. The paper failed to mention that the truck in question had a history of killing people, or that the families of Walker and Cole had no money to bury their two men, or that the city had no contractual obligation to compensate the widows beyond a rudimentary one-month severance. Earline Walker, the pregnant widow of Robert Walker, decided to have her husband buried in what amounted to a pauper's grave in Tallahatchie County, Mississippi, down in the Delta, where their families had been field hands.

Instead, the headlines that morning were reserved for Memphis's most famous citizen—Elvis Presley—whose wife, Priscilla, had given birth to a six-pound fifteen-ounce baby girl at Baptist Hospital less than an hour after Walker and Cole met their deaths. The Presleys' daughter had dark hair and blue eyes, and they'd named her Lisa Marie. For the rush to the hospital that morning, Elvis had orchestrated an elaborate caravan at Graceland, complete with a decoy vehicle to throw off reporters. Dressed in a pale blue suit and blue turtleneck, Elvis greeted well-wishers at the hospital while Priscilla rested—then blazed off again in a convoy of Lincolns and Cadillacs.

"I am so lucky, and my little girl is so lucky," Elvis said. "But what about all the babies born who don't have anything?"

■

JUST OVER A week later, on February 12, thirteen hundred employees from the city's sanitation, sewer, and drainage departments went on strike. Though the deaths of Walker and Cole provided the catalyst, the strike organizers had a long list of grievances that went well beyond the immediate question of safety. They wanted better pay, better hours, the right to organize, a procedure for resolving disputes. They wanted to be recognized as working professionals—and not as boys. Theirs was a labor dispute with unmistakable racial overtones, since almost all the sanitation and sewer workers were black.

February was an inauspicious time to begin a garbage strike; conventional wisdom had it that a work stoppage should occur in the summer, when the refuse would rot faster and produce an unholy stench. But the strike preyed on an old dread lodged deeply within the civic memory: Ever since the yellow-fever epidemic of 1878—which was then thought to have been spawned by putrescent garbage heaped in open cesspools—the city had been extremely attentive to public cleanliness.

From the start, the city refused to acknowledge the garbagemen's cause, or even their union's existence. Soon a few scabs were brought in, but they couldn't keep pace, and the garbage began to pile up all around the city. Municipal employees could not go on strike, Memphis's mayor, Henry Loeb, insisted. "This you can't do," he told them. "You are breaking the law. I suggest you go back to work."

Henry Loeb III was a garrulous, square-jawed man, six feet four, who had commanded a PT boat in the Mediterranean during World War II. He came from a family of millionaires who owned laundries, barbecue restaurants, and various real estate concerns. His wife, Mary, the daughter of a prominent cotton family, was Queen of the Cotton Carnival in 1950. It couldn't be said that Loeb was a racist—certainly not in the raw, Bull Connor sense—and he was by no means a typical cracker politician. For one thing, he'd been schooled in the East, at Phillips Andover and Brown; for another, he was Jewish, a biographical quirk that made him unfit for the Memphis Country Club (even though he'd recently converted to Christianity and joined his wife's Episcopal church).

Like many white business leaders in the South, Mayor Loeb approached the entwined subjects of labor and race with a paternalism reminiscent of the plantation. Although always outwardly courteous to blacks, he called them "nigras" despite his best efforts, and he seemed to believe that his fair city, having avoided the messy troubles of Little Rock, Birmingham, and Montgomery, didn't have a race problem. During an earlier term as mayor, Loeb had presided over the integration of the city's public establishments, schools, and restaurants without incident. Reinforced by that mostly positive experience, Loeb's position was that black folks in Memphis were *content*—and would remain so, as long as Northern agitators didn't come down and stir things up.

This was a prevalent attitude among white Memphians, in fact, an attitude perhaps best summed up by a popular cartoon that ran in the *Commercial Appeal* every morning. The creation of a Memphis editorial cartoonist named J. P. Alley, *Hambone's Meditations* featured the home-spun wisdom of a lovably dim-witted black man, a kind of idiot savant. The grammatically challenged Hambone would say things like: "Don' make no diff'unce whut kin' o' face you's got, hit look mo' bettuh *smilin'*!!"

The garbage workers didn't seem so different from Hambone; many of them were older men who talked and carried themselves not unlike the cartoon character. They were "the world's least likely revolutionaries," the journalist Garry Wills said at the time. Unschooled in the ways of protest, they were lowly Delta "blue-gums," as some whites still called them—men who scratched where they didn't itch and laughed at things that weren't funny. Yet these men were playing fiercely against type. They refused to listen to the mayor, and they would not go back to work. Instead, they were out there each day, marching down Main Street, past glowering police and unsympathetic merchants, on the way to city hall to lay their grievances before the massuh.

Mayor Loeb, stubborn as John Wayne, didn't see what was coming—even after it had arrived. Memphis, which had been run for generations by the well-oiled machine of an all-powerful political boss named E. H. Crump, was an orderly, quiet, and well-mannered town of leafy parkways and beautiful cul-de-sacs. Crump had died in 1954, but his punctilious spirit lived on. Affairs were supposed to run smoothly, and people were supposed to be nice. It was not only discourteous to honk your horn in Memphis; it was *illegal*. "This is not New York," Loeb told the strikers. "Nobody can break the law. You are putting my back up against a wall, and I am not going to budge."

The nominal leader of the strike was a blunt, overweight former garbage worker named T. O. Jones, a firebrand whose considerable courage did not quite make up for his lack of savvy or experience. Eventually, the sanitation workers attracted more sophisticated national leadership in the form of labor representatives from the American Federation of State, County, and Municipal Employees. The real moral force behind the strike, however, proved to be a local Memphis minister, a cerebral man who happened to be a legendary tactician of the civil rights movement. His name was James Lawson.

An old friend of Martin Luther King's, Lawson had studied the tenets of civil disobedience while living in India, had played a crucial role in leading the successful Nashville sit-ins of 1960, and had traveled to Vietnam on an early peace-seeking mission. Lawson saw the sanitation strike not merely as a labor dispute but also as a civil rights crusade, and soon he made his influence felt. "You are human beings," he told the striking workers. "You deserve dignity. You aren't a slave—you're a man."

One day a few weeks after the start of the strike, the garbage workers began carrying a placard whose slogan, echoing Lawson's words, neatly summed up their fight. The slogan caught on in Memphis, and then around the nation. It said: I AM A MAN.

THROUGH THE MONTH of February 1968, as Martin Luther King stepped up his travels around the country to promote the Poor People's Campaign, it became clear to everyone close to him that he desperately needed a vacation. His doctor said so, and so did Coretta. Friends and colleagues noticed the bags under his eyes, the despair in his voice, the worry on his face. He nursed ever-deepening doubts about himself and the direction of the movement. His insomnia worsened. In speeches and sermons, he touched increasingly on morbid themes. He even made the SCLC draft new bylaws declaring that his closest friend and right-hand man, Ralph Abernathy, would succeed him should anything happen to him. King, clearly, was about to snap.

Finally his staff prevailed. It was time for their leader to head for somewhere sunny. Abernathy would go with him. Their usual habit, this season of the year, was to spend a week in Jamaica. This time, though, King had a different idea: they would fly to Acapulco.

They left the first week of March. On the initial flight, to Dallas, King fell into an argument with a segregationist white man from North Carolina. Ordinarily, King never engaged in pointless one-on-one jousts, but something about the man ignited his temper. Uncharacteristically aggressive in pressing his points, King talked about the Poor People's Campaign as an alternative to riots this summer. The argument predictably went nowhere, but when they landed in Dallas, the segregationist wished King good luck in Washington, saying, "It may be the last chance for your brand of non-violence."

On the ramp, Abernathy questioned King about the argument. *Why do you even bother with those guys?* he said. *You know you can't convince them.*

"I don't play with them anymore, Ralph," King said testily. "I don't care who it offends."

In the Dallas airport, King and Abernathy stopped off in a men's clothing shop. When he noticed Abernathy admiring a collection of fine neckties, King lapsed into an effusively generous mood. "Here, take this," he said, handing Abernathy his American Express card. "Buy one for me, and four or five for yourself, whatever you want." He set off down the terminal to place a call at a pay phone while Abernathy bought nearly fifty dollars' worth of ties.

They landed in Acapulco that afternoon and checked in to a suite at the El Presidente Hotel with a balcony that looked out over Condesa Beach and the brilliant blue Pacific. King and Abernathy spent the day watching the famous cliff divers and then ducking into the shops of La Costera. King remained in a sentimental and ultra-generous mood, one that Abernathy found sweet but strange. Anything that met Abernathy's fancy, King tried to buy.

After a long day, they collapsed in their suite. Abernathy woke up in the dead of night, around three o'clock in the morning, with a stab of foreboding. In the dim light, he noticed that King wasn't in his bed. Worried, he checked the bathroom and the common room, but his friend was nowhere to be found. He thought about calling hotel security. Then he remembered the balcony.

He opened the sliding door and found King there, in his pajamas, leaning over the railing, lost in thought. Even as Abernathy drew near to his side, King didn't seem to register his presence.

Abernathy and King had been together since the beginning—

since the Montgomery bus boycott and the formation of the Southern Christian Leadership Conference. They'd met in 1951 when Abernathy, a native Alabaman and World War II veteran, was a student pursuing a master's degree in sociology. Since then, they'd marched together, tasted tear gas together, gone to jail together. And nearly everywhere they went in their ceaseless travels, they shared the same hotel room. They were inseparable friends—"a team," as Abernathy put it, "each of us severely crippled without the other." But in all those turbulent years, Abernathy had never been so worried about his friend. He feared that King might have received another letter from the FBI, urging him to commit suicide. He worried that suicide was what King vaguely had in mind now, as he leaned out over the balcony.

"Martin," he said. "What you doing out here this time of night? What's troubling you?"

King didn't reply at first. He just stood there, arms draped over the railing. He stared and stared at the ocean. "You see that rock out there?" he finally said.

Abernathy looked over the dark water and saw a huge rock in the bay, waves frothing around it. "Yeah, I see it," he said, puzzled.

"How long you think it's been there?" King asked.

"I really don't know. Centuries and centuries. I guess God put it there."

The waves smashed and hissed. "You know what I'm thinking about?" King said.

"No, I really don't." Abernathy's concern was edging into annoyance. "Tell me."

"You can't tell me what I'm thinking about, looking at that rock?"

Abernathy only shook his head—he was irritated by this cryptic guessing game.

In the silence, King started singing a hymn. "Rock of ages, cleft for me, let me hide myself in thee."

Now Abernathy understood. It was the old hymn they'd sung together many times before, a reverie about approaching death, about finding comfort in the final hours. Though he was now thoroughly spooked, Abernathy joined in, and for a time the old friends sang out over the sea breeze of Acapulco:

While I draw this fleeting breath,
When mine eyes shall close in death
When I soar to worlds unknown,
See thee on thy judgment throne,
Rock of ages, cleft for me,
Let me hide myself in thee.

ONE OF THE self-help books that the Reverend Xavier von Koss recommended to Eric Galt, *Psycho-Cybernetics*, by Dr. Maxwell Maltz, was a slender paperback with a blazing orange cover. The book claimed to offer "a new technique for using your subconscious power" by incorporating recent discoveries from the emerging world of computers.

Galt studied *Psycho-Cybernetics* closely. Throughout this strange little book, Dr. Maltz drew an analogy between the human personality and "servo-mechanisms" like the electronic computer. He proposed to show how a person could lead a happier, more fulfilled life by following some of the same ruthlessly goal-oriented processes that "servo-mechanisms" use to accomplish assigned tasks and solve computational problems.

"Your brain and nervous system constitute a goal-striving mechanism which operates automatically," he wrote. Maltz's basic point was that, much like a computer, the human personality craves a central, organizing goal. Said Maltz: "The automatic creative mechanism within you can operate in only one way: It must have a target to shoot at."

The trick to happiness and fulfillment, Maltz argued, is "to purge all memory of past failures" while developing what he called a "nostalgia for the future." All along, one must keep "the desired end-result constantly in mind," aggressively seizing every opportunity to move toward it. "You must go on the offensive," Maltz stressed, while focusing the mind much like the electronic brain that drives a self-guided weapon. The goal-striving mechanism, he said, "works very much as a self-aiming torpedo or missile seeks out its target and steers its way to it."

In *Psycho-Cybernetics*, Dr. Maltz was fond of quoting a line from Emerson: "Do the thing and you will have the power." The goal cannot be some far-off abstraction that one loosely dreams and procrastinates about; it must be a sharp goad for intense activity and applied effort.

"Don't think before you act. *Act*—and correct your actions as you go along," Maltz advised. "It is the way all servo-mechanisms *must* work. A torpedo does not 'think out' all its errors in advance. It must *act first*— start moving toward its goal—*then* correct any errors which may occur."

Oddly, Dr. Maltz was neither a psychologist nor a computer specialist but a plastic surgeon. For years he had cut away on the faces of burn victims, sufferers of congenital birth defects, survivors of traumatic car accidents, and unlucky souls cursed with harelips and cleft palates.

Dr. Maltz loved his work and claimed that the personalities of his patients often changed dramatically after their procedures—they brightened, blossomed, and began to move successfully toward their goals. "When you change a man's face you almost invariably change his future," Maltz wrote. "A plastic surgeon does not simply alter a man's face. He alters the man's inner self. The incisions frequently cut deep into the psyche."

■

On March 5, perhaps prompted by his reading of *Psycho-Cybernetics*, Galt visited a prominent plastic surgeon, Dr. Russell Hadley, in his medical office on Hollywood Boulevard. A bearish, likable man, and a former medic in World War II, Dr. Hadley now taught on the staff of the USC Medical School. Galt was scheduled to have a rhinoplasty— a nose job.

Galt wanted the tip of his nose sculpted to make it appear less bulbous. When Dr. Hadley asked why, Galt replied that he was an actor seeking cosmetic improvements because he had begun to land some enticing roles in TV commercials. "I casually told him," Galt later said, "that I thought the surgery would enhance my prospects, and the doctor saw nothing out of the ordinary." Galt had other features he wanted to alter—most notably his prominent ears, which always had been a source of embarrassment to him—but he'd save those procedures for another day. "The ears," Galt said, "would have to wait."

Hadley informed him that the fee for the rhinoplasty procedure was two hundred dollars, and Galt promptly paid in cash. On the medical form, Galt gave his address as "the St. Francis Hotel" and listed his nearest relative as a "Carl L. Galt," of Birmingham, Alabama.

As he customarily did, Dr. Hadley snapped a "before" picture of Galt, which he planned to compare with an "after" picture he would take once the patient's scars were fully healed. Then Hadley, donning a mask and surgical gown, put Galt under local anesthesia, packed his nostrils with gauze and cocaine strips, and, with his fine scalpels and suctioning tools at the ready, performed the rhinoplasty in a small operating room adjacent to his office. The procedure took about an hour. After suturing the incisions and bandaging the abraded flesh, Dr. Hadley sent Galt on his way.

The operation had gone flawlessly, but Galt was not quite satisfied. Back home at the St. Francis, he ripped off his bandages. Standing in front of a mirror, Galt resolved to improve on things. He pressed and shaped the inflamed cartilage of his nose, bending it slightly to the right. This little exercise in self-manipulation must have smarted terribly, but Galt, wincing through the pain, was determined to accentuate the work that Hadley had done. Then Galt retaped his nose, as he later put it, "in a position that would apply more pressure to the end of my nose," in the hope that it would "heal in a more Roman, aquiline fashion."

Galt met the doctor for a follow-up appointment on March 7 to have the nasal pack removed, and then again on March 11, when Dr. Hadley undid the stitches. The doctor noted that the wounds were "healing well."

The patient was scheduled for one last appointment several weeks later—a checkup in which he was supposed to pose for the "after" photo—but Eric Galt never returned to the offices of Dr. Russell Hadley.

Although Galt had spent several long hours in his close care—and Hadley prided himself on rarely forgetting a face—the details of his patient's visage would soon vanish from his memory. "I'm a fairly observant person," Hadley later said. "Faces are my business. But what amazes me is that, try as I might, I cannot remember anything at all about Eric S. Galt."

■

LATER THAT SAME week, Martin Luther King was also in Los Angeles, staying in a hotel only a few miles from the St. Francis. On March 16, King gave a talk to the California Democratic Council at the Disneyland Hotel in Anaheim, where he praised the cheering crowds for endorsing Senator Eugene McCarthy's presidential bid (even though King himself had not formally endorsed McCarthy). He then made disparaging comments about Lyndon Johnson that were widely quoted in the news. "The government is emotionally committed to the war," King said, but "emotionally hostile to the needs of the poor." King made the local television news, as well as the *Los Angeles Times*, but his statements were largely overshadowed by Robert Kennedy's formal declaration, made that same day from Washington, that he would run for the presidency.

The next day, Sunday, March 17—St. Patrick's Day—King delivered a sermon titled "The Meaning of Hope" at a church in Los Angeles. He said that hatred, whether practiced by whites or blacks, was becoming a national disease. "I've seen hatred," he told the congregation, "on too many faces—on the faces of sheriffs in the South and on the faces of John Birch Society Members in California. Hate is too great a burden to bear. I can't hate."

Sometime that day, the Reverend James Lawson in Memphis reached King by telephone in his hotel. Lawson had an urgent invitation: he wanted his old friend to swing through Memphis and give a talk to the striking garbage workers. The sanitation strike was now over a month old and reaching a crisis stage, Lawson said. During a recent peaceful march down Main Street, the police had attacked the garbage workers with Mace and billy clubs. Mayor Loeb was digging in, and things were getting ugly. Could King lend a hand?

King asked Lawson when he'd like him to be there.

Lawson said the sooner the better, noting that a mass meeting was scheduled for the very next night, March 18. Lawson told King that if he came, he could expect to address a crowd of at least ten thousand people. What was happening in Memphis, Lawson said, was the perfect illustration of what he was trying to accomplish with the Poor People's Campaign—a spirited fusion of racial and socioeconomic issues. King needed to see it for himself.

As it happened, King was already scheduled to travel through Mississippi all the next week. A brief detour through Memphis wouldn't be too taxing on his itinerary, King agreed.

Even as he said this, Lawson could hear some of King's staff members grumbling in the background. Andrew Young, the executive vice president of the SCLC, was one of the grumblers. He worried that Memphis was a distraction, if not a trap. King needed to stay focused on the main goal, the march in Washington. Their month was already seriously overbooked, and King was exhausted from ceaseless traveling. Young knew that King had an incorrigible habit of ensnaring himself in local conflicts by accepting "just one little invitation to give just one little speech."

But King overruled Young and the rest of the staff. He told Lawson what he wanted to hear. They would rework the itinerary, and King would fly to Memphis the next day in time for the mass meeting. It would only be one night—what could be the harm in that?

■

AT THE SAME moment that King was giving his Sunday sermon only a few miles away, Eric Galt walked down to the front desk of the St. Francis Hotel and gave notice that he would be vacating his room. He filled out an official postal service card to have his mail forwarded to "General Delivery, Atlanta." This venue change was more than a little strange: Eric Galt had no personal connection to the state of Georgia. Apparently, he'd never been to Atlanta in his life.

It had been one week since his last appointment with Dr. Hadley. The stitch marks on his nose were almost gone, and Galt felt more comfortable out in public. That day, he took care of a number of last-minute errands in preparation for his cross-country trip. The next morning, Monday, March 18, he threw all his belongings in his car—the Channel

Master transistor radio, the portable Zenith television, the photographic equipment, the sex toys, and the self-help books. He stopped by Marie Tomaso's place and picked up a box of clothes that she'd asked him to drop off for her family in New Orleans.

Then he pointed the Mustang east, toward Martin Luther King's hometown.

King flew east late in the afternoon of March 18, landing in Memphis just in time to speak to the rally that had assembled at Mason Temple, a massive black Pentecostal church downtown. Lawson hadn't lied about the turnout—in fact, he'd significantly underestimated it. When King entered the cavernous hall and stepped up to the podium, he found more than fifteen thousand cheering fans packed inside.

After the roar subsided, King greeted the sanitation workers and congratulated them for their struggle. "You are demonstrating," he began, "that we are all tied in a single garment of destiny, and that if one black person is down, we are all down. You are reminding not only Memphis, but you are reminding the nation that it is a crime for people to live in this rich nation and receive starvation wages."

King was invigorated by this crowd. The energy in the great hall was intoxicating. No one booed, no one heckled. This audience unequivocally loved him, and everyone seemed united behind the strike—in lieu of collection plates, enormous garbage cans were passed around and filled with donations. "I want you to stick it out," King said, until "you can make Mayor Loeb say 'Yes,' even when he wants to say, 'No.' "

King spoke for an hour, almost entirely without notes. He explained that the Memphis strike fit into the larger fight that was now central to the movement—the fight for economic justice symbolized by his upcoming Poor People's Campaign. "With Selma and the voting rights bill," he said, "one era came to a close. Now our struggle is for genuine equality, which means *economic* equality. What does it profit a man to be able to eat at an integrated lunch counter if he doesn't earn enough money to buy a cup of coffee?"

King moved toward a broad indictment of American society—how could a nation so rich and technologically innovative fail to recognize the misery of its poorest citizens? "We built gigantic buildings to kiss the sky," King said, and "gargantuan bridges to span the seas. Through our spaceships we carve highways through the stratosphere. Through our submarines we penetrate oceanic depths. But it seems I can hear the God of the universe saying, 'Even though you've done all of that, I was hungry and you fed me not. I was naked and ye clothed me not. So you cannot enter the kingdom of greatness.' "

King left the microphone for a moment to confer with Lawson, then returned to the podium to close his address with an announcement that did not please his staff: he was coming back to Memphis in a few days to conduct a massive march downtown on behalf of the garbage workers. "I will lead you through the center of Memphis," he said. "I want a tremendous work stoppage, and all of you, your families and children, will join me."

The crowds went wild, and King's face lit up. He loved the spirit here in Memphis. It seemed that everyone in the vast hall was smiling— everyone except Ralph Abernathy and Andrew Young, who could only roll their eyes and think: *Just one little speech.*

■

IN TRUTH, KING had conflicted feelings about Memphis, a town he had visited many times before. It was a very different city from Atlanta, rougher around the edges, funkier, with a population that was poorer and closer to the cotton fields. The last time King had stayed any length of time here was in 1966. In June of that year, James Meredith, who'd become nationally famous four years earlier as the first African-American man to attend the University of Mississippi, was leading a solitary march—the March Against Fear, he called it—from Memphis to Jackson, Mississippi, to protest brutality against blacks when he was struck down by a white sniper wielding a shotgun; seriously but not fatally hurt, Meredith had become a victim of the very thing he was marching against. King joined a clutch of civil rights leaders in Memphis to pick up where Meredith had fallen—and to trudge through sultry heat all the way to Jackson, Mississippi. Though they reached their destination, the march ended with tear-gas dousings and a deepening rift between King and Stokely Carmichael's emergent black-power movement. King's memories of the episode were not fond ones.

On that stay in Memphis, King had briefly lodged at his usual hangout, the black-owned Lorraine Motel, located a few blocks from the river on the south end of downtown. True to habit, King and his entourage returned to his old haunt on this night, after the speech at Mason Temple.

The Lorraine had long been popular among Stax musicians, gospel singers, and itinerant ministers. Count Basie had stayed here, as had Ray Charles, the Staple Singers, Otis Redding, Aretha Franklin, Cab Calloway, Sarah Vaughan, Louis Armstrong, and Nat "King" Cole. The old part of the lodge—the Lorraine *Hotel*—had once been a white whorehouse. In the mid-1940s the husband-and-wife team of Walter and Loree Bailey bought the place and worked hard to make it respectable, building a new wing that was a modern motor court.

King liked the homey feel of the place, the way you could wander into the kitchen at odd hours and order whatever you wanted. Over the years, King had stayed at the Lorraine at least a dozen times, and the Baileys had become like family. The room rate was thirteen dollars a night, but the Baileys refused to charge King.

King usually stayed in room 306, on the second floor of the motel in the middle of the long balcony. Abernathy referred to it as "the King-Abernathy suite." Furnished with twin beds, a television, cheap Danish furniture, and a black rotary telephone, 306 was a modest-sized paneled room appointed in a 1960s contemporary style that Andrew Young later described as "seeming so modern then and so frightful today."

King, Abernathy, Young, and the few others in the entourage stayed up far into the night, meeting with local ministers and planning the coming demonstration: it was decided that they would march down Beale Street, the fabled avenue of the blues. Lawson, along with AFSCME leaders, would organize the march, and King would drop into the ranks in the mid-morning to lead the procession. Given everything he'd seen at Mason Temple that night, King was tremendously optimistic. Not since Selma had he been a part of something that felt so auspicious.

The next morning King and his crew rose early and headed south into the poorest precincts of the Delta, to begin a brief whirlwind through Mississippi and parts of Alabama.

The day started in Clarksdale, in the heart of blues country—the town where, according to one version of the legend, the young Robert Johnson met the devil at midnight at "The Crossroads" and sold his soul to learn to play guitar. King was brought to tears by the poverty he saw in the plantation settlements of shotgun shacks, surrounded by wet, fallow cotton fields.

Later in the day, King and his entourage worked their way down to a rally at Jennings Temple Church in Greenwood, Mississippi, a town also steeped in the Robert Johnson story. Just outside of Greenwood, in 1938, the itinerant bluesman, still in his late twenties, died a horrible death, likely of strychnine poisoning, said to have been slipped into his whiskey by an angry juke-joint owner. A fellow musician said Johnson "crawled on his hands and knees and barked like a dog before he died."

It was, for King, haunted country, country just a few steps from slavery, and a natural place for his Poor People's Campaign to take root.

He would return to Memphis in three days.

■

ON THE BLUSTERY spring day of March 22, Eric Galt swung his Mustang into Selma, Alabama. He was exhausted from his transcontinental journey and eager to clean off the grunge of the road. The drive from Los Angeles had taken four days. He'd followed a southerly route across the prickly deserts of the Southwest, and then down into Texas.

He stopped for one night in New Orleans, where, true to his promise, he dropped off the box of clothes for Marie Tomaso's family.

Entering the Selma city limits, he turned in to the parking lot of the Flamingo Motel, on Highway 80, not far from the heart of town—and checked in, signing the register book "Eric S. Galt."

Galt moved into his room and peered out the window at the traffic on the highway. The Flamingo was just a few blocks from the Edmund Pettus Bridge, where three years earlier Martin Luther King had helped lead several hundred marchers into the teeth of Governor Wallace's mounted state troopers.

A gritty agribusiness town on the Alabama River, Selma had been a major Confederate rail hub and manufacturing center for war matériel—including shells, saltpeter, even ironclad warships. Nathan Bedford Forrest led a doomed effort to save the town's munitions factories from the Union torch in the very last days of the war. But it was the civil rights movement that had made Selma famous around the world, a fact that Galt must have known. The spirited marchers had tramped by this very motel, down this very road—Highway 80—en route to the state capitol in Montgomery to lay their grievances at the feet of Galt's beloved Governor Wallace. The Selma-to-Montgomery march was in some ways the acme of the civil rights movement. The confrontation at the Pettus Bridge shocked the nation and resulted in President Johnson's signing of the historic Voting Rights Act of 1965.

Why had Galt come to Selma? What business did he have with this racially freighted burg in the Black Belt of Alabama, this arsenal of the dead Confederacy, with its crumbling antebellum mansions and live oaks gauzed in Spanish moss? He was no Civil War buff, and certainly no fan of the civil rights movement. One didn't easily wander into Selma on the way to someplace else; it was not on the main roads between New Orleans, Birmingham, and Atlanta, Galt's ultimate destination. Yet something about Selma interested him enough to make a detour— of nearly sixty miles—to stay the night here.

There is one clue. That morning Galt had awakened in New Orleans, where the *Times-Picayune* reported a curious fact: Martin Luther King was scheduled to make a public appearance in Selma that very day to drum up recruits for his Poor People's Campaign. Other newspapers and TV stations across the South reported King's plans as well.

The conclusion was unavoidable: in making his detour and speeding his way up to little Selma on this particular day, Eric Galt appeared to be *stalking* Martin Luther King. But stalking him for what purpose? Armed only with his Japanese-made Liberty Chief revolver, he surely was not thinking of killing King—at least not yet. That was far too risky. With a handgun, he would have to shoot close in, and unless King was entirely alone, Galt would run a high risk of being captured.

Yet the potent symbolism of killing King in Selma must have registered with him. To many who thought as Galt did, it would seem a delicious irony that George Wallace's nemesis should be cut down in the very spot where the most famous insult to the governor's authority, and to the honor of his state, had taken place.

Far more likely, though, Galt had come to Selma just to get a sense of King's entourage. He wanted to take note of the style in which the minister traveled, his habits of movement, the presence or absence of bodyguards or police details. What were King's most obvious vulnerabilities? What car did he ride in, and in what sort of convoy? How long did he linger with the crowds? King's appearance in Selma would be, for Galt, a kind of dry run.

On a deeper level, it is also possible that Galt wanted to see King for himself and hear his message firsthand, to stoke his rancor for the man and his movement. But Galt's anticipated encounter with his target was not to be. King never reached Selma that evening, and his talk was canceled. Mustering recruits for the Poor People's Campaign, he was delayed in the tiny town of Camden, thirty-eight miles away, and ended up spending the night there. (It's possible, of course, that Galt somehow learned of this late-breaking revision in the SCLC itinerary in time to catch King's appearance in Camden, but there's no evidence for it.)

When a frustrated Galt woke up the next morning in Selma, he began to weigh his options. The papers were now reporting that the Nobel laureate would be heading home. If King would not come to Galt, then Galt would go to King. So Galt checked out of the Flamingo Motel the next morning and headed northeast, on dry roads, in the direction of Atlanta.

■

On March 22, the day of the proposed march down Beale Street, Memphis awoke to an extraordinary spectacle. Overnight, seventeen inches of *snow* had fallen, and the city was a wonderland, with a heavy wet slurry smothering the jonquils, freezing the azalea blossoms, and bending the branches of magnolia trees. Serious snow was a rarity in Memphis, especially in the month of March, but this one was for the record books: it was the second-largest snowstorm in the city's history. Memphis shut down. Schools and factories and government offices closed, with power outages reported throughout the region. Nature, as one wag put it, had gone on strike.

Lawson told King the news: an act of God had intervened, and the march would have to be postponed. "We've got a perfect work stoppage, though!" he quipped. Lawson and King set a new date for the march—Thursday, March 28.

The papers called it, simply, "The Day of the Big Snow." A prominent black minister in Memphis said, "Well, the Lord has done it again—it's a white world." While many people in Memphis welcomed the great storm and the respite it provided from civil tensions, others saw it as a bad omen. "It had never snowed that late in March," said one strike supporter. "And some of us felt that something was just in the air, and that something dreadful was going to happen."

■

Two days later, Eric Galt rolled into Atlanta, and though he knew nothing about the city, he soon found his kind of neighborhood—which is to say, slatternly, sour smelling, and cheap. No matter where he was in the world, his radar for sleaze remained remarkably acute. It was March 24, a Sunday. He located a rooming house at 113 Fourteenth Street Northeast, just off Peachtree Street near Piedmont Park in midtown. It was a somewhat disheveled part of Atlanta that had lately been turning into a hippie district—or at least what *passed* for one in this starched-collar, business-oriented, Baptist-conservative boomtown, which a few years earlier had adopted the boosterish slogan "The City Too Busy to Hate." Home of Coca-Cola and Delta Air Lines, among other large national companies, Atlanta had become the proud epitome of the New South; it was a city of unapologetic commercialism and an often ersatz sophistication, but also, in many quarters, a city of surprising racial tolerance—so much so that one prominent Southern essayist, John Shelton Reed, would remark: "Every time I look at Atlanta, I see what a quarter million Confederate soldiers died to prevent."

Galt's new neighborhood in midtown cut against the city's conventional grain, however; it was a shaggy precinct of head shops and pawnshops, street buskers and panhandlers, co-op houses and record stores, with the first strains of what would become known as Southern rock seeping from the late-night bars along Peachtree. Not that Galt was interested in any of this; he couldn't stand "longhairs," as he called hippies, or their music—and he especially detested their protest politics, one of the constant subjects of George Wallace's ridicule. Except for illicit drugs, which Galt both sold and used, the ways of the counterculture were foreign to him—and antithetical to everything Wallace preached.

Still, Galt felt at home in this part of town, with its familiar undertow of petty criminality. It was a neighborhood, Galt wrote, where he "wouldn't have to answer too many questions." He might have looked like a square with his alligator loafers and his nicely laundered dark suit, but he was a canny hustler who knew how to live on these streets. Here, he could beg, borrow, or steal what he needed, watch his pennies, and lie low as long as circumstances required.

He eased the Mustang into the gravel parking area and walked through the weedy lot to the rooming house, where vines of brown ivy clung lifelessly to the cheap asbestos siding. For a buck fifty a night, he rented a forlorn little room with a marshmallowy bed, a stained washbasin, and a tiny dresser marred with dents and scratches. The room, number 2, was on the first floor, its windows slatted with metal venetian blinds.

Galt coughed up enough money for a week's rent—a grand total of $10.50. He hauled in his portable Zenith, his transistor radio, and his clothes—as always, tidy and clean—and set up housekeeping among the filth.

The manager of the place, a wino from Mississippi named Jimmie Garner, was in the midst of a prolonged drunk. Because so many of his previous tenants had been scruffy squatters—"this place was just *infested* with hippies," Garner later admitted—the landlord was duly impressed by the clean-cut Galt. He thought the well-dressed new roomer looked "like a preacher"—adding that "there was nothing whatever about this man that was unusual." He was quiet and mannerly and didn't cause any trouble. Garner did notice that the guest was always alone, and not at all forthcoming about his circumstances.

"What do you do for a living?" Garner asked him one day.

"Jack of all trades—done some welding in the Carolinas," Galt replied with a curtness that conveyed an unwillingness to endure questioning. For the next four days, the guest came and went, sometimes on foot, sometimes in his Mustang. Mostly, though, he kept to his room, with the blinds drawn.

What was Galt doing *in camera* for those four days and nights? If he was following his usual routine, he was reading the newspaper, watching TV, listening to his transistor radio, and subsisting on saltine crackers, tinned meats, and powdered soups. He also bought a can of Carnation milk, a bottle of French salad dressing, and a bag of frozen lima beans. He had his self-help books, including his beloved *Psycho-Cybernetics*. He was settling in for a long haul, it seemed, and the figures he jotted on an envelope indicated that he was growing short on cash.

At some point he bought a detailed map of Atlanta and began studying it closely. He must have spent a considerable amount of time driving around town, checking specific locations that he circled on the map with a pencil. He was endeavoring to learn the lay of the land—or, as Galt later put it, "to bone up on Atlanta's street system."

One of his circles marked the location of his rooming house. Two others were more ominous. Pencil in hand, he circled addresses on Sunset Avenue and Auburn Avenue: the residence and the church, respectively, of Dr. Martin Luther King Jr.

ON THE MORNING of Thursday, March 28, King boarded a flight at Newark, bound for Memphis. He'd spent several exhausting days in the New York area, drumming up support for his Poor People's Campaign, still determined to wage his "War on Sleep." He tried to catnap on the plane, but he couldn't.

Perhaps he was worried about the Beale Street march, set to begin as soon as he touched down in Memphis. Or perhaps the unpleasantness of the previous night played in his head: After a fund-raiser at the apartment of Harry and Julie Belafonte, he'd ended up staying at the Manhattan home of Arthur and Marian Logan (she was a civil rights activist and a member of the SCLC board). There he'd fallen into an argument about the merits of the Poor People's Campaign that lasted for hours and turned sour. The Logans tried to convey their sincere doubts about his Washington project, but King would hear none of it. Downing glass after glass of sherry, he argued with his hosts until three in the morning. Marian Logan worried that he'd become unreasonable; he drank so much that he seemed to be "losing hold" of his faculties, she said. She'd never seen him so wound up before. She noticed that he gripped his glass with one hand and made a clenched fist with the other.

As his plane sped across the country, King was bleary-eyed, restive, and a bit hungover. He was traveling with an aide, Bernard Lee, a young bespectacled Howard University graduate who'd helped lead the sit-in movement in Alabama and was now a devoted SCLC staffer. Abernathy was already in Memphis and would meet King and Lee at the airport. The plan was for King to stay no more than a few hours in Memphis. He would fulfill his vow to march with the striking garbage workers—and then fly straightaway to Washington to continue raising funds and solidifying support for his Poor People's Army. The march would be a mere whistle-stop.

He worried about Memphis, but he knew that his old friend James Lawson was an ace at organizing these sorts of events, adept at training marshals and disciplining the marchers. A first-rate communicator and strategist, Lawson would take care of things. On King's visit to Memphis ten days earlier, the mood had seemed so right, so united and strong. The esprit de corps of the sanitation workers reminded King of the movement's early days, in Montgomery, Birmingham, and the March on Washington.

The plane touched down at around 10:30. King and Lee disembarked and met Abernathy at the gate. The flight was nearly an hour late, so Abernathy hurried them through the airport and out to the modern terminal to a waiting white Lincoln Continental that whisked them downtown. It was a humid spring day, and the sun was just beginning to burn through the morning haze. More than ten thousand people had been gathering in the hot side streets, waiting for King to arrive.

Now the Continental nosed through the crowds outside Clayborn Temple, the African Methodist Episcopal church that was the starting point of the march, a few blocks off Beale Street. People pressed their noses against the car windows to get a look at King, and for a while he and Abernathy were pinned there in the backseat.

Once he was able to dislodge himself from the limo, King looked around and immediately sensed that something was "off" about the crowd. The atmosphere, he told Abernathy, was "just wrong." People trampled on King's feet and swarmed all around him. The garbage workers were dutifully lined up, carrying their I AM A MAN posters, but King could sense that this was no longer the garbage workers' show. The event was all but hijacked by young rowdies who sang and shouted expletives and seemed generally to have come to raise hell. Many thousands were teenagers playing hooky. Cries of "Black power" filled the air. Though it was still morning, people were drinking. A number of kids wore shirts that said "Invaders," a local organization of militants. Some had scrawled their own signs—LOEB EAT SHIT, one of them read. One firebrand carried a noose in his hand.

The crowds were growing hot and irritable. "All the police would have to do is look the wrong way and the place would have blown up," recalled a spokesman for the Invaders. "Some youngsters in high schools had been led to believe this could be the day, man, that we could really tear this city up."

King and Abernathy found Lawson and pointedly asked him what was going on. *Where were the marshals? Why were all these young folks so riled up?* Lawson didn't know, exactly, but he said some of the crowd's restiveness could be attributed to a false rumor, spreading like a virus, that the police had killed a high-school girl.

King and Abernathy briefly considered canceling the march, but they worried this might precipitate the very thing they most feared—a riot. So much spite surged through the crowd that it seemed imprudent to try to stop it now. King's experience was that usually these things worked themselves out; simply putting one foot in front of the other had a way of dissipating negative energy.

■

THE MARCH BEGAN. King, Abernathy, Lee, and Lawson locked arms in the front, and began walking, as police helicopters whirred overhead. They left Clayborn Temple and slogged along Hernando Street for a few blocks, jerking and halting, trying to find the right pace. Then they turned left onto Beale, the avenue of the blues, and marched west, in the direction of the Mississippi River.

In the rear, no one bothered to form orderly lines. The kids were jostling and shoving, sending forward wave after wave of people stumbling and stepping on heels. "Make the crowds stop pushing!" King yelled. "We're going to be trampled!"

Soon they passed W. C. Handy Park, named for the prosperous bandleader and composer who first wrote down the blues and shaped the form into an internationally recognized genre. As it happened, this very day was the tenth anniversary of W. C. Handy's death, and someone had laid a wreath beside the bronze statue of the beaming bluesman standing with his trumpet at the ready.

But this Beale was a faded version of the street that the Father of the Blues had known; had he been alive to see it now, he would have despaired at its mirthless state. In Handy's heyday, it was the Main Street of Negro America, a place of deep soul and world-class foolishness, of zoot suits and chitlin joints, of hoodoos and fortune-tellers, with jug bands playing on every corner. The street smelled of tamales and pulled pork and pot liquor and lard. Day and night, Beale throbbed with so much authentic and sometimes violent vitality that, as Handy put it in one of his famous songs, "business never closes 'til somebody gets killed."

For more than a century, blacks from across the Mississippi Delta came to Beale to experience their first taste of city life. Workers came from the levee-building camps, from the lumber and turpentine camps, from the cotton fields and the steamboat lines. The only confirmed studio photograph of Robert Johnson was taken on Beale—a ghostly image of the long-fingered bluesman posing in a fedora and pin-striped suit with his well-worn guitar. Muddy Waters, Howlin' Wolf, and B. B. King came here to play some of their first city gigs. The South's first black millionaire, Robert Church, made his real estate fortune on Beale. Black doctors, black photographers, black dentists, black insurance companies, black mortuaries, black newspapers, hotels and restaurants "for coloreds only," African-American parades as a counterpart to the all-white Cotton Carnival—Beale was a place where the concept of "separate but equal" had one of its more spirited and convincing runs.

"If you were black for one Saturday night on Beale, you'd never want to be white again," the Stax Records legend Rufus Thomas once quipped.

By the spring of 1968, however, most of the great clubs and theaters—the Daisy, the Palace, the Monarch, P. Wee's Saloon, Club Handy—were boarded up or gone altogether. Though there were still reputable businesses closer to Main, much of Beale had become a drab drag of busted concrete and liquor stores and pawnshops, populated by winos and petty thieves. As King tramped west on Beale, past Handy's statue, separate was most assuredly *not* equal. The blues was on its sickbed, it was said—a moribund music, an era dead and gone. Now a column of proud but anxious men carried signs in the direction of city hall, headed for an uncertain future.

◼

THE TROUBLE STARTED when King, Lawson, and the others in the vanguard approached the intersection of Beale Street and Main. King heard a crashing sound somewhere behind him and jumped reflexively. They turned right onto Main Street and King heard it again. It sounded to him like shattering plate glass—and it was.

Some of the younger marchers had taken their placards, ripped off the wooden pickets, and started smashing store windows along Beale. This ignited a chain reaction. Now people hurled bottles, bricks, stones, any projectile at hand. Someone yelled, "*Burn it down, baby!*" Screaming bystanders bolted in all directions. The sidewalks glittered with glass shards.

Then came the looters, dashing into stores, grabbing whatever they could on the run, and dashing back into the chaos. Abe Schwab's dry-goods store was robbed and vandalized, as were Uncle Sam's Pawn Shop, Lansky Brothers men's clothing store, York Arms sporting goods, and dozens of other businesses along Main and Beale. Soon incongruous objects from the storefront windows lay about the sidewalks—a broken violin, a washboard, a naked mannequin.

King couldn't see all of this, and he didn't know exactly what was going on behind him, but he smelled trouble. The march had become a mob. He turned to Lawson. "Jim—there's violence breaking out."

Lawson looked worried. Up ahead, a line of policemen in riot gear blocked Main Street. By their implacable stance, they indicated that the march would go no farther. Some of them fastened on gas masks.

Grabbing a bullhorn, Lawson wheeled toward the crowd and made his displeasure known: "Turn around! All marchers, young and old, go to the temple! You have hurt the cause—we don't want violence!"

Then Lawson said to Lee and Abernathy, "Take Dr. King out of the way."

King balked. "Jim, they'll say I ran away."

"I really think he should go," Lawson yelled to Abernathy, this time in an adamant tone. Lawson was worried that King's life might be in danger—and if not his life, certainly his reputation.

King soon realized how ruinous it would be for him to appear to be *leading* a riot. "You're right," he finally said. "We got to get out of here."

Abernathy and Lee linked arms with King and pushed through the crowds to McCall, a side street. There they flagged down a white Pontiac driven by a black woman, who, upon recognizing King, waved them inside the car. A police lieutenant on a motorcycle rolled up and offered to escort them from the chaos. They wanted to go to the Lorraine Motel, but the officer said that would only take them into the teeth of the riot once again.

"Just get us away from trouble," Lee yelled.

"Follow me," barked the policeman, and he led them to the Holiday Inn Rivermont, a new high-rise luxury hotel on the city's south bluff overlooking the Mississippi. The policeman promptly checked King and his entourage in to a suite, room 801. King switched on the television and morosely watched the live coverage from Beale Street. He couldn't believe what flickered across the screen.

Looters darting from buildings . . . canisters of tear gas . . . riot police in wedge formation . . . nightsticks . . . blood streaming down faces . . . squirts of Mace. At Lawson's urging, the garbage workers had fallen back to Clayborn Temple and taken refuge there to plan their next move while bathing one another's burning eyes with wet sponges. They remained disciplined and true to their cause—one police official freely admitted that his cops "never had trouble with the tub-toters." But some of the young hellions, wanting more of what they'd tasted on Beale, ventured out into the streets in search of trouble. When some of them threw rocks at the police and then ran back into the sanctuary, officers fired tear-gas canisters at the church, staining the walls and sending people gasping.

The rioting on Beale soon spread to other precincts. It took police another hour to gain control of the city. When the mayhem finally smoldered out, scores had sought treatment at local hospitals, and hundreds had been arrested. Two hundred buildings were vandalized, with total property damages that would later be estimated at $400,000. A policeman killed—some said cold-bloodedly murdered—a suspected looter named Larry Payne, shooting the teenager at point-blank range with a shotgun. Numerous cases of police brutality were reported. Many responding officers clearly had overreacted in a show of overwhelming force, but others had performed bravely and practiced restraint in a situation they'd never encountered before, a situation that could have escalated into a Southern reply to Watts.

Mayor Henry Loeb, arguing that "the march was abandoned by its leaders," announced on television that three thousand soldiers of the National Guard would soon take control of downtown Memphis to restore order and enforce a seven o'clock curfew. "We have a war in the city of Memphis," added the fire and police director, Frank Holloman, in a fit of hyperbole. "This is a civil war." So tense was the atmosphere around Memphis that a spokesman for the Panama Limited, the Illinois Central passenger line running between Chicago and New Orleans, announced that the train would forgo its customary stop in Memphis. On this night, the Panama Limited's engineer would speed right through the troubled city.

King spent the afternoon watching his nightmare unfold on the screen. He crawled under the bedcovers with his clothes on, smoked cigarettes, and kept his eyes locked on the television. He'd never been so depressed, never so unable to move or speak or react in any way. For hours, he lay in an almost catatonic daze.

Everything he had worked for was in jeopardy, he realized. His marches had always attracted violence, had always served as magnets for turmoil and hate. That was their purpose, in fact—to expose through choreographed drama a social evil for all to see, preferably with cameras rolling. One could only hope for the appearance of a Bull Connor and his police dogs, or redneck Klansmen on the sidelines, burning the usual "nigger" in effigy. Violent opposition only bolstered the demonstration's message.

But in all of King's marches, the participants had never before *caused* violence. This was a new and troubling turn. He realized that what had happened in Memphis that day played right into the hands of the critics of the Poor People's Campaign. How could he stage a peaceable mass protest in Washington when he couldn't bring off a modest-sized march through a modest-sized city in his native South? Memphis had become a litmus test—and he'd failed.

■

LATE THAT AFTERNOON, King came out of his shell long enough to begin a postmortem on the march. He spoke to James Lawson and another prominent Memphis minister, the Reverend Billy Kyles. They told King about the Invaders, a group of young black-power militants who had the reputation and aura of a gang but also aspirations to be a grass-roots social welfare organization that did serious work in the community. If the Invaders hadn't caused the violence, then they had declined to exert their influence to stop it. As elsewhere in the country, a generational divide existed in Memphis between the older ministers and the younger militants. Differences in style, lingo, aims, and education meant that they had trouble working together—the clerical collar came up against the dashiki. On some level, the day's violence was a reflection of those generational frictions.

King hadn't known about the Invaders. He listened carefully and began to process what Kyles and Lawson had to say. "Until then, King really didn't have any idea of what had happened," recalled Kyles. "He wasn't angry, he was just very disturbed, and upset."

That evening King began a telephone blitz, trolling for opinions from his closest friends and advisers. He called Coretta, who tried without much success to console him. He called Stanley Levison, his attorney friend in New York, who told him that more than anything he needed to get some sleep. He called the SCLC board member Marian Logan, in whose house he had stayed the previous night. Her advice was succinct: "Get your ass out of Memphis."

King was sunk in profound doubt about his role and his identity. On the phone, he told one adviser that people would now declare that " 'Martin Luther King is dead. He's finished. His nonviolence is nothing, no one is listening to it.' Let's face it, we do have a great public relations setback where my image and my leadership are concerned."

Ralph Abernathy tried to lift King's spirits but failed. They went out on the balcony and looked over the Mississippi River. Abernathy had never seen his friend this dejected before. "I couldn't get him to sleep that night," Abernathy recalled. "He was worried, worried. Deeply disturbed. He didn't know what to do, and he didn't know what the press was going to say."

The more Abernathy tried to console him, the deeper King descended into his funk. "Ralph," he said, "we live in a sick nation. Maybe we just have to give up and let violence take its course. Maybe people will listen to the voice of violence. They certainly won't listen to us."

THE FOLLOWING MORNING, Friday, March 29, Eric Galt walked into the Long-Lewis hardware store in Bessemer, Alabama, a blue-collar suburb of Birmingham, about 160 miles west of Atlanta. He made his way over to a salesman named Mike Kopp, who stood beneath an enormous moose head mounted on the wall—a trophy that advertised the hardware store's sideline business in big-game hunting equipment.

Galt inquired about the store's selection of high-powered rifles.

"We've got a few 30.30s," Kopp said.

Galt cut him off. "I need something more powerful than that," he said.

He then peppered Kopp with questions about various kinds of ammunition. How many inches would a certain kind of bullet drop in fifty yards? Or one hundred yards? What was the knockdown power? What about the recoil?

The questions were too detailed for Kopp to answer with authority. Galt started to leave, but then eyed the large bearded ungulate scowling from the wall and mused, "I once tried to bring down a moose, but I missed."

Kopp studied the pale, fidgety man and concluded to his own satisfaction that Galt had never hunted moose—or any species of big game.

■

J. Edgar Hoover had been monitoring the events in Memphis, and that morning, March 29, he came to work with a feeling of vindication. To him, the mayhem on Beale Street was a fulfillment of all his earlier warnings: King might talk nonviolence, but it was an act. The Memphis debacle only foreshadowed what would happen if King was allowed to march on Washington. Hoover's ties to the Memphis authorities were unusually close—fire and police director Frank Holloman had been an FBI agent earlier in his career, and had even served as Hoover's "office manager" in Washington. Hoover made sure his COINTELPRO agents were on the case, working with the Memphis police to gather all the information necessary to heap maximum blame on King—and make every accusation stick.

Early on the morning of March 29, the FBI field office in Memphis was in high dudgeon. The assistant director William Sullivan called from Washington and spoke with the second-in-command in the Memphis office, Special Agent C. O. Halter. Sullivan wanted Halter's men to find out if King had been sleeping around, drinking too much, or engaging in any other "improper conduct" or "activities both official and personal" while in Memphis. "Mr. Sullivan requested that we get everything possible on King and that we stay on him until he leaves," Halter later recalled. Among other things, agents tried to learn the identity of the woman whose Pontiac Lee and Abernathy had flagged down the previous day—presumably on the suspicion that she and King might have had a tryst.

Sullivan wanted the Memphis agents to prove that King was personally responsible for much of the Beale Street fracas. Agents were instructed to answer such questions as: "Did Martin Luther King do anything to trigger the violence? Did he make any statements which could have had an effect on the crowd? Did King do anything to prevent violence? . . . Although Martin Luther King preaches non-violence, violence occurs just about everywhere he goes."

The FBI in Memphis was unable to find anything suggesting that King had in any way provoked the violence, but specialists with the

Racial Intelligence Division did seize on one potential line of attack: King, who had urged Memphis blacks to boycott white businesses downtown, was "a hypocrite" for securing a room in the white-owned Rivermont when he could have stayed at the black-owned Lorraine Motel only a few blocks away.

The FBI sent out a blind memorandum to what it termed "cooperative media"—pro-Hoover newspapers around the country. "The fine Hotel Lorraine in Memphis," the memo stated, "is owned and patronized exclusively by Negroes, but King didn't go there from his hasty exit. Instead, King decided the plush Holiday Inn, white-owned, operated, and almost exclusively white patronized, was the place to 'cool it.' There will be no boycott of white merchants for King, only for his followers." (The memo made no mention of the fact that it was a Memphis motorcycle cop, on orders from police headquarters, who had chosen the Rivermont, led King there, and personally checked him in.)

In the end, the FBI succeeded in making only minor hay out of this "hypocrisy" charge, but the smear had a more consequential effect: it ensured that the next time King and his party came to Memphis, they would stay at his old hangout, the thoroughly exposed, open-courtyard (but black-owned) Lorraine Motel.

The violence in Memphis, meanwhile, prompted the FBI's leadership to renew its age-old request to wiretap the SCLC offices in Atlanta and Washington. William Sullivan sent a memo to Cartha DeLoach outlining "the gravity" of King's upcoming Poor People's Campaign and the need for enhanced intelligence on King. The Washington demonstrations, he said, "could end in great violence and bloodshed. This being the capital city, it would do us irreparable propaganda damage around the world. We have been girding ourselves for this task ever since King's announcement to march on Washington. We should leave no stone unturned."

DeLoach and Hoover concurred with Sullivan's assessment. A wiretap request signed by Hoover promptly landed on Ramsey Clark's desk, but the attorney general refused to dignify it with a reply.

■

LATER THAT MORNING, around 10:00, King awakened in his Rivermont suite and pulled himself together. He knew it would be a bad day. He cringed at the prospect of reading the morning papers. In fact, the reaction in the news that morning—and for several days to come—would be even worse than he'd feared.

The epithets were as prolific as they were colorful. The *Memphis Commercial Appeal* called him "Chicken à la King." The *Dallas Morning News*: "The headline-hunting high priest of nonviolent violence." The *St. Louis Globe-Democrat*: "A Judas goat leading lambs to slaughter."

Senator Robert Byrd of West Virginia described King as "a man who gets other people into trouble and then takes off like a scared rabbit." The Memphis riot was "a powerful embarrassment to Dr. King," argued the usually sympathetic *New York Times*, calling the disturbance further indication that he should call off the Poor People's Campaign. Senator Howard Baker of Tennessee said that in view of the Beale Street violence, King's proposed march on Washington would be "like striking a match to look in your gas tank to see if you're out of gas."

King read enough of the offerings to get the gist of it. Disgusted, he took a shower and pulled on some clothes. He was just buttoning his shirt when Abernathy knocked on his bedroom door. "Martin," he said, "we have visitors."

King padded out to the common room to greet three young men in their twenties. "We're with the Invaders," one of them said. "We've come to explain what happened yesterday." They were Charles Cabbage, Izzy Harrington, and Calvin Taylor—leaders of the organization widely blamed for the Beale Street violence.

King took a seat with his guests. He offered cigarettes, and they had a smoke. Bright light from the balcony streamed in through the sliding glass doors. The Mississippi River swirled eight stories below them. The conversation got off to an awkward start when Charles Cabbage mentioned that a man had knocked on his door the previous night and warned him of a plot on King's life.

King replied dismissively that he got those kinds of threats every day. "If someone really wants to kill me, there's nothing I can do about it," he said. Indeed, Cabbage was amazed that King had no security at the Rivermont—and that no one had bothered searching him or his fellow Invaders for weapons.

They finally circled around to the subject at hand. The Invaders claimed they had not caused the previous day's violence. None of the Invader leaders was even present on Beale. But they knew the young militants who had started the trouble, and they had done nothing to discourage it. This was because Jim Lawson had insulted them, they said. He'd refused to allow the Invaders to be part of the planning; he'd kept them out of the discussions altogether. The ministers didn't understand the young brothers and what was really going on in the streets.

King listened with a sorrowful expression. He seemed to see right through them. He wasn't entirely buying their story, but he appreciated the spirit of their gesture—dropping by and speaking face-to-face. He was puzzled, though. He said he couldn't believe anyone would resort to violence. "We should have sat down and talked before the march," he said. "Jim didn't tell me about the black power elements in the city. He led me to believe there were none."

King was less interested in determining the riot's precise cause than in ensuring that violence didn't break out again: he had already decided to return to Memphis.

"What can I do to have a peaceful march?" he asked. "Because, you know that I have got to lead one. There is no other way." King vowed that the SCLC would thoroughly plan the next event and that the Invaders would be included in the discussions. "You will be in on it," King promised. "You will not be left out."

The meeting concluded, and the three Invaders left the Rivermont touched with awe. Even if they didn't subscribe to King's philosophy of nonviolence, they agreed they had been in the presence of a great man. "He wasn't raising his voice," Calvin Taylor recalled. "He wasn't bitter. When he came into the room it seemed like all of a sudden there was a real rush of wind and calm settled over everything. You could feel peace around that man. He *looked* like peace."

■

A FEW HOURS later, Eric Galt drove his Mustang to a large sporting goods store in Birmingham called the Aeromarine Supply Company. Located by the Birmingham airport, it boasted one of the South's largest selections of firearms of all descriptions. As an avid newspaper reader, Galt had likely seen the large classified advertisement that Aeromarine had been running all that week in the *Birmingham News*. "Guns—Guns—Guns," the ad announced. "Browning, Remington, Colt. Over 1,000 arms in stock for your selection. Buy, sell, trade. 5701 Airport Hiway."

Now Galt wandered over to the Aeromarine counter and was met by a man named U. L. Baker (who would later relate the conversation in detail to authorities). This time, Galt seemed to have more definite ideas about what he wanted. "Let me look at that Winchester there," he said. It was a bolt-action Model 70 .243-caliber rifle designed for shooting deer at mid- to long range.

Baker pulled it off the rack for Galt to inspect. After a while, Galt set it aside and asked Baker to take down several other models. Galt studied the rifles for a few minutes but then declared, "I like that one there," pointing to a Remington Gamemaster .243 caliber. "You got a scope that'll fit it?"

Baker brought out a variable scope manufactured by Redfield. Galt liked the look of it and asked what the price tag would be for the rifle and scope.

Baker tallied it up. "That'll be $248.59, sir."

Galt said he'd take it, and while Baker went to work mounting the scope to the rifle, another customer, a local gun enthusiast and NRA stalwart named John DeShazo, sidled up to Galt and gave him a start. "What're you gonna do with *that*?" DeShazo said.

"Oh," Galt replied, "I'm going deer hunting . . . with my brother."

DeShazo thought he smelled liquor on Galt's breath. "That one's powerful," he said.

Galt stammered something about going hunting up in Wisconsin. DeShazo thought the customer didn't look like an outdoorsman and concluded, after watching him handle other weapons in the store, that he didn't know much about rifles. "You've really got quite a gun there," DeShazo said. "You'll have to learn how to use it."

Galt chose some boxes of ammo for the rifle and told Baker he was ready to pay up. He signed the sales slip "Harvey Lowmeyer" and said he lived at 1907 South Eleventh Street in Birmingham. He opened his wallet and paid the bill in cash—all in twenties—and shambled out of the store with the rifle box under his arm.

Later that afternoon, Galt called Aeromarine Supply Company

and said he wanted to exchange the rifle. "My brother says I got the wrong one," he told Don Wood, the storeowner's son, who answered the phone. "I'm going to need a heavier gun."

Wood told Galt he would gladly accept an exchange. However, the store was closing up, so Galt would have to drop by in the morning. Galt took a room at the Travelodge motel in Birmingham, with the intention of returning to Aeromarine with the .243-caliber rifle first thing the next morning.

■

AFTER HIS MEETING with the Invaders, King finished dressing and headed down to a Rivermont conference room to face the media. He looked sharp, dressed in a green-blue silk suit and a razor-thin tie, but Abernathy worried about his friend; King was too exhausted and too depressed to perform before hostile journalists. They were going to destroy him.

Once he entered the brightly lit room, however, King seemed to undergo a transformation. He was poised, forceful, brimming with cautious optimism. The cameras caught no hint of the doubts that had washed over him the previous night. Astonished, Abernathy thought King showed a "lion quality."

Why did you run away from the march yesterday?

"I did *not* run away from the march," King insisted in a level tone. It was a matter of principle: "I have always said that I will not lead a violent demonstration."

The trouble, he pointed out, was caused not by legitimate participants but by a few undisciplined young people on the sidelines. His decision to lend a hand to the Memphis cause was predicated on "a miscalculation," he said. "When I spoke here two weeks ago, thousands of people [were] assembled inside and outside. Nobody booed, nobody shouted Black Power. I assumed the ideological struggles that we find in most cities, particularly in the North, were non-existent here."

King said he now understood his mistake. If he could do it over again, he would sit down and confer at length with the city's black youth. They were "just angry," he said, "feeling a sense of voicelessness in the larger society and at the same time a sense of voicelessness in the black community."

One of the journalists asked King whether the Beale Street violence presaged another long summer of riots across the nation.

"I cannot guarantee anybody that Memphis or any other city in this country will not have a riot this summer," King replied. "Our government has not done anything about removing the conditions that brought riots into being *last* summer."

So you can't give the country a guarantee?

"I don't know what you mean by 'guarantee.' I don't want to put myself in the position of being omniscient. I can only guarantee that *our* demonstrations"—ones fully vetted and organized by the SCLC—"will not be violent."

What had happened in Memphis the previous day was disappointing and even tragic, he said, but he had not lost faith. The philosophy of nonviolence was still the only hope for America and the world—it was, in fact, the only alternative to human annihilation. "Nonviolence can be as contagious as violence," he insisted, and that was something he aimed to prove next month during the Poor People's Campaign on the Mall. "We are fully determined," he vowed, "to go to Washington."

After the reporters dispersed, King turned to Abernathy and Lee, relieved that the ordeal had gone as well as it had. "It was perhaps his finest performance with the press," Abernathy thought. Lee said that King "must be called to do what he is doing—he could not have changed as he did in one night if God had not put His hands on him."

Yet King's thoughts were already somewhere else. "Can you do something for me, Ralph?" King asked.

"What's that?"

"Can you get me out of Memphis?"

■

WHEN THEIR PLANE arrived in Atlanta early that night, Abernathy retrieved his car at the airport and dropped King off at the Butler Street YMCA. King hoped a steam bath and a rubdown from his blind masseur would lift his spirits.

Afterward, King, Abernathy, and their wives had a somber dinner at the Abernathy house. Juanita Abernathy cooked fish and a special casserole she prepared only once a year—a concoction made from pig's ears, pig's feet, and pig's tail. Following the heavy meal, they lounged around the house. Coretta and the Abernathys tried to cheer King up, to little effect. He was still licking his wounds.

He talked about going on a fast, as Gandhi had done, to purify the movement. He talked about the old times in Montgomery, dredging up names long forgotten and reliving youthful triumphs from the halcyon days of the struggle. He tried to snooze on a love seat in the Abernathy family room, gently grousing that the chair was too small.

■

IN BIRMINGHAM the next morning, Eric Galt returned to Aeromarine Supply Company as the doors opened at 9:00. Don Wood waited on him. Something about this customer didn't seem right, and Wood wanted to oversee every aspect of the transaction. He quickly deduced, as John DeShazo had, that Galt knew little about rifles—and even less about deer hunting.

Galt told Wood he'd like to look at the Remington Gamemaster 760 .30-06-caliber rifle. Wood took it down from the rack, and Galt immediately liked the look and feel of it. It was a pump-action rifle, "the fastest hand-operated big game rifle made," according to the Remington literature.

As Galt handled the Gamemaster, Wood asked him, "What you need that one for? That .243 there will kill anything in Alabama."

"Well, see, I'm going to hunt in Wisconsin," Galt replied.

The implication was that the bucks were bigger up that way, so he needed a rifle that could fire bigger ammo. Certainly the .30-06 version of the Gamemaster 760 fit the bill. It had prodigious amounts of "knockdown power," enough to kill anything in Alabama and Wisconsin, too. The ammunition the Gamemaster fired had real heft—it weighed twice as much as the .243-caliber round Galt had purchased the day before.

Galt asked some technical questions about the velocities and trajectories of various rounds. Wood recommended the Remington-Peters

.30-06 soft-pointed Springfield High Velocity Core-Lokt cartridge—
150 grain—which he noted would travel 2,670 feet per second. Mush-
rooming on impact, the bullet would bring down the biggest buck on
earth at three hundred yards. At one hundred yards, it was said to be
capable of stopping a charging rhinoceros. And it was astonishingly accurate, Wood said: for a target standing a hundred yards away, the bullet would drop only one-hundredth of an inch.

The rifle's pump-action feature especially appealed to Galt. It would
allow him to keep his finger poised on the trigger and his eye fixed on the
sight while smoothly pumping the rifle's slide mechanism to reload. As
the Remington brochure put it, "The pump-action aids the shooter in
staying on-target during second- and third-shot situations . . . helping
you to put that buck in the freezer."

Galt said he'd take it, even though the Gamemaster .30-06 cost a little more than the .243. For a scope, Galt decided on a Redfield 2x7. Wood
asked Galt to give him a few hours to mount the scope, and Galt took off.
Wood mounted it himself, setting it to 7x, the maximum magnification—
so a deer viewed through the Redfield's crosshairs would appear seven
times closer than it was. The Redfield company boasted that its 2x7 offered
a "wide enough field of view for tracking moving animals [but] good com-
promise power for varminting." Another nice feature was the magnesium
fluoride film coating on the scope's lens, which enabled a shooter to see his
target in low-light situations—even at late dusk.

The only problem with the scope was that, once mounted, its high
profile prevented the Gamemaster from fitting into its original box. At
three o'clock, when Galt returned, Wood suggested that he might want
to buy a nice leather gun case, but Galt didn't want to spend any more
money. So Wood improvised a solution: he rummaged around in the
back of the store and found an old box for a Browning rifle, which was
slightly bigger than the Gamemaster box. Wood stuffed the scope-
mounted rifle into the carton—it just fit—and secured the slightly cumbersome assemblage with Scotch tape.

Pleased enough with the jury-rigged packaging, Galt selected a
twenty-round box of the Remington-Peters .30-06 cartridges and told
Wood he was ready to settle up. He took out his wallet and completed

the exchange, paying the difference from the previous day's purchase in cash.

Again, Galt gave his name as "Harvey Lowmeyer" with a Birmingham address. Wood did not ask his customers to show identification—nor was he required by any law to do so. Galt smiled awkwardly, picked up the package, and turned toward the door.

THAT SAME MORNING, in Atlanta, King held an emergency meeting of his SCLC executive staff to discuss what to do about Memphis. The all-day conclave was held in a paneled conference room on the third floor of the Ebenezer Baptist Church on Auburn Avenue. Key advisers had flown in from all over the country: Chauncey Eskridge, one of King's legal counselors, came in from Chicago; Stanley Levison, from New York; Walter Fauntroy, from Washington; a labor delegation from Memphis. All King's regular staff was there, too: Andrew Young, James Bevel, Dorothy Cotton, Hosea Williams, James Orange, Jesse Jackson, and, of course, Abernathy.

All through the morning, King sat at a cramped Sunday-school desk, a creaky affair with a tiny wooden writing surface attached by a slender arm. He listened quietly to his staffers as they deconstructed the disaster in Memphis. They bickered and hurled accusations and named names. They agreed on little—except that Memphis was a catastrophe, and that under no circumstances should King go back to that troubled river town. The situation in Memphis, said one adviser, "was a set up," possibly orchestrated by the FBI to ruin King once and for all. It was a detour, a dangerous left turn. And it was a drain on resources that the SCLC did not have.

King listened to the dissension with growing agitation and distress. More painful to him was that many members of his staff clearly were not on board with the Poor People's Campaign. The Washington project, they said, was too ambitious, too logistically complicated, too diffuse in its goals. King held his tongue as staff members put forward their own ideas about what they should be doing. Jim Bevel wanted to concentrate on the Vietnam War. Jesse Jackson thought grassroots economic initiatives like the one he headed up in Chicago—called Operation Breadbasket—were the most promising use of the SCLC's time and energy. Hosea Williams said the real secret to gaining power was voter registration drives to elect leaders sympathetic to their cause.

After a while the discussion became a blur to King. His young staffers were headstrong. They were growing restless and wanted to take the movement in their own directions. Some of them thought they were smarter than King—and that he'd lost his touch.

Slowly, King rose from his Sunday-school desk and vented his feelings. "We are in serious trouble," he said. "The whole movement is doomed." Couldn't they see? It wasn't about Memphis anymore, or even Washington. It wasn't about the fine points of protest strategy. It was about the very foundation of nonviolence itself. Their flame was in danger of flickering out. Everything they'd worked for since Montgomery was on the line. Forget Washington. They couldn't even think about going there until they had proved to the nation that they could bring off a nonviolent march and redeem their mistakes and reestablish the primacy of their central creed.

"Memphis," he said, "is the Washington campaign in miniature." They had no choice. They *had* to go back there before they could go anywhere else. "The Movement lives or dies in Memphis," he said.

The staff would not relent. As far as most of his advisers were concerned, both Memphis *and* Washington were mistakes.

King finally lost patience with his staff. They were too impressed with themselves, too full of private ambition. He was especially angry with Jesse Jackson, who seemed to be trying to create his own fiefdom in Chicago. "You guys come up with your projects," King said, "and you always pull me in. If I sensed that this was important to the movement and to you, it always had my full support. Now, I'm not getting *your* full support. Now that I want you to come back to Memphis to help me, everyone is too busy."

Finally he turned to Abernathy. "Ralph, give me my car keys. I'm getting out of here."

Abernathy looked puzzled. During the conversation, he'd been playing with King's keys on the table, and he'd absentmindedly stuffed them in his pocket. Now he handed them over, and King stormed down the hall toward the stairs.

Abernathy followed him. "Martin," Ralph said. "What's bugging you?"

"Ralph, I'll snap out of it. Didn't I snap out of it yesterday?"

"Will you let me know where you'll be?"

King didn't answer.

Then Jesse Jackson tried to follow King down the stairs. "Doc, don't worry," he said. "Everything's going to be all right."

King paused on the landing and wheeled on Jackson. "Jesse," he said. "Everything's *not* going to be all right. If things keep going the way they're going now, it's not just the SCLC but the whole country that's in trouble. If you're so interested in doing your own thing that you can't do what this organization's structured to do, if you want to carve out your own niche in society, go ahead. But for God's sake, don't bother me!"

Jackson stood speechless as King climbed in his car and took off, leaving the staff flummoxed and heartsick. Abernathy tried to pick up the pieces. "The leader is confused," he said somberly. "He's under great stress. We need to rally around him in this difficult time." What happened in Memphis had shaken him to the core. He was experiencing a spiritual crisis. They had no choice now—they *all* had to go back to Memphis and make things right.

Everyone in the room agreed. "We had never seen Martin explode that way, not with us," recalled Andrew Young. "After he left, people were so stunned they finally began to listen. Finally, the team of wild horses was one."

They talked about Memphis. They would send some of their best people ahead of King to work with the Invaders and plan every aspect of the march. They would give King everything he wanted.

The transformation was so complete that some board members thought the Holy Spirit had been in the room. There were war whoops and hallelujahs. Andrew Young danced a little jig. Out of dissension, a consensus had formed.

Yet for several long hours they couldn't locate King to tell him the good news. What he did during his absence remains a mystery. Some said he met one of his mistresses in an apartment hideaway. Others said he conferred with his father, Martin Luther King Sr.—Daddy King, as he was known. Still others said he experienced a kind of Gethsemane moment, a period of private doubt and soul-searching in some favorite place of seclusion.

When he showed up late that afternoon, King was immensely relieved to hear the staff had come together. He now had to pack for a quick trip to Washington—he was giving an important sermon the next day. When he returned, his time and energies would be focused on one place: Memphis.

■

AT SHORTLY AFTER eleven o'clock the following morning, King stepped into the grand white pulpit of the Washington National Cathedral. Cloaked in black clerical robes, he seemed to have emerged from the depths of the previous day's despair. He addressed an integrated crowd of more than three thousand worshippers packed inside the vast Gothic hall. A thousand more were gathered on the grounds outside, listening to a public address system. It would be King's last formal sermon.

King spoke in fulminous tones about Vietnam, calling it "one of the most unjust wars in the history of the world." The conflict has "strengthened the military-industrial complex, it has strengthened the forces of reaction in our nation, it has played havoc with our domestic destinies, and it has put us in a position of appearing to the world as an arrogant nation."

The central theme of the sermon was poverty in America—and the moral imperative to address it. "Ultimately," he said, "a great nation is a compassionate nation. But America has not met her obligations to the poor." He likened poverty in America to "a monstrous octopus, spreading its nagging, prehensile tentacles." In recent months, he'd been to Appalachia, he said, and to the ghettos of Newark and Harlem, and to many other impoverished places in America where he'd seen conditions so squalid that "I must confess I have literally found myself crying." He told the crowd that in Marks, Mississippi, in the nation's poorest county, he'd seen so much hunger on the faces of sharecroppers there that he concluded something radical had to be done to acquaint the nation's leaders with the ravages of systemic, multigenerational poverty.

"We are coming to Washington in a Poor People's Campaign," he vowed. He would bring an army of people from all races and backgrounds, people "who have come to feel that life is a long and desolate corridor with no exit signs, people who have never seen a doctor or a dentist in their lives." Although King said that the members of his Poor People's Army "do not seek to tear up Washington," they will nevertheless engage in what he called "traumatic nonviolent action." Fighting would accomplish nothing—not in Memphis, not in Washington, not in Vietnam. "We must learn to live together as brothers," he said, "or we will perish together as fools." Nothing will ever be done about poverty in America "until people of goodwill put their hearts and souls in motion."

Afterward, King held a brief press conference in which he said outright that he could not support President Johnson for reelection. "I see an alternative in Senator McCarthy and Senator Kennedy," he said, and though he had already privately concluded that Kennedy was the better choice, he stopped short of making an endorsement. As in Memphis, reporters pressed him to make a pronouncement on the prospect for riots over the summer. "I don't like to predict violence," King replied, "but if nothing is done between now and June to raise ghetto hope, I feel this summer will be not only as bad, but worse, than last year." This would be terrible, not only for the ghettos, but for the very health of American democracy. "We cannot stand two more summers like last summer without leading inevitably to a rightwing takeover and a fascist state."

What would it take for you to call off your Poor People's Campaign? one journalist asked. *What would Congress or the president have to do?*

King said he would gladly cancel the whole demonstration if Congress would adopt the recommendations recently proposed by the Kerner Commission, a bipartisan body that had made a thorough study of the riots in Watts, Newark, Detroit, and other cities. But King saw little cause for optimism. "I would be glad to talk to President Johnson or anyone else," King said. "We're always willing to negotiate."

■

AT THAT MOMENT, President Johnson was decidedly not in the mood to negotiate with Martin Luther King. Johnson was only a few miles away at the White House, planning an important speech he would give that night on national television. The address was primarily about Vietnam, but Johnson was toying with the idea of tacking on a bombshell at the end. He was thinking about announcing to the nation that he was withdrawing from the 1968 presidential race.

For months, Johnson had been secretly thinking of leaving office at term's end. There were many reasons for this, but the truth was he'd become miserable in the White House. He'd been having nightmares about his health. His Gallup approval rating had plummeted to 36 percent. He had enemies on all sides. Trying to describe the White House mood, Lady Bird Johnson paraphrased Yeats: "A miasma of trouble hangs over eveything."

Vietnam, the war that King so stridently criticized, lay at the center of Johnson's woes. The quagmire in Southeast Asia had become the president's obsession. It occupied most of his time and energy, and it hogged so much national treasure that he could no longer pursue the Great Society programs he had once doted on. Besieged by war critics, Johnson had become paranoid, distrustful of old friends, imprisoned in the office he once loved.

He wanted out.

"I felt that I was being chased on all sides by a giant stampede coming at me from all directions," he later told the historian Doris Kearns Goodwin. "Rioting blacks, demonstrating students, marching welfare mothers, squawking professors, and hysterical reporters. And then the final straw. The thing I feared from the first day of my Presidency was actually coming true. Robert Kennedy had openly announced his intention to reclaim the throne in the memory of his brother. And the American people, swayed by the magic of the name, were dancing in the streets."

Relinquishing power went against every grain of Johnson's being. Yet he had a hunch that by stepping down now, he could regain political capital and close out his term with a measure of grace, perhaps devoting his final months to extricating the country from Vietnam. It would be a retreat with honor, a magnanimous exit. His speechwriters composed two endings for that night's speech, and it was up to Johnson to decide which one to use.

The president spent the afternoon and early evening fretting over what to do. By dinnertime, no one, not even Johnson, was certain which ending he would pick. At 9:00, he went on the air. For twenty-five minutes, Johnson spoke of Vietnam and his desire for peace. He was halting the bombing over most of North Vietnam, he said, and was now proposing serious talks with Ho Chi Minh.

Then, with a change in tone that caught millions of viewers off guard, the president stared straight into the teleprompter. "With the world's hopes for peace in the balance every day," he said, "I do not believe that I should devote an hour or a day of my time to any personal partisan causes or to any duties other than the awesome duties of this office. Accordingly, I shall not seek, and I will not accept, the nomination of my party for another term as your President."

When the address was over, a euphoric Johnson leaped from his chair and bounded from the Oval Office to be with his family. "His air was that of a prisoner let free," the First Lady wrote. "We were all fifty pounds lighter and ever so much more lookin' forward to the future."

The president described his mood this way: "I never felt so right about any decision in my life."

AFTER BUYING THE rifle and scope in Birmingham, Eric Galt returned to his Atlanta rooming house, taking care to keep his new acquisition hidden from other tenants and his landlord. He spent much of his time reading the *Atlanta Constitution*, which gave extensive coverage to King's troubles in Memphis and reported, on April 1, his vow to return in a few days for a peaceful demonstration down Beale Street.

Suddenly Galt knew where he needed to be. King's frenetic pace, combined with the constant, improvisational changes to his schedule, had made him nearly impossible to track; the peripatetic minister had scarcely been home in Atlanta during the time Galt had been living at the rooming house. But on this occasion the papers had neatly forecast the precise location of King's next appearance—on historic Beale in downtown Memphis—and conveniently gave Galt several days to plan ahead.

"You must have a goal to shoot for, and a straight course to follow," Dr. Maltz had urged in *Psycho-Cybernetics*. "Do the thing and you will have the power."

A straight course was exactly what Galt had now; one could detect in his patterns a sudden sense of focus. He began to accelerate his movements, to concentrate his formerly fevered and desultory thoughts, to make clear and cogent preparations. He paid another week's rent at his Atlanta rooming house. He bought a map designated "Georgia-Alabama," another of the entire United States, from which he planned his route to Tennessee. On April 1, at about 10:00 a.m., he dropped off a bundle of dirty clothes at the Piedmont Laundry around the corner at 1168 Peachtree Street—giving fastidious instructions to the counter clerk about items he wanted dry-cleaned, including a black-checked suit coat. As always, he said he wanted his regular laundry folded, with no starch. The laundry's desk clerk, Mrs. Annie Estelle Peters, wrote his name on the ticket in perfect Palmer penmanship cursive—"Galt, Eric."

On April 2, Galt threw a few belongings together and placed his Gamemaster rifle, still awkwardly nestled inside its Browning box, in the trunk of his car. He tossed some toiletries and clothes in a cheap, Japanese-made leatherette zippered bag, as well as his Remington-Peters ammo, his camera equipment, and, the better to monitor King's movements, his Channel Master transistor radio. Galt left most of his other belongings—including his Zenith television—in his room. Fearing a break-in, he decided to hide his snub-nosed .38 revolver in the flophouse's basement.

It was a warm spring morning, and the sun shone at his back as Galt drove the Mustang west out of Atlanta, toward Memphis. As the road spooled into the Georgia piney woods, he was alone with his thoughts and the hypnotic thrum of the V-8 engine. He hurtled over country roads, past Indian mounds and termite-chewed barns and rutted ditches of rust-red soil. Spring had arrived in earnest. Buds appeared on the deciduous trees, and the warming earth swelled with bright new blooms—jasmine, wild cherry, forsythia. It was the time of year when newly hatched bugs snapped from the greening thickets and splattered on windshields, and the skies swarmed with great black clouds of starlings.

Galt cut a jagged crease across the kudzu-strangled Southland, across countryside that Nathan Bedford Forrest and his marauders had prowled during the Civil War. Keeping to the Lee Highway—Highway 72—he shot past Huntsville and Madison and Muscle Shoals, past Tuscumbia and Cherokee and Iuka. Galt angled ever closer to the Tennessee state line, at one point passing not far from Pulaski, birthplace of the KKK. Along the way, he discovered that one of his tires had a slow leak, and he pulled over to change it.

As he drew nearer to Memphis, he must have regretted that he hadn't had an opportunity to test-fire his new rifle. Outside the old Confederate rail crossroads of Corinth, Mississippi, just a few crow miles from the Tennessee border and not far from the battlefield of Shiloh, Galt pulled off the road and found a secluded place.

The bloodbath at Shiloh had begun 106 years earlier to the week, on an early April day much like this one. Lasting a mere two days, the engagement ended with twenty-four thousand dead and wounded—more than all the American casualties of the Revolutionary War, the War of 1812, and the Mexican War *combined*. This battle, fought in the vicinity of a small country church, affirmed everyone's worst fears, North and South—that madness would prevail, that the War Between the States would descend into a protracted horror of staggering loss.

The writer Ambrose Bierce, who fought here as a young man, described the woods around Shiloh as a "smoking jungle" so deep and dark that "I should not have been surprised to see sleek leopards." Now, behind a scrim of similar woods just south of the battlefield, Galt cut the engine and opened the trunk. Studying the Gamemaster in the filtered light, he familiarized himself with its components, with the contour of its walnut stock, with the heft of its butt and the feel of its pump-action mechanism. The moving parts of the gun worked seemingly without friction, thanks to a proprietary burnishing process the Remington company called "vibra-honing."

Galt was loath to draw attention to himself—a farmer, a Civil War buff, or even a Mississippi state trooper could be within earshot—but he knew he had to test the Gamemaster's accuracy. He needed to make sure the Redfield scope was properly aligned and showing no idiosyncrasies. He wanted to acquaint himself with the rifle's powerful kick, and examine the trajectory to see for himself how much the bullet dropped over long distances.

Galt leveled the Remington and trained his scope on a target off in the hazy woods. Then he curled his finger around the trigger.

Deer hunting season had ended months earlier, so any knowledgeable sportsman who happened to be passing through that drowsy stretch of the Magnolia State might have been surprised to hear, in the first week of April, the ragged concussions of a high-powered hunting rifle as a succession of .30-06 shells whined through the trees.

AT 7:00 ON the morning of Wednesday, April 3, Ralph Abernathy dropped by the house on Sunset to pick up King and drive to the Atlanta airport. Coretta offered breakfast, but the men were late for their plane to Memphis. King tossed some books into his briefcase, packed a few suits, and headed for the kitchen. "I'll call you tonight," he said, giving his wife a kiss.

King was nursing a slight cold, but other than that Coretta didn't sense that anything was amiss. "It was an ordinary goodbye," she later recalled, "like thousands of other times before."

The two men hopped into Abernathy's 1955 Ford and sped to the airport, arriving just in time for the flight. At the gate, they met a few other SCLC staff members—Dorothy Cotton, Bernard Lee, and Andy Young—and they all scurried aboard the Eastern Air Lines jet.

They needn't have rushed: for nearly an hour the plane remained idling at the gate. People began to grumble and crane their necks to learn the cause of the holdup. Eventually, the pilot's voice broke over the intercom to apologize. "We have a celebrity on board this morning," he said, "and we're required to check every piece of luggage in the entire cargo hold for explosives." An anonymous caller had phoned

Eastern Air Lines with a threat to blow up Martin Luther King's plane.

King cut a worried look at Abernathy. "Ralph," he said, "I've never had a pilot say that before."

Eastern Flight 381 finally pushed off from the gate and taxied down the runway. "Well," King said with a mordant grin, "looks like they won't kill me this flight."

"Nobody's going to kill you, Martin," Abernathy replied. He could tell the episode had rattled his friend. King stared pensively out the window as the plane rose over Atlanta and circled west.

The jet landed at 10:30 Memphis time and pulled up to Gate 17. King stepped off the plane and was met by a small entourage that included the Reverend Jim Lawson and a chauffeur named Solomon Jones, who was driving a big white Cadillac provided for King's use by the R. S. Lewis Funeral Home. King moved briskly through the terminal, walking a gauntlet of television cameras, police officers, undercover detectives, and FBI agents. Lawson did not trust the cops, though they were ostensibly there for King's protection. When one of the Memphis Police Department officers stepped forward to ask Lawson where they were headed, the minister tried to shoo him away, saying, "We have not fully made up our minds."

Among the plainclothes policemen posted in the terminal were two black officers, Detective Edward Redditt and Patrolman Willie Richmond. They had been assigned to work as an undercover team and follow King everywhere he went during his Memphis stay. But some of the Memphis strike organizers were onto Redditt (he had been conducting surveillance on strike activities for weeks), and they took him for a spy if not a traitor to his race. That morning, a prominent female activist named Tarlease Mathews approached Redditt in the airport and fairly hissed at him: "If I were a man I would kill you."

■

KING AND HIS party stepped outside and approached a waiting convoy of cars. The weather was turning blustery—thunderstorms were in the forecast, and meteorologists announced that the mid-South was under a tornado watch. With plainclothesmen Redditt and Richmond following close behind, the motorcade drove downtown so King and Abernathy could check in to the Lorraine Motel.

Nearly all of King's staff members were lodging at the Lorraine—James Bevel, James Orange, Jesse Jackson, Hosea Williams, Chauncey Eskridge, Bernard Lee, and Dorothy Cotton, as well as Young and Abernathy. A South African filmmaker named Joseph Louw, working on a PBS documentary about the Poor People's Campaign, was also staying in the motel, as was a black *New York Times* reporter named Earl Caldwell. A few rooms had been reserved for the Invaders, with whom King's staff was intensely negotiating. Then, too, King was expecting the arrival of his younger brother, A. D. King, who was a minister in Louisville, Kentucky. AD had been on a road trip with his girlfriend, Lucretia Ward, in Fort Walton Beach, Florida. They were driving her baby blue Cadillac convertible, and were bringing along a young black state senator from Louisville named Georgia Davis, one of Martin Luther King's mistresses. They were supposed to arrive late that night.

Now a cameraman from Channel 5, the NBC affiliate in Memphis, took a shot of the SCLC entourage standing on the balcony, in front of 306, the brass numerals gleaming in the sun. King was set up in his familiar digs—if not in his favorite city, at least in his favorite room at his favorite hotel, with his staff and closest confidants around him. Whatever might happen in Memphis that week, his world was in place at the Lorraine.

■

SHORTLY AFTER LUNCH, King and much of the staff took off in a convoy for the Reverend James Lawson's Centenary United Methodist Church to discuss strategies for the coming march. There King learned that the City of Memphis had succeeded late that morning in obtaining a federal injunction effectively preventing him from staging *any* demonstration for the next ten days. Among the many arguments raised by the city attorney, Frank Gianotti, was the legitimate worry that King could be in mortal danger should he lead another march down Beale Street. "We are fearful," Gianotti said in U.S. District Court, "that in the turmoil of the moment someone may harm King's life, and with all the force of language we can use we want to emphasize that we don't want that to happen."

Despite the city's profession of concern for his safety, King was dejected by this new obstacle. Over the course of his career he had violated many local injunctions, but never a *federal* one, and he was uncertain how to respond. "Martin fell silent again," Abernathy recalled. "Nothing was going right in this town."

Soon reporters found King and pressed him for a response to this latest development. King put on a game face. "Well," he said, "we are not going to be stopped by Mace *or* injunctions. We stand on the First Amendment. In the past, on the basis of conscience, we have had to break injunctions and if necessary we may do it in Memphis. We'll cross that bridge when we come to it."

King returned to the Lorraine at 2:30 that afternoon, only to be met by federal marshals, who served him with a formal copy of the injunction. King accepted the documents good-naturedly—he even laughed before the cameras, as though to suggest that no mere piece of paper could stop the movement now.

The ACLU, meanwhile, had found King a good Memphis attorney to help him fight the injunction, and within an hour he showed up at the Lorraine to introduce himself. His name was Lucius Burch, an irascible white liberal in a conservative town who had always come down on the progressive side of the race question. Burch lived in an antebellum mansion in the country east of Memphis, flew his own plane to work, and had by some miracle survived several aviation crashes. He was frequently away on hunting trips, diving adventures, and horse-packing sojourns in the mountains, and he had a house in Ireland to which he often retreated. Burch, Porter & Johnson was considered the preeminent law firm in Memphis. Burch had a reputation for being brilliant, literary, cocky, and touched with a certain incorrigible style of persuasion, in and out of the courtroom.

Flanked by two junior attorneys from his firm, Burch sat across the bed from King in room 306 and interrogated him. "Dr. King, I'm going to get right to the point. I need to know how important this march is to you and your movement. I need to know, fundamentally, what it *means* to you." Burch had never met King, and wanted to make sure that he and his group "were what they purported to be."

King was taken aback by Burch's directness, but he liked him from the start. "It's simple," King answered. "My whole future depends on it. The tenets of non-violent protest are on the line."

Andy Young stepped in to add that the proposed march was exactly what it was represented to be: the constitutional right of people to express by assembly and petition what they felt was a just grievance. The strike was now in its fifty-second day, and unless they could successfully stage this "Redemption March," as it was being called, there was little hope of a peaceful resolution.

After drawing King out a little more, Burch recalled, "I had no second thoughts or looking back. The white community didn't realize that Martin Luther King was the answer to the firebombing and he was the answer to the looting and he was the answer to Black Power. He was the best friend they ever had."

Lucius Burch would fight the injunction tooth and nail, and he would push for a modified march—disciplined, heavily self-policed by marshals, devoid of placards that could serve as weapons, and assembled in tight formations, four abreast, from start to finish. Burch took off for his office on Court Square, where he would spend all night working on arguments to present in court the following morning.

■

TRUE TO THEIR assignment, the plainclothes officers Edward Redditt and Willie Richmond had been watching King all day. From the airport, to the Lorraine, to Lawson's church, then back to the Lorraine again, they had stayed on King's tail, taking note of all comings and goings, copying license plate numbers, trying to identify all persons with whom he came in contact.

Now they were inside Fire Station No. 2, a new firehouse of white brick and glass just across Mulberry Street from the Lorraine. Here they had set up a semipermanent spy nest so they could keep an eye on doings around the motel. They cut viewing slits into a few sheets of newspaper, which they taped to a window panel in the locker room's rear door. Then, holding up binoculars, they took turns watching all afternoon and into the early evening. They saw the federal marshals, they saw Lucius Burch arrive, they saw the Invaders coming and going. They saw members of King's staff walking along the balcony, going on ice runs, holding what appeared to be brown bags of liquor.

It was growing dark outside, unnaturally dark for six o'clock, making it harder for Redditt and Richmond to see anything. The forecasted storm was sailing in from the west, and now the wind was whining through the power lines and driving rain sideways. They could hear the wail of the Civil Air Defense sirens. A tornado had been spotted in Arkansas, another one in Tennessee, twenty miles north of the city.

At 6:30 police headquarters radioed Redditt and Richmond and told them to head to Mason Temple, where King was supposed to speak at a rally that night. They needed to get there early and secure good seats.

When they arrived at the cavernous Mason Temple around 7:00 p.m., the rain was pounding on the roof and the wind howled. The foul weather was taking a toll on attendance—fewer than a thousand people were listening to Lawson, the first in a roster of speakers that was supposed to crescendo with King, around nine o'clock.

Not long after Redditt and Richmond arrived, a black minister walked over and whispered to them that they had better leave—whatever cover the officers thought they had was blown. "This is the wrong place for you," the minister said. "The tension of the young people is already high." Word was out that Redditt had been using binoculars to spy on King from the fire station behind the Lorraine—apparently some black firemen working at Fire Station No. 2 had ratted on them. Now some of the young militants were growing agitated. "People started looking at us," Richmond later recalled, "and they knew we were policemen. We thought it was best to leave so there wouldn't be any trouble."

AROUND 7:15 P.M., as the rainstorm kept pelting the city and thunderheads menaced the sky, Eric Galt coasted into the parking lot of Vic DuPratt's New Rebel Motel at 3466 Lamar Avenue on the southeastern outskirts of Memphis. The main drag in from Birmingham, Lamar was a bustling byway on the rednecky edge of the city, cluttered with tire dealerships, body shops, honky-tonks, drive-in BBQ joints, and a string of motor courts much like the New Rebel. It was the long, gritty Appian Way into Memphis, a road awash in acrid lights and crowded with mud-barnacled pickup trucks.

He had pulled in to Memphis sometime earlier that day—a city he had apparently never spent any time in before. Not all of Galt's movements are known, but he certainly spent much of the day tooling around the southern edges of the city, along the Mississippi-Tennessee state line. He got a haircut. He picked up a six-pack of Schlitz beer at a bait shop in Southaven, Mississippi. Shortly before noon, he bought a Gillette shaving kit at a Rexall drugstore in Whitehaven, not far from Graceland. (Though Priscilla was home with her new baby daughter, Elvis was off in Hollywood the whole month.)

The New Rebel's bright red sign sported a Confederate plantation owner who, with his high leather riding boots, white gloves, and battle sword dangling at his side, closely resembled Colonel Reb, the impressively mustachioed mascot of the Ole Miss football team. Despite the Dixie atmospherics, and the George Wallace-esque ring to its name, the New Rebel was not exactly Galt's kind of place. The motel was clean, modern, and well run—as Galt himself later put it, "the kind of place where more or less legitimate people's around." It had a new swimming pool and a decent restaurant that offered room service. Its spick-and-span rooms cost $6.24 a night—a good bit more than he usually liked to pay. Not only that, the motel management requested too much personal information from its guests. The layout of the premises was overly conducive to desk-clerk nosiness: the New Rebel had an enclosed courtyard that required patrons to drive through a narrow entrance, so the attendant at the front desk, sitting behind a large plate-glass window, could keep a close eye on all comings and goings.

Still, Galt realized this was no time to be wandering around at night in an unfamiliar town hunting for lodging while a storm raged. The wind was howling with such force around the New Rebel that one guest later said he "thought the roof of the motel might blow off." So Galt put his money down, signing the registration card "Eric S. Galt, 2608 Highland Avenue, Birmingham, Alabama." He filled out the standard form, dutifully noting that he was driving a Mustang bearing Alabama plate number 1-38993.

The desk clerk, Henrietta Hagermaster, put him in room 34. After paying the nightly rate in cash, Galt pulled his car through the narrow entranceway and parked directly in front of his door. He inserted the key into the lock, turned it, and stepped inside.

■

AT THE LORRAINE, King and Abernathy looked out the window and grimaced at the gravid skies and listened to the eerie sound of the air-raid sirens. They knew what this kind of weather meant: the turnout for the rally at Mason Temple was going to be low—maybe anemically low. How many people could be expected to brave a tornado warning to come out tonight? This was not good for King, they both realized; the media would note the low attendance, and possibly use it to suggest that his local support was waning. Besides, King desperately needed to rest. His cold was worsening, his throat was scratchy, and he thought he might have a slight fever. This was not his night.

"Ralph," he said, "I want you to go speak for me tonight."

Abernathy balked. "Why don't you let Jesse go? He loves to speak."

King dismissed the idea. "Nobody else but you can speak for me."

"OK, OK," Abernathy said. "But can I bring Jesse?"

"Yes, but *you* do the speaking."

At about 8:30, Abernathy arrived at Mason Temple and was startled to behold nearly three thousand people, most of them garbage workers and their families, gathered in the large hall. It was clear they had come to see King, not him. They were clapping and singing in anticipation—struggling to be heard over the din of the pummeling rain and thunder.

Abernathy found a phone in the church vestibule and called the Lorraine. "Martin," he said, "you better get over here right now. There's two thousand people braved the storm for you. This is *your* crowd."

■

It was going to be a perfunctory appearance, a courtesy call. King was just going to slip on a suit and go over and acknowledge the crowd, say a few words, and get back to the Lorraine to nurse his cold. When he walked into Mason Temple at around 9:00 p.m., however, the spirit of the crowd caught him. He was wearing a long black raincoat over his suit, and as he walked down the aisle, people reached out and touched his sleeves, his lapels, his coattails.

Abernathy gave a meandering introduction that went on for nearly half an hour, his words echoing through the vast hall as the tornado sirens keened outside. With a slightly embarrassed smile, King sat on the platform, puzzled by what sounded more and more like a eulogy. Periodically, the shutters high in the gallery would bang in the lashing wind, and King would flinch. There would be a spate of thunder and lightning, and then—*bang*—the shutters would slam once more, and King would jump again.

Finally Abernathy was done. King rose and approached the podium without notes. After the usual salutations, he settled into an ominous tone. "Something is happening in Memphis," he said. "Something is happening in our world. The nation is sick, and trouble is in the land." Still, he said, he would rather be alive today than in any epoch of history—because the stirrings in Memphis were part of a larger movement across the globe. "The masses of people are rising up," he said. "And their cry is always the same: *We want to be free!*"

The crowd was a mix of sanitation workers, church folk, and admiring preachers; representatives from the Invaders were also present. At least one FBI agent was there, too, dutifully taking notes in the back. As King fell into the familiar rhythms, people periodically erupted with calls of "Amen!" "Tell it!" "Preach it!" The television news cameras whirred. The shutters banged. The thunder grumbled on.

King made it clear that his lawyers were going to fight the injunction in court the next day and that the march would go on no matter what. "Let us develop a kind of dangerous unselfishness," he said. "We're not going to let any injunction turn us around."

He seemed tired and harrowed, his nerves frayed, but slowly he began to ease into a groove. He reached for metaphors from the book of Exodus, metaphors that resonated with this churchgoing crowd, so close to the river and to slavery themselves. "You know," he said, "whenever Pharaoh wanted to prolong the period of slavery in Egypt, he had a favorite formula for doing it. What was that? He kept the slaves fighting amongst themselves. But whenever the slaves get together, something happens in Pharaoh's court. When the slaves get together, that's the beginning of getting out of slavery."

Outside, the thunder and lightning seemed to be dissipating, the worst of the storm passing to the east. The banging noise stopped, and there was only the hissing hush of steady rain on the corrugated roof.

King spoke of the bomb threat on his plane that morning, and the delays it had caused. "And then I got into Memphis," he said. "And some began to talk about the threats that were about—about what would happen to me from some of our sick white brothers." With a slow trolling gaze, he surveyed the audience, as if to say to any would-be assassin, *Are you out there?*

For ten minutes, he veered off on a theme of thanatopsis, exploring different angles of his own mortality. He recalled the time a decade earlier when a deranged black woman plunged a letter opener into his chest at a book signing in a Harlem department store, and how the blade nearly punctured his aorta. The doctor told him that if he had sneezed, he would have ruptured his artery and drowned in his own blood.

King went on to reminisce about the glorious events that had happened since 1958—Birmingham, Selma, the March on Washington, and the other benchmarks of the civil rights movement—all the things he would have missed had he died from his stabbing wound. "And I'm so glad," he said, "that I didn't sneeze."

Sweat poured off his face now, and his eyes seemed to moisten, as he moved toward a crescendo. "We've got some difficult days ahead. But it really doesn't matter with me now. Because I've been to the mountaintop."

Tell it!

"And I don't mind. Like anybody, I would like to live a long life. Longevity has its place."

Amen!

"But I'm not concerned about that now. I just want to do God's will. And he's allowed me to go up to the mountain, and I've looked over, and I've *seen* the Promised Land."

Hallelujah preach it uh-huh.

"I may not get there with you. But I want you to know tonight that we as a people will get to the Promised Land. So I'm happy tonight. I'm not worried about anything. I'm not fearing any man. Mine eyes have seen the glory of the coming of the Lord."

Drowned in rapturous applause, King turned and collapsed in Abernathy's arms. Other ministers swarmed the stage, awed by the pathos of King's words. A local pastor noticed that King had tears in his eyes—"it seemed like he was just saying, 'Goodbye, I hate to leave.'"

In the audience, the mood was triumphant. People were crying, shouting, chanting. One striking sanitation worker recalled, "It seemed like he reached down and pulled everything out of his heart." Said another: "I was full of joy and determination. Wherever King was, I wanted to be there. It seemed to me from where I was sitting, his eyes glowed."

■

AT THE NEW REBEL Motel, Eric Galt apparently never emerged from his room. He placed no phone calls through the motel switchboard and made no requests of any kind. He was a thoroughly unremarkable guest: he rode out the tornado warnings, sipped a few cans of Schlitz, and watched TV in his room.

Aside from reporting on the tornado's destruction, the local ten o'clock telecasts were filled with news that night about the sanitation strike and King's efforts to reverse the injunction so he could march again down Beale Street. The reports noted that King and his aides might have to linger in town for quite some time as lawyers hashed out the legal nuances of the proposed march. One newscast showed footage of King and his entourage standing on the balcony of his downtown lodgings; the clip showed the door to King's room at the Lorraine. The room number, 306, was clearly legible.

Whatever else Galt did that night is unknown. But the staff at the New Rebel noticed that he kept the lamps inside his room switched on; through the evening, a milky luminescence seeped around the edges of his window blinds. Perhaps fueled by amphetamines, Galt appeared to be burning through the small hours of the night. From midnight on, Ivan Webb, the night clerk, made his hourly rounds of the motel property and at each inspection found to his surprise that Galt's room remained brightly lit.

■

AFTER THE SPEECH, King ventured into the Memphis night. The storm had passed, and now a light, fine rain saturated the air. He was lighthearted, reinvigorated, in a playful spirit. His fever seemed to have broken. "He was like a kid again," Billy Kyles recalled. "He'd preached the fear out, he'd just laid that burden down."

King, Abernathy, and Bernard Lee went out to a late dinner at a friend's house and didn't return to the Lorraine until after 1:00 a.m. Emerging from his taxi, King saw a familiar blue Cadillac convertible parked in the parking lot. He knew that his brother, AD, had arrived from Florida with AD's girlfriend, Lucretia Ward, who owned this excellent road car. And he knew that the Kentucky state senator Georgia Davis must be here, too, waiting for him.

"Senator!" he called out in the Lorraine parking lot. "Where's the *senahhtahh?*" He spoke in his deepest baritone—rounded, unmistakable, irresistible. Georgia always called it "the Voice."

King, Abernathy, and several others went into AD's room, where Georgia embraced King. Everyone in the room knew about her—there was nothing to hide. They all stayed up for a while, joshing and visiting, talking about the night's speech, the storms, and tomorrow's big day in court. Around three in the morning, Georgia excused herself and walked in the misting rain toward her room, 201. As she approached her door, she heard King's footsteps, just behind her, on the concrete walkway. Outside, they didn't speak or acknowledge each other—they didn't know who from the press or the police or the FBI might be spying on them.

Georgia turned the key to the lock and walked into her room, leaving the door slightly ajar. King slipped in and shut the latch. She studied his face, as a lover, as an equal, her desires unclouded by awe. "I didn't idolize him like a lot of other people did," she later said. "To me he was just a man."

King turned and sat on the bed next to Georgia. Opening his arms, he said, "Senator, our time together is so short."

ON THE BRIGHT, warm morning of April 4, Eric Galt slept in at the New Rebel Motel. Around 9:30 the maid knocked on his door to pick up his bed linen. "Yes?" he said, slightly startled, and she replied, "Oh, I'll come back later."

Galt ate breakfast, most likely at the New Rebel restaurant, and then checked out, taking several small bars of Cashmere soap from the bathroom. He bought a copy of the *Memphis Commercial Appeal*. In its copious coverage of the strike, the paper featured a page-one photograph of King standing in front of room 306 at the Lorraine.

Through the middle of the day, Galt spent some time "just stalling around," as he later put it, in the Memphis suburbs. He went to a tavern—he referred to it as a "beer house"—and made a long-distance call from a phone booth. The call was to his brother who lived in the suburbs of Chicago. According to a journalist who later interviewed the brother at length, Galt said: "Soon it will all be over. I might not see you for a while. But don't worry about me. I'll be all right."

▪

THAT MORNING, KING woke up early for an eight o'clock staff meeting to discuss the day's efforts in the U.S. District Court of the Western District of Tennessee. Even after the late night, he ran the meeting with a sense of urgency and moment. Andrew Young would serve as King's plenipotentiary before Judge Bailey Brown. It would be the job of attorney Lucius Burch to marshal Young's considerable eloquence and experience. Through deft examination on the witness stand, Burch would use Young (as well as Lawson, who would speak for the local cause) to show how vital this march really was, not just for King, but for the concept of peaceful protest in America and the world. If necessary, it would become a symposium on the First Amendment. King's vision of the future was on the line.

■

JUST ONE BLOCK west of the Lorraine, on South Main Street, stood a tumbledown rooming house run by a middle-aged woman named Bessie Brewer. The sign in front of the soot-darkened brick building at 422½ Main blandly announced APARTMENTS/ROOMS beneath an advertisement for Canada Dry's Wink soda—THE SASSY ONE.

A resident of Bessie Brewer's rooming house would later describe the place as "a half-step up from homelessness." Its long corridors were narrow and dark, with blistered walls and cracked linoleum floors that smelled of Pine-Sol. Mrs. Brewer's establishment was a haven for invalids, derelicts, mysterious transients, riverboat workers, and small-time crooks—rheumy-eyed souls who favored wife-beater T-shirts and off-brand hooch. Mostly white middle-aged men, they blew in on wisps of despair from Central Station a few blocks to the south and from the nearby Trailways and Greyhound terminals.

The guest rooms were upstairs on the second floor, above a grease-smeared joint with striped awnings called Jim's Grill that sold Budweiser and homemade biscuits and pulled-pork BBQ. Rich smells from Jim's kitchen curled upstairs, coating the flophouse tenants in a perfume of charred carbon and year-old frying oil. The tiny rooms, furnished with scuffed Salvation Army furniture, sweltered through the heat of the afternoon, even though many of the windows were crammed with ventilation fans that vigorously thunked away. For eight bucks a week, Mrs.

Brewer's tenants were satisfied with what they got and rarely complained. Among the long-term guests in her establishment were a deaf-mute, a tuberculosis patient, a schizophrenic, and an unemployed drunk who had a deformed hand. A homemade sign on the wall near Mrs. Brewer's office admonished, "No Curseing or Foul Talk."

■

AT AROUND THREE o'clock that afternoon, Eric Galt spotted Mrs. Brewer's shingle on South Main and pulled the Mustang up to the curb alongside Jim's Grill. A few minutes later, Loyd Jowers, the owner of Jim's Grill, looked through the grimy plate-glass windows and saw the Mustang parked out front.

Galt had apparently been casing the neighborhood for the past half hour or so and noticed something: some of the rooms at the back of Mrs. Brewer's rooming house enjoyed a direct view of the Lorraine Motel. He observed that while a few of the rear windows were boarded up, several remained in use; their panes, though dingy and paint smudged, were intact.

Galt stepped out of the car, opened the door at 422½ Main, and climbed the narrow stairs toward Bessie Brewer's office. At the top of the stairs, he opened the rusty screen door.

Galt rapped on the office door and Mrs. Brewer, her hair done in curlers, opened it as far as the chain would allow.

"Got any vacancies?" he asked.

A plump woman of forty-four, Mrs. Brewer wore a man's checked shirt and blue jeans. She had been the rental agent at the rooming house for only a month. The previous manager had been forced to leave after a sordid incident that was covered in the local papers: apparently, he'd gotten into a quarrel with his wife and ended up stabbing her.

Mrs. Brewer appraised the prospective tenant. Slim, neat, clean shaven, he sported a crisp dark suit and a tie and looked to her like a businessman. She wondered why such a well-dressed person would show up at her place—and what he was doing in such a raw part of town. "We got six rooms available," she said. "You stayin' just the night?"

No, Galt replied, for the week.

Mrs. Brewer promptly led him back to room 8, a kitchenette apartment with a refrigerator and a small stove. "Our nicest one," she said. "It's $10.50 a week. You can cook in there."

Galt glanced at the room without venturing inside and shook his head: this room wouldn't do. The window was on the west side of the building, facing Main and the Mississippi River.

"No, see, I won't be doing any cooking," he mumbled. "You got a smaller one? I only want a room for sleeping."

Mrs. Brewer studied Galt. He had a strange and silly smile that she found unsettling. She described it as a "smirk" and a "sneer," as though he were "trying to smile for no reason." She padded down the hall to 5B and turned the doorknob, actually a jury-rigged piece of coat-hanger wire. "This one's $8.50 for the week," she said, throwing open the door.

Galt stuck his head inside. The room had little to recommend it—a musty red couch, a bare bulb with a dangling string, a borax dresser with a shared bathroom down the hall. A little sign over the door said, "No Smoking in Bed Allowed." The ceiling's wooden laths peeked through a large patch of missing plaster. Yet one attribute immediately caught Galt's eye: the window *wasn't* boarded up. A rickety piece of furniture partially blocked the view, but with just a glance he could see the Lorraine Motel through the smudged windowpanes.

"Yeah," Galt abruptly said, "this'll do just fine."

Mrs. Brewer did not bother to mention that her last long-term tenant in 5B, a man known as Commodore Stewart, had *died* several weeks earlier and the room had not been rented since. She was happy to fill it again, but being naturally suspicious, she was a little surprised by how quickly her new guest had made up his mind.

While they stood talking in the corridor, one of the tenants across the hall emerged from his room and got a look at his new neighbor. Charlie Stephens, a balding former heavy-equipment operator and a disabled World War II veteran, had been severely wounded during the liberation of Italy and still had shrapnel embedded in his left leg. Now unemployed, he was fifty-one years old and sickly. That afternoon, Stephens was trying to repair an old radio that had been on the fritz. He'd been living at Mrs. Brewer's for some time, sharing room 6B with his common-law wife, a mentally disturbed woman named Grace Walden who spent most of her days in bed.

Charlie Stephens, for his part, suffered from tuberculosis and was a bad alcoholic—in fact, he was already well in his cups as he eyed, through thick tortoiseshell glasses, the new guest across the hall. Down the hall, out of earshot from Stephens, Mrs. Brewer told Galt under her breath that the people who lived around 5B were usually quiet, but that the guy next to him—Stephens—drank a bit too much.

"Well," Galt volunteered, "I take a beer once in a while myself."

Mrs. Brewer told him that was fine as long as he stayed in his room and kept quiet. Then she led Galt back to her office, where he presented her with a twenty-dollar bill, snapping it crisply. She gave him $11.50 in change. She did not give him a key—the door to 5B, rigged as it was with a bent coat hanger in lieu of a knob, had no lock.

"And what's the name?" Mrs. Brewer asked, pointing to her spotty registration book.

"It's John Willard," he replied. He did not volunteer any information about himself—where he was from, what he drove, what brought him to town. As she jotted the name in her logbook, she noticed that he flashed his smile once again.

KING AND ABERNATHY went down to the Lorraine restaurant that afternoon and ordered a mess of fried Mississippi River catfish for a late lunch. The waitress slightly botched the order—instead of bringing two plates, she brought one giant platter, piled high with crunchy fish. That was fine with King. "We'll just share," he said, and so the two old friends ate together, washing the catfish down with big glasses of sugary-sweet iced tea.

They brought the fish back up to 306 and kept nibbling while King placed a series of telephone calls around the country. He was worried about what was going on in court that day. "Where is Andy?" King fretted. "Why hasn't he called us?"

▪

GALT BROUGHT UP some toiletries from the Mustang in his blue plastic zippered bag and settled into his new digs at Bessie Brewer's flophouse. The room was indistinguishable from a hundred others he'd frequented over the years. There was a small defunct fireplace, cracked floors that vaguely smelled of uric acid, walls of peeling paper, and a low wainscoting of smudged white bead board. Galt hardly noticed the lumpy mattress, the sagging springs, the faded bedspread.

Galt was much more interested in what was *outside* the room. He slid the blond dresser to the side, adjusted the curtains, and savored a mostly unobstructed view of the Lorraine. He dragged a straight-backed chair to the window and surveyed the scene more closely. The rooming house's backyard was grown up in spindly leafless brush and littered with liquor bottles and other trash. At the far edge of the unkempt lot, Galt could make out the lip of a large retaining wall that dropped eight feet down to Mulberry Street. Across Mulberry, a finny Cadillac glimmered in the Lorraine parking lot next to the drained swimming pool, which was partially hidden by a privacy wall.

Rising above it all was the two-story motel with its mustard yellow cinder-block walls and metal-framed windows and doors of soft turquoise. A bright arrowed sign, a classic piece of roadside Americana, stood at the corner, its neon tubes not yet turned on. The main wing of the motel, styled in a kind of modern-deco minimalism, was dominated by a long balcony—the same balcony where King stood in the photo Galt had seen in the *Commercial Appeal*. King's room was only two hundred feet away—and some twelve feet lower than Galt's perch inside 5B.

The view of the Lorraine was even better than Galt had guessed from his initial inspection. More study revealed a small problem, however: to get a bead on the area right in front of King's door, Galt would have to open his window, lean over the sill, and fire his weapon with the rifle tip protruding several feet outside the rooming house's walls. Exposing his position in this way would run a high risk of detection.

Galt found a solution: just down the hall, the moldy communal bathroom afforded a more promising angle. There, all he'd have to do was crack the window, rest the rifle barrel on the sill, and take aim. It was a direct yet largely concealed shot, and an easy one at that—through the magnification of a 7x scope, a man standing on the balcony would appear to be only thirty feet away.

Galt couldn't have asked for a better vantage point than Bessie Brewer's rooming house. From the privacy of 5B, Galt could monitor the goings-on at the Lorraine—and from the shared bathroom a mere thirteen paces away, he could raise his rifle with little fear of detection and fire directly at, and slightly down upon, his target.

Then he realized he was missing something, a lookout's most

important tool. The Lorraine was just far enough away that he couldn't make out faces or other details with the naked eye. Galt could use the Redfield scope on his Remington, but he didn't want to bring his rifle up yet—lugging the weapon in its cumbersome box might draw too much attention, especially in broad daylight. In any case, a rifle scope was impractical for long-term surveillance work. For all Galt knew, he could be stuck here for days, possibly a whole week, snooping on the SCLC entourage. He would have to improve on his equipment.

■

THROUGHOUT THE AFTERNOON, King held meetings to talk about what to do with the Invaders. Two members of his staff—Hosea Williams and James Bevel—had been negotiating with the Invaders for days, trying to extract a promise that they would help with the march and not resort to violence. King wanted the Invaders to be included in the planning and to serve as marshals along the march route. But the Invaders were unwilling to make any promises unless King's SCLC gave them a significant sum of cash—by some accounts, they demanded ten thousand dollars. Hosea Williams refused to commit any money, but he did provide the Invaders with a room at the Lorraine while suggesting to one Invader leader, Charles Cabbage, that he come on board for the week as hired SCLC staff.

King grew angry when he learned of these developments. "Hosea," he fumed, "no one will be on our payroll who accepts violence as a means of social change." When he found out that the Invaders were trying to extort money from the SCLC, King became even more furious, saying, "I don't negotiate with brothers."

Cabbage and his Invaders were told they were no longer welcome at the Lorraine, that their room had been promised to someone else. Cabbage stormed out of the Lorraine late that afternoon, toting a small arsenal of rifles and guns wrapped in a blanket under his arm.

■

AROUND 4:00 P.M., Galt trundled down the narrow staircase of Bessie Brewer's rooming house and got in his car. He drove the short distance to the York Arms Company, a sporting goods store located several blocks north at 162 Main, close by a movie theater that was showing *The Graduate*. York Arms, which carried rifles and shotguns among other merchandise, was one of the stores that had been looted the previous week when King's march turned ugly. This afternoon, as Galt walked in the front door, a clutch of striking garbage workers—many carrying placards that said, I AM A MAN—strolled down Main Street, not far from the York Arms storefront.

"Got any binoculars?" Galt asked the first salesman he met, Ralph Carpenter. "I'd be interested in some infrared ones if you got any—for night vision."

Carpenter looked at the new customer and would later describe him as having an "average face, average hands, average neck—he was a neat, average-looking fellow and there was nothing outstanding about him." The man wore a dark, smooth-finish suit, a wide-collared white shirt, and a tie whose knot was slightly off center.

Carpenter told the customer he didn't carry any infrared binoculars, then showed the customer several brands of regular, high-end binoculars that cost upwards of $100. Galt balked at the prices. Then Carpenter remembered that he had several cheaper pairs in the show window. They were 7x35 Banners, manufactured by Bushnell, with fully coated optics. "These only cost $39.95," Carpenter said brightly as he retrieved a pair from the window. "They're imports, from Japan."

Galt seemed to like the price and put the binoculars up to his eyes. He said they were acceptable.

Carpenter tallied the tax and said the total would be $41.55.

Galt retrieved a roll of neatly folded bills from his right front pants pocket, from which he peeled off two twenties and a one, and then found fifty-five cents in another pocket. The salesclerk demonstrated how to focus and adjust the eyepieces on the Bushnells and then began to box up the merchandise, noting that the binoculars also came with a black leather case and accompanying straps. Carpenter slipped the box into a gray-blue paper sack—marked "York Arms Company." As Galt aimed for the door, Carpenter said, "Hurry back."

Galt said something in reply, but Carpenter couldn't quite catch what he said—he spoke in a soft mumble.

■

AT FIRE STATION No. 2, across Mulberry Street from the Lorraine, the black police officers Ed Redditt and Willie Richmond were back at their surveillance post, keeping a close eye on the comings and goings at the motel. Holed up in the locker room, they took turns with the binoculars, peering through the slits in the newspapers that were still taped to a rear window. Off in the background, they could hear the murmur of a television in the station's lounge and occasionally the friendly commotion of Ping-Pong matches.

There was a pay telephone in the firehouse, and that afternoon, to everyone's surprise, the phone rang. One of the firemen picked up the receiver to hear a woman on the line. She didn't say her name, but her voice had a distinct edge. "We know Detective Redditt is in there, spying on King. You tell him he is doing the black people wrong. Now we're going to do *him* wrong." Then the caller hung up.

Ed Redditt's superiors at police headquarters, interpreting the call as a possible death threat, decided it best to remove him from the situation; his cover had been blown, at the very least. Redditt wanted to stay, but headquarters was adamant. His boss took him off the case, assigned him an armed police guard, and advised him to go into hiding with his family for a few days.

Willie Richmond was told to remain in the firehouse and stay on the job for the rest of the afternoon. Since the anonymous caller hadn't mentioned him, Richmond's department superiors felt he was safe, his usefulness uncompromised.

He raised the field glasses to his face and turned his gaze back on the Lorraine.

■

KING EMERGED FROM 306 and walked down the balcony toward the stairs. After their late lunch together, Abernathy had fallen asleep, and King had made a few calls, but he was bored now and in search of company. He was anxious to hear from Andy Young and learn how the day's courtroom session was faring. He wandered down to Georgia Davis's room, 201, where he found his brother, AD, and Lu-

cretia Ward, as well as Senator Davis. They all sat around joking, gos-
siping, mimicking different preachers. King lay across the bed, his eyes
closed, half following the dance of conversation.

After a while, he and AD decided to call their mother in Atlanta.
Once Mama King answered, they played a little prank, each pretending
to be the other, thoroughly confusing her. King was pleased to hear the
delight in her voice when she realized that her two boys were together in
Memphis. They spoke for nearly an hour. Near the end Daddy King got
on the line as well.

Through the afternoon, Georgia thought King seemed distracted
and tired but happy. She saw a look of resignation on his face, a look of
acceptance, that she'd seen many times the past year. "He really sensed
his time was not long," she said. "He felt he'd fulfilled his mission on
earth. He said on many occasions that he would not live to be an elderly
person. He'd say, you know, there are a lot of kooks out there. Sometimes
I thought that he almost welcomed it."

That night, King and a large entourage were supposed to go to the
home of the local minister Billy Kyles for dinner. The word was that
Kyles's wife, Gwen, was making a soul food feast. "Senator," King now
said, "you like soul food?" Georgia said she did, and he said she should
come to dinner as his guest.

Finally, about five o'clock, Andy Young, fresh from court, arrived at
the Lorraine, with the SCLC lawyer Chauncey Eskridge soon following
on his heels. King was in a teasing mood, and he assaulted Young with a
mock tirade: *Where you been all day? How come you never call? Why do you
keep your leader so ill informed!* Abernathy, aroused from his nap, came down
and joined in. King hurled mock invectives at Young, then he hurled a pillow, and then Young hurled it back. Soon they were in a full-scale pillow
fight and wrestling match—the King brothers, Abernathy, and Young—
the men all yelling, snorting, horselaughing like a scrum of kids.

Once things settled down, Young and Eskridge gave their report from
the U.S. District Court. Attorney Lucius Burch had been masterful. After
listening to nearly eight hours of heated testimony on both sides, Judge
Bailey Brown had agreed to modify the federal injunction to accommodate
a tightly controlled demonstration. King and Lawson would have to make

myriad assurances as to the route, size, organization, and policing of the march, and they would have to cooperate with authorities at every turn. The details would be hammered out the next day, but here was the essence of it: the show would go on as scheduled for Monday morning, April 8.

They'd won.

■

ERIC GALT RETURNED to the area around Bessie Brewer's rooming house about 4:30 to find that he'd lost his parking space in front of Jim's Grill. He was forced to park some sixty feet farther away, just south of Canipe's Amusement Company, a shop that leased and serviced jukeboxes and pinball machines all over town. He took the binoculars up to his room but almost immediately returned to his car, apparently with the idea of retrieving the Remington from the trunk. He realized that with this new parking space, he'd have to be much more careful about hauling up the rifle; on this busy street, toting a long narrow box could be risky. So he remained in his car awhile—fifteen minutes or more—and waited for the traffic on South Main to ebb.

Two women who worked across the street at the Seabrook paint and wallpaper company saw him sitting in his Mustang. Having just completed the day's work shift at 4:30, they were standing by the large showroom window, gazing out on the street, waiting for their spouses to pick them up. One of the workers, Elizabeth Copeland, thought the man inside the Mustang was "waiting for someone or something." Copeland's colleague, Peggy Hurley, stood by the window until 4:45, when her husband arrived. As she walked toward her husband's car, Hurley noticed that the man in the Mustang was still there, patiently sitting behind the wheel. He was a white man, wearing a dark suit.

It is likely that Galt had spotted the two women as they lingered by the window and thought it prudent to wait until they left before undertaking his risky errand. Whatever the case, sometime between 4:45 and 5:00, Galt opened up his trunk and wrapped the long box in an old green herringbone bedspread he'd stashed in the car. Clutching the bundle, he moved briskly toward the rooming house.

Once inside 5B, Galt laid down the Gamemaster and removed his new field glasses from the York Arms bag. Sitting in the straight-backed chair by the window, he fiddled with the Bushnells and trained the lenses on the Lorraine. He never bothered with the straps designed to attach to the leather binocular case—he merely tossed them aside.

Galt adjusted the Bushnells to their highest setting, 7x, the same magnification power as his Redfield scope. People were standing in the Lorraine courtyard by a white Cadillac. The parking lot was splotched with rain puddles, remnants of the previous night's storm. In the fore-ground, down in the rooming house's backyard, tangled branches bobbed in the faint breeze. The binoculars must have created the illusion of an odd intimacy: enlarged through Galt's lenses, King's comrades in the parking lot appeared to be less than twenty feet away, and yet they be-trayed no awareness of his presence as they joked and milled about. Sweeping the Bushnells slightly upward, Galt could easily make out the number affixed to King's room—306—but the door was closed and the orange window drapes were drawn. Just outside his door, a fire extin-guisher, slightly askew, was lodged on the wall.

■

AT THAT MOMENT, King was inside the room with Abernathy, getting ready for dinner at the Reverend Billy Kyles's house. The room was cluttered with newspapers and coffee cups and other detritus of the day. The bony ruins of King's catfish lunch clung to a plate. King's heavy black briefcase squatted like an anvil on the table, the gold initials "MLK" embossed near the latch. The orange bedspreads lay rumpled and twisted. *The Huntley-Brinkley Report* flickered on the TV.

King was half-listening as he shaved in the bathroom—a process that, for him, was both laborious and smelly. King, who had a thick beard but sensitive skin, had found years earlier that shaving with a conven-tional razor and cream caused him to break out in a bumpy rash. So he had taken to using a potent depilatory called Magic Shaving Powder, a product widely used by Orthodox Jews whose strictures forbade them to touch a razor to the face. King's elaborate shaving ritual was said to be one of the reasons he so often ran late.

Now King, standing before the mirror in his suit slacks and an un-dershirt, was mixing the fine white powder in a cup of warm water and stirring it into a thick paste. The concoction gave off the sulfurous stench of rancid eggs. King, who'd become inured to the smell, spread the goop over his face and let the hair-removing chemicals (bearing ghastly names like calcium thioglycolate, guanidine carbonate, and nonoxynol-10) do their work.

Abernathy shrank from the smell as he always did—he grabbed a chair across the room by the window and teased King about it. From the bathroom, King asked Abernathy to call the Kyles home and see what was on the menu for tonight. Abernathy balked at the assignment but then picked up the phone and soon had Gwen Kyles on the line. He hung up and reported to King: "Roast beef, candied yams, pig's feet, neck bones, chitlins, turnip greens, corn pone."

It would be a down-home dinner, King's favorite. The news seemed to put him in an even better frame of mind. After a few minutes, he meticulously scraped off the Magic Shaving Powder paste with a spatula-like tool. The gunk swirled down the drain, taking a thousand little hairs with it. He patted his face dry with a towel, only to be interrupted by a crisp knock at the door. The Reverend Billy Kyles, a tall, gangling extrovert wearing dark-rimmed glasses, stood at the threshold and said they'd better hurry—the hour was getting late, and Gwen was expecting everyone.

Pastor of the Monumental Baptist Church in Memphis, Kyles had known King and Abernathy for ten years. The two men began to gang up on their old friend. "Billy," Kyles later recalled King saying, "we're not going to get *real* soul food at your house. Gwen's just too good-looking to make soul food—she can't cook it."

Kyles feigned hurt and displeasure: "*Who* can't cook soul food?"

Abernathy chimed in: "All right now, Billy. If she's serving up *feel-ay meen-yuns* or something, then you're gonna flunk."

King was in the bathroom slapping Aramis aftershave lotion on his face—masking the harsh sulfur smell with fine notes of sandalwood, leather, and clove.

Kyles said, "Man, we're gonna be late. You just get ready, Doc, and don't worry about what we gonna have."

Moderately chastened, King got into gear. He put on a dress shirt and tried to fasten the collar button, but it was too tight—he'd gained weight since he last wore it, or perhaps the shirt had shrunk at the cleaners.

One thing was certain, Kyles said in riposte as he walked out the door, they'd be having more food than King's waistline needed. *Doc*, he said, *you getting fat*.

"That I am," King agreed, and, his vanity pricked, he cut a glance at Kyles, who fidgeted out on the balcony. Then King changed the subject: "Do I have another shirt here?" He pulled a freshly laundered button-down from his belongings, a white Arrow permanent-press dress shirt, and quickly put it on—finding that the collar buttoned more easily.

"Now," he said, his eyes scanning the room. "Where's my tie? *Somebody's* moved it." He was looking for his favorite one, a crisp, slender brown silk tie with gold and blue diagonal stripes. King at times enjoyed the role of absentminded professor—dependent on Abernathy to mother him and manage the minutiae of his life—and now he played the part to the hilt. It was the kind of whimsical repartee they'd enacted in a thousand hotel rooms over the past decade, a banal conversational style informed by the real possibility that FBI moles might be listening in. "Hmmm," King said, "someone's *definitely* moved it."

"Martin," Abernathy scolded, "why don't you just look down at that chair?"

The tie was there, of course, right where he'd left it. King, an adept and fastidious tie tier, quickly threaded the knot and cinched it up to his fleshy neck. He fixed a silver tiepin in place and studied himself in the mirror. About five minutes before six o'clock, he stuffed in his shirttails and ambled out the door to see what was going on with the rest of the party at the Lorraine.

■

PATROLMAN WILLIE RICHMOND, watching through his binoculars, saw King emerge from his room onto the balcony. The firehouse was full of commotion, and Richmond found it hard to concentrate. A special "tactical" unit of the Memphis Police Department—TAC Unit 10—had pulled in to the station's parking lot and come inside for refreshments. The unit was composed of three squad cars, with four men to a car. The twelve officers were hanging out in the lounge, drinking coffee, and joking among themselves. Some of the firemen joined in on the fun.

One of the firemen, a thirty-nine-year-old white lieutenant named George Loenneke, passed through the locker room and saw Richmond standing with his binoculars. "There's Dr. King right there," Richmond said. "I presume he's going to supper."

Loenneke walked over to Richmond. "Let me see," he said. "I haven't seen Dr. King since he was in town to do the Meredith march." Richmond handed over the binoculars, and Loenneke got a glimpse through the peephole. "That's him alright. He hasn't changed a bit."

■

WHAT ERIC GALT did inside 5B between five o'clock and a little before six is not precisely known. Perhaps he read the *Memphis Commercial Appeal*—he had brought up the paper's first section from the car. Perhaps he listened to the news on his Channel Master pocket radio or mashed a bead of Brylcreem onto his fingertips and worked the unguent through his freshly cut hair. Perhaps he contemplated wrapping his fingertips with the Band-Aids that were among the toiletries in the outer compartment of his zippered blue leatherette bag; it was an old trick to avoid leaving fingerprints, a precaution he customarily liked to take before committing a crime.

But he had no time to fool around with Band-Aids. Suddenly, at about 5:55 p.m., a familiar figure floated across his binocular glass. To Galt's astonishment, Martin Luther King had emerged from his room and was standing on the balcony, right in front of 306, next to a metal service dolly. Standing in his shirtsleeves and a tie, he looked down into the Lorraine parking lot. Above him, a light fixture dangled loosely from the ceiling.

It must have given Galt a start: at last, the man he'd been chasing since he left L.A. was in his sights, suspended in the jittery, fuzzy-edged world of coated optics. He was a perfect target, fully exposed, almost as though he were speaking at a dais.

At 7x magnification, the details would have been startlingly vivid. Galt would have been able to see everything—the pencil mustache on

King's face, the laces on his black wing-tip shoes, the gold watch on his left wrist, the crisp diagonal stripes on his silk necktie.

Galt had to make a lightning-fast decision. He might never get a chance like this again. He ran to the communal bathroom to check the view. Charlie Stephens, the sickly drunk across the hall in 6B, could hear the new roomer's footsteps as he clomped down the corridor's linoleum floor. The rooming house walls were paper-thin, and Stephens, whose bed backed up to the bathroom wall, listened as "Willard" fumbled around in there. Then Stephens heard him emerge from the bathroom and clomp right back to his room.

The view from the bathroom must have convinced Galt that it was now or never. Back in 5B, Galt frantically pulled together his blue zippered bag, the binoculars, and the boxed rifle still wrapped in its green bedspread. (In his haste, he left behind the two binocular-case straps he'd tossed on the floor earlier.) He scooped up his belongings and dashed down the hall toward the bathroom. Once inside, he slammed and locked the door.

It was about 6:00.

KING LOOKED OUT over the drained swimming pool and inhaled the fresh air. The night was partly cloudy and cool—fifty-five degrees—and a crescent moon climbed in the sky. A slight wind blew off the Mississippi River, only a few blocks to the west but slightly hidden behind the natural rise of the bluff. All around the Lorraine stood the old cotton lofts and classing rooms, the drab brick warehouses of South Main's industrial grid. Off to the north, the Memphis skyscrapers rose over the city—the Gothic Sterick Building, the spectral white Lincoln American Tower, the Union Planters Bank with its revolving restaurant, forty stories up. The downtown lights were just beginning to glitter. On the roof of the Peabody Hotel, the resident mallards were happily ensconced in their mansion for the evening.

As King took in the Memphis night, he leaned against the railing for several long minutes. He was completely vulnerable, but King had refused a Memphis police detail as he nearly always did—"I'd feel like a bird in a cage," he said. He did not believe in bodyguards, certainly not armed ones. No one in his entourage was allowed to carry a gun or nightstick or any other weapon. The very concept of arming oneself was odious to him—it violated his Gandhian principles. He wouldn't even let his

children carry *toy* guns. In an almost mystical sense, he believed nonviolence was a more potent force for self-protection than any weapon. He
understood the threats that were about but refused to let them alter the
way he lived. So no one was on the balcony to shield his movements, to
shepherd him along, to survey the sight lines and vantage points and anticipate the worst.

If he'd had premonitions of an early death the previous night—*sick
white brothers*—he seemed to have flushed them from his consciousness.
Now he was in a jovial mood. Last night's darkness had dissipated. The
tornadoes all around Memphis had killed six and injured more than one
hundred people, but the storms had passed, leaving nothing more men-
acing than rain puddles. King had much to look forward to, and he
seemed buoyed to have his entourage with him. He was about to head
out with comrades to his favorite kind of dinner, to celebrate a victorious
day in court. *Memphis*—maybe the place was redeemable after all.

Walter Bailey, the owner of the Lorraine, noticed King's ebullient
mood as he stood there with his staff. "He just act so different, so happy,"
Bailey said. "It looked like they had won the world."

■

A LITTLE BEFORE six, a guest at Mrs. Brewer's flophouse named
Willie Anschutz was sitting in his room, 4B, with another tenant, Mrs.
Jessie Ledbetter. Anschutz, a nondrinker, was a fifty-seven-year-old laborer at a local moving company. Mrs. Ledbetter, a deaf-mute widow
who'd lived in the rooming house for seven years, was short and stout and
wore a bright floral-print dress. The two old friends—Anschutz affection-
ately called her "the dummy"—had been whiling away the afternoon, sip-
ping Cokes and eating cookies and watching a movie on television. At
some point, Anschutz took a small tub of dirty dishes down the hall to
rinse them in the common bathroom, but he found the door locked. Five
minutes later he returned and found that it was *still* locked. He jiggled the
faceted-glass doorknob to let the person inside know he was hogging the
lavatory. Slightly peeved, he stuck his head inside Charlie Stephens's room.
"Who the hell's in the bathroom?" he griped. "He's been in there a while."

Stephens, still tinkering with his broken radio in the kitchen area of
his room, had heard the guy from 5B traipsing into the bathroom and

was aware that he'd been in there "an undue length of time." Through the thin walls, he could hear all comings and goings at his end of the flophouse. Oddly, the whole time the 5B guest had been in there, he hadn't run any water or flushed the commode.

"Oh, that's the new guy from 5B," Stephens told Anschutz.

"Well, I gotta get in there!" Anschutz complained.

■

"You comin', Ralph?" King asked, slightly impatient. He had ducked back into room 306 to get the tailored Petrocelli suit coat, made of fine black silk, he'd bought at Zimmerman's in Atlanta.

"In a second—thought I'd get some of that Aramis, too," Abernathy said, rummaging through King's shaving kit.

"I'll wait for you out here," King replied, slipping on his jacket. In the pockets of his coat he had a silver Cross pen and a scrap of paper scrawled with notes for a speech he planned to give in Memphis later that week on the Poor People's Campaign. On it was the line "Nothing is gained without sacrifice."

King rejoined his post, leaning on the balcony just in front of the door. He stood there for a while, looking down at the small crowd again. Solomon Jones, the driver, cranked the Cadillac to get it warmed up.

From the group, Jesse Jackson greeted King. "Our Leader!" he said, in exaggeratedly regal tones.

"Jesse!" King boomed in return. "I want you to come to dinner with me tonight." It was a small gesture, but everyone in the entourage knew what it meant; inviting Jackson to dinner was King's first step toward making up with his headstrong apprentice after their fight in Atlanta. King was *forgiving* him.

Kyles, still standing on the balcony, interrupted. "Doc, Jesse took care of that before you did. He got himself invited!"

Jackson had in fact finagled an invitation for himself, but he didn't look like he was going to a dinner party. He was wearing a mod olive turtleneck sweater and a leather coat, a fashion decidedly out of step with the tie-wearing squares of the inner circle. When someone in the Lorraine parking lot gave him a once-over as if to question his attire, Jackson quipped, "All you need for dinner is an appetite."

King laughed at Jackson's hipster threads and his resourcefulness at adding himself to the guest list. On this night the Leader was full of charity. He zestfully tugged at his coat lapels, as was his habit when he felt confident and ready for the world. He was clean shaven, sweet smelling, and dressed to the nines. He looked at Jackson and flashed a broad smile.

Georgia Davis was down in 201 with the door slightly ajar. As she fixed her hair in the bathroom mirror, she could hear King carrying on with his staff, could hear the Voice, rich and melodious, booming across the courtyard. She could tell he was in a good mood. She wished he would stop jabbering—she was getting hungry. She looked at her watch: 6:00. They were all supposed to be at Kyles's house by now. Then she glanced out the window and saw King on the balcony. He just stood there, the life of his own party, smiling and joking and talking away.

■

INSIDE THE MILDEWY bathroom, Galt removed the Gamemaster from its box and loaded it with a single Remington-Peters .30-06 round. Galt must have felt he was running out of time—otherwise he would have loaded the clip with more bullets. He jerked the window up with such force that it jammed after opening only five inches. Probably using his rifle tip, he poked the rusted window screen and dislodged it from its groove; the screen tumbled to the weedy lot below.

The bathroom was disgustingly dirty; the toilet bowl was streaked, and a dented piece of wainscoting trim ran along peeling walls the color of a robin's egg. Galt climbed into the old claw-footed bathtub, which was scuzzy and stained, its tarnished drain clogged with a tangle of hairs. A flimsy contraption dangling over the tub's rim held a shrunken nub of soap. Galt leaned his body against the wall and rested the rifle on the paint-flaked windowsill.

Squinting through the Redfield scope, he found King, still standing there on the Lorraine balcony. Galt's loafers must have squeaked as they rubbed on the surface of the bathtub, leaving black scuff marks. A television murmured somewhere down the hall; a ventilation fan thumped in a nearby window. The smell of charred burgers tendriled up from Jim's

Grill, where happy-hour Budweiser was flowing and intense games of barroom shuffleboard were in session.

Galt likely heard Willie Anschutz rattling the bathroom door, a disruption that doubtless tried his concentration. He had to move fast. He brought King's head within the crosshairs. It was starting to grow dark outside, but the chemical emulsion on his scope's lens enhanced targets in twilight. In the distance behind the Lorraine was the immense gray post office building, a hazy monstrosity looming in the crepuscular light.

King continued to hold court, oblivious to danger. His face nearly filled the scope's optical plane. He was 205 feet away, but with 7x magnification, he appeared only 30 feet away. It was an easy shot, a cinch.

Galt leaned into the rifle and took aim. At 6:01 p.m., he wrapped his index finger around the cool metal trigger.

■

THE CADILLAC WAS still idling down below, and the various members of the party were edging toward their cars. King did not move from his perch on the balcony—he seemed transfixed by the evening, enchanted by the scene in the courtyard. Andy Young was shadowboxing with James Orange, a wild bearish man as big as an NFL linebacker. "Now you be careful with preachers half your size!" King called out to Orange.

Jackson, standing beside the Cadillac, introduced King to Ben Branch, a saxophonist and bandleader originally from Memphis, who had come down from Chicago to play music in support of the sanitation workers; he and his band had a gig that night over at Mason Temple, where King and his entourage were headed after the Kyles dinner.

"Oh yes," King said. "He's my man. How are ya, Ben?"

"Glad to see you, Doc," Branch called up.

"Ben, I want you to sing for me tonight at the meeting. I want you to do that song, 'Take My Hand, Precious Lord.' " King had loved the great gospel standard for years. It was a tragic, sweet song written in the depths of the Depression by a black composer named Thomas Dorsey after his wife and baby died in childbirth:

When the darkness appears and the night draws near
And the day is past and gone
At the river I stand
Guide my feet, hold my hand.

"I want you to sing it like you've never sung it before," King told Branch. "Sing it *reeeeeal* pretty."

"I sure will, Doc."

Solomon Jones hopped out of the Caddie and yelled up to King. "It's getting chilly," said Jones. "I think you'll need a topcoat."

"Okay, Jonesy," King answered. "You really know how to take good care of me." He fished for a pack of Salem menthols from his pocket and grasped a cigarette in his hand. He straightened up and stepped back from the railing. He was just turning, perhaps to retrieve his cashmere topcoat inside the room, when a ragged belch rang out over the parapets.

■

THE MEMPHIS POLICEMAN Willie Richmond, watching the Lorraine from inside the firehouse, heard the noise. It did not register with him as the report of a rifle—it was just a loud noise, perhaps a backfiring truck, and it seemed to come from somewhere off to the northwest. But fireman George Loenneke saw everything. Through Richmond's field glasses, through the little peephole in the newspapered window, the scene reeled out in slow motion before Loenneke's eyes: King falling backward from the handrail. King tumbling to the balcony floor. King staying there and not getting up. Loenneke gave Richmond the binoculars for a look. No one else inside the station had heard anything or had an inkling of what had happened.

Richmond turned and ran through the firehouse, yelling: "He's been shot! The Reverend King has been shot!"

■

CHARLIE STEPHENS, STILL trying to repair the old radio in his room just a few feet away from the bathroom, heard the concussion through the thin plywood wall. Even in his alcoholic stupor, he instantly knew what it was. Having fought in Europe, he was well acquainted with the sound of weapon fire. "I know a shot when I hear one," he later said. "When that explosion went off, it sounded like a German 88."

Inside the bathroom, Eric Galt withdrew the rifle from the cracked window. He knew he'd made a serious hit to King's head. The aerosol mist of blood would have been visible through the scope. King had been knocked back and had largely disappeared from view on the balcony's concrete floor.

Galt scrambled out of the bathtub and threw the still-warm Gamemaster and his other belongings into the bedspread. He wrapped it all up in a bundle, unlocked the bathroom door, and took off down the hall, heading for the stairs.

Charlie Stephens opened the door and saw a man in a dark suit leaving the bathroom hallway with a long package under one arm. He assumed it was the stranger in 5B, but he saw him only from the back.

Willie Anschutz, who like Stephens had heard the alarming noise from the bathroom, was standing farther down the corridor. The roomer in 5B brushed past him, carrying a bundle under one arm. "He had something about three and a half foot long," Anschutz recalled, "wrapped up in something, it might have been an old piece of blanket." He was walking at a businesslike clip, but not quite running. A smirky smile curled across his face.

"Hey, that sounded like a *shot*!" Anschutz said to the man.

Covering his face with his free hand, the tenant who called himself John Willard calmly replied, "It *was*."

THE BULLET STRUCK the right side of King's face at a velocity of 2,670 feet per second. The soft-nosed projectile shattered his mandible and, following the downward angle of its path, exited from the underside of his jaw only to reenter, burrowing into the flesh of his neck. As it did so, it sliced through his shirt collar and coat lapel and cleanly sheared away the taut cinch of his brown necktie just back from the knot.

The bullet worked its violence precisely as it was designed to do: soft-pointed rounds, forbidden by the Geneva Conventions, hotly expand upon striking their target. Considered a humane agent of dispatch for hunted animals, the bullets are designed to rupture tissue and wreak maximum trauma, so a victim has little chance of survival even when no major organ or artery has been hit.

The bullet's impact knocked King backward, spraying a fantail of blood on the balcony floor and the ceiling above him. Shards of jawbone skittered across the cement floor. Instinctively, he grasped at his throat with his right hand and fumbled for the railing with his left. Within a second, King was splayed on his back, his legs crimped at awkward angles, his wing-tip shoes caught in the bottom rungs of the metal railing. His right pants leg was hitched up to mid-calf, exposing his ribbed black socks. His eyes rolled. His head moved slightly, from left to right.

The wound gushed with his pulse, the blood forming an expanding pool around his head and shoulders. A Salem menthol was crushed in one hand. His arms spread out wide on the cold concrete; he had come to rest in a posture that some at the Lorraine would later compare to crucifixion. One witness said, "His arms went out to the sides like he was a man on a cross."

Abernathy, applying Aramis aftershave on his face inside 306, heard what sounded like a firecracker or a backfiring car outside, but he thought little of it. The astringent lotion tingled on his hands and cheeks. *Firecracker?* he thought again, and glanced out the door, which was slightly ajar. He saw King's wing-tip shoes on the floor of the balcony, tucked under the railing. His first thought, alarmed but optimistic, was that King had taken cover in reaction to the popping noise outside. Then, when Abernathy got to the door, he saw the blood and knew.

"Oh my God, Martin's been shot!" he screamed. He headed for the balcony, but feared the sniper might still be out there somewhere. He glanced down into the Lorraine courtyard and saw the others stooped behind vehicles, hugging tires, taking cover. Abernathy could hear screams and shouts from down below: *My God, my God, my God! Duck! Get down! Hit the ground!. . . Don't get up—he's still out there!*

A few seconds passed before Abernathy emerged onto the balcony, and he stayed in a crouch. King lay diagonally on the cement floor, to the left of the door. Carefully stepping over him, Abernathy saw that his friend looked afraid and tried to comfort him by patting his left cheek. The wound on his right jaw was worse than Abernathy had feared. Ragged and torn, it was, he thought, as large as a fist. A slash of bone shone through. The blood "glistened," Abernathy later said, and it steadily pooled around King's head, soaking his shirt and suit coat.

King breathed with a raspy difficulty. His quivering lips appeared to be forming the word "Oh," but produced no sound. He seemed to be trying to say something. His eyes wobbled in their sockets, then steadied and sharpened. His gaze fell on his friend. Abernathy thought King was trying to communicate something through his eyes.

"Martin," Abernathy said softly. "It's all right. Don't worry. This is Ralph. This is *Ralph*."

■

WITHIN FORTY-FIVE seconds of firing the shot, Eric Galt had scrambled down the rooming house stairs—twenty-five steps in all—and thrown open the door. It was 6:02 p.m. when he emerged into the twilight on South Main. The night was cold and damp, the street strangely deserted. Most of the businesses had closed for the night, and the brick and glass storefronts simmered in a thin soup of neon. With the Gamemaster still bundled under his arm, Galt turned left and dashed south along the cracked sidewalk. His fake-alligator loafers clopped on the cement as he aimed for his Mustang, parked sixty feet away.

It was all too easy. South Main was ghostly quiet, and there was no indication of the carnage he'd just created a block away. No one even noticed him—let alone tried to stop him. But as he approached his Mustang, he saw the three Memphis police cars of TAC Unit 10 parked just ahead. They were angled toward the Lorraine, at the Butler Avenue fire station. Just around the corner, several policemen stood outside the fire station brandishing weapons.

If Galt continued down South Main, one of these officers would see the suspicious-looking package under his arm. The odds of his reaching the Mustang undetected were slim. He made an impulsive decision he would later rue: he would have to ditch the rifle.

He was passing by Canipe's Amusement Company, the cluttered shop at 424 South Main that leased and serviced jukeboxes and pinball machines. The storefront had a recessed entry; its plate-glass windows angled in from the sidewalk, creating a triangular vestibule, so the doorway was slightly hidden from the cops' line of sight. This fortuitous cavern might buy him a minute. It's not clear whether Galt noticed, but the owner, Guy Canipe, was seated at his desk. Farther back in the shop, two black patrons were rummaging through the store's collection of second-hand 45 records, which Canipe sold for a quarter apiece. From somewhere in the store, music droned from a jukebox.

Instinct told Galt what to do. Within seconds, he jettisoned the whole incriminating bundle in the entryway. The rifle box, wrapped in its dingy bedspread, made a solid thunk as it crashed against the Canipe's door.

■

"MARTIN, CAN YOU hear me?" Abernathy asked. "Are you in pain?"

The life was leaching from King's face. Within minutes, his skin turned an ashen hue. He was slipping into shock. His blood pressure was plummeting, his lips turning blue, his skin clammy and cool. He seemed to stare into space, his pupils dilated. "The understanding," Abernathy said, "drained from his eyes."

The corona of warm blood oozed outward over the concrete slab. Earl Caldwell, the *New York Times* reporter staying at the Lorraine, thought that the blood was strangely thick and viscous—that instead of flowing, it layered upon itself, like "crimson molasses." Marrel McCullough, an undercover policeman who had been spying on the Invaders, cradled King's head in a white motel towel and wrapped one end around the wounds to stanch the bleeding. King's eyes were open but tracked independently of each other.

Now he was surrounded by people—Andy Young was there, and Jesse Jackson, and McCullough. Young knelt at King's side and felt his right wrist for a pulse. He thought he detected a beat—faint and thready, but still there. Studying King's eyes, Young wondered whether he was aware of what had happened, whether he'd heard the report of the rifle, whether he felt anything at all. "Ralph," he said softly. "It's all over."

"Don't say that," Abernathy replied with a grimace. "Don't say that."

Inside room 306, Billy Kyles was leaning against the wall, screaming and crying. He held the telephone receiver in one hand and pounded the wall with the other. He had been trying to call an ambulance but couldn't get through. He pounded and pounded the wall, screaming, "Answer the phone! Answer the phone! Answer the phone!" But the Lorraine operator, who had left her desk and hurried outside to investigate the commotion, wouldn't pick up.

"Let's not lose our heads," Abernathy told Kyles, adding that surely someone else had called an ambulance by now. Kyles pulled himself together and went onto the balcony with a hotel bedspread and a pillow for King's head. Kneeling down to cover King in the orange bedspread, he spotted the Salem cigarette crumpled in his hand. Thinking that King wouldn't want people to see cigarettes, Kyles discreetly slipped it out of his grip.

A few doors down, in room 309, Joseph Louw trembled with a manic rage. He wanted to grab a gun and kill the first white person he saw, but the only thing he had to shoot with was his still 35 mm camera, hidden in his dresser. He yanked open the drawer and scooped up the camera. Then he emerged onto the balcony and began furiously shooting in all directions, his index finger firing in pure reflex.

His camera found the courtyard of the Lorraine plunged into confusion. Like swarms of agitated hornets, firemen and policemen could be seen scattering from the engine house. Most of them dropped down the retaining wall and came running for the Lorraine. In the parking lot, no one seemed to know what to do, where to go, how to help. People ran in all directions—moaning, crying, praying, cursing. Some stayed crouched, half expecting another shot, fearing this might be a mass assassination attempt. Others labored under the mistaken idea that the explosion had been a bomb and that King had been hit by shrapnel.

Solomon Jones, King's chauffeur, aimlessly screeched the Cadillac back and forth over the parking lot, rubber crying over asphalt. In the confusion, Jones looked across Mulberry Street and thought he saw a man wearing what looked like "something white over his head" standing in the brushy area beneath the brick rooming house.

In the motel office, the Lorraine's co-owner Loree Bailey began "shaking like a leaf," according to her husband. She wandered around the premises, moaning, "Why? Why? Why?" A few minutes later, a blood vessel to her brain ruptured, causing a massive cerebral hemorrhage. She collapsed on the floor of her office, fell into a coma, and would die in the hospital a few days later.

Now the parking lot was filled with screams, shouts, wails, pleas, accusations: "*Motherfuckers. . . Call an ambulance!. . . Oh Jesus, oh Jesus. . . Police shot him. . . Don't move him—don't move his head!. . . Motherfuckers finally got 'im.*" Helmeted policemen, weapons drawn, streamed into the Lorraine courtyard.

At first, many in King's entourage thought the police were attacking *them*—that the Lorraine was under siege. Then the cops yelled, "Where'd the shot come from? Where'd the shot come from?" Young, Abernathy, and the others standing over King raised their arms and pointed up and slightly to the right, toward the northwest and the brick rooming house half-obscured by brush. As they did so, Joe Louw snapped a black-and-white image that would run in papers around the world, a photograph suffused with palpable urgency and thinning hope.

It's not clear how Abernathy and the others so accurately intuited the sniper's location—none of them had *seen* anything, no puff of smoke or gleaming barrel, no suspicious flash in a window. The crack of the rifle had reverberated off so many brick facades and concrete surfaces, and with such muddying force, that it seemed impossible to pinpoint the direction from which the trouble had originated. The angle of King's splayed and twisted body provided only a general clue. Yet in that moment when the policemen asked the question from below, a basic deduction took place, a group reflex informed by instant apprehensions. Without hesitation or pause for parley, the arms shot up. Louw's camera captured it succinctly: a line of index fingers pointed one way, accusing in a single gesture.

Over a police radio, an officer relayed this information to police headquarters: "We have information that the shot came from a brick building directly east—correction—directly *west* from the Lorraine." Now more policemen flooded into the courtyard, and so many radios were switched on that the police dispatcher at headquarters began to hear only a whining hum. "Cut off some of the radios at the Lorraine, cut them off!" the dispatcher demanded. "We're getting too much feedback."

The sheriff's deputy William DuFour, a vigorous man in his mid-thirties, trundled up the Lorraine balcony steps and tried to take control of the situation. "Where's he been hit?" he asked. People on the balcony were unsure how to take DuFour's arrival—at this moment, especially, they were deeply suspicious of any white man in a police uniform. In seeming response to DuFour's voice, the muscles of King's face faintly pulled and twitched, as though he were trying to rise from his shock to answer DuFour's question. "Dr. King, don't move!" shouted the deputy sheriff, cutting King off before he could further injure himself.

As DuFour tried to ascertain the severity of the wounds, James Bevel padded about the Lorraine courtyard, lost in a rambling soliloquy that veered from the senseless to the savant: "Murder! Murder! Doc said that wasn't the way. Yet you knew he'd never be old. You couldn't think of him as an old man. It ended as it had to end. It was written this way."

GUY CANIPE, the owner of Canipe's Amusement Company, was sitting at his desk near the front of his shop, facing south, and listening to a selection of scratchy old 45s he'd punched into one of his jukeboxes for the two black customers in his store. An appraising man in his late fifties who wore a checked flannel shirt and spoke in a slow Texas drawl, Canipe liked any kind of music, his friends said, "so long as it made him money."

Surrounded by the carcasses of broken-down nickelodeons and pinball machines, he was sucking on a wad of tobacco and sifting through paperwork when he heard a thud in the enclave at the front of his store. Ordinarily, the noise wouldn't have registered with him. This was the sort of neighborhood where derelicts were always tossing trash—and where all manner of flotsam ended up on doorsteps; a year earlier, in fact, someone had left a perfectly good television on his doormat. But this time Canipe sensed something. He stood up, stepped over to the threshold, and beheld a curious bulge in his entryway, wrapped in a cloth that looked to him like a curtain.

Canipe looked up and spied a man heading south down Main Street. The stranger walked swiftly but did not break into a full run. Canipe could only see his back, but could tell he was a white man of medium build, neat in appearance, bareheaded, around thirty years old, and wearing a dark suit. He was, as Canipe put it, "not like the kind of people you see down here." By this time, the two black customers in Canipe's store, Julius Graham and Bernell Finley, had come forward, and they, too, got a look at the mysterious man.

He slipped behind the wheel of a white late-model Mustang about four or five spaces south of the shop, parked next to a large liquor billboard that said, VERY OLD BARTON, a popular brand of bourbon. The man cranked the motor and peeled off into the street heading north, passing right in front of the shop. Finley thought the Mustang made a "screeching" sound and then sped off, "like it was going to a fire—laying rubber down the street." As far as Canipe, Graham, and Finley could tell, the driver was the only person in the vehicle, but the Mustang was going too fast for any of them to take down a license plate number.

Now Canipe inspected the bundle at his doorstep. At one end, a black pasteboard box peeked from the fabric. Canipe, who was an avid hunter, could see the word "Browning" printed on the box and imagined for a second that someone had presented him with a generous lagniappe—a brand-new shotgun. The barrel glinted steel blue from the box. It was pointing at him.

Finley and Graham, curious, moved toward the door, but Canipe blocked their exit. He could see a policeman racing down South Main, his pistol drawn as he approached the bundle. "Get back," Canipe told his two customers. "There's some kind of trouble out here and I don't want no part of it."

The officer, Lieutenant Judson Ghormley of the Shelby County Sheriff's Department, had missed Galt and the squealing Mustang by no more than a minute. The forty-year-old Ghormley, who wore a khaki shirt and green uniform trousers, thought the little amusement shop was closed for the night and seemed surprised when Canipe cracked the door and poked his head out.

"You see who put this down?" Ghormley asked Canipe.

The shop owner told Ghormley he'd just missed the guy, and offered his description, with Finley and Graham chiming in. Finley could only say he was "medium height, medium weight, medium complexion" and that he wore a "dark suit—what color, I couldn't say." Graham was sure of one thing: the man had driven off in a Mustang, a white late-model Mustang.

Soon Ghormley got on his walkie-talkie and conveyed the information to police headquarters. "I have the weapon in front of 424 Main, and the subject ran south on Main Street!" he squawked excitedly.

The dispatcher shot back over the scratchy airwaves: "You are not to touch the weapon! *Repeat*—the weapon is not to be touched! You are advised to seal the area off completely. Any physical description on the subject?"

Ghormley radioed back over his walkie-talkie: "All we know is, he's a young white male, well dressed, dark colored suit."

Within minutes, the police dispatcher broadcast the very first description of the shooter and the probable getaway car: "Suspect described as young white male, well dressed, believed in late-model white Mustang, going north on Main from scene of shooting."

It was 6:10.

■

INSIDE THE ROOMING house, Charlie Stephens dashed back to his room and peered out the window. Across the way, the courtyard of the Lorraine Motel was pure chaos. On Mulberry Street, policemen scurried this way and that, and a line of officers advanced on the rooming house and formed a cordon.

From down below, in the brambled rear lot of the rooming house, a helmeted policeman gave Stephens a start. "Hey!" the cop yelled. "Get back from that window!"

Although Stephens had heard the gun go off in the bathroom, he had no idea what was really going on—he didn't even know Martin Luther King had been staying at the Lorraine.

The policeman eyed Stephens suspiciously. "Stay in your room," he commanded. "No one is allowed to leave the building!"

"But what is it?" Stephens yelled back. "What's happening?"

The look of pure befuddlement on Stephens's booze-reddened face must have convinced the cop that this man could not be judged a serious suspect. "It's Martin Luther King," the policeman said. "He's been shot."

■

AT THAT MOMENT, the sound of an approaching siren punctured the night. Fire department ambulance 401—a long-finned modified red Cadillac that looked rather like a hearse—screeched around the corner and pulled into the Lorraine courtyard. Emergency technicians hopped out and removed a stretcher from the rear doors of the ambulance. They hauled it up to the balcony and, with Abernathy and the others helping, managed to slide King onto the soft white bedding. The gurney stays were cinched in place, and firemen administered oxygen to King from a portable tank. Then a group of about six men, including Andy Young and the sheriff's deputy William DuFour, guided King's stretcher down the steps, negotiating the sharp turn of the staircase.

Young, for one, believed there was no hope for King, that this frantic press of medical attention was probably a useless formality. He thought King was already dead, or at least irretrievably on his way.

In the parking lot, concerned onlookers parted for the stretcher as it jounced over the asphalt. Georgia Davis, her eyes brimming with tears, threaded her way through the small crowd. She stood transfixed as the medics threw open the twin doors and eased King into the ambulance. Abernathy climbed in the back and crouched at King's side. On instinct, Davis followed Abernathy's lead and started to get into the ambulance, eager to be with her lover. But Andy Young touched her shoulder and said softly, "Georgia, I don't think you want to do that."

She seemed puzzled for a moment, her face caught in the flashing red dome light, but she realized Young was right: this was not her place. Any photographer could capture her there at King's side, and the awkward truth of a mistress would become part of history forever. She backed away from the ambulance and melted into the crowd.

The rear doors slammed shut, and at 6:09 the ambulance roared off for St. Joseph's Hospital, the nearest emergency room to the Lorraine. The driver, J. W. Walton, got on the radio and yelled to a dispatcher, "Give me the loop lights!" At Memphis Fire Headquarters, a city engineer threw a master switch that held the traffic lights at green on all north and south streets, while all the cross streets remained red. Now

Walton could race to the hospital without having to slow down at even the busiest intersections.

The ambulance, escorted by several policemen on motorcycles, sped through downtown Memphis. One of the medics hovered over King, taking his pulse and blood pressure. A different oxygen mask was placed over his mouth, and the resuscitator pump soughed away. As the siren wailed in the twilight, Abernathy wondered if his friend could hear it, and if he was frightened.

"Is he alive?" Abernathy asked.

The medic gave a perfunctory nod. "Barely," he said. "Just barely."

After four breakneck minutes the ambulance pulled up to the St. Joseph's emergency room—the same emergency room that had treated James Meredith two years earlier after he'd been shot on his ill-fated march from Memphis. Catholic-run St. Joseph's Hospital was one of the largest and most prominent institutions in Memphis, but it had been chosen for one simple reason: it was closest to the Lorraine.

At 6:15 p.m., Martin Luther King, unconscious but with his heart still beating, was wheeled through the swinging double doors and down a long corridor toward the emergency room. Abernathy walked briskly at his side.

■

In front of Canipe's Amusement Company on South Main, Lieutenant Judson Ghormley stood sentinel over the curious bundle the stranger had dropped on the ground. Faithful to the dispatcher's command, Ghormley had not laid a finger on it, but had simply parked himself in front of the door with his pistol drawn and awaited instructions from farther up the chain of command.

Captain Jewell Ray of the police department's Intelligence Division raced down Main Street and halted in front of Canipe's. Thirty-six years old, a native of Memphis with a slow, custardy drawl, the craggy-faced Ray wore plain clothes—a sport coat and a tie. "Captain," Ghormley told Ray. "The guy dropped this."

Captain Ray crouched on a knee and studied the bundle. A dingy green bedspread was loosely twirled around a black cardboard box. He could also see a blue zippered satchel. Not wanting to taint the evidence with fingerprints, he removed a pencil from his breast pocket and used it to pull back the edge of the box cover. On the box he could plainly see the word "Browning." Next to the rifle, he saw a box of ammunition.

Impressed but also puzzled by the trove, Captain Ray ordered two other policemen, armed with shotguns, to guard it until homicide detectives arrived. As more police flooded the area, he had them block the doors to Canipe's and all the adjoining businesses along South Main, including Jim's Grill.

"No one leaves the area," he barked. "This entire block is to remain secure until Homicide gets here."

At that, Captain Ray, accompanied by Lieutenant Jim Papia, clambered up the narrow steps of Bessie Brewer's rooming house. On the second floor, they found tenants circulating in the dim halls, animatedly discussing what had happened. They first met a wild-eyed middle-aged man named Harold Carter who said he heard something "that sounded a mighty lot like a shot, but I'm crazy—don't pay any attention to what I say." Captain Ray then moved on to the deaf-mute, Mrs. Ledbetter, who gestured and made guttural mumbling sounds that made no sense, but she pointed down the hall. Willie Anschutz stepped into the conversation and told Captain Ray the shot had come from the bathroom. There was a guy in the bathroom who wouldn't come out, Anschutz said. "Then I heard what sounded like a shot in there. He took off down the hall with something in his arms. I told the guy, 'That sounded like a shot.' And he said, 'It *was*.'"

Then Captain Ray met Charlie Stephens, who appeared to be drunk and agitated by all the commotion. "Yeah, the shot come from the bathroom," Stephens said. "It was the new tenant, the guy in 5B. This afternoon, when he moved in, I heard a noise in there—sounded like he was moving furniture."

Ray and Papia raced down the hall and turned the coat-hanger "doorknob" of 5B. The door screaked open, revealing a cheerless room devoid of personal belongings or luggage. The two officers had a sinking feeling, an eerie sense that they'd missed their man by a matter of minutes. The bed was tidily made, but there was still a depression on one side of the mattress, as though someone had just been sitting there. The window overlooking the Lorraine was open. The curtains had been slid to one side and now rippled faintly in the breeze. A straight-backed chair was by the window, facing toward the Lorraine, and a large rickety dresser had been scooted across the floor, evidently to make room for the chair.

Ray and Papia walked to the window and tried to figure the sight lines. "Looks like he was settin' here watching," Lieutenant Papia said. "But it's not a good angle to shoot from."

Captain Ray tried to picture the shooter standing there and agreed. He began to think that Stephens was right—maybe the shot came from the bathroom.

As they turned to leave, however, Papia spotted something: on the floor were two short black leather straps. Papia thought they had come from a camera.

Now Captain Ray and Lieutenant Papia clomped down the linoleum hall to the bathroom. They opened the door and moved toward the window, which was cracked open about five inches. Ray tried to open the window farther, but it was jammed. He peered down into the littered yard and spotted a wire-mesh screen directly below, as though it had been jimmied from its groove.

Outside, through the gloaming, Ray and Papia could see the Lorraine dead ahead, about two hundred feet away. The motel parking lot was a confusion of swirling squad-car lights and chattering radios. Unlike in 5B, the sight line from this window to the Lorraine was a direct one. "Yeah," said Papia, "he could get a good shot from here."

Captain Ray discovered that the wooden windowsill had a curious marking, a half-moon indentation that appeared to him to have been freshly made; thinking it *could* have been caused by the recoil of a firing rifle barrel, he made a note of it, and later that night homicide detectives removed the sill and took it into evidence. By the look of things, the sniper would have had to stand in the bathtub to squeeze off the shot. Indeed, there appeared to be new scuff marks in the tub. Above the tub, higher along the wall, was a large palm print. It seemed likely to Captain Ray that the sniper, while climbing into the tub, had used one hand to steady himself against the wall.

Captain Ray ordered a policeman to guard the bathroom, and

another to stand watch over 5B and secure the crime scene until homicide detectives and FBI agents could take over the case.

"Where's the landlord?" Captain Ray asked. Eventually comprehending him, Mrs. Ledbetter tugged at his sleeve and led him down the corridor to Bessie Brewer's room and office in the flophouse's adjoining wing. The deaf-mute gestured toward the door of room 2 and groaned.

"Open up!" Ray commanded, pounding on the door. "Police!"

A bolt slid open, and a nervous-looking Mrs. Brewer appeared at the door. In the room, an episode of *Rawhide* flickered on the television.

"Who rented room 5B?" Captain Ray wanted to know.

Mrs. Brewer couldn't remember the man's name. Flustered, she began to rummage around her office for the receipt book. She had heard the shot, she volunteered, or at least what *sounded* like a shot. She had stepped out into the hall and run into Willie Anschutz, who told her, "Your new roomer ran down the stairs with a gun!" She'd dashed down to 5B only to find it empty, just as Captain Ray and Lieutenant Papia would find it a few minutes later. Then, worried about her safety, she'd scurried back to her office and bolted the door.

The man in 5B had checked in around 3:00 or so, Mrs. Brewer said, and paid for a week's rent. He was dressed in a sharp-looking dark suit, like what a businessman would wear. She first showed him a nicer room toward the front of the building, but he turned it down.

"Here it is," Mrs. Brewer said, grasping the receipt book. She opened it up and found the stub for $8.50 made out earlier that day.

The roomer's name, she told Captain Ray, was John Willard.

AT THE LORRAINE, Jesse Jackson was on the phone, frantically trying to get word to Coretta. He sat on the edge of the bed and dialed the number over and over again on the black rotary telephone. He didn't want her to have to hear the news over the airwaves, through the sterile voice of a news announcer. When he finally caught her, at about 6:20, she had just returned to the King home at 234 Sunset. She'd been shopping most of the afternoon in downtown Atlanta with her twelve-year-old daughter, Yolanda, to buy her a new dress for Easter Sunday. Coretta was lying down in her bedroom, resting her feet, her ankles crossed, when she picked up the beige receiver from the bedside phone. "Hello?"

"Coretta, Doc just got shot," Jackson said, indelicately blurting out the news. The report he gave her contained a hopeful fib: her husband had only been hit *in the shoulder*.

"I . . . understand," she said, after a long pause. There was a formality to the way she said it. Jackson thought she bore the news with stoic reserve, almost as though she'd been expecting it. This was a phone call, she later said, that she'd been "subconsciously waiting for" nearly all her married life.

As she talked with Jackson, her sons, Dexter and Marty, came racing into the room. They'd been watching TV elsewhere in the house, sitting on the floor, when a news bulletin flashed across the screen, saying their daddy had been shot in Memphis.

"Mama?" Dexter interrupted excitedly. "You hear that? What do they mean?"

Coretta raised her finger to her lips to shush the boys, and they waited impatiently at the foot of the bed as their mother finished hearing what Jackson had to say.

"They've taken him to St. Joseph's Hospital," he told her.

"I understand," she replied again. "I . . . *understand.*" As he recalled years later in his memoir, Dexter didn't understand why his mother kept saying those words, but he dreaded the tone in her voice.

"I don't know how bad it is," Jackson said. "But you should get a plane out right away."

"I'll check for the next flight," she told Jackson, and calmly hung up.

■

INSIDE ST. JOSEPH'S, a team of nurses and ER orderlies wheeled King into a small, harshly lit chamber with pale green walls. They transferred King to an operating table and snipped away his blood-stiffened jacket, shirt, undershirt, and tie—giving the clothing to Memphis Police Department witnesses as possible evidence. King lay with his head turned slightly to his left, the gaping wound at the base of his neck no longer bleeding. His face was still partially covered with a towel. A crucifix hung on the wall, the dying Christ's visage brooding over banks of medical machines and arrayed instruments.

Among the first physicians on the scene was Dr. Ted Galyon, who, using a stethoscope, detected a clear heartbeat and a radial pulse. An IV tube was inserted into King's left forearm to administer vital saline fluids, another in his ankle to infuse blood.

At 6:20, Dr. Rufus Brown, a young white physician from Mississippi still in his surgical residency, entered the room. Dr. Brown could see that King was having trouble breathing—the bullet had ravaged his windpipe, and the lungs weren't getting sufficient air. Without a moment's hesitation, Dr. Brown picked up a scalpel. "Tracheotomy," he said to the hovering staff, and pressed the blade into the base of King's throat. Several minutes later a cuffed endotracheal tube was inserted into the new hole, and King was connected to a respirator.

Ralph Abernathy was there in the emergency room, watching all this. He leaned against a wall, along with the Reverend Bernard Lee. Dr. Brown eyed the two men uneasily—it was against hospital policy for loved ones to be present in the room. A nurse sidled up to Abernathy and said, "You really *must* go."

Abernathy was adamant. "I'm staying," he said, with enough declarative force to end the matter. He and Lee stood against the wall and watched the frantic proceedings. Abernathy was amazed by the size of the wound—it extended from King's jaw down his neck toward the clavicle.

Within minutes, nearly a dozen doctors were crowded into the room—including a thoracic surgeon, a heart surgeon, a neurosurgeon, a pulmonary specialist, a renal specialist, and several general surgeons. Examining the injuries, the doctors found blood bubbling in the chest. Probing further, they could see the apex of King's right lung bulging up through the wound. They clamped various severed vessels deep inside King's right chest cavity and inserted a tube that quickly drew nearly a thousand cc's of pooled blood.

At around 6:30, the neurosurgeon Dr. Frederick Gioia stepped into the fray. A Sicilian-American from upstate New York who had trained in Geneva, Switzerland, Dr. Gioia was an endearingly gruff, intense man with delicate surgeon's hands. Over the years, he had treated countless cases of gunshot trauma. Dr. Gioia quickly confirmed that the bullet had damaged King's jugular vein and windpipe, and then had driven down into the spinal cord, cutting it completely—apparently ricocheting through several vertebrae and lacerating the subclavian artery in the process. As Dr. Gioia later put it, "A defect in the vertebral bodies of C-7 to T-2 was present with a complete loss of spinal cord substance." Along its zigzagging path inside his body, the fraying bullet had torn loose shards of bone that became, in effect, tiny projectiles, wreaking further internal damage. The main part of the bullet had come to rest along his left shoulder blade; Dr. Gioia could feel the hard mass of metal—or what was left of it—just under the skin, wedged against the scapula.

Shortly after making this determination, Dr. Gioia set down his instruments and shook his head. He came over to speak with Abernathy and Lee. "It would be a blessing if he did go," the doctor said, his piercing blue eyes peering over his surgical mask. "The spine is cut and he has sustained awful brain damage." Shards of bullet, he noted, had severed prominent nerves near the base of the skull.

If King did survive, he would be paralyzed from the neck down and would probably live in a vegetative state. There was very little Dr. Gioia could do, very little anyone could do at this point. By most medical definitions, King was already brain-dead. The organs were alive, and the lungs drew breath thanks to the respirator, but King's vital systems had ceased to function as an organic whole.

Yet his heart kept beating.

■

EVER SINCE THE first dispatcher alerts around 6:10 p.m., the Memphis police had been on the lookout for a late-model Mustang driven by a well-dressed white man possibly answering to the name John Willard. Cruisers were placed at nearly every major thoroughfare leading from the city, and all across Memphis policemen pulled over every Mustang they saw. This was no mean task, as the wildly popular Mustang was one of the most common cars on the road. A quick check with area Ford dealers would reveal that some four hundred light-colored Mustangs had been sold over the past three years in Memphis and Shelby County.

Still, several promising leads soon developed. At 6:26, a sheriff's department dispatcher broadcast an alert, based on information of uncertain origin, that put the assailant's Mustang heading north and east out of the city: "Subject now believed north of Thomas from Parkway, dark hair, dark suit."

Ten minutes later, a police lieutenant named Rufus Bradshaw, driving car 160, was flagged down by an agitated young man named Bill Austein at the corner of Jackson and Hollywood in north Memphis. The twenty-two-year-old Austein, who drove a white and red Chevrolet Chevelle and worked for a heating and air-conditioning company, was a licensed citizens-band radio enthusiast (FCC call letters KOM-8637). Lieutenant Bradshaw described him as "looking like the deacon of a church." Austein said he was just now receiving an extraordinary transmission over the CB radio in his Chevelle—a transmission on Channel 17, one of the lesser-used frequencies, that urgently concerned the shooting of Martin Luther King.

His curiosity piqued, Bradshaw pulled his cruiser alongside Austein's car in the parking lot of a Loeb's Laundry and listened with fascination to the chatter on his radio. For the next twelve minutes Bradshaw heard a live narration purportedly being transmitted from a blue 1966 Pontiac hardtop barreling toward the northeastern precincts of the city—a Pontiac that was in hot pursuit of a fast-fleeing white Mustang. The broadcaster claimed the man he was following was "the man who had shot King."

As he attempted to decipher this unfolding story, Bradshaw got on his own radio and excitedly relayed to the central police dispatcher what he was hearing. The headquarters dispatcher, who could not directly raise the CB signal himself, listened to Bradshaw and, in spurts and fragments, broadcast an often garbled version of his narration. "White male, east on Summer from Highland, in white Mustang, responsible for shooting," the dispatcher began. The minutes slipped by, and the chase escalated from seventy-five miles per hour, to eighty, ninety, ninety-five, as the Mustang and pursuing Pontiac hurtled east through rush-hour traffic and ran red lights by the dozen. The CB operator in the Pontiac, who spoke with brisk officiousness in a cracking adolescent voice, said he had two companions in the car.

Several times the transmission faltered due to atmospheric conditions, distorting the voice to the point of incoherence, but then the signal would regain its clarity. The chase progressed to the city's far eastern outskirts, then into the suburbs of Raleigh and on toward the naval air base at Millington. As night fell over Memphis, Martin Luther King's assailant appeared to be making for the honeysuckled hill country of rural Tennessee.

Austein kept breaking in and requesting the name or call number of the CB operator in the Pontiac, but the man refused to answer. All he would volunteer was the make and year of his vehicle. On the strength of the gripping transmissions relayed by Bradshaw, police dispatchers diverted cruisers to northeast Memphis in the hope of intercepting the speeding vehicles. Roadblocks were erected, highway patrolmen alerted.

As Fire and Police Director Frank Holloman and his staff listened to this white-knuckled narrative, a palpable excitement began to run through headquarters, a gathering hunch that they might be zeroing in on the mysterious John Willard. Other people listening in over the airwaves got caught up in the chase. At one point some other CB operator, obviously not a fan of the civil rights movement, broke in over the static and stated, "Let him go, as this may be the subject that shot Martin Luther King."

At 6:47, as the cars headed out Austin Peay Highway, the chase seemed to turn from dangerous to potentially lethal: the witness in the blue Pontiac suddenly screamed over his CB, "He's shooting at me! He's hit my windshield!"

Squawked Bradshaw: "The white Mustang is firing at the blue Pontiac! The white Mustang is firing at the blue Pontiac!"

Austein broke in and asked the CB operator in the Pontiac if he could make out the license plate number on the Mustang, but the driver said he was leery of getting that close—he feared the shooter in the Mustang might open fire again.

Then, at 6:48, Austein's CB receiver fell silent, the staticky reports mysteriously terminated, and Holloman's hottest lead went ice-cold.

■

THE SCENE OUTSIDE St. Joseph's Hospital was one of deepening chaos and confusion. People shouted and cursed, they cried and prayed, they stood quietly at the edge of the parking lot and held vigil by candlelight. Helmeted policemen stood at attention, wearing riot gear, loaded shotguns at the ready. Weird rumors hatched, intensified, and rippled through the milling crowds. The assassin had been caught and killed on the Mississippi River bridge, it was said. President Johnson was on his way to Memphis on Air Force One. Ralph Abernathy had been shot, too, and was dying alongside King. One of the more far-fetched and optimistic pieces of gossip had it that King had walked into the ER under his own power while holding a towel over his face, that the bullet had only grazed his jaw, and that he would be meeting with the press momentarily to assure the world he was safe.

By 6:30 the crowds outside grew so unruly that hospital officials, fearing a riot, requested more police to set up barricades. Only the closest of King's staff—Young, Bevel, Chauncey Eskridge—were able to enter the facility. A resourceful reporter for the *Commercial Appeal*, realizing he was following one of the biggest stories of his career, suddenly complained of chest pains—"I think I'm having a heart attack!" he moaned—and gained admittance to the ER.

In the waiting room, Andy Young sat with his head in his hands, and an FBI agent paced the corridors. Eskridge leaned on the wall in the waiting room and said, "Why, why would anybody want to do this? I just don't understand it." Young found a phone booth down the hall and called Coretta, not knowing that Jackson had just reached her from the Lorraine. She was hurriedly packing, planning to hop on the next flight to Memphis. A television newscast droned somewhere in the background of the King home.

Young disabused her of the hopeful idea that King was merely shot in the shoulder. "The *neck*," Young corrected her. "It's very serious. But he's not dead, Coretta. He's not dead."

"I understand," Coretta said again—Young thought she sounded "almost serene." She was scheduled to depart Atlanta on the 8:25 flight, she told him.

"All right," Young replied. "We'll be looking for you at the airport. But, Coretta, bring someone with you."

She said she would—in fact, Ivan Allen, the mayor of Atlanta, had offered to drive her to the airport, and Dora McDonald, King's personal secretary, was ready to fly with her to Memphis. Hanging up the beige receiver, she turned to Yolanda, Dexter, and Marty, who'd been trying to follow the conversation. Coretta opened her mouth to speak, but Yoki, as Yolanda was nicknamed, cupped her hands over her ears and ran out of the room, screaming, "Don't tell me! Don't tell me!"

Coretta gathered her two boys in her arms and took a deep breath. "Your father—there's been an accident."

■

JESSE JACKSON EMERGED from his room at the Lorraine and, looking deeply distracted and in disarray, roamed about the courtyard in the swirling lights of the squad cars.

"I need to see Dr. King!" Jackson yelled impatiently to someone off in the distance. "Can I get a ride to the hospital to see Dr. King?" He saw a gaggle of reporters attempting to interview the musician Ben Branch. "Don't talk to them!" Jackson yelled. Branch agreed, thinking Jackson meant that they should all decline interviews until Abernathy and Young returned from the hospital. They, after all, had been closest to King and had seen the most. Branch told the reporters, "No comment," and walked away.

A few minutes later one of the television crews spotted Jackson. "Jesse? Reverend?" a reporter said. "Could you tell us just what happened, please?"

Jackson demurred at first—"Can you excuse us, Jack? Can it wait a little while?"—but the reporter persisted. "Would you tell me just what happened so we can get this film in, please?"

Finally Jackson relented. More than anyone else in the SCLC (aside from King himself), the twenty-six-year-old Jackson was a natural before the klieg lights, and when the cameras began to whir, he brightened just a little. "The black people's leader," he began, "our Moses, the once in a 500-year leader, has been taken from us. Even as I stand at this hour, I cannot allow hate to enter my heart at this time, for it was sickness, not meanness, that killed him. The pathology and the neurosis of Memphis, and of this racist society in which we live, is what pulled the trigger. To some extent Dr. King has been a buffer the last few years between the black community and the white community. The white people don't know it, but the white people's best friend is dead."

When the reporter pressed him for details about what happened at the Lorraine immediately after the shot, Jackson replied, "People were, uh, some were in pandemonium, some in shock, some were hollering, 'Oh God.' And uh . . ."

He glanced off camera and hesitated a moment. Perhaps the stress of the tragedy was getting the better of him, or perhaps he sensed an opportunity, but at this point Jackson began to spin a small fiction that would grow in the days ahead, one in which he imagined himself playing the approximate role that Abernathy had in fact played on the balcony. "And I immediately started running upstairs to where he was," Jackson said. "And I caught his head. And I tried to feel his head. I asked him, 'Dr. King, do you hear me? Dr. King, do you hear me?' And he didn't say anything. And I tried to—to *hold his head*. But by then . . ."

The SCLC staffer Hosea Williams glanced from his room window and saw Jackson speaking to the press. Curious, he wandered out to the courtyard and listened. Jackson's account gave Williams pause, because in all the confusion he couldn't remember Jackson ever getting near the fallen King, let alone cradling his head in his arms. Some people at the Lorraine couldn't remember seeing Jackson at all after the shot was fired, while others said he'd hidden somewhere behind the swimming pool's privacy wall until the ambulance arrived.

Williams was thus already suspicious when he thought he heard Jackson tell the television reporter, "Yes, I was the last man in the world King spoke to."

It's possible that the older and more seasoned Williams felt a stab of jealousy over the brazen way in which the young Jackson assumed the limelight. But the baldness of this apparent lie so infuriated Williams that he climbed over a railing and pushed his way toward him, yelling, "You dirty, stinking, lying . . . !" People standing around the Lorraine had to physically restrain him to keep him from assaulting Jackson. "I was gonna stomp him in the ground!" Williams fumed.

Even as King clung to life in the hospital, internecine dissension seethed in the ranks; the young Turks were beginning to fight for proximity, real or imagined, to the heat of the drama. "It's a helluva thing to capitalize on, especially one you profess to love," Williams later told a reporter. "The only person who cradled Dr. King was Abernathy. I have no hang-ups about Jesse talking to the press. But, *why lie?*"

The conflict with Williams seemed to rattle Jackson. He told another SCLC staffer that he was sick and had decided to leave for Chicago later that night. "This whole thing's really shot my nerves," Jackson said, noting that he planned to check in to a hospital back home.

Yet his account was already gaining purchase in the media, and his star as King's logical successor was beginning to rise. As the NBC correspondent David Burrington reported from the Lorraine, only minutes later: "The Reverend Jesse Jackson of Chicago, one of King's closest

aides, was beside him when he was shot while standing on a veranda outside his motel room."

■

INSIDE THE St. Joseph's ER, the attending doctors could tell that
King's heart was faltering. At 6:45 p.m., Dr. Ted Galyon ordered a medical technician to wire King's bare chest to an EKG machine. The heartbeat was desperately weak—the electric needle scratched languid zigzags
across the slow-spooling paper. Dr. Galyon requested an Adrenalin in-
jection directly into the heart muscle, while another physician initiated
closed-chest cardiac massage—using the heels of his hands to rhythmi-
cally knead the lower sternum. High along King's rib cage, right beside
his breastbone, the doctors could see an impressive old scar—the cross-
shaped wound left from the surgery King had undergone in 1958 to remove the letter opener the demented lady had plunged into his chest at
the book signing in Harlem.

King did not react to the resuscitative efforts now under way, and
when a doctor shone a bright penlight in his eyes, his pupils were massively dilated and unresponsive. One of the surgeons, shaking his head,
turned and spoke under his breath to Ralph Abernathy and Bernard Lee.
"He won't make it," he said.

Abernathy looked dazed and puzzled. "Then why are they all still
in here?" he replied, casting his eye over the busy team of physicians,
nurses, and orderlies.

The doctor said gently, "With somebody as well-known and important as Dr. King, you try everything. But nothing's going to work
now."

The doctors continued to massage King's heart for more than fifteen minutes, but the EKG needle stopped scribbling altogether. The
tape emerging from the machine showed no cardiac function at all. The
same doctor came over to Abernathy and Lee again and said, "He's
going. If you'd like to spend a few last moments with him, you can have
them now."

Abernathy took King in his arms and held him. His breathing was
"nothing more than prolonged shudders," Abernathy said. "The breaths

came farther and farther apart. Then, a pause came that lengthened until I knew it would never end."

Dr. Jerome Barrasso entered the room and at 7:05 p.m. pronounced Martin Luther King dead.

Abernathy joined hospital officials outside in making a brief statement to Memphis, and the world. As they did so, the St. Joseph's chaplain, Father Coleman Bergard, was summoned to the emergency room. Following the hospital's protocol, Bergard leaned over the body and gave conditional absolution, praying for the soul of Martin Luther King.

Then, gently, Father Bergard closed King's eyes.

■

IN ATLANTA, KING's parents listened to the radio at Ebenezer Baptist Church. They knew their son had been shot and seriously wounded, but they still held out hope. Martin Luther King Sr. had a little radio set up near his desk in his upstairs study. As he prayed aloud, Alberta King cried in silence. She had grown up in Ebenezer and had been the church's organist since 1932; Ebenezer was her home, and her sanctuary, the best possible place for her to be in such a crisis. "*Lord, let him live, let him live!*" King senior moaned as the minutes drained away.

Then the somber bulletin came over the airwaves. King turned to his wife, but neither said a word. For years they had feared the coming of news like this—its possibility had lurked behind every late-night phone call, behind every startling noise. Daddy King recognized that in the face of concerted evil, his son had nowhere to hide. "No matter how much protection a person has, it will not be enough if the enemy is hatred," he would write. His son's fate, he realized, had been sealed years earlier. "To avoid it was impossible, even as avoiding the coming of darkness in the evening."

The Kings held each other in the study and tried to absorb the blow. Mrs. King recalled her conversation with both her sons earlier in the day, how from the motel room in Memphis they had teased her by each pretending to be the other. It had meant so much to her to hear from them, to know they were together and safe.

Daddy King removed his glasses, and the tears coursed down his cheeks, toward his gray-flecked mustache. "I always felt I would go first," he said over and over. He could only think of his son as a child, growing up, like his mother before him, in this very church, his young life revolving around Ebenezer. "My first son, whose birth had brought me such joy that I jumped up in the hall outside the room where he was born and touched the ceiling—the child, the scholar, the boy singing and smiling—all of it was gone. And Ebenezer was so quiet; all through the church, the tears flowed, but almost completely in silence."

■

A FEW MILES away, at the FBI headquarters in Atlanta, the news of King's death came flooding in over the radio. Reaction in the office hallways was mixed. Over the past decade, agents in the Atlanta field office had probably exhausted more man-hours on King—following and wiretapping and bugging and attempting to smear him—than they'd spent working on any other single subject. Code-named "Zorro," King was the office bogeyman, the subject with the most voluminous file, and the quarry of a thousand investigatory trails.

Two agents, who happened to be standing next to each other when the news came in, succinctly captured the office's divergent opinions on King. The first, Arthur Murtagh, allowed as how he thought King's death was a tragedy. "He was a credible person," he said. "He was doing what he could to help his people."

The agent standing next to him, James Rose, chastised Murtagh for his naïveté, and the two colleagues became embroiled in a heated argument. Rose said King was a Commie, a charlatan, and a threat to the nation's security; he was trying to take over the country and give it to the Russians.

According to Murtagh, Rose exclaimed, "They got Zorro!" and nearly jumped up and down with joy. "Thank God, they finally got the S.O.B.!"

AT POLICE HEADQUARTERS, Director Frank Holloman received word of King's death within seconds and alerted his highest-ranking officers to brace the entire force for the storm he expected would soon rage in the streets—looting, arson, possibly a full-scale race riot. Right now, though, his attention was focused on the incredible high-speed pursuit that had just taken place out on Summer Avenue.

Holloman had some of his best men analyze a recording of the broadcast. Several things about the episode began to seem glaringly strange. Not a single bystander or motorist anywhere along Summer called to report a car chase or gunshots. This was an amazing fact, for Summer was one of Memphis's busiest thoroughfares and the chase had taken place at rush hour, just after the first news bulletin of King's shooting was broadcast—a time, that is, when the city was on edge and primed for trouble.

As officers analyzed the tape and plotted times and locations on a map, they realized that the chase would have had to keep up an *average* speed of eighty miles per hour, nearly impossible on that traffic-snarled artery. Surely such a high-speed pursuit would have produced accidents, or near accidents, while creating a spectacle no motorist driving along Summer could forget.

Furthermore, sheriff's department officers in cruisers parked at several key intersections farther out Summer insisted that they never saw or heard anything unusual—no blue Pontiac, no white Mustang, no squealing tires or revving engines, no windshields shot out. It seemed to them like a phantom car chase.

Bill Austein, the CB enthusiast who had originally flagged down Officer Rufus Bradshaw, nursed doubts of his own. After the transmission fizzled off the airwaves, he and Bradshaw sat in the parking lot of Loeb's Laundry and sifted the extraordinary narrative they'd just heard. Austein realized that the broadcaster's voice sounded oddly calm and steady for a young man purportedly speeding at eighty miles an hour, swerving from lane to lane, with gunfire shattering his windshield.

It was also strange that the transmitter never identified himself, despite repeated urgings by Austein and other Memphis CB operators to do so. If the guy was willing to risk so much to catch a speeding car, and even put his life in danger, why wouldn't he say who he was?

Austein had additional questions about the signal itself. Throughout the broadcasts, he had repeatedly checked the little floating needle on his radio—the S-meter, it was called—and noticed that the signal strength never diminished, even though the pursuit was supposedly taking the Pontiac many miles to the northeast, well beyond the city limits, where the signal should have faded to nothing.

This was extremely fishy, Austein realized, for it meant that the broadcaster, whoever he was, had to have been stationary for much or all of the transmission—either parked in his car or radioing from a home base. The more he thought about it, the more Austein became convinced that the chase was "entirely a hoax," most likely perpetrated by a teenage CB enthusiast, just for yuks. The prankster had doubtless been listening to the police radio, where he picked up the first report that the getaway car was a white Mustang—and then let his imagination run wild.

Holloman's men soon reached more or less the same conclusion. Of course, the possibility remained that the CB radio enthusiast was *not* some random practical joker, but rather some nefarious individual who, as part of an elaborate plot, had manufactured a bogus car chase to throw the Memphis police off the killer's scent. Holloman briefly considered this possibility—it was well known in law-enforcement circles that many members of the United Klans of America communicated through citizens-band radios—but he had no time to speculate about that now. As a precaution, he would later have his detectives check every auto body and glass repair shop in Memphis to learn whether any blue Pontiac owners came in with a shattered windshield. For now, all Holloman could say with certainty was that for a few vital minutes, his police department had been had.

■

WHATEVER THE RADIO prankster intended, his hoax had only one beneficiary, and that was Eric S. Galt. The spectacular story of the car chase diverted attention to the wrong part of the city and in all likelihood helped buy Galt a precious fifteen minutes.

Having thrown down his bundle and peeled off in his Mustang—missing the first onrushing wave of police officers by as little as thirty seconds—he sped down Main Street past Huling Avenue, then headed off on one of the most far-flung and convoluted getaways in American history.

Galt's immediate goal was to exit the state as quickly as possible, which was an easy thing to do from downtown Memphis, since the city lay along the river at the alluvial convergence of Arkansas, Mississippi, and Tennessee. Galt could have sped west and taken the immense iron-truss bridge over the Mississippi River, which would have spilled him out into Arkansas in no more than three or four minutes. Instead, he headed southeast toward Mississippi on Highway 78—Lamar Avenue, the same route he'd come in on earlier that day from the New Rebel Motel.

By 6:10, when the first bulletin describing the make of his car squawked over police radios, Galt was on his way out of town. For a white-knuckled ten minutes, he found himself crawling in bumper-to-bumper traffic—a few slow miles of congestion caused by a road construction project. According to his memoirs, Galt turned on his car radio and scanned the AM stations for bulletins.

The traffic jam had cleared by 6:30, and he passed the New Rebel Motel, with its neon Confederate colonel flickering on the sign out front, lighting up the dusky highway. Minutes later, he crossed into rural Mississippi, aiming in the direction of Birmingham and Atlanta, his Mustang boring into the rust red hills under the mantle of darkness. Except on Summer Avenue, Memphis police did not erect roadblocks along the major thoroughfares leading out of the city. Galt had managed to keep just ahead of the ever-enlarging dragnet by the thin margin of a few minutes and a few miles.

As Galt cut across the Magnolia State, the bundle must have weighed on his mind, the nagging realization that he'd left a constellation of things behind at the crime scene that could lead to him. With growing alarm, he tried to recall just what, besides the weapon, was stuffed in that ungainly pile he'd dropped on the sidewalk.

But for now, Galt could savor his triumph. Through an exquisite confluence of timing, dumb luck, and the idiosyncrasies of geography, Eric Galt had slipped safely from the orbit of metropolitan Memphis and was now pushing with impunity deep into the Mississippi hill country.

There was something else, too. The broadcasters now broke in over the airwaves to announce a stunning piece of news: Martin Luther King Jr. was dead.

■

AT THE AIRPORT in Atlanta, Coretta King hurried down the long corridor, with Mayor Ivan Allen and Dora McDonald at her side. As they neared the gate for the Memphis flight, she heard her name called out over the airport's PA system.

Coretta was optimistic at first. "Someone is paging me," she said brightly. Then she was seized by a "strange, cold feeling," she later wrote, "for I knew it was the word from Memphis and that the word was bad."

When Mayor Allen took off to retrieve the page, Dora said, "Come on, we need a room where we can sit down," and led Coretta to the outer entrance of the ladies' room, where they waited a few awful minutes, holding hands. Then Mayor Allen returned, with a stricken expression on his face. Assuming a peculiar formality, he walked up to Coretta, looked her in the eyes, and said, "Mrs. King, I have been asked to tell you that Dr. King is dead."

The words hung in the air as passengers pressed toward their gates. Dora and the mayor tried to comfort Coretta. For a time they stood weeping together in a clutch. But the plane was about to leave. "Mrs.

King," Mayor Allen said, taking her hand in his. "What do you want to do? Do you want to go on to Memphis?"

She shook her head. "I should get back home," she said, "and see about the children."

■

IN A FIFTH-FLOOR conference room at the U.S. Justice Department building in Washington, Attorney General Ramsey Clark received word of King's death just moments after it was announced in Memphis. Fearing that the nation was about to come apart at the seams, Clark viewed King's death as "a tragic setback and stunning on a personal level."

The attorney general instantly knew that the FBI would have to take over the case—although murder, even the murder of a nationally prominent citizen, was not a federal crime. But the assassination of Martin Luther King was too momentous to leave to the Memphis Police Department. Clark also realized there was a strong likelihood that King's assailant had already crossed state lines, thus making this a multi-jurisdictional case.

Clark assigned a phalanx of Justice Department lawyers the task of finding workable legal grounds for the FBI's immediately taking on the case. They hastily zeroed in on Title 18, section 241 of the U.S. Code, which "prohibits conspiracies to injure, oppress, threaten, or intimidate any citizen in the free exercise or enjoyment of any right or privilege secured to him or her by the Constitution or laws of the United States."

Attorney General Clark next put in a call to Cartha DeLoach, the assistant director of the FBI, who had just arrived at home. "I think the bureau should investigate," he told DeLoach, briefly outlining the "conspiracies to injure" clause Justice planned to invoke. No expense should be spared, Clark insisted. "Get as many facts as you can. I'll call the White House."

Clark's unspoken implication was that DeLoach should call Hoover, since Clark's relationship with the FBI director was so bad that the two were hardly on speaking terms. DeLoach took the cue and got Hoover on his private line. He recalled the conversation years later in his memoir.

"Some idiot shot Martin Luther King," DeLoach said.

The director had heard all about the assassination, of course, and wouldn't let DeLoach get a word in edgewise. "Do *not* accept responsibility for this investigation," Hoover demanded in his machine-gun sputter. "This is a local matter. Offer Memphis whatever help they need—ballistics, fingerprints, criminal records. But this case falls under the jurisdiction of city and state police."

Eventually, DeLoach was able to interrupt the Old Man's tirade long enough to say that he'd already heard from the attorney general. "Clark says he wants us to take over the case."

After a long pause, Hoover heaved a sigh. "Well he *would*," he said in exasperation. Hoover must have shuddered at the thought that his bureau was now charged with the responsibility of solving the murder of a man he detested, a man he and his COINTELPRO agents had so determinedly tried to smear, sabotage, and "neutralize."

DeLoach explained that Justice had already ginned up some sort of legal rationale. DeLoach said he thought Clark's decision was sound. Even though King was a private citizen, how odd it would seem, to the country and to the world, for the FBI *not* to take charge of the most prominent national murder case since the JFK assassination. It was, he said, "a crime of immense importance to the nation" and one characterized by great "external pressures."

"OK, go ahead," Hoover curtly said, recognizing the futility of his argument. "But I want *you* to take charge. Don't let Clark turn this into a political circus. You make it clear this is the FBI's case."

Then, without another word, he hung up.

With this awkward and decidedly herky-jerky start, the FBI's search for MLK's killer began, a manhunt that would become the largest in American history, ultimately involving more than thirty-five hundred FBI agents and costing the government nearly two million dollars. From the moment of its inception, the investigation into King's assassination was characterized by a certain cognitive dissonance at the top: a hidebound FBI director charged with finding the assassin of a man he loathed, all the while answerable to (yet barely on speaking terms with) a liberal young attorney general who revered the deceased. Cartha DeLoach, as usual, found himself in the middle of it all. "Hoover remained at war with Clark," he later wrote, "and I was in the line of fire." It was an arrangement, DeLoach said, that would often leave his "pressure gauge registering in the red."

DeLoach believed that despite Hoover's hatred of King, the Old Man was committed to using every ounce of the bureau's considerable power to chase the assassin down. As DeLoach put it, "He was as anxious as anyone to find King's killer, even though he disapproved of the man. We had a job to do and we were prepared to do it. The case was handled in a very intensified manner, and everyone in the FBI was called upon to help out."

Ramsey Clark agreed: "The FBI's reputation was at stake, and there was nothing more important to Hoover than the bureau's reputation. Hoover was afraid people were going to say *he* did it. So he was all out for finding the killer. And from the start you could feel it in the pace and the seriousness of the people in the bureau."

DeLoach called Robert Jensen, special agent in charge of the FBI's Memphis field office. Jensen had already visited the crime scene and had been in close consultation with Memphis homicide detectives only minutes after King's shooting was first reported. "The AG wants us to take over the case," DeLoach announced. Jensen understood immediately what that meant: as the field office of origin, Memphis would serve, along with Washington, as the command center of the national investigation. Until the case was resolved, Jensen would have to play the formidable and thankless role of bureau point man—"the guy," as DeLoach put it, "with a thousand opportunities to screw up."

But DeLoach had faith in Jensen, whom he viewed as "very experienced and thorough." Born in Denmark and raised in Detroit, Robert G. Jensen had served as a navigator in World War II, flying twenty-five missions over Europe. After attending the University of Michigan, he'd spent twenty-one years in the FBI, serving in Philadelphia, Miami, Birmingham, and Washington, D.C. A bit of a golf nut, Jensen was taciturn, levelheaded, and equipped with a wry wit that was accentuated by slightly crooked front teeth. Most of all, he was calm, a quality that stood him in good stead as he faced the likely hysteria of the coming weeks.

DeLoach ordered Jensen to gather the crime scene information and get the physical evidence on a plane straightaway so forensic experts at the FBI's crime lab could begin to analyze it. "As you well know," DeLoach told Jensen, "this has to be solved as soon as possible. We need to full-court press this—all your people on the job till they drop."

■

When Inspector Nevelyn Zachary of the Memphis Police Department's Homicide Bureau arrived at 424 South Main Street, the bundle was still there in the vestibule of Canipe's Amusement Company, guarded over by a policeman holding a shotgun. Zachary had the bundle photographed just as it was found. Then he put on gloves so as not to tamper with the evidence and took the bundle into his possession. But Zachary's custody of this extraordinary little trove would only last several hours, while Clark, DeLoach, and Hoover conferred about whether the FBI should fully enter the case. Some time after 8:00 p.m., the bundle was raced to the downtown field office of the FBI and placed in the hands of Special Agent Jensen.

Now Jensen removed the faded green herringbone bedspread that was loosely wrapped around the contents. To him, it looked like an old bedspread that had come from a cheap motel somewhere. He laid out the material on a well-lit table in an examining room and put on a pair of latex gloves. Then, sensing that the solution to the case might well be contained in these very belongings, Special Agent Jensen began to take a careful inventory.

The first and most obvious thing that drew his attention was the black cardboard rifle box. It was originally made for a Browning but now contained a Remington Gamemaster .30-06 rifle. Jensen quickly ascertained that it was a Model 760, serial number 461476, and it seemed to be newly purchased: it hardly had a scratch on it. The weapon was mounted with a Redfield telescopic sight. The magazine was empty, but inside the chamber he found a spent casing, which he carefully removed.

Jensen also found a twenty-round box containing nine cartridges. They were Remington-Peters .30-06 soft-pointed, metal-jacketed Springfield High Velocity cartridges—150 grain.

Beside the box of ammo was a blue plastic zippered suitcase approximately twenty by thirty inches, stuffed with an odd miscellany of objects. Among other things, Jensen removed a magnetic tack hammer, a pair of flat-nosed duckbill pliers with the words "Rompage Hardware" stamped on the handle, and two road maps—"The United States" and "Georgia-Alabama." He also found that morning's front section of the

Memphis Commercial Appeal. On page one, the newspaper conspicuously carried reports about Dr. King's efforts in Memphis and mentioned that King and his entourage were staying at the Lorraine Motel.

Then, from deeper inside the bag, Jensen retrieved a pair of binoculars, which seemed brand-new and were packed with an instruction booklet and lens cloth as well as a box and a black leather carrying case. The binoculars were made by the Bushnell company, serial number DQ 408664. Jensen confirmed that two slender buckled leather straps that Memphis police had earlier found in John Willard's room fit the binoculars perfectly—evidence that whoever dropped the bundle outside had almost certainly been in 5B.

There was little mystery when and where the binoculars had been purchased—Jensen found a paper sack that said, "York Arms Company," with a receipt for $41.55, dated that very day. York Arms, Jensen knew, was just down Main Street from the rooming house, on the same stretch of the street where the striking garbage workers had been picketing each day with their I AM A MAN sandwich boards.

The bag held a few clothing items, too—a pair of long black socks, a gray cloth belt, a pair of gray and white undershorts rather clumsily darned in the crotch with brown thread, a white handkerchief, a Jockey Power-Knit T-shirt. Picking further into the folds of the suitcase, Jensen found a brown bag containing two aluminum cans of Schlitz—"The Beer That Made Milwaukee Famous," the labels said. Stickers affixed to the can bottoms indicated that the six-pack had been taxed and purchased in Mississippi.

Jensen found that most of the remaining items in the suitcase were drugstore sundries—a tube of Colgate toothpaste, a Pepsodent brand toothbrush, an aerosol can of Gillette shaving cream, Right Guard deodorant, razor blades, Bufferin tablets, a bar of Dial soap, Palmolive Rapid Shave, One A Day vitamins, Mennen Afta aftershave lotion, Head & Shoulders shampoo, a box of Band-Aid sheer strips, Brylcreem, a can of Kiwi brown shoe polish. There were also two small hotel-size bars of soap—Cashmere and Palmolive—that the assailant had perhaps taken from a motel bathroom somewhere along his travels. Whoever he was, Jensen thought, the guy was frugal and very keen on personal hygiene and the maintenance of his clothes—an incongruous fact, given the slovenly standards at Mrs. Brewer's flophouse. Some of these toiletries had been bought in the Memphis area, Jensen realized: they bore adhesive price stickers stamped "Oliver Rexall, Whitehaven."

There was one final item in the suitcase, a piece of merchandise that gave Jensen pause: a pocket-sized transistor radio made by Channel Master. The radio looked as though it had some miles on it; the maroon plastic housing was smudged and scratched, and the perforated silver grille over the speaker had a few dings.

On the side, faintly scratched in small numerals, the radio bore a curious aftermarket identification number. But Special Agent Jensen couldn't make out the numerals; to him, it looked as though the number had been deliberately tampered with in order to make it illegible.

PRESIDENT JOHNSON SAT at his mahogany desk in the Oval Office, staring in disbelief at a one-page typed memo that had just been handed to him by an aide. "Mr. President," it succinctly said, "Justice has just advised that Dr. King is dead." It was 8:20 eastern time.

For the next few minutes Johnson turned toward his bank of three television screens built into the wall, his eyes shifting restlessly from NBC to ABC to CBS. In a corner, the wire-service Teletype machines nattered away. Drinking a Fresca, the president paced the green carpet and digested the reports steadily seeping into the Oval Office. He had brief phone conversations with Clark and then DeLoach. A familiar dread settled over him: having been ushered into office by an assassination, he now confronted another momentous rip in the national fabric. "A jumble of anxious thoughts ran through my mind," Johnson later recalled. "What does it mean? Was it the act of one man or a group? Was the assassin black or white? Would the shooting bring violence, more catastrophe, and more extremism?"

Johnson instantly knew that his ambitious plans for the evening, for the week, possibly for the month, were wrecked. At 8:00 p.m., he was supposed to attend a $250-a-plate Democratic fund-raising dinner at the Washington Hilton on Connecticut Avenue, then fly all night to Honolulu aboard Air Force One to confer with General Westmoreland about possible Vietnam peace negotiations. Since withdrawing from the presidential race four days earlier, Johnson had been on a high, basking in wide praise for his statesmanlike decision, full of new optimism about the chances for ending the war and energetically turning attention back to his beloved Great Society programs for his final months in office. Just as he'd hoped, abdicating the throne had seemed to ease all his problems. Staffers noticed a new spring in his step as he dove back into the fray, blessed with what seemed to be fresh political capital.

Yet now, with the King assassination, LBJ understood his brief reprieve was over. "Everything we've gained in the last few days we're going to lose tonight," Johnson said morosely.

Johnson met with his staff and frantically began to make plans. He would postpone, if not cancel altogether, his trip to Hawaii. First thing the next morning, Friday, he would dispatch Attorney General Clark to Memphis to spearhead the FBI investigation. Later in the morning, he would meet at the White House with the nation's most prominent black leaders to discuss the future of civil rights. Then he would attend a King memorial service that was now being planned at the National Cathedral, where King had spoken on Sunday. A White House telegram of condolence would go out to Martin Luther King Sr. and his wife. That Sunday—Palm Sunday—would be declared a day of national mourning. All federal flags in the land would fly at half-staff—the first time in American history that a private citizen would be so honored in death.

But right now, Johnson realized he had to go on live television and talk to the nation. While speechwriters crafted a statement, he slipped down to the White House barbershop for a quick trim and then a dab of makeup. From the barbershop, he called Coretta King at home in Atlanta—she'd just returned from the airport—and offered her his condolences. At just before 9:00 eastern time, he strode out to the West Lobby and stood at the podium before a nest of microphones. The night air was heavy with moisture—rainstorms were in the forecast. Framed by a set of French doors, President Johnson wore a dark suit, the crisp fold of his handkerchief peeking from his pocket.

"America is shocked and saddened by the brutal slaying tonight of Dr. Martin Luther King," he told the cameras. "I ask every citizen to reject the blind violence that has struck Dr. King. I pray that his family can find comfort in the memory of all he tried to do for the land he loved so well. I have just conveyed the sympathy of Mrs. Johnson and myself to his widow, Mrs. King."

Johnson paused and gathered strength for the larger message he wanted to convey. "I know that every American of goodwill joins me in mourning the death of this outstanding leader and in praying for peace throughout this land. We can achieve *nothing* by lawlessness. It is only by joining together that we can continue to move toward equality and fulfillment for all of our people."

The president returned to the Oval Office and made calls to governors and mayors across the land. He wanted to impress upon them the importance of police restraint and worried that too large a show of force out in the city streets would only escalate the violence. *We're not at war with our own people*, he kept saying. "Don't send your skinny little rookies out with great big guns all by themselves—if the shooting starts it may never stop." Johnson feared his message wasn't sinking in. "I'm not getting through to them," he told a staffer. "They're holed up like generals in a dugout, getting ready to watch a war."

Even as he said this, fires were beginning to break out, within a few miles of the White House. Until that point, conventional wisdom had it that Washington, D.C., was more or less riot-proof, that larger, northern cities like Chicago, Cleveland, and Boston would be the first to "go." Yet smoke now rose over the District, and alarming reports flooded into the Oval Office—"*The D.C. Civil Defense says crowds forming at 16th and Newton Streets NW and at 14th and T Streets NW . . . A gunman has taken up a position on the roof of the Hawk and Dove bar . . .*"

Black militants around the city were sounding the clarion call. "King was the last prince of nonviolence [and] nonviolence is now a dead philosophy," the Congress of Racial Equality's Floyd McKissick told journalists covering a disturbance on U Street. "The next Negro to advocate nonviolence should be torn to bits by the black people!" In the Columbia Heights neighborhood, black youths shattered store windows, reportedly yelling, "Let's kill the honkies—burn this town down!"

But the ever-quotable Stokely Carmichael, a Howard graduate who lived in Washington, would attract the most attention in the press. "When white America killed Dr. King," he told a reporter, "she declared war on us. The rebellions that have been occurring around this country—that's just light stuff compared to what is about to happen."

Rainstorms would somewhat dampen the night's rioting in Washington, but over the next few hours eighteen fires would be set and some two hundred stores vandalized or looted—and the police would make more than two hundred arrests. Inevitably, the chaos turned lethal: a hapless white man named George Fletcher, who got lost driving through the District, was set upon by a gang of rioters; he was stabbed in the head and died later that night.

Similar disturbances were beginning to flare up elsewhere—in Chicago, Baltimore, New Jersey. Violence was all over the news; the whole nation, it seemed, was on the brink of a nervous breakdown. Johnson's words to the country had seemingly produced little effect. The president glanced at the three flickering television screens and buried his head in his hands.

The black-tie fund-raiser at the Washington Hilton, Johnson learned, had broken up early—nearly three thousand $250-a-plate dinners went cold, with Vice President Hubert Humphrey, ashen faced, telling the Democratic faithful to head home. Before leaving the Hilton, Senator Frank Church said, "The nation is steeped in violence—it is the curse of the land."

One place that didn't erupt in violence that night was Indianapolis, where Robert Kennedy, on a campaign stop before a mostly black audience, broke the news to the stunned crowd with an off-the-cuff speech in which he invoked the memory of his own assassinated brother and then quoted Aeschylus: "Even in our sleep, pain which cannot forget falls drop by drop upon the heart, until, in our own despair, against our will, comes wisdom through the awful grace of God."

President Johnson continued reading and watching the heartbreaking reports from around the nation until Lady Bird called him to a late dinner. A few close advisers joined the Johnsons at the table, including Secretary of Defense Clark Clifford. The family beagles wandered in and out of the room. Johnson's granddaughter Lyn squirmed in the president's lap, her frivolity doing little to brighten the mood.

"It was one of those frozen moments, as though the bomb had fallen on us," Mrs. Johnson later recalled. "Dinner was a strange, quiet meal. We were poised on the edge of another abyss, the bottom of which we could in no way see."

■

As news of King's assassination spread, the city of Memphis began to prepare for racial apocalypse. Fire and Police Director Frank Holloman readied his riot squads for duty and dispatched helicopters into the city skies—both to search for the killer and to monitor the streets for the first signs of civil unrest. Holloman had been informed that the FBI would be taking over the investigation, but for now he had his own force on the case, working every possible angle. MPD detectives fanned out to interview the owners of every light-colored Mustang in the city and to track down every citizen unfortunate enough to have the surname Willard. Room 5B at Bessie Brewer's rooming house was swept for fingerprints, hairs, and fibers, as was the communal bathroom from which the shot had apparently been fired.

The crime scene was measured, photographed, and analyzed. Near the Lorraine, police arrested and briefly detained several potential suspects, while other officers combed the brushy area beneath the rooming house for footprints, shell casings, and other clues. Meanwhile, detectives began to call every motel in the city to learn if anyone named Willard, or anyone with a white Mustang, had registered for a room over the past few days.

Holloman appeared on local television to announce that he was placing the city on a strict 7:00 p.m. to 5:00 a.m. curfew and closing down all gas stations and liquor stores. There would be roadblocks, shoot-to-kill orders to halt looters, peremptory searches and arrests. All major sporting and festive events would be canceled, including Saturday night's planned coronation of the 1968 King and Queen of the Cotton Carnival at the Crown and Scepter Ball, one of the most vaunted bashes on the city's social calendar. The first of what would be weeks of threats came flooding into the carnival offices. "You've killed our King," one reportedly said. "Now we're gonna kill your queen." The carnival's planners were already preparing for the unthinkable: they were considering canceling the entire carnival, something that hadn't been done since World War II.

Memphis, for all intents and purposes, was girding for war. The National Guard, Holloman announced, had already been called back to Memphis. "I and all the citizens of Memphis deeply regret the murder of Dr. King today," Holloman said. "Every resource of the Memphis police department, Shelby County's sheriff's office and the Tennessee Highway patrol is dedicated to identifying and apprehending the person or persons responsible."

Although he said "or *persons*," Holloman noted that "from the evidence we have at this time, only one man was involved." He said the probable assassin was a white man, neat, well dressed, six feet tall, 165 pounds, between twenty-six and thirty-two years old—this rather bland description a composite of the descriptions offered by all the different people in and around the rooming house and Canipe's Amusement Company who'd gotten a glimpse of him. Holloman thought it was too soon to release the name John Willard to the public—for the time being, he and other law-enforcement officials were simply referring to the probable assassin as "the man in 5B."

"Certain evidence has been found which we believe will be helpful," Holloman added. In addition to the gun—a Remington .30-06—the suspect had left behind a suitcase filled with numerous items, one of which was a pair of binoculars that the man in 5B had apparently bought in Memphis that very day.

William Morris, the sheriff of Shelby County, revealed a little more information about the sniper's location when the shot was fired. "We feel," he told reporters, "that the assassin crouched in a second-floor window, sighted through the trees, and fired the shot that killed Dr. King. He got a straight shot."

■

MAYOR HENRY LOEB had been on his way to Oxford, Mississippi, to give a talk at Ole Miss Law School, when he received the news of King's shooting over a portable telephone. He immediately canceled his appearance and had his driver wheel the car around and speed back to Memphis. Within twenty minutes he arrived at city hall, a shining new edifice of white marble surrounded by beds of nodding tulips one block from the river. Once inside his office, Loeb turned on the police inter-com and learned that King was dead.

He decided that he should give his own live television statement, and soon the cameras were set up in his office; its walls were decorated with the city's official seal—featuring a tufted cotton boll and a steam-boat. "We of Memphis are deeply saddened by the tragic event that has just occurred in our city," he began. "And we extend our deepest sympa-thies to Dr. King's family." In the harsh lights, Loeb looked shaken and wan, but tried to project an air of steely calm. He wore a white oxford cloth shirt that fairly crinkled with starch—one that had been pressed, no doubt, by a steady black hand in one of his family's many commercial laundries. On the wall behind him, television viewers could see a framed picture of the PT boat he'd served on in World War II.

"Every conceivable effort is being made to apprehend his assassin," Loeb continued. "We call upon all citizens of our community, as Dr. King would have wished, to maintain peace and honor." Loeb called for three days of mourning and ordered flags at all municipal buildings flown at half-staff. The next day, all Memphis schools would be closed. While urging his city to refrain from violence, the mayor neglected to mention that on the carpeted floor by his shoes, concealed in the foot well of his desk, was a loaded shotgun.

Shortly after giving his statement, Loeb sat in a near-catatonic state in his office huddled with several city leaders, white and black. The city councilman Jerred Blanchard, a blustery Republican attorney who had played football at Yale, thought Memphis was now "damned to hell all over the world—the man who was recognized as the Negro leader of all the leaders, slain, assassinated. Just a modern form of lynching."

Loeb called in a chaplain to pray for the city, for the country, and for the soul of Martin Luther King. Then Mayor Loeb did something no one had ever seen him do in public life, something that seemed almost inimical to his bull-moose demeanor: he broke down and cried.

"I'm so sorry it had to happen like this," he told the black city coun-cilman Fred Davis. Tears rolled down the mayor's cheeks.

"We tried to comfort him," Davis later recalled. "He talked about God. He was just stunned."

∎

A LITTLE LATER, Loeb rose from his gloom, stuffed a pearl-handled .38 revolver in his pocket, and ventured out in a convoy of unmarked police cars for a tour of the anguished city. The white neighborhoods, he found, were ghostly quiet. Most families were locked inside their homes, many with newly purchased shotguns and handguns at the ready—during the previous weeks, gun shops in Memphis had enjoyed a sensationally brisk business, especially among white customers. "Our neighborhood was like a tomb," one white city councilman later recalled. "We were armed, ready for anything. If a Negro had stopped to change a tire, I don't know whether he'd be left alive or not."

Most white Memphians seemed genuinely shocked by the murder—or at least shocked that it had happened in their city. ("This is the darkest day I've ever seen," said the city council chairman, Downing Pryor. "I am sad, sad, sad.") But there were already a few hints of celebration in the white community, too. Through the night, racist wags repeatedly called in a song request to a popular white radio station: "Bye Bye Blackbird." Lucius Burch, the Memphis attorney who'd successfully argued the SCLC position in court that day, received repeated hate calls from a half-demented white lady who gleefully chastised him for representing "that nigger King."

When Loeb's police convoy passed through Orange Mound and other black neighborhoods of Memphis, he found hundreds and then thousands of people emerging onto the streets. Most were simply seeking to absorb the shock of the news, to grieve in the safety of numbers, but others were clearly hunting for trouble. Fires were starting to break out around town, including one at a large lumberyard. The night air shrieked with sirens and burglar alarms. Across Loeb's police radio came reports of sniper shootings, smashed window fronts, rock-throwing clashes. People were reportedly shooting at police cars—even police *helicopters*—and several city buses had been stoned.

Much of the rage was aimed directly at the mayor himself: a Molotov cocktail exploded at a Loeb's dry cleaner, and city hall received numerous death threats. It was all Loeb's fault, many declared in the loudest tones: if he hadn't been so intransigent in his Old South ways, so tone-deaf to the cry of history and the irreproachable dignity of I AM A MAN, then King would never have needed to come in the first place, to be made a martyr on Memphis soil.

Loeb took the death threats seriously and arranged to have his family moved from the mayor's residence to an undisclosed location.

At Mason Temple, where King would have appeared after dinner for yet another garbage strike rally, hundreds gathered in despair. A number of black militants showed up, and the mood turned ugly, especially after rumors began to circulate that the Memphis Police Department had orchestrated King's assassination. An elderly church lady, crippled with arthritis, told people she was ready to go out and fight. "The Lord," she said, "has deserted us." One unidentified member of the Invaders tried to intervene, pleading for calm—at least until Dr. King was in the ground. "Just respect the man enough not to go out and do it tonight," he told the growing crowds. "Wait till he's buried. That's just what the honkies want us to do. Come right out there like a bunch of wild Indians, and they could wipe us out like they did the Indians."

At police headquarters, Director Holloman, closely monitoring news of the events erupting across the city, grew alarmed to the point of panic. He reported that "rioting and looting is now rampant . . . we are in a very critical emergency situation—the city is under attack." The feeling of panic was made worse by a general breakdown in telephone communications. The lines were so jammed that many callers found it difficult to get a dial tone; during the first few hours after the assassination, more than thirty thousand long-distance calls went out of Memphis. As the first units of what would amount to four thousand National Guardsmen began to roll into the city, the situation seemed to be spiraling out of control.

Police shot a twenty-six-year-old black man named Ellis Tate nine times and mortally wounded him—the officers claimed he fired a rifle at them from the shadows of a liquor store. Fearing that an all-out racial war was imminent, T. O. Jones, leader of the garbage strike, barricaded himself in a room in the Peabody Hotel. A black worker at the Memphis Firestone plant grabbed a rifle and some ammunition, went to a cemetery near his house, and took charge of a hill, commando style. "That's what I thought everybody else was going to do," he later said. "I just expected to go to war."

The Reverend James Lawson, anticipating the mayhem from the moment he heard of King's shooting, went straight to WDIA, Memphis's most popular black radio station, and began to broadcast messages through the night. "Stay calm," Lawson urged. "It would be a compounding of this death if people around our country should decide that now is the time to let loose an orgy of violence. It would be a denial of Dr. King's life and work. Stay calm. *Stay calm.*"

At Billy and Gwen Kyles's house, meanwhile, the soul food dinner still simmered on the stove. The dressed-up guests gathered in silence, in rooms heavy with succulent smells. No one had an appetite. "I went numb," Gwen Kyles said. "I felt like somebody had knocked all my senses out." She paced the floor of her dining room, past the long line of empty chairs, crying, "They've torn it now—they've torn it."

■

ERIC GALT KEPT driving through the Mississippi night, hewing to back roads wherever possible, putting miles between himself and the turmoil emanating from Memphis. The news on the radio surprised him—there were scattered reports of riots and looting, not only in Memphis, but all across the country. Federal troops and National Guardsmen were now marching into major cities, the president had made a televised statement, the nation's capital was on fire. The sheer magnitude of what he'd done must have begun to dawn on Galt. He could feel the heat of the whole country coming down on him: he was, he realized, the most wanted man in America.

Sleep was certainly not an option now—he would have to stay up through the night and make a beeline for Atlanta, where he planned to pick up whatever belongings he'd left at Garner's rooming house. What he would do after that was uncertain, but given his familiarity with Mexico, he was probably thinking of driving *south*, perhaps toward Puerto Vallarta. Lit with the success of his deed, and the adrenaline rush of flight, Galt didn't need amphetamines to keep him burning around the clock.

Although he was headed for Georgia, and possibly Mexico, Galt's larger goal was to reach southern Africa. "Rhodesia"—the word dangled before him like a banner. He knew that under the pariah government of Ian Smith, Rhodesia observed no extradition treaties with the United States. Galt had been toying with the idea of immigrating there for several months, ever since he first moved to Los Angeles from Puerto Vallarta. Galt liked what Smith was doing in Rhodesia, and he had an idea that if he could ever reach Salisbury, the people there would welcome him as a hero, grant him instant citizenship, and harbor him from any American attempts at prosecution. "I thought I was going to get away," he later said. "I thought I could get to Africa and those folks over there wouldn't send me back." And because it was an English-speaking country, he thought he could "blend in with the population." He wasn't exactly sure what he would do once he got there. Become a bartender, perhaps? A locksmith? Serve in a mercenary army? But the idea of Rhodesia burned in his imagination, the promise of sanctuary and refuge, the possibility of living in a society where people understood.

Before he could get there, however, Galt was determined to make this brief detour to Atlanta. It may have seemed brazenly risky to head straight for the hometown of the man he'd just killed, yet there was also a clever counter-intuition in such a course. The main thing was Galt had left a few items in his rooming house that he felt he needed—his .38 revolver, some self-help books, and probably some money he'd stashed away, as well as the pile of clothes that he'd checked at the cleaners around the corner on Peachtree Street.

As he passed through Holly Springs and New Albany and Tupelo, Galt kept trolling the radio waves for news. Somewhere along the way, he heard a bulletin that the police were looking for a white Mustang driven by a "well-dressed white man." This must have given him a shock, for until that point he was confident he'd gotten away scot-free, that no one had spotted him or his car. Hearing this bit of bad news changed everything: he knew immediately that he'd have to ditch the Mustang, and he somehow thought that without a car, Mexico would not be a plausible destination. Instead, he would head for Canada and then try to get to Rhodesia from there.

Though this newest twist ratcheted up the pressure, there was nothing Galt could do about it. Until he reached Atlanta, all he could do was keep his cool. "I had to drive slow," he later wrote, "and be careful so as not to attract attention and get arrested for speeding."

By nine o'clock he had passed into Alabama—"Heart of Dixie"— where at least his license plate would attract no notice. He harbored a vague hope that George Wallace's Alabama, like Ian Smith's breakaway state of Rhodesia, would protect him, that the majority of its citizens would praise him for his act and shield him from pursuers. That was one of the main reasons he had chosen to live for a time in Birmingham before his adventures in Puerto Vallarta—staying there long enough to secure an Alabama driver's license, buy a car, and get it titled, licensed, and registered there. That, too, was the reason he had bought the gun and scope in Birmingham. It was a pitifully naïve train of reasoning, but Galt believed that Wallace would likely smile on his crime, viewing him as an Anglo-Saxon patriot from Dixie's finest state. If Galt were ever caught and convicted, he was confident that Governor Wallace, if not *President* Wallace, would grant him a full pardon after a short prison sentence.

When Galt passed through Florence, Alabama, he considered abandoning the car and taking a bus the rest of the way to Atlanta, but then he thought better of it. He paused only twice during the night. At one point, he got out beneath the crescent moon and tried to wipe the Mustang's surfaces clean of fingerprints. "I knew that the car could be hot for some time," he would write, "and I didn't want to leave any calling cards in or on the vehicle before abandoning it once I got to Atlanta." Then somewhere in Alabama, Galt pulled off at a secluded spot, opened his trunk, and dumped his camera equipment in a ditch, all the expensive gear he'd bought with an eye to becoming a porn director—the projector, the splicer, the movie camera, everything but the Polaroid, which was light and portable enough. Porno was one career dream he'd just have to set aside. "I just wanted to get rid of everything that would connect me with the Mustang—or with anything, anything that would leave any type of trail to me or help the police in any manner," Galt later said.

As soon as he reached Atlanta in the morning, he knew he'd have to park the Mustang and travel light; the camera gear would only slow him down.

AT THE LORRAINE Motel, most of the members of King's entourage reconvened—the inner circle, now bereft of their leader. Slumped and spent, they sat together in 306, with King's briefcase and personal effects still scattered about the room. Andy Young was there, as well as James Bevel, Bernard Lee, Hosea Williams, James Orange, and Chauncey Eskridge. As sirens cried through the night, the men gathered around their organization's new president, Ralph Abernathy, whose election, according to SCLC bylaws already in place, was automatic. Abernathy didn't have King's charisma or organizational élan, yet his succession was beyond question. "King wouldn't make a decision without him," Williams said. "He trusted Ralph like he trusted Jesus."

Around them, Memphis roared and raged. Helicopters whirred in the sky, and the half-tracks of the National Guard grumbled down Main and Beale, their metallic treads leaving enormous zippers in the pavement. Downstairs, a gang of young black thugs backed two white newsmen into a corner and briefly scuffled with them, shouting, "You're going to get yours next, and it ain't going to be too long!" On the Lorraine balcony, noted one reporter, "flashbulbs still blinked repeatedly against the room number, like summer lightning."

In those awful hours immediately following the murder, people in the King entourage didn't quite know what to do or how to comport themselves. They made a few calls to friends of the movement. They talked about the future. They tried to catch some news on the television, but most of the broadcasts had flickered off the air. All they could really do, Andy Young said, was "sleepwalk through the night"—trying as best they could to process what had happened that terrible day. Seldom do organizations suffer such a profound and surreal shock: to be gathered in one place with their leader, only to see him struck down from above, as though the tragedy were a ritual enacted upon a public stage.

Thoughts of the previous night's speech turned over in their minds. *Longevity has its place. . . . I may not get there with you . . . I'm not fearing any man.* Over the past year, King had often invoked similar themes in other speeches and sermons—but never quite so forcefully, never with such pathos in his voice. Had King foreseen his own death? Had he felt the sniper's presence as he tarried for so many dangerous minutes on the Lorraine balcony? Abernathy, for one, was convinced that his friend not only had a premonition but in fact had been forwarded specific information about his impending death. As Abernathy later testified before the U.S. Congress, he believed King "had received, through letter or telephone, some knowledge that something was going to happen . . . some word from some source that he was going to be assassinated."

Andy Young thought it was clear that King wasn't the only intended victim of the murder. Others in the group may have been in danger, and in a larger sense the entire civil rights movement was in the assassin's crosshairs. King had often said that after any horrible setback—like the death of Medgar Evers or the shooting of James Meredith—others must immediately rush in to take up the fallen person's cause or else the enemy gathers the impression that by killing the leaders he can kill the movement. Therefore, that night the group at the Lorraine resolved that the work must go on: the Beale Street march, the garbage strike, the Poor People's Campaign in Washington, all of it. "We can't let Martin down by staying in the graveyard with him," James Bevel told the group. "He wouldn't want that. Everything he planned has to go forward. Ralph Abernathy is our leader now and we have to go to work behind him."

Everyone at the Lorraine began to mourn in his own manner. "People freaked out and did strange things that reflected their own insecurities," Young recalled. A. D. King had become seriously drunk and was now storming around the Lorraine, screaming and swearing. "They got him, the motherfuckers finally got my brother!" King shouted. He vowed to get a pistol and "kill all the motherfuckers who killed my brother." But then he would punctuate his tirades with moments of recognition. "My God, what am I talking about?" he'd say. "We've got to be nonviolent. That's what Martin would want." AD was so unstable that friends in the group took turns shielding him from reporters so he wouldn't embarrass himself.

Downstairs, Georgia Davis went back to her room, 201, the room she and King had shared the night before. King's whispered words rang in her ears: "Our time together is so short." "I touched the pillow, searching for some lingering contact, some connection with him. But all I felt were the cold, clean sheets." Suddenly she felt a consuming dread. "The vision of his body flashed through my mind," she later wrote. "I remembered all the preachers I had ever heard, describing the fiery furnaces." And she thought: *I am descending into hell.*

At one point, Abernathy emerged from room 306 holding the cardboard backing from a laundered shirt and began scraping King's congealed blood into a jar. As he did so, he wept, and said to those assembled on the balcony, "This is Martin's precious blood. This blood was shed for us." The Memphis photographer Ernest Withers took several shots of the blood—to his eyes, the puddle's shape bore a curious resemblance to King's silhouette. Using a small vial, Withers scooped up some of the blood for himself; he would keep it in his refrigerator for many years.

Jesse Jackson went a step further. Young recalled seeing Jackson leaning over and pressing his palms down flat in the pool of drying blood. Then he stood up, raised his crimson hands to the sky, and wiped them down the front of his shirt. Minutes later, Jackson, not bothering to change his stained shirt, left for the airport to catch the last flight to Chicago. "There's nothing that unusual about it," Young later said. "We Baptists, you know, we believe there's power in the blood—power that's transferable."

■

CORETTA KING RETURNED home from the Atlanta airport and began to deal with the avalanche of phone calls and telegrams while greeting the tearful well-wishers who streamed into her house. Within hours, a greenhouse's worth of flowers had materialized, and phone company workmen came to install a bank of three telephones to handle the swelling volume of calls.

A newspaper reporter described the newly widowed Mrs. King as "composed but dazed" as she moved through the rooms at 234 Sunset, brushing past the portrait of Mahatma Gandhi on the wall and the bouquet of fake carnations King had recently given her. Financially, she had serious concerns about how she was going to carry on—King had not written a will, had only a minimum life insurance policy, and left scarcely any savings, other than this cozy little brick home on the southwest side of Atlanta, not far from the slums. The house, together with two joint checking accounts he shared with Coretta, would be judged too small in value to probate.

Yet already Coretta seemed profoundly resigned to her husband's death. "I do think it's the will of God," she said. "We always knew this could happen." It was something she had been preparing for, and even publicly speaking about, for years. Three years earlier, in Seattle, she had told a crowd, "If something happens to my husband, the cause will continue. It may even be helped."

All his campaigns had been dangerous, she said, "but there was something a little different about Memphis. Martin didn't say directly to me that it's going to happen in Memphis, but I think he felt that time was running out." Coretta said her husband had long felt "a mystical identity with the meaning of Christ's Passion" and that it seemed appropriate that his death should come during the Easter season.

After President Johnson's call, the newly installed phones began to ring ceaselessly. The governor of New York, Nelson Rockefeller, called, offering a chartered plane for her use. The comedian Bill Cosby called, offering to come and entertain her kids. Senator Robert Kennedy called, offering *another* plane. Attorney General Clark conveyed his condolences and assured her that the FBI was on the case. Harry Belafonte, the calypso singer, phoned to say he'd be there the next day, "just to do any little menial thing—I want to share this sorrow with you."

Among the offerings from Western Union, a telegram arrived from the Ethiopian emperor, Haile Selassie, in Addis Ababa. "It is with profound grief," the Lion of Judah said, "that we have learned the shocking news of the death of Dr. Martin Luther King whose valiant struggles for the cause of human dignity shall long be remembered by all peace loving peoples."

Coretta slipped away from the commotion and went back to the kids' rooms to put them to bed. As she later recalled in her memoir, it was clear that Dexter didn't fully comprehend what had happened. "Mommy," he said, "when is Daddy coming home?"

"He was hurt very badly," Coretta answered, realizing she was unable at this late and frantic hour to face a conversation about death. "You go to sleep, and I'll tell you about it in the morning."

Then she spoke with Yolanda, her eldest child, with whom she'd been shopping all afternoon for an Easter dress. "Mommy, I'm not going to cry," Yoki said resolutely. "I'll see him again in heaven."

But something was bothering her, something clearly nagged at her young conscience. "Should I hate the man who killed my father?" she asked.

Coretta shook her head. "No, darling, your daddy wouldn't want you to do that."

■

WITHIN AN HOUR of King's death, authorities transported his body across town to the office of the chief medical examiner at John Gaston Hospital on Madison Avenue, where it was promptly taken to a pathology suite in the basement. The corpse was placed on a stainless steel table in a room with a sloping tile floor equipped with a drain. A set of implements lay gleaming beneath the bright lamps—chisels, vibrating saws, an array of scalpels and forceps. The body was covered with a sheet of thick, crinkly medical paper. From beneath the sheet, a tag marked "A-68-252" dangled from the subject's big toe.

The Shelby County medical examiner, the pathologist Dr. Jerry Francisco, emerged in a white lab coat. He was a tall, punctilious, soft-spoken man whose voice was tinged with the gentle twang of the hill country of western Tennessee. Although he was only in his mid-thirties, Dr. Francisco had already conducted many hundreds of autopsies; later in his career he would investigate the deaths of numerous Memphis-area celebrities—including that of Jerry Lee Lewis's fifth wife, Shawn Michelle, and, most famously, Elvis Presley.

By temperament and training, Dr. Francisco was a stickler for detail and loved to recite the arcane lore of his profession from the time of its Norman origins in medieval England. Dr. Francisco took relish in pointing out that in addition to dissecting the cadavers of important people who'd died under mysterious circumstances, the coroners of ancient London were required by law to serve as "the Keeper of the Royal Aquarium."

At around 9:00 p.m., Abernathy was summoned from the Lorraine and ushered into the lab to identify the body, in accordance with legal protocol. An attendant removed the sheet of medical paper, producing a harsh crackling sound. Gazing at the body on the sterile metal table, Abernathy thought his friend "somehow looked more dead" than he had seemed when he'd left him in the hospital just two hours earlier. "I stared for a moment," Abernathy wrote in his memoirs, "a mute witness to the final dehumanization of Martin Luther King, Jr., his transformation from person to thing. I knew in that moment that I could leave this body now, leave it forever."

Abernathy nodded and curtly told Dr. Francisco what he needed to hear. "This," he said, "is the body of Martin Luther King, Jr.," and he signed the requisite form.

Then Francisco asked Abernathy to reach Coretta King by phone to secure her permission to conduct the autopsy. Abernathy hesitated. He failed to understand why an autopsy was necessary; no one doubted for a moment what had killed his friend. "It seemed incredible to me," Abernathy later wrote, "that such a procedure could make any difference now." He hated to trouble Coretta with such a gruesome request and wanted to spare her the shock of yet another indignity.

"How important is it?" he asked.

"*Very*," Dr. Francisco assured him—in fact, it was required by law. He explained that for forensic purposes he needed to determine with greater specificity the angle of the bullet's path. Any future prosecution of King's assailant would legally require an autopsy to determine with absolute certainty that King had died as a direct result of the gunshot wound. A host of secondary questions might be answered, too: Could there have been a *second* bullet? Could the wound have been caused by a pistol, fired at close range? Could the doctors at St. Joseph's have done anything to save King's life? "It might tell us something we didn't know before," Dr. Francisco added, according to Abernathy. "Something that could save another person's life."

Reluctantly, Abernathy made the call to Mrs. King and then handed the phone to Dr. Francisco. She readily gave her consent, speaking in a voice that seemed to Dr. Francisco remarkably calm and composed.

After Abernathy left the autopsy suite, Dr. Francisco's first task was to remove the bullet from King's body. About 9:30 p.m., with three Memphis police officers serving as official witnesses, Dr. Francisco excavated the main fragment from an area just beneath the skin of King's left shoulder blade. He attached a tag to the lump of metal, labeling it "252." The police witnesses described the badly marred and distorted bullet as "giving the appearance of being a 30-06," but it had mushroomed almost beyond recognition. It had a copper jacket and a nose composed of soft lead, the police officers surmised, "as it was very flattened."

Dr. Francisco wrapped the deformed bullet in cotton and gave it to the police witnesses, who tagged it with a receipt and dropped it into a brown manila envelope. The three police witnesses then left the examining room to deliver the package to Inspector Zachary of the MPD's Homicide Bureau—who, in turn, would hand it over to Special Agent Jensen of the FBI.

Dr. Francisco prepared to go about his macabre work, feeling the weight of history upon him. He recalled that, after the assassination of President Kennedy, alleged irregularities associated with the autopsy became the subject of much speculation—and ultimately helped to hatch any number of conspiracy theories. "More than any case I'd ever been assigned to, I knew the work had to be without flaw," he later said. "I said to myself, 'Not a single mistake, Francisco.'" In a literal sense, history *was* watching him: photographers, working in both color and black and white, diligently captured every stage of the procedure on film.

The autopsy was unusual in another respect—the high level of security under which it was conducted. The Memphis authorities feared that plotters in a conspiracy, or a hostile mob, might try to sabotage Dr. Francisco's examination or even steal King's body. So while he worked,

Memphis policemen, armed with shotguns, were stationed on both sides of the examining room door. Dr. Francisco later recalled, with characteristic understatement: "I felt very safe."

Now Dr. Francisco examined his subject, noting the various scars and bruises on King's body, the blood spatters, the needle marks from the emergency room. "This," he later wrote, "is a well developed, well nourished Negro male measuring 69½ inches in length. The hair is black, the eyes are brown. There is a line mustache present."

Following the usual protocol, Dr. Francisco systematically removed, examined, and weighed the various organs—including the spleen, pancreas, liver, gallbladder, and brain—all of which he judged to be healthy and normal. Then he made a close inspection of King's injury, with the aid of X-ray images that had been taken at St. Joseph's Hospital. Around the wound's entrance, he found and collected on slides trace amounts of a black substance that, upon microscopic examination, was later determined to be a residue of lead left by the soft nose of the bullet. Dr. Francisco described the path of the bullet through King's body as "from front to back, above downward, and from right to left"—an important orientation, for it went far in confirming the suspected location of the fired rifle.

He regarded King's wounds as almost immediately catastrophic and felt certain that no amount of medical intervention could have saved him. "Death," Dr. Francisco summarized in his autopsy narrative, "was the result of a gunshot wound to the chin and neck with a total transection of the lower cervical and upper thoracic spinal cord and other structures of the neck. The severing of the spinal cord at this level and to this extent was a wound that was fatal very shortly after its occurrence."

"This," he succinctly concluded, "was *not* a survivable gunshot wound."

King's body was wheeled out of the autopsy suite and given over to the custody of the R. S. Lewis Funeral Home—the same black-owned mortuary that had provided King with a Cadillac and chauffeur during his stay at the Lorraine. The Lewis morticians had been hired to conduct the embalming, makeup, and other tasks necessary to prepare the body for public viewing.

Around 11:00 p.m., as the shotgun-wielding policemen stood guard outside the Tennessee Institute of Pathology, King's body was loaded into the rear of a hearse and driven across the desolate city on curfew-flushed streets prowled only by the occasional tank. The downtown was ghostly quiet but blindingly bright. "Every light in every store was on (the better to silhouette looters)," observed Garry Wills, who'd just arrived on assignment for *Esquire*. "Jittery neon arrows, meant to beckon people in, now tried to scare them off. Nothing stirred in the crumbling blocks. Even the Muzak in an arcade between stores reassured itself, at the top of its voice, with jaunty rhythms played to no audience."

At 11:15, King's body arrived at R. S. Lewis and the morticians began their work.

■

PRESIDENT JOHNSON, a bit of an insomniac even on peaceful nights, padded down to the Oval Office sometime in the early morning hours, dressed in his bathrobe. All through the night, the news stories and telegrams had been flooding into the White House. World reaction to King's death was immediate and far-reaching. Johnson was not quite prepared for the magnitude of the shock King's death was causing around the globe. In this nerve center of the world, the Situation Room memorandums and State Department telexes kept piling up, and the news-ticker machines steadily hammered away.

On one of the wire services, the Reverend Billy Graham, traveling in Australia, was quoted as saying that "tens of thousands of Americans are mentally deranged. [King's slaying] indicates the sickness of the American society and will further inflame passions and hates." In New Delhi, the Indian prime minister, Indira Gandhi, said Martin Luther King's slaying "is a setback to mankind's search for light. Violence has removed one of the great men of the world."

The governor of California, Ronald Reagan, said the whole nation "died a little" with King's murder. The retired baseball legend Jackie Robinson, reached in New York, was practically speechless: "I'm shocked. Oh my God, I'm very frightened, very disturbed. I pray God this doesn't end up in the streets."

A telegram from an analyst at the American embassy in Paris summarized the French reaction to King's slaying that morning: "Press and radio, which in recent months had almost lost sight of King in the glare of the more flamboyant [Stokely] Carmichael, now proclaim King as the only truly great leader among American negroes and agree he cannot be replaced."

The London papers quoted the British pacifist philosopher Bertrand Russell as saying that the murder of Dr. King is only "a foretaste of the violence that will erupt in America because the U.S. government cannot finance a full-scale war in Vietnam and alleviate the misery of its most oppressed citizens."

The morning paper in Nairobi said King's death "once again reminds the world of the sick society America is . . . It may well be that the era of non-violence has died with its prophet."

Not all the incoming commentary praised the fallen King or his methods. The South Carolina senator Strom Thurmond told a wire service reporter: "I hesitate to say anything bad about the dead, but I do not share a high regard for Dr. King. He only *pretended* to be nonviolent." Texas's governor, John Connally, concurred. While acknowledging that King "did not deserve this fate," Connally insisted that the civil rights leader "contributed much to the chaos and turbulence in this country."

The presidential candidate George Wallace could not be reached for comment, but Bob Walters, California chairman of Wallace's campaign, had this to say about the deceased: "Although he claimed to be a nonviolent man, he spread seeds of violence which are now in the country. You shall reap what you sow."

The wires also reported that the racist J. B. Stoner of the National States Rights Party was giving a speech in Meridian, Mississippi, when he heard the news of King's death. Gloating, the bow-tie-wearing demagogue told a crowd of like-minded segregationists: "Martin Lucifer Coon is a good nigger now."

■

SOME TIME AFTER midnight, Memphis time, Special Agent Jensen finished reviewing and tagging all the physical evidence now in the FBI's possession: the bullet removed from King's body, the rifle and scope and ammunition, the binoculars, the transistor radio, the suitcase with all its miscellaneous contents, King's shorn necktie and bloodied shirt, photographs from the autopsy, the old windowsill with the tiny half-moon indentation that Homicide Bureau detectives had removed from the communal bathroom. There were also three twenty-dollar bills that FBI agents had obtained from Bessie Brewer—one of which she believed the man in 5B had given her when he signed in.

Jensen sealed the contents in clear plastic and boxed them up, writing on the outside of the package, "FBI Crime Laboratory, Washington, DC." He gave it to Special Agent Robert Fitzpatrick, who would serve as a personal courier for this important parcel. Fitzpatrick rushed to the airport, where a chartered jet was waiting. Shortly before 1:00 a.m., he boarded the plane and flew through the morning hours, the package at his side at all times. The jet landed at Washington's National Airport just before dawn. An armed escort met Fitzpatrick at the terminal and sped him to the city.

At 5:10 a.m. eastern time, Friday, April 5, Fitzpatrick personally delivered the evidence to Special Agent Robert A. Frazier of the FBI Crime Lab on Pennsylvania Avenue. Ballistics, fiber, and fingerprint experts were already waiting.

BOOK TWO

WHO IS ERIC GALT?

■ ■ ■ ■ ■ ■ ■

For murder, though it hath no tongue, will speak
With most miraculous organ.

SHAKESPEARE, Hamlet

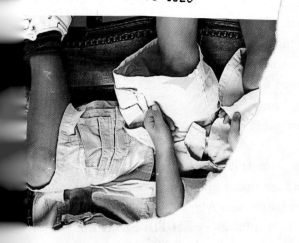

JUST AFTER DAWN on Friday, April 5, a Lockheed Jetstar taxied from
the immense hangar that housed presidential planes and then shot down
the runway at Andrews Air Force Base in Maryland. On board the
twelve-seat business jet were Ramsey Clark, Cartha DeLoach, and several
other government officials, including the brilliant young black Justice Department lawyer Roger Wilkins. On this early morning, they were has-
tening to Memphis on a vital mission: to officially kick off the federal
investigation into Martin Luther King's assassination—and to assure the
city, and the nation, that the Justice Department would expend every resource to find and prosecute King's killer.

That morning Clark wore a crisp black suit with a thin tie of diagonal blue and white stripes. He already felt exhausted, and the day was
only beginning, a day that promised to be as stressful as any he'd experienced as attorney general. Clark had hardly slept the night before—no
one at the Justice Department had.

The jet banked over Prince Georges County and climbed west over
Washington, where the fires from the previous night's rioting still smoldered. Clark looked out the window at the city where he had been largely
raised and schooled.

DeLoach tried to brighten the mood. He was confident that the FBI would find the killer—or killers—within a matter of hours. While the plane was in the air, he was in constant communication with the bureau and would periodically share the latest bulletins with Clark. The probable murder weapon, he said, was safely ensconced in the crime lab, two floors above Clark's office in the Justice building, and was now undergoing analysis. Working off the serial number on the rifle—461476—FBI officials had already called the Remington Arms Company in Bridgeport, Connecticut, and traced the weapon to a gun wholesaler in Alabama and finally to a gun shop in Birmingham called Aeromarine Supply Company; FBI agents in Birmingham would soon be dispatched to question the employees who sold the gun.

Then DeLoach learned of a tantalizing new lead: in 1958 the Memphis Police Department had arrested a white male fugitive named John Willard who had committed arson and whose last known whereabouts were in Mississippi. MPD sleuths, as well as FBI agents from Memphis and Jackson, were already combing the region in hopes of tracking the man down.

DeLoach had been in such a hurry this morning that he hadn't had time to eat. Now he opened his briefcase and found a sandwich next to his large revolver. As he tucked into his breakfast, he looked out the window at the Shenandoah Valley, which was now sharpening with the vivid greens of spring. The jet hurtled past the mountains of Virginia at four hundred miles per hour and headed over Tennessee.

Two hours later, at 7:20 a.m. central time, the Jetstar landed in Memphis. Stepping off the plane, Clark and DeLoach saw that the place had a decidedly martial cast. National Guardsmen and riot police ringed the perimeter of the runway, and military planes were parked along the tarmac. Flags flew at half-staff.

Special Agent Robert Jensen met Clark and DeLoach on the tarmac and drove them into the troubled city, which was just now stirring from the curfews.

■

AT THAT SAME moment, Eric Galt eased his Mustang into the parking lot of a forlorn housing project in Atlanta called Capitol Homes.

It was about 8:20 eastern time on a drizzly Friday morning, and the city was waking up to the banner headlines in the *Constitution* proclaiming that Atlanta's most famous citizen had been slain. Galt had been driving through the night, worried all the while that some state trooper might notice the make and color of his car and end his escape before he even got out of the South. From Birmingham to Atlanta, he had avoided main highways and driven strictly on back roads. "At daybreak I stopped for gas on the outskirts of Atlanta," he later said; he then went to the Capitol Homes project—a location he had scoped out two weeks earlier.

Galt hated giving up his loyal Mustang—over the past seven months he had driven it some nineteen thousand miles. Ditching it like this violated his sense of frugality. "I sure hated that I didn't have time to sell it for at least $1,000," he wrote. But he knew there was no time to put an ad in the paper and fool around negotiating with customers and all the usual rigmarole; the whole world, it seemed, was searching for this car.

Capitol Homes was a complex of old redbrick buildings occupied almost entirely by white tenants. Trash was heaped in one corner of the parking lot, and a playground slide lay toppled on the ground. The general drabness of the eight-hundred-unit complex was relieved by a flower garden near the entrance off Memorial Drive. Rising over the neighborhood, as if to mock its dreariness, was the elegant neoclassical Georgia state capitol, with its massive gold-ribbed dome shimmering through curtains of rain.

That morning a woman named Mary Bridges, who lived in apartment 550 of Capitol Homes, was in a rush to get her twelve-year-old daughter, Wanda, off to school. Through her front window, Mrs. Bridges spotted a white two-door Mustang hardtop with whitewall tires pulling in to the parking lot. The car abruptly stopped, then made a screeching sound as it jerked rearward into a vacant parking place a few yards from her door. The Mustang had Alabama plates, and the car windows were affixed with Mexican "Turista" stickers.

Mrs. Bridges opened her door and stood at the threshold with Wanda, watching the man emerge from the Mustang, lock the door, and hurriedly scuffle away. He seemed nervous, wary. She had never seen the man before, or the car. He had "soot-black hair" and wore a dark suit—

the coat dramatically flared out in the morning breeze. Without a rain-coat or umbrella, and carrying no luggage, he hurried along the wet side-walk, turned left at the flower garden, and disappeared down Memorial Drive.

She thought he might be a traveling insurance salesman, but some-thing about the mystery visitor disturbed her. Mrs. Bridges turned to Wanda and said, half-joking, "He might have a gun."

Galt was relieved to have shed his car, severing himself from the most conspicuous piece of evidence that tied him to Memphis. What he did next is not precisely known, but in all likelihood he flagged down a taxi. At 8:41 a.m., a United Cab Company driver named Chuck Stephens was heading west on Memorial Drive when he was hailed by a white man Stephens later described as about thirty years old, six feet tall, slender, and neat. The man was standing in the spitting rain on Memo-rial near Fraser Street—just a few blocks from Capitol Homes. Stephens pulled over, and the man hopped in, asking to be taken to the Greyhound bus depot. Stephens nodded and headed downtown, thinking it odd that his passenger was going to the bus station without any luggage. The man didn't say a word during the short drive. Upon reaching the Greyhound terminal, he paid the fare—ninety-three cents—and climbed out into the drizzly street.

Galt's plan was to take the first bus north to Detroit. But when he got to the station, he inquired about the times and found the next coach bound for the Motor City wasn't scheduled to leave until around 11:00 a.m.—and that bus was running late. Realizing he still had a few hours to spare, Galt decided to make a dash for his flophouse neighborhood around Peachtree Street to pick up his laundry and a few things from his room.

■

AT THE LORRAINE Motel, a stunned and deeply sleep-deprived Ralph Abernathy started off the morning by giving a brief press confer-ence in the motel parking lot, just below the now-infamous balcony, where janitors had scrubbed off the last of King's blood to make way for enormous wreaths of flowers. "This is one of the darkest days in the history of this nation and certainly in the life of my people," Abernathy said, although in the end he had no doubt that "non-violence will triumph." He never had any desire to lead the movement, he said. "No living man can fill his shoes. I always wanted to stand with him and not ahead of him."

But as the new president of the SCLC, Abernathy wanted to assure the world that the cause would go on—starting with the Beale Street march that King had planned in support of the garbage workers. He announced that he would return on Monday to lead it. Not only would the demonstration be nonviolent, he vowed; in deference to King, it would be utterly *silent*. To run this memorial march, Bayard Rustin would be called in—the old pro, the bespectacled impresario of the civil rights movement, who, among other things, had stage-managed the March on Washington in 1963 where King had given his "Dream" speech.

When a reporter asked Abernathy if he was worried that returning to Memphis might provoke another assassination attempt—perhaps on *his* life—Abernathy replied, "We're all willing to die for what we believe in."

All the members of the inner circle rallied around Abernathy— except Jesse Jackson. He was in Chicago, where he had hired a public relations agent and was now giving a live interview to NBC's *Today* show. Reiterating his hyperbolic story from the previous night, he told the national audience that he was the last person to speak with King, and implied that he'd cradled King's bleeding head in his final moments. "He died in my arms," he said. As if to prove it, he still wore the blood-streaked turtleneck. Jackson failed to mention the odd way the blood got there. He then left for a busy itinerary of other interviews and public appearances, wearing his bloody shirt through the day. By inventing this halo-glow moment with the fallen King, Jackson apparently was trying to make the point that *he*, not Abernathy, had inherited King's mantle.

The *Today* show was blaring from several rooms at the Lorraine, and some of King's entourage who saw Jackson's interview found the spectacle repugnant. Said James Bevel: "To prostitute and lie about the crucifixion of a prophet within a race for the sake of one's own self-aggrandizement is the most gruesome crime a man can commit."

When he heard about it, Abernathy was much more charitable, even though he had cause for greater outrage. The only possible explanation, he said, was that Jackson "was somehow in shock, reliving the whole scene in his mind, and acting out what he might have *wished* to do during those last seconds."

■

SHORTLY AFTER THE *Today* show went off the national airwaves, FBI special agent Neil Shanahan walked through the door of Aeromarine Supply Company at 5701 Airport Highway in Birmingham. There he met Donald Wood, the son of the store owner and an experienced salesman of firearms. Shanahan began to question Wood about a certain Remington .30-06 rifle that had come into the FBI's possession the previous night in relation to the Martin Luther King assassination.

"Well, I sold a Gamemaster to a guy about a week ago," Wood volunteered, according to a report Shanahan filed shortly after the interview. Wood remembered the man well. In fact, he said, when he'd read in the paper this morning that the weapon left at the crime scene was a Remington .30-06, his thoughts turned immediately to this particular sale.

"Would you happen to have a record of it in your files?" Shanahan asked.

Wood said he did, and he soon retrieved from the Aeromarine office a sales invoice, dated Saturday, March 30. Shanahan felt a frisson of recognition, for there it was, in a clear and legible hand: Remington Model 760 Gamemaster .30-06, serial number 461476, with mounted Redfield variable scope—the exact weapon found outside Canipe's Amusement Company the previous night.

The man who bought the rifle had stated that he lived in Birmingham, at 1907 South Eleventh Street. The name he gave was Harvey Lowmeyer. His signature was scrawled across the bottom of the invoice. By the messy way it was chicken-scratched, Shanahan couldn't tell for sure whether the name was spelled "Lowmeyer" or "Lowmyer."

Agent Shanahan phoned this information to his superiors, and soon agents were dispatched to the address on Eleventh Street, only to discover that no one named Harvey Lowmeyer had ever lived there. Meanwhile, Shanahan asked Wood if he'd be willing to offer an official statement. Wood readily consented, and Shanahan brought him to the FBI field office, where he underwent several hours of questioning.

Wood said that Harvey Lowmeyer had first come into Aeromarine the day *before* the date on the invoice. On that day—Friday, March 29—he purchased a Remington Model 700 .243, but called back later to say he wanted to exchange it for something more powerful. "My brother says I got the wrong one," Lowmeyer had said. Wood told Lowmeyer he could come back the following morning and make the exchange.

As agreed, Lowmeyer had walked into Aeromarine the next morning. Wood told Lowmeyer it would take a while to remove the scope from the .243 and mount it on the .30-06. Around three o'clock, Lowmeyer returned. Wood put the Gamemaster in an old Browning box. Lowmeyer bought some Remington-Peters ammunition and completed the transaction—paying in cash.

What did this Lowmeyer look like?, Agent Shanahan asked.

To Wood, he seemed like a "meek individual"—soft-spoken, mumbly, nervous. He recalled that Lowmeyer wore a slightly rumpled dark brown business suit with a white shirt and a tie. He was approximately five feet eight inches tall, weighed about 160 pounds, and looked to be in his mid-thirties. He had a medium complexion. His dark brown hair was swept back from his forehead.

Through Wood, Shanahan located a regular Aeromarine customer named John DeShazo who had spoken with Harvey Lowmeyer in the store the day he bought the original .243 rifle. An NRA loyalist who often spent hours at a time inside Aeromarine, DeShazo confirmed Wood's version of events, as well as his description of Lowmeyer, but he added a few details. DeShazo had smelled alcohol on Lowmeyer's breath. "He wasn't drunk, bleary-eyed, or slurring his speech," DeShazo said, "but he'd definitely been drinking."

DeShazo went on: "The man gave the impression that he was not from Alabama. He didn't look like a hunter or an outdoorsman. He appeared out of place in the store, didn't know a thing about rifles and had no business getting one. I thought at the time that this is the type of guy who buys a rifle to kill his wife—the type of guy who gives the use of weapons a bad name."

AT THE FBI Crime Lab in Washington, the fingerprint expert George Bonebrake spent the early-morning hours of April 5 poring over the contents of the package that had been couriered up from Memphis. A slight, fastidious man, Bonebrake was one of the world's foremost authorities on dactyloscopy, the study and classification of finger and palm prints. Bonebrake had worked as a fingerprint examiner for the FBI since 1941. His was an esoteric profession within the crime-fighting universe—more art, it was said, than science, a closed world of forensic analysis predicated on a foundation of facts so incredible that a thousand bad TV detective shows over the decades had done little to diminish the essential mystery: that the complex friction-ridge patterns on human fingertips and palms, unique to every individual on earth, carry trace amounts of an oily residue excreted from pores that, when impressed upon certain kinds of surfaces, can be "raised" through the use of special dusting powders or chemicals—and then photographed and viewed on cards.

As far-fetched as the discipline seemed to most laymen, fingerprint analysis by 1968 had been the standard technique of criminal identification for more than half a century. It replaced a bizarre and not terribly accurate method of French origin called the Bertillon system, which required the careful measuring of a criminal's earlobes and other anatomical parts. Fingerprinting wasn't perfect, but it was the best system in existence for narrowing the pool of potential culprits in many situations. In many cases, fingerprinting was a godsend, providing the breakthrough that solved the crime.

In 1968, the FBI categorized fingerprints according to the Henry classification system, which was developed by Britain in the late nineteenth century. The system recognizes three primary friction-ridge patterns—arches, loops, and whorls. Loops, the most common pattern, are assigned a numerical value according to the number of ridges contained within each pattern found on each digit. Loop patterns can be further described as "radial" or "ulnar," depending on which direction their microscopic tails point.

Bonebrake got started with his meticulous work shortly after dawn. Most of the prints that he found were fragments or smudges that contained little or no information of value. The twenty-dollar bills that Mrs. Bessie Brewer had provided yielded no usable prints whatsoever. Eventually, however, Bonebrake was able to lift six high-quality specimens from the Remington rifle, the Redfield scope, the Bushnell binoculars, the front section of the *Commercial Appeal,* the bottle of Mennen Afta aftershave lotion, and one of the Schlitz beer cans.

Most of these prints appeared to come from different fingers, but already Bonebrake could tell that two of the prints—those taken from the rifle and the binoculars—were from the same digit of the same individual. Both seemed to have been deposited by a left thumb, and, upon further study, the print pattern would turn out to be unmistakable: an ulnar loop of twelve ridge counts.

This was an important find. The FBI had the fingerprints of more than eighty-two million individuals on file—a number obviously too large to work with, as fingerprint examiners had to do all matching the old-fashioned way, by hand, eyeball, and magnifying glass. This tiny little detail, however, narrowed the search considerably: an ulnar loop of twelve ridge counts on the left thumb. Bonebrake's task was still formidable, but now he had something definite on which to draw comparisons. He made large black-and-white blowups of all six of the latent prints, and then he and his team got started.

■

ON ANOTHER FLOOR of the FBI Crime Lab, Robert A. Frazier spent the morning examining and test-firing the Remington Gamemaster after it had been dusted for fingerprints. A ferociously methodical man with nearly three decades' experience, Frazier was the chief of the FBI's Firearms Identification Unit, where a team of ballistics experts worked around the clock in what was widely considered the world's preeminent weapons-testing facility. Here technicians fired rifles into water recovery tanks, examined bullet fragments and firearms components under high-powered microscopes, and subjected objects to arcane tests to detect such things as the presence of gunpowder and lead.

Within a few hours, Frazier and his team had made a long list of important preliminary findings.

First, the projectile which Dr. Francisco had extracted from Martin Luther King's body only a few hours earlier was a .30-caliber metal-jacketed, soft-nosed bullet made by the Remington-Peters Company—identical in manufacture to the unused Remington-Peters .30-06 rounds found in the ammo box that was part of the bundle.

Second, Frazier was able to ascertain the kind of barrel from which the bullet was fired. The barrels of modern firearms are "rifled" with spiral grooves that are designed to give bullets a rapid spinning motion for stability during flight. The raised portions between the grooves are known as lands. The number, width, and direction of twist of the lands and grooves are called the class characteristics of a barrel, and are common to all firearms of a given model and manufacture. Frazier determined that the bullet that killed King had been fired from a barrel "rifled with six lands and grooves, right twist," and that the Gamemaster, analyzed under a microscope in his laboratory, exhibited the same land-and-groove pattern.

Third, the spent cartridge that Special Agent Jensen had removed from the chamber had been fired in the same Gamemaster rifle, as evidenced by a tiny "extractor mark" Frazier found imprinted on the metal casing. At the base of this spent cartridge case, Frazier discovered a head stamp that said, "R-P .30-06 SPRG," indicating that it was a Remington-

Peters round of the same caliber as the ammunition found in the ammo box.

Frazier concluded, based on the "physical characteristics of the rifling impressions" as well as other factors, that the bullet removed from King's body *could* have been fired from the Remington Gamemaster. However, he could not say with scientific certainty that the bullet came from this rifle, "to the exclusion of all other rifles." This was because the bullet, as he described it in his report, "had been distorted due to mutilation" as it struck hard bone while passing through King's body.

Frazier knew that the mechanical components of individual firearms (such as the firing pin and breech face) have distinctive microscopic traits that can engrave telltale markings on bullets. The tiny striations often found on fired bullets are known as individual identifying characteristics and are, in effect, the ballistics equivalent of a fingerprint. Frazier had hoped the bullet that killed King would exhibit these telltale markings, but it didn't: the round, having been chipped, dented, warped, and broken into several discrete parts, was missing the critical information.

Though a dismaying discovery, it was not uncommon; bullets often came to Frazier's lab in sorry condition. Such was the secondary effect of firearms violence: projectiles, in doing their damage, themselves became damaged.

Frazier also studied the windowsill that had been removed from the communal bathroom at Bessie Brewer's rooming house. Making microscopic comparisons between the half-moon indentation in the windowsill and various markings on the rifle barrel, he determined to his satisfaction that the dent could have been caused by the Gamemaster's recoil upon firing—it was "consistent" with the barrel's contours and appeared to have been created recently—but again, he stopped short of an absolute confirmation.

Finally, Frazier examined King's bloody clothes, subjecting them to chemical tests. He found "no partially burned or unburned gunpowder" on King's dress shirt, suit coat, and necktie, which conclusively confirmed what everybody who'd been at the Lorraine already knew—that King had *not* been shot at close range. But when Frazier tested the clothing with sodium rhodizonate, he found lead particles on King's coat lapel, the right

collar of the shirt, and the severed tie. This lead residue was composition-
ally consistent with the lead in the bullet extracted from King's body—and
consistent with what Frazier would expect a high-velocity .30-06 round to
deposit around the site of a wound.

■

WHILE THE FBI pored over King's mangled clothes, Eric Galt
was in Atlanta, only a few miles from King's church and birthplace; he,
too, had clothes on his mind. Around 9:30 a.m. eastern time, Galt
dropped by the Piedmont Laundry on Peachtree Street to pick up the
clothes he had left before he went to Memphis. The laundry's counter
clerk, Mrs. Annie Estelle Peters, had waited on Galt when he dropped
off the clothes on April 1, and she immediately recognized the returning
customer when he walked through the door. As before, he was neatly
dressed and clean shaven; this time, though, he seemed to be in a hurry.
He was abrupt in his speech and impatient when she left the counter to
locate his clothes.

She returned with his items—three pieces of dry cleaning and an
assortment of regular laundry totaling $2.71, which he paid for in cash.
There was a black-checked coat, a pair of gray trousers, a striped brown
tie, four undershirts, three underdrawers, a pair of socks, and a wash-
cloth. All his laundry items were affixed with tiny identifying tags that
said, "EGC-83"—which was Galt's permanent "laundry mark" for all his
dealings with Piedmont. Hastily, Galt picked up the folded laundry,
neatly stacked in a rectangular package of stapled paper, and slung the
hangered dry-cleaning items over his shoulder. He walked out of the
shop and headed up Peachtree, in the direction of his rooming house on
Fourteenth Street.

Galt didn't barge into the rooming house—he watched and waited
from a distance until he was "satisfied there was no unusual activity
around the place." Then he moved quickly. Neither the tenants nor the
owner, Jimmie Garner, saw him. He tidied up his room a bit, throwing
some trash in a plastic bag and dropping it into a garbage can out back.
He also threw out the manual typewriter he'd had since his time in Puerto
Vallarta—it would be too cumbersome, he realized, for his fugitive travels
to Canada. He packed a suitcase with his clean laundry and his self-help

books and his Polaroid camera. He retrieved his .38 Liberty Chief revolver from its hiding place in the basement and stuck it in his belt. He
assembled a wad of bills that he later estimated to be slightly more than a
thousand dollars—money saved, he later claimed, from various smuggling
and fencing schemes over the past year. He stamped and addressed an envelope to the Locksmithing Institute in Little Falls, New Jersey, containing the final lesson in his locksmithing correspondence course, an
envelope he would mail later that morning. Then he dashed off a short
note for Mr. Garner on a piece of cardboard—a note clearly designed to
throw authorities off his scent. He said he unexpectedly had to go to
Birmingham but would come back for his remaining belongings—he
specifically mentioned the portable Zenith television—in a few days. He
placed the note on his bed and left his key in the lock. Then Galt grabbed
his suitcase and never returned to 113 Fourteenth Street Northeast.

Probably hailing another cab, he headed for the bus station.

■

At the R. S. Lewis Funeral Home just a few blocks from Beale
Street, Martin Luther King's corpse lay in a temporary bronze casket in a
viewing room of purple drapes and lurid stained glass. He was clothed in
a fresh dark suit.

No public viewing had been announced, yet hundreds of people
had been lining up since dawn outside the funeral home, hoping to view
the body. The Lewis specialists, listening to crackling recordings of
King's speeches, had labored through the night—embalming, grooming,
dressing, and beautifying the body. "There was so much to do," the mortuary's co-proprietor Clarence Lewis told a reporter. "The jawbone was
just dangling. They had to reset it and then build all that up with plaster."
They'd had to work in such a rush that Ralph Abernathy, having been in
Dr. Francisco's autopsy suite the night before, worried that his friend
might not be presentable. "I didn't know whether the funeral home
would attempt to repair the indignity of the autopsy," he said. But when
he arrived from the Lorraine, Abernathy was amazed at what the Lewis
cosmetologists had done with their tinting powders and restorative
waxes. "The body appeared unblemished," Abernathy said. "The morticians had done their job well."

Before the crowds were admitted, Abernathy and others from the SCLC inner circle lingered a few minutes with their leader. "We all wanted to be there," Andrew Young wrote. "Even though we all knew that we, the living, must move on with our lives, with our movement, we wanted to be near Martin for as long as we possibly could."

Then the doors opened, and the long, solemn line of visitors shuffled through. They were an eclectic mix of humanity—"from company presidents to field hands," one newspaper reporter put it. Photographers from around the world snapped pictures. When a woman kissed King's right cheek, Clarence Lewis grew concerned. "It will spoil the makeup job," he said. Many of the mourners were garbage workers and their families, who, as they peered into the still face of the martyr, were touched both by sadness and guilt, a feeling that he had died for them. They leaned over, they spoke to King, they touched his face, and they wept.

"I wish it was Henry Loeb lying there," one woman said.

"Why'd this happen to you, Dr. King?" said another, leaning into the coffin. "What are we going to do now?"

For several hours, people marched through the funeral home. They moaned and wailed and prayed and sang. Abernathy said, "The Lord is my light and my salvation." Billy Kyles said, "I am the resurrection and the life." The cameras kept flashing.

Finally the lid was lowered, and the coffin was placed in the back of the long limousine. When Abernathy shut the hearse doors, he placed his hand on the glass and said, "Long live the King."

A two-mile procession of cars followed the hearse as it crept through the city streets and then motored out to the Memphis Metropolitan Airport, escorted by National Guardsmen and police. The convoy turned toward the tarmac, where an Electra four-engine prop jet had just landed, a plane that had been provided to the King family by Senator Robert Kennedy. The aircraft's hatch door was open. Standing at the lip, hatless, wearing a black dress and black gloves and staring out over the approaching motorcade with a queenly rectitude, was Coretta Scott King.

RAMSEY CLARK AND Cartha DeLoach spent most of the morning making the rounds in Memphis. They dropped by the local FBI office to bolster the morale of Jensen's already beleaguered cadre of field agents. They paid a visit to the U.S. attorney's office, to reassure prosecutors that the FBI would work hand in glove with them to build a successful case against King's assailant, if and when he was caught. Then they met with some of the top National Guard officers. Clark told the commanders they were doing a fine job but urged them not to use excessive force. He was particularly troubled by the use of tanks. "I thought it was a provocation," Clark said, "and it was also a kind of sorry sign as to what kind of country we are. I mean, what's around here that calls for *tanks?*"

Clark's entourage quickly moved on to city hall for a meeting with Mayor Henry Loeb. Outside the building, some of the garbage strikers were marching with their I AM A MAN signs. Clark was clearly moved by the succinct clarity of the slogan. "What a message that was," he later said. "It was one of the most imaginative demonstrations and one of the most powerful symbols that came out of the civil rights movement." The Justice Department official Roger Wilkins was similarly touched by the sight of the garbage workers, solemnly parading on the morning after King's assassination: "To see these men walking in a very orderly fashion, asserting, 'I should be treated as a human being'—you couldn't *not* be moved by that. I stood there with tears rolling from my eyes."

Clark and Wilkins strode inside the white marble halls for their visit with Mayor Loeb, which went nowhere. Wilkins described Loeb as "gracious in a Southern kind of way, but staunch as a brick wall." Clark tried to persuade Loeb to do whatever it took to resolve the strike—it was not only in the city's best interests but in the nation's as well. Loeb dug in his heels even as he lavished his Washington visitors with hospitality. "We did not move him one inch," recalled Wilkins, "and he did not have one inch of sympathy for these men who were out there pacing around the building."

Finally, Clark and DeLoach met with Fire and Police Director Frank Holloman, in his smoke-filled office. Holloman had some bad news. The enticing "John Willard" lead his detectives were bird-dogging that morning had already dried up. This particular John Willard, it turned out, had an airtight alibi: he was still in jail.

Clark and DeLoach tried to brighten the mood by sharing some of the positive information they'd gleaned from FBI headquarters that morning: that the murder weapon had already been traced to Birmingham, where agents had obtained a good physical description of the buyer; that analysts in the fingerprint unit had lifted several high-quality latent prints they were now comparing with the prints of known fugitives; that right here in Memphis, Jensen's men had interviewed the York Arms clerk who had sold the binoculars to the man in 5B. Jensen, meanwhile, had hired an artist to interview witnesses at Bessie Brewer's and Canipe's to prepare a preliminary sketch of "John Willard." All in all, they were making brisk progress, DeLoach thought. It was only a matter of time before they'd catch the killer.

But Director Holloman remained surly. The stress King's assassination was putting on his already overstrained department showed on his pale and furrowed face. He'd been up all night and was now so wired on nicotine and coffee that he could scarcely complete a thought. He kept running his fingers through his strands of gray hair. "He was just about out on his feet," said an aide. "He was whipped and numb."

Holloman deeply resented the rumors circulating around the city, and the nation, that his department was somehow involved in King's murder—rumors intensified by the public knowledge that Holloman had once worked directly for Hoover at the FBI headquarters in Washington. Clark and DeLoach assured him the federal government had no such suspicions, but the accusation clearly stung—and would continue to trouble him the rest of his life. "I had not a scintilla or an iota of a desire to see any harm come to Dr. King," Holloman testified in Washington years later. "One of the greatest disappointments in my life has been that Dr. King was assassinated and that he was assassinated in Memphis."

Holloman apprised Clark and DeLoach of other developments around the city—that night's curfew plans, preparations for Abernathy's "silent march" down Beale, the various leads his own department was pursuing. He mentioned that Memphis's two daily Scripps Howard newspapers had offered a combined reward of fifty thousand dollars for information leading to the killer's arrest, and that the Memphis City Council had responded by putting up another fifty thousand dollars. Holloman was mildly optimistic that a hundred grand would produce a raft of new leads, but he also knew that posted rewards of this sort have a way of bringing out the nutcases and cranks.

■

CLARK BROKE UP his mid-morning meeting with Holloman to call a press conference. More than a hundred journalists and film crews from around the world—including Sweden, Australia, Yugoslavia, and Japan—gathered in a nondescript federal suite downtown to hear the attorney general's delicately worded remarks. "All of our evidence at this time," Clark said, "indicates that it was a single person who committed this criminal act."

He was not free to divulge any details lest he jeopardize the ongoing investigations. But he wanted to assure the nation that investigators had already compiled a considerable amount of evidence, and that every effort was being made to catch the killer. The dragnet, he said, extended well beyond Memphis. "It has already spread several hundred miles from the boundaries of Tennessee now." Investigators were working on several names, some of which might be aliases, and they were hunting for a white Mustang. "We have a name we're working on. Whether it is the right name we'll have to see. We're very hopeful. We've got some good breaks." He said he hoped to have an early conclusion to the investigation, followed by an indictment, trial, and conviction.

"We are getting close—we've got one man on the run," Clark confidently announced. But as the nation's highest law-enforcement official, he was worried about violence erupting around the country. He advised the nation's mayors, governors, and police chiefs that "either overreaction or under-action can lead to rioting. You have to exercise a very careful control."

Throughout his remarks, Clark was repeatedly interrupted by militants from the Invaders and other groups. Some were suspicious of Clark's quick pronouncement that no conspiracy was involved in the shooting. How could he possibly *know* this already? Their criticisms quickly devolved into shouting and incendiary diatribes for the benefit of the cameras. When Clark left the room, he was livid. "A lot of phonies," he vented to DeLoach. "They'll just make things worse."

Clark soon received word that Coretta King's plane had arrived, so he and DeLoach made for the airport. When they got there, the bronze casket was being loaded onto the rear of the Electra prop jet, by means of a hydraulic conveyor belt ramp. Clark and Roger Wilkins climbed on board to greet Mrs. King, A. D. King, Abernathy, and the others gathered sorrowfully on the plane. DeLoach lingered on the tarmac. "In view of Mr. Hoover's longtime feud with her husband," he said, "I thought she might resent my coming"—probably a prudent assessment on his part.

On board, Clark offered his deepest sympathy, both on his own behalf and on that of the government. Wilkins thought Coretta was "courageous and calm and gracious" as she received them. "People were crying—it was all very hard. But Coretta was simply regal." Farther back in the cabin, A. D. King was having a rough time. To Wilkins, he looked like "a bloated and faded version of Martin—it was said AD drank too much."

Outside, in the bright humidity of the forenoon, DeLoach awkwardly sidled up to Andy Young, who was standing on the hot pavement. Over the whine of jet engines, DeLoach tried to express his condolences. "We'll do everything we can," he told Young. "I'm sure we'll get him."

Young nodded blankly. Exhausted and grieving, he was, at that moment, emphatically uninterested in exchanging pleasantries with any FBI official—especially DeLoach, who Young knew was complicit in many of the dirty tricks the FBI had pulled on King over the years. DeLoach thought Young was "somewhere else," which was true enough. Finding and punishing the assassin were surprisingly low in the SCLC's scheme of priorities. Young felt that carrying on King's work was a far more important task than fixating on the crime itself, or on legal retribution. Throughout the movement, King had seldom vilified individuals—even Bull Connor or George Wallace; instead he'd tried to focus on engaging the larger social forces at work in any given situation. This same strain of transcendent "love-your-enemies" thinking guided Young, Abernathy, and the others as they began to contemplate their leader's death. As Young put it, "We aren't so much concerned with who killed Martin, as with *what* killed him."

It was the kind of sentiment that mystified a G-man like DeLoach.

In a few minutes, Ramsey Clark stepped off the plane and rejoined DeLoach on the tarmac. Coretta never left the plane; she had no interest in putting a toe on Memphis soil. Amazingly, no city official—neither Mayor Loeb, nor Director Holloman, nor a single city councilman, black or white—had come to greet her at the airport. She had flown here for one errand only: to claim her husband's body and get home.

Now the Electra's hatch doors heaved shut, and the plane taxied and climbed into the bright hazy skies, banking southeast toward Atlanta. Along the runway, several hundred mourners, some with fists held high, bade their farewell to Martin Luther King. Some tried to sing a stanza of "We Shall Overcome," but the spirit wasn't there, and the song soon withered into silence.

■

AT THE CAPITOL HOMES project in Atlanta, the white Mustang sat parked all day, its windshield beaded with rain—the car that held hard clues and hidden imprimaturs that might lead to the identity, if not the whereabouts, of Martin Luther King's killer. Mary Bridges and her daughter Wanda weren't the only ones who had seen the mystery car pull in to the parking lot that morning. A few buildings away, Mrs. Lucy

Cayton had been standing on her front stoop with a broom in her hands, when she saw the driver emerge from the Mustang. "He was nice looking," she thought. "That's why I stood with my broom and watched."

Several doors down, Mrs. Ernest Payne had also gotten a glimpse of the man who parked the Mustang that morning, had watched him step out and "fool with the car door" before heading off toward Memorial Drive. He wore a dark suit and carried what she thought was a "little black book" under his arm.

Mrs. John Riley lived in a unit just across the parking lot from the Mustang. She too had spotted the car but didn't pay much attention to it. But her thirteen-year-old son, Johnny, a car buff, feasted his eyes on it as soon as he got home from school. He noticed the Alabama tag, the rust red mud inside the car, and the two stickers in the window that said, "Turista." The teenager observed that the Mustang, unlike every other car in the Capitol Homes lot, was *backed* into its parking space; he could only surmise that the guy who left it didn't want passersby to readily spot the out-of-state tag.

Mrs. Riley sat in her kitchen, visiting with a few neighbors over coffee. They got to talking about the assassination and the riots. One neighbor said she'd heard the authorities were looking for a white Mustang.

Mrs. Riley tittered and pointed out the window. "Why," she said, "it's sitting right out there in the parking lot." Everyone laughed a nervous laugh—a laugh that said, *Wouldn't that be something?*—and then the ladies resumed their klatch without another thought.

LATER THAT AFTERNOON, in Washington, President Johnson was taking a late lunch in the White House with the Supreme Court justice Abe Fortas and several advisers. The King assassination had taken a toll on everyone at the White House, and President Johnson looked haggard as he sat down at the table in the White House residence. He'd already had a long and exhausting Friday. After attending a King memorial service at the National Cathedral, he'd spent most of the day in the Cabinet Room meeting with a conclave of the nation's most prominent black leaders—among them Justice Thurgood Marshall, the great civil rights stalwart Bayard Rustin, the D.C. minister Walter Fauntroy, and the heads of the established civil rights organizations. Johnson had invited Martin Luther King Sr. to the meeting as well, but the minister was too racked with grief to contemplate such a trip. He did send a telegram, which Johnson read aloud to the assembled group. "Please know," King said, "that I join you in your plea to American citizens to desist from violence so that the cause for which my son died will not be in vain."

Moved nearly to tears, Johnson looked up from the telegram and spoke off the cuff. "If I were a kid in Harlem," he said, "I know what I'd be thinking. I'd be thinking that whites had declared open season on my people—that they're going to pick us off one by one unless I get a gun and pick them off first."

After a few hours, the solemn and awkward meeting broke up with promises of goodwill but no hard-and-fast resolutions. With some of the black leaders around him, Johnson made a brief statement on national television. "Violence," he said, "must be denied its victory."

Now ravenous, Johnson tried to steal a few minutes to grab a bite. He bowed his head with the others at the table and said a perfunctory but heartfelt grace: "Help us, Lord, to know what to do."

Justice Abe Fortas, who, oddly enough, was born and raised in Memphis, talked to the president for a while about the search for King's killer, but the main topic of conversation was the fragile state of security in the nation's capital. Through much of the day, troubling reports from the White House message center had been piling up, rumors that a full-scale riot was being planned for the streets of downtown Washington. The word flowing into the White House was that the previous night's disturbances were mere child's play; tonight, the whole city was going to blow.

Though the morning had started off peacefully enough, by midday the feel on the streets had begun to change. Following a viral logic, the city descended into fear and then hysteria. The rhetoric turned ugly. Stokely Carmichael had been outdoing himself, feeding the press out-landish calls to violence—at one point urging Washington blacks to "take as many white people with them as possible." All whites, he in-sisted, were complicit in King's death: "The honky, from honky Lyndon Johnson to honky Bobby Kennedy, will not co-opt King. Bobby Kennedy pulled that trigger just as well as anybody else."

Through the early afternoon, the feverish rumors grew. Black store owners began to cover their plate-glass windows with plywood and scrawled entrances with the words SOUL BROTHER in hopeful attempts to differentiate their businesses from white-owned stores—the mercantile equivalent of Israelites smearing their door frames with lamb's blood.

Finally, as though belatedly reading the path of a glowering storm, people panicked. The large department stores downtown discreetly began to close up, removing merchandise from windows. Hundreds and then thousands simply got up and left their places of work, yanked their kids from school, and began to walk, then run down the streets, hurrying to bus stops and train stations and the Potomac River bridges. Idling in clogged traffic, frightened motorists abandoned their cars on the streets and took off on foot. It looked like a Hollywood disaster film—as Washingtonians, black and white, evacuated the District en masse.

As Johnson tried to eat lunch, an aide who'd been looking out the window toward Pennsylvania Avenue interrupted the president and his fellow diners. "Gentlemen," he said. "I think you better see this."

Johnson stood up and, with a hint of trepidation in his step, wandered over to the window. The president didn't say a word; he only pointed: toward the east, an immense pillar of fire climbed over the cornices of downtown Washington and billowed in the sky. Soon the corridors of the White House smelled of smoke.

The president was almost philosophical. "What did you expect?" he later told one adviser. "I don't know why we're so surprised. When you put your foot on a man's neck and hold him down for three hundred years, and then you let him up, what's he going to do? He's going to knock your block off."

■

A FEW HUNDRED yards away, at FBI headquarters in the Justice Department building, the crime lab technicians remained burrowed in their work. While fingerprint experts combed through hundreds of thousands of stored print cards, other analysts sifted through the physical evidence that had been flown up from Memphis. Taken together, these dozens of objects formed a vast puzzle. The significant and the random, the potentially crucial and the probably meaningless, were all assembled in a forensic riddle on a well-lit table in the crime lab. The search for the man in 5B was moving not only outward into the country but downward into the close realm of slides and tiny threads teased from artifacts, downward into the swimming lenses of laboratory microscopes. Quite apart from fingerprints, the assailant had left faint trails that he was not aware of—traces of his physiology, hints of his movements, windows into the habits of his mind.

That afternoon, the fiber expert Morris S. Clark began to microscopically examine the green herringbone bedspread that was twirled around the gun in front of Canipe's. He found human hairs—dark brown Caucasian hairs—entangled in the picked and faded fabric, as well as in the teeth of "Willard's" hairbrush, in the clothes, and on some of the other belongings in the bundle. The hairs, oily and fine, all seemed to come from the same man.

Down the hall, meanwhile, another search was in progress. On the handle of the duckbill pliers found in the blue zippered bag, FBI investigators took note of a little price sticker stamped with the word "Rompage." A quick telephone call to the National Retail Hardware Association in Indianapolis revealed that Rompage was a large hardware store in Los Angeles, located at 5542 Hollywood Boulevard. This presented something of a left turn: suddenly, in a single phone call, the manhunt had been enlarged two thousand miles to the West Coast.

Agents from the Los Angeles field office were quickly dispatched to Rompage, armed with the crude portrait of "John Willard" that Jensen's artist had sketched in Memphis. Tom Ware, the Rompage manager, didn't recognize the unprepossessing man in the sketch, which was no surprise. But he knew the pliers well. In October 1966, his logbook showed, he had bought a large "seconds" order of duckbill pliers at a bargain-basement price. He'd slapped the "Rompage" stickers on them and displayed them in a big barrel of discounted items near the store entrance. They were hot sellers.

And so the niggling but possibly salient question arose: Did the slayer of Martin Luther King buy a pair of pliers in Los Angeles sometime over the past year and a half? Did he once *live* in Los Angeles, perhaps in the vicinity of the store? FBI agents began to interview every known regular customer of Rompage Hardware—contractors, plumbers, carpenters, electricians. Their efforts proved little more than a goose chase.

But another hunt now under way at FBI headquarters was leading somewhere. Examiners had found laundry tags stamped in the inseams of the undershirt and the pair of boxer shorts left in Willard's bag. The tiny tag was made of white tape and bore the number "02B-6." Investigators contacted experts in the laundry industry and eventually reached the Textile Marking Machine Company in Syracuse, New York, whose representatives soon confirmed that the laundry tag in question was made by a stamping appliance manufactured by their plant. The tag was a relatively new proprietary material known as Thermo-Seal Tape, and the Syracuse company kept a thorough log of all the laundries throughout the nation that had bought the Thermo-Seal marking machine. Digging deeper into their books, company accountants found no record of any purchases by laundries in Memphis or Birmingham—the two cities the FBI was mainly focusing on. Most of the Thermo-Seal machines now in use were on the West Coast.

Where on the West Coast? the agent following up this particular lead wanted to know.

The Thermo-Seal rep consulted his records and replied, "Out in California. Mainly in the Los Angeles area." In fact, he said, close to a hundred laundries in Los Angeles had adopted the Thermo-Seal system. At the FBI's request, the company quickly began to compile a comprehensive list of them all.

■

THE ELECTRA PROP jet sped for Atlanta, bringing Martin Luther King home to the city of his birth, the city of his alma mater and his church and his family. About thirty-five people sat on the plane, with the coffin parked in the rear, where several seats had been removed. The short journey of 398 miles seemed long and tedious, and most people just stared out the window as the engines droned on. In one hour, the plane arced over the same rural countryside that Eric Galt had taken twelve hours to drive across, on meandering back roads, the previous night.

Ralph Abernathy sat in silence, thinking of the curious and dreadful turn of fate that had transpired over the past three days. He remembered how King had reacted to the bomb threat on the flight from Atlanta to Memphis that Wednesday morning. "I thought of the brittle smile on his face when the captain announced the threat and reassured us that everything was safe," Abernathy said in his memoirs. "There had been a normal and very human fear behind that smile." Now, three days later, King lay in a coffin in the rear of a plane going in the opposite direction. Abernathy peered out the window, at the wet Southland surging with spring. "Martin was unworried, at peace," he said. "For just an instant, staring at the greening woods below and thinking of what was to come, I almost envied him." Abernathy knew he'd be returning to Memphis in three days to lead the memorial march down Beale Street, and the thought occurred to him that he might end up flying home in his own bronze box.

The plane landed in Atlanta, where the rain had turned to a gentle, all-suffusing mist. Coretta's four children, all dressed up, had been brought to the airport tarmac, and now they climbed the portable stairs and boarded the plane. Bernice, who was five, practically skipped down the aisle, seemingly without a care. Andy Young gathered her up in his arms. Bunny—as everyone called her—looked around the cabin, and then a puzzled expression formed on her little face. "Where's Daddy?" she said. "Mommy, where is Daddy?"

Coretta's heart ached. "Bunny," she said, taking her daughter in her arms. "Daddy is lying down in the back of the plane. When you see him, he won't be able to speak to you. Daddy has gone to live with God, and he won't be coming back."

Little Dexter, who was seven, understood the meaning of the big box in the rear of the plane but was leery of confronting the full truth. "I'd look around at the plane's interior, anywhere but at the coffin," he later wrote. "I didn't want to think about my father in there, unable to get out." He kept asking Coretta random questions—"What's *this*? What's *that*?"—while fidgeting and pointing to different features of the aircraft. "Mother knew I was avoiding the fact of our father's corpse. I was curious about him being in the casket, but I didn't want to face it."

The casket was removed from the rear of the plane and loaded into a hearse. Everyone disembarked, formed a motorcade, and followed the King family to the Hanley Bell Street Funeral Home, where crowds were already forming outside.

Coretta asked the funeral director to open the coffin. She fretted that the morticians in Memphis had botched their work, that they'd failed to "fix his face," as she put it. But when the lid swung open, she was pleased. His countenance "looked so young and smooth and unworried against the white-satin lining of the casket," she wrote. "There was hardly any visible damage."

The children were brought in to see their father. They stared and stared, in disbelief, in curiosity, in dread. Andy Young was standing nearby when Dexter said, "Uncle Andy, this man didn't know our Daddy, did he?" speaking of King's killer.

Why do you say that? Young asked.

"Because if he had, he wouldn't have shot him. He was just an ig-norant man who didn't know any better."

■

AS THE HANLEY Bell Street Funeral Home was taking delivery of King's body in Atlanta, Eric Galt was only a few miles away, at the Greyhound bus terminal, buying a one-way ticket for points north. The waiting room was the usual sweaty swirl of humanity—soldiers on leave, itinerant workers, mothers comforting croupy babies. People sat smoking on the molded plastic benches, half listening to the shrill squawk of the loudspeaker announcing delays and cancellations, the buses now boarding for Charleston, New Orleans, and Tallahassee.

Galt had a few belongings in a single suitcase—some clothes, whatever toiletries he hadn't dumped in Memphis, a book on self-hypnosis, and his dog-eared copy of *Psycho-Cybernetics* by Dr. Maxwell Maltz. Probably he bought a copy of the *Atlanta Constitution* and, secreting himself behind the broad, inky sheets, read of all the destruction he had wrought from coast to coast. On the front page, the immense banner headline read: DR. KING SHOT, DIES IN MEMPHIS; RIFLE FOUND, HUNT FOR KILLER PRESSED.

The *Constitution* noted a number of details about King's suspected slayer—more details than Galt would have felt comfortable with, perhaps, but nothing that pointed directly to him. The physical description was vague and somewhat inaccurate. The suspect, the *Constitution* reported, was "a young, dark-haired white man who dashed out of a flophouse across the street from King's hotel, dropped a Browning rifle on the sidewalk and fled in a car." The paper also noted, in an eerie juxtaposition, that a group of "old-line Georgia segregationists" had succeeded in raising a considerable war chest for George Wallace's presidential campaign—"so there will be a man in the White House who recognizes the viewpoint of the southern white people."

The *Constitution*'s progressive editor and publisher, the legendary Ralph McGill, had an editorial on page one. Whether Eric Galt read it is doubtful, but it was aimed right at him: "The moment the triggerman fired, Martin Luther King was the free man. The white killer was the slave—a slave to fear, a slave to his own sense of inferiority, a slave to hatred, a slave to all the bloody instincts that surge in a brain when a human being decides to become a beast."

Around one o'clock, Galt boarded the coach that said "Cincinnati" on the destination marquee, with the familiar lean hound lunging across the length of the cargo compartments. Galt crept down the narrow aisle and took a seat. Like most cross-country Greyhound coaches, the bus had a tiny rear lavatory that was doubtless ripe with the smell of chemicals losing the fight against cidered urine.

That afternoon the bus churned north out of Georgia in clouds of diesel fumes, grinding up through the striated limestone foothills at the border with Tennessee. The bus stopped in Chattanooga, and Knoxville, and then pressed on toward Kentucky. With every mile he put behind him, Galt must have felt a deepening relief. He was out of the Deep South now, burrowing into regions of the country that carried no association with himself or his crime. He was likely starting to breathe easier, knowing that his jag from Memphis, to Birmingham, and then to Atlanta was growing colder as he vanished into the murky inseams of the country.

Yet no matter how far north the bus ventured, he found that no place was untouched by King's death, no stop along the dreary string of terminals was immune from uncertainty and anger and fear. Galt could escape from his crime but not from its powerful recoil.

By nightfall Galt was in the hills of Kentucky, gliding through bluegrass and bourbon country toward Lexington, then crossing the muddy Ohio into Cincinnati, where he got off at the Greyhound terminal.

In his memoirs, Galt said he had a layover of two hours, so he checked his suitcase in to a locker and went to a nearby tavern—not only for drinks to ease his nerves, but also to gather some news. Cooped up on the bus, and lacking his pocket radio, he was starved for information on the manhunt. He must have been relieved to learn from the evening papers that authorities had made no substantial new breaks in the case. The Mustang had not been found, and there was no mention of a rooming house in Atlanta. Late that night, he boarded a second bus, bound for Detroit.

■

WHILE GALT'S GREYHOUND motored north, Attorney General Ramsey Clark and his small entourage boarded the Jetstar in Memphis and took off for Washington. Clark had been getting disturbing reports of incipient rioting in D.C. throughout the day, so they cut short their time in Memphis. Around five o'clock, the jet rose into the Memphis sky and arrowed toward the capital.

On board, Cartha DeLoach continued to be a font of optimism. The search for the man in 5B was proceeding crisply, in his estimation. Thus far, it seemed nearly a textbook operation. DeLoach had been in repeated contact with FBI headquarters and had all the reports in hand—laundry tags, ballistics, fibers, hairs, fingerprints, gun receipts, physical descriptions—the case was coming together with rapid efficiency. The new Los Angeles twist presented some unexpected complications, he had to concede, but otherwise all evidence seemed to be pointing to one suspect, or possibly two, living and plotting the crime out of the Southland. DeLoach assumed of course that both "Lowmeyer" and "Willard" were fictitious, but to be sure, FBI agents were checking every permutation of those names throughout the South.

DeLoach was so confident, in fact, that he was willing to make a wager with Attorney General Clark: the bureau would catch King's killer within twenty-four hours—that is, by five o'clock Saturday night—or he would present Clark with a bottle of the finest sherry he could find. Clark shook on the deal, even though it was a bet he sincerely hoped to lose.

Though he was more skeptical, Clark had to admit that the case was shaping up well. "We had considerably more evidence, considerably earlier, than we ever expected," he recalled. "But we didn't realize the suspect was one of these unique types of people who tends to do just the *opposite* of what you'd expect. You'd think he'd go right, and he goes left. He was intent on giving us a merry chase—to put it mildly."

As Clark sped toward Washington, he thought about America's historical penchant for gun violence. Like many liberals across the nation, he hoped that the King assassination might quicken the gun-control debate on Capitol Hill, and he vowed to push for a policy requiring a permit to own a gun—especially high-powered rifles like a

.30-06. "We are virtually unique among nations in our failure to control guns," he would write. "Destroyers of life, causers of crime, guns had once again scarred our national character, marking another terrible moment in our history."

DeLoach rode in silence most of the flight to Washington, absorbed in very different thoughts. The day in Memphis had been long and stressful, and his head was throbbing from lack of sleep and the pressure of the investigation. J. Edgar Hoover's long-standing "feud" with King, as DeLoach called it, would inevitably stir deeper doubts within already suspicious segments of the American public, who wondered if the FBI had been involved in the assassination—or if Hoover had directly ordered it. DeLoach realized that even if he won his bet and the FBI *did* catch King's killer by tomorrow, it still wouldn't be enough "to dam the flood of criticism and abuse that was coming our way."

It was past ten o'clock when the Jetstar began its approach into Washington. The plane was twelve miles out, over the horse country of Virginia, when Clark and DeLoach first spotted the smoke—a long, doomed finger extending all the way from the District. Since all commercial flights into National Airport had been banned, Clark asked the pilot to drop down and fly low along the Potomac. What they saw stunned them.

"I looked down at a city in flames," Clark recalled. Smoke engulfed all of downtown and the Mall. Only the great illuminated dome of the Capitol and the sharp white obelisk of the Washington Monument punctured the seething blankets. Clark could see infernos blazing up around U and Fourteenth streets, and also within a few blocks of his own office at the Justice Department building, the same building where FBI Crime Lab analysts were burning midnight oil, poring over the King assassination evidence.

The spreading conflagrations made the previous night's scattered rioting seem tame—the pilot of the Jetstar thought it looked like Dresden. All told, more than five hundred fires had been set throughout the city. At President Johnson's behest, much of the District was now occupied by federal troops, spearheaded by the Third Infantry Regiment, the so-called Old Guard, a corps of elite troops out of Fort Myer specifically trained, like the loyal Praetorians of ancient Rome, to protect the seat of government in the event of crisis—a Russian invasion, presumably, or the landing of Martians.

The White House was reinforced with sandbags and ringed with troops, its great lawns bathed in blinding floodlights. Machine-gun nests were erected all around the Mall and the Capitol building, where soldiers, some fresh from Vietnam, stood in nervous vigil, their rifles fixed with bayonets. One reporter thought the scene on Capitol Hill had "the air of a parliament of a new African republic."

The Jetstar made several low passes over the District. Looking down at the city where he grew up, the city he loved, Clark recalled accounts he'd read of the British sacking and torching Washington during the War of 1812. "In all my life," he said, "I never thought we'd see Washington *burning*."

THROUGH THE EARLY morning hours of April 6, Eric Galt's Greyhound continued to grind north through flat Ohio farm country, creeping toward Detroit. According to his memoirs, the coach reached the Motor City around eight that morning, a bright warm Saturday. Galt bought a fresh copy of the *Detroit News*, whose pages were dominated by reports of the assassination and the riots it had ignited. Detroit itself had been particularly hard-hit: though nothing like the riots in Washington, or the massive riots that hit Detroit in the summer of 1967, looting and arson had been widespread since Friday. The previous night, police had fired on several crowds of rioters, killing one man. Now three thousand National Guardsmen patrolled the streets, and Detroit's mayor, Jerome Cavanaugh, repeated for the media what had effectively become a national mantra: "It is better to overreact than underreact."

As he scanned the paper, Galt must have been relieved by the vagueness of the reports on the manhunt. It seemed that no new leads had developed. The articles made no mention of an Eric Galt or a Harvey Lowmeyer, no mention of a Mustang found in Atlanta. The authorities seemed to be concentrating on a nonexistent man named John

Willard. Now that he was poised on the border, only miles away from Windsor, Canada, Galt could breathe a little easier.

He knew that crossing between the United States and Canada was a lax affair requiring no documentation, and that travelers were seldom stopped and questioned. But in the wake of the King assassination, he worried that the border guards might be taking special precautions. Galt checked himself in the bathroom mirror and decided he looked too much like a fugitive to cross the border into Windsor. His dark beard had come in strong over the past two days, and he feared that unless he got cleaned up, he might arouse suspicions should a customs agent stop him. Unfortunately, he had dumped all his shaving toiletries with the bundle back in Memphis.

Galt later claimed that he stashed his suitcase in a locker at the Greyhound terminal, took off across a grassy park, and found an old-fashioned barbershop where he requested a shave. The barber hesitated—he'd stopped shaving customers years ago—but Galt prevailed upon the man and climbed into his chair. Soon the barber was working up the lather with a mug brush and sharpening the blade on his leather strop. If the subject of Martin Luther King's assassination came up, what might have been said between the two men is not known. But for the next ten minutes or so, without realizing his customer's identity, the barber gingerly dragged his straight razor over the face and neck of Martin Luther King's assassin.

Clean shaven, Galt returned to the terminal for his suitcase and hailed a taxi. His worries about the border proved unwarranted—his cab crossed under the Detroit River through the fumy Windsor Tunnel without so much as a glance from the authorities. (It was a point of local interest that the Detroit-Windsor crossing was the only major border crossing where one had to go *south* to pass from the United States into Canada.) The cabbie drove to the Windsor train station. For a one-way fare of $8.20, Galt took the noon train on Canadian National Railways. The four-hour trip was an easy one, making a northeastern stitch across the farm country of Ontario, roughly paralleling Lake Erie, passing through the city of London. At around four o'clock the train pulled in to his destination, Canada's largest city—Toronto.

Galt stowed his suitcase at Union Station and set off on foot in search of a cheap place to stay. As usual, his radar was keen—according to his memoirs, he made his way to a rooming place at 102 Ossington Avenue, in a polyglot neighborhood, sometimes called Little Italy, on the west side of downtown Toronto. Owned by a middle-aged Polish couple, the old redbrick walk-up apartment was not far from the Trinity-Bellwoods Park, and only a few blocks from a mental hospital. Across the street from the apartment was a sparring gym where, two years earlier, Muhammad Ali, then Cassius Clay, had trained for his winning bout against the Toronto boxing legend George Chuvalo.

Mrs. Feliksa Szpakowski, a bosomy middle-aged woman with a broad face and horn-rimmed glasses who wore her gray hair in a bun, opened the aluminum storm door and greeted Galt at the front steps. In broken English, she told him she could let him a room on the second floor for eight Canadian dollars a week.

Mrs. Szpakowski showed him up to the room, which was, by Galt's standards, clean and well-appointed. The floors were tiled in new linoleum, the walls were painted a cheery canary yellow, the curtains and matching bedspread done in a bright red floral pattern. The only art on the wall was a picture of Christ and a framed needlepoint that said, "Home Sweet Home." In the alcove of the bay window was a big console television, its rabbit-ears antenna waiting to take in the news of the world.

Galt liked the room and paid Mrs. Szpakowski a week's rent. She didn't ask for a name at first, and he didn't volunteer one. But she *did* ask him, in her thick Slavic accent, what he did for a living.

"Real estate," Galt told her. He said he worked for Mann and Martel, a local firm.

That was good enough for Mrs. Szpakowski, though it seemed a little odd to her that such a well-dressed real estate agent—he was wearing his usual suit—would be interested in a room in this ethnic working-class part of town.

■

IN ATLANTA THAT same day, the King home was a hive of round-the-clock planning. Trying to decide how best to eulogize the fallen monarch of black America was testy, high-concept business. Titanic egos had flown in to offer Coretta their creative vision. The services must be flawlessly choreographed, letter-perfect. Some of King's friends wanted a massive rally to be held in Atlanta's largest football stadium; others preferred a small dignified ceremony for a select few; still others envisioned a *movable* funeral—a march to honor the man who'd accomplished so much by putting one foot in front of the other. Emotions ran high. During one of the planning sessions, Sidney Poitier and Harry Belafonte fell into an argument so bitter that the two West Indian friends wouldn't speak to each other for several years.

This funereal strategizing was going on in a house jam-packed with mourners and well-wishers. Probably the most noteworthy of the callers at 234 Sunset that afternoon was Senator Georgia Davis, who had driven to Atlanta with A. D. King's lover, Lucretia Ward, in Ward's baby blue convertible Cadillac. "I didn't want to face Coretta," Davis said, but AD thought a ritual of meeting and forgiveness was necessary for everyone's healing. They walked dolorously through the house until they found Coretta. Davis took her hand and simply said, "I'm sorry."

Coretta silently nodded, casting a beatific expression that was impossible to read. Davis knew she shouldn't be there—it was an excruciatingly awkward moment. "Sorry for what?" Davis later wrote, analyzing her own apology. "I was sorry she had lost her husband; I was sorry the world had lost a savior; and, on some level, I think I was apologizing for my relationship with her husband." She regretted hurting Coretta, but, she said, "I have never regretted being there with him. I would come whenever he called, and go wherever he wanted."

■

GALT LEFT HIS room to retrieve his suitcase from Union Station. When he returned about an hour later, he switched on the big television in his room. The rest of the weekend, he didn't leave his room except to buy newspapers and pastries at a local bakery. He'd close his door and stay there night and day. The television was always on.

Little had changed in the news since Galt had left Detroit that morning. Though many American cities still lay smoldering, the worst of the rioting was over. To Galt's relief, the weekend seemed to bring no fresh developments in the manhunt. Ramsey Clark appeared on *Meet the Press* on Sunday morning, and while he said he was confident that the killer would be found, the attorney general offered no details that indicated the FBI had a suspect. Clark didn't say so, but the case was losing some of the momentum it had enjoyed in its opening hours.

Galt, for now, was safe. That morning, Palm Sunday, was quiet across the United States, a time of sorrow and reflection after three days of convulsions. The America that Galt had left behind now seemed to be grinding to a halt for a prolonged period of mourning. The papers announced that the Academy Awards, scheduled for that night, would be postponed until after King's funeral—as would the National Hockey League play-off game in St. Louis and the season openers of at least seven Major League Baseball teams, from Cincinnati to Los Angeles.

The only person who seemed to be observing any sense of normalcy was the man ultimately in charge of the investigation—J. Edgar Hoover. The FBI director, it was reported, was spending the weekend as he often did. He was in Baltimore, at the horse races.

Much of the news that Palm Sunday came out of Memphis, where a nearly spontaneous racially mixed crowd of some ten thousand people gathered in Crump Stadium for a kind of town hall meeting. This soul-searching event, called Memphis Cares, was put on by a prominent local businessman named John T. Fisher. It went on for hours, and was, by turns, beautiful and haunting and cathartic. The Reverend Jim Lawson, the man who had invited King to Memphis in the first place, took the stage and assumed the angry tone of a biblical prophet: "This man, in the full prime of his life, is dead, shot down, executed in cold blood. We have witnessed a crucifixion in the city of Memphis. Is it a sign from God? If it *is* a sign, it is an awful one: that God's judgment is upon our land. That the time is now upon us when not one stone will be left upon another, but that this city and this nation which we love dearly will become nothing more than a roost for vultures and a smoldering heap of debris."

The television kept blaring from Galt's room; Mrs. Szpakowski thought it was odd how much time her new tenant spent in there, apparently watching TV and reading the papers. She spoke with him once during the weekend, as he was returning with newspapers bundled under his arm. "I noticed how worried he looked," she recalled. "I thought maybe he was worried about his family. I really thought he might be from the mental hospital down the street."

CORETTA SCOTT KING wore a bittersweet smile behind her widow's veil as she marched along Main Street in downtown Memphis. It was a gray, gloomy Monday, the morning after Palm Sunday, and raindrops spat at the crowd of some twenty thousand marchers following behind her. Dressed in a funereal black gown and holding hands with her now-fatherless children, Coretta held her head high as she kept up a solemn, steady pace. She gazed straight ahead, with faraway eyes that were full of sadness but spilled no tears. Keeping just in front of the Kings, step for step, was Director Holloman, who anxiously scanned the parapets and side streets for snipers.

Coretta's daughter Yolanda marched in a pink dress, while the two boys, Martin III and Dexter, wore natty sport coats and ties (the youngest, Bernice, was back home in Atlanta). The children looked all about them, distracted and awestruck, at the crying people and the soldiers and the overflying helicopters and the signs that said, HONOR KING—END RACISM and DR. KING: NOT IN VAIN and I AM A MAN. It was such a strange experience for them to be a part of, such a beautiful grim pageant—not a funeral procession, exactly, and certainly not a celebratory or cathartic New Orleans-style dirge, but its own kind of hauntingly purposeful piece of political theater. "The people were kind," Dexter King wrote years later, "yet Memphis seemed like a forbidding place, a different evil kingdom where my father was killed."

Coretta King hadn't really planned on coming back to Memphis to join Abernathy's great silent march. She had a funeral to organize in Atlanta, she had a family to look after, and she had her own world of grief. But Memphis needed her there, she realized; the movement needed her, the garbage workers needed her. So that morning, Harry Belafonte had arranged a plane for her to return to the city of her husband's murder. She arrived with the children, and her motorcade sped downtown, escorted by good-ol'-boy policemen astride fat Harley-Davidsons in swirls of flashing lights, and she saw for the first time the world of shadows that Memphis had become. She joined the march at Main and Beale—the literal and figurative intersection of white and black Memphis. It was the very spot where King had been when the rioting erupted during the March 28 demonstration, the violence that had swept King toward the dark eddy that overwhelmed him.

This time around there was no violence whatsoever. The march was silent, just as Abernathy had promised it would be: only the sound of soles scuffing on pavement. Bayard Rustin had carefully choreographed every inch of the march—and had done so with his usual good taste and raptor's eye for detail. He was thrilled and relieved by the outcome. "We gave Dr. King what he came here for," he said. "We gave Dr. King his last wish: A truly non-violent march."

It had come about through meticulous planning. The Reverend James Lawson had personally trained the hundreds of marshals of the march—many of them members of the Invaders, who only a few days earlier had been calling for burning the city down. Lawson had had flyers printed up that were handed out to the marchers: it was to be a solemn and chaste affair, a requiem. There was to be no talking, no chanting, no singing, no smoking, no chewing of gum. "Each of you is on trial today," Lawson said. "People from all over the world will be watching. Carry yourself with dignity."

Almost no uniformed policemen could be found along the route of the march. Holloman, rightly figuring his men in blue had outworn their welcome in the black community, did not want to risk provoking another confrontation. Instead, several thousand National Guardsmen lined the street—projecting a federal and presumably more neutral presence. The guardsmen's M16s were fixed with bayonets, but (though the marchers didn't know this) the rifles were kept *unloaded*.

Holloman, for his part, was much less worried about potential violence from within the ranks of the marchers than from outsiders who might be "intent on discord," as he put it. He genuinely feared that King's killer was still in Memphis and that he might attempt an encore, setting his sights on Abernathy, or Mrs. King, or any one of the score of powerful dignitaries and popular celebrities marching in the procession. His fears were well-grounded. Jim Lawson, for one, had received a death threat the previous night; someone had called his house and vowed that "once you reach Main Street, you'll be cut down." Abernathy said he was worried about people out there for whom "the spilling of one man's blood only whetted their appetite for more."

All morning, before the march started, Holloman had his men sweep the entire march route clean: All office building windows were to remain closed, and no one would be allowed to watch from a rooftop or balcony. Every potential sniper's nest was investigated and blocked off. Hundreds of undercover cops and FBI agents were posted throughout the march to look for suspicious movement.

All their precautions proved unnecessary, it turned out. The march was beautiful, pitch-perfect, decent. It moved forward without incident, a slow river of humanity stretching more than a dozen city blocks. Arranged eight abreast, the mourners silently plodded past department store windows that had been carefully cleared of lootable items, which were replaced with discreet shrines honoring King. Coretta marched at the front, with Abernathy, Young, Jackson, and Belafonte. There were clergymen, black and white, and then labor leaders and garbage workers. Farther back could be found such celebrities as Sammy Davis Jr., Bill Cosby, Ossie Davis, Dr. Benjamin Spock, Isaac Hayes, and Sidney Poitier (whose racially charged *In the Heat of the Night* was up for Best Picture in the now-postponed Academy Awards).

Most of the marchers were black, but there was also a surprising sprinkling of prominent white Memphians—some of them well-known conservatives. Foremost among these was Jerred Blanchard, a lawyer and staunch Republican city councilman who'd gotten drunk on whiskey the previous night and then awakened with something of an epiphany. "I guess it was my mother speaking to me, or my wife," Blanchard said. "I really am a right-wing Republican. I've fought in several wars . . . I've never liked labor unions. But it was decency that said, 'You get your old south end in that march. To *hell* with the country club.'"

The long column of mourners kept snaking north on Main Street toward city hall, with Mrs. King still in the lead. "There she is, there she is!" bystanders exclaimed under their breaths.

Among the businesses that Mrs. King passed was the York Arms Company, the same sporting goods store Eric Galt had visited just four days earlier. The shop's owners had removed all the hunting rifles from the windows and locked the place up tight in advance of the march. One of the items left in the window, however, was a pair of binoculars: they were Bushnell Banners, 7x35, with fully coated optics.

■

THAT SAME DAY, as Mrs. King and her legions of marchers slowly approached city hall, two of Robert Jensen's G-men, Agents John Bauer and Stephen Darlington, were driving out on Lamar Avenue, near the city's border with Mississippi. Bauer and Darlington, two rookies who both happened to hail from Pennsylvania, had been stopping at scores of economy inns all over Memphis, trolling for scraps of information— mainly about the models and makes and colors of the automobiles that motel guests had been driving the past week. It was hard, tedious work, and so far their efforts had turned up nothing promising. Now the agents pulled their bureau sedan in to the puddled parking lot of the New Rebel Motel. In the misty rain, the wipers slapped the windshield. The Confederate colonel glowered down from his sign.

Bauer and Darlington walked into the office and had a word with Anna Kelley, the New Rebel's owner. "We're with the FBI," Darlington said, and asked if she'd mind if they asked some questions. Mrs. Kelley nodded her consent.

Darlington and Bauer especially wanted her to concentrate on the night of April 3, the night before Martin Luther King was killed. Had anyone checked in to the New Rebel driving a white Ford sports car?

Anna Kelley consulted her records and soon found someone. His name was Jerry Goalsby, from Ripley, Mississippi. He had checked in to the New Rebel that night, April 3, and had left the following morning. According to the registration card, Goalsby was driving a Ford of some type.

Agent Darlington pressed her. What color? What model?

Mrs. Kelley frowned. The card only said, "Ford."

"Anyone else driving a Ford that night?" Darlington asked.

Kelley riffled through the other registration cards from April 3. "Well, yes," she said. "Here's one." A man from Alabama had checked in to the New Rebel at 7:15 p.m. that same evening. As she recalled, it was a rainy night, tornado warnings in the forecast. She never saw the man herself, and couldn't give any sort of physical description. But according to the card, he drove a Mustang with Alabama tags, license number 1-38993. The card didn't specify the car's color.

The guest—what was his name? Agent Bauer demanded.

She showed him the card. It said, in plain block lettering, "Eric S. Galt, 2608 Highland Avenue, Birmingham, Alabama."

■

AFTER HOLING UP in his room all weekend at the Szpakowski rooming house in Toronto, Eric Galt finally emerged that Monday morning and, according to his memoirs and other accounts, made his way down to the offices of Toronto's *Evening Telegram*. He told the front desk that he had come to look at back issues of the newspaper.

Soon he was led to the paper's reading room. How far back you interested in? the librarian asked.

Galt said he was interested in the 1930s, and the librarian indicated that would be on microfilm.

Galt was shown the microfilm machines, and soon a box arrived with reels dating back to the early 1930s. The librarian demonstrated how to work the machine, threading the brittle ribbon of plastic through the guides and sprockets. Galt flipped on the light and adjusted the focusing knob until a grainy world of black and white swelled into view.

For the next several hours, Galt advanced through the early 1930s, through the initial years of the Great Depression. He skipped over the headlines about Roosevelt, the Lindbergh baby kidnapping, the imprisonment of Al Capone, Amelia Earhart's transatlantic solo flight. Galt wasn't interested in news or sports, wasn't interested in history at all. With each day's paper, he always spun back to the same section: births and obituaries.

Galt was trolling for names—specifically, the names of baby boys born in the early 1930s in Toronto. As he scrolled through 1932, ten or more birth announcements caught his eye and he jotted down the particulars. One of them was named Ramon George Sneyd. "At the Women's Hospital," the paper said, "on Saturday, October 8th, to Mr. and Mrs. George Sneyd (née Gladys Mae Kilner), a son, Ramon George." Communing with these faded names in the murky light of the microfilm screen, Eric Galt was frantically looking for a way to cease being Eric Galt: he was hunting for a new identity.

It's possible that he had gathered valuable tips from someone about how to obtain a new alias, but if so, Galt never revealed who it was. In any case, the methods Galt used were ludicrously simple. "I'd read somewhere," he later said, "that Soviet spies in Canada routinely assumed the names of actual Canadians [by] taking them from gravemarkers or from the birthing notices in old newspapers. I'd been trying for years to get out of the United States on some system like this." It was a clever technique, but not exactly an esoteric one. A Royal Canadian Mounted Police report noted at the time, "Teenagers are adopting this practice to obtain birth certificates for persons over twenty-one years in order that they can frequent beverage rooms."

Satisfied with the day's catch, Galt left the reading room around noon with his collection of names and headed back for the Szpakowski rooming house. On his way, though, he likely made a brief expeditionary detour—to roam through one of Toronto's graveyards.

■

THE GREAT SILENT march in Memphis came to rest at an echoey marble plaza beside city hall, where an aluminum stage and a powerful public address system had been erected beneath the city's official insignia—cotton boll and steamboat. Rosa Parks, the grandmotherly prime mover of modern civil rights, sat on the platform with Mrs. King, Teddy Kennedy, and other dignitaries as the rear of the march caught up and filled in the public square. It was still spitting rain, but occasionally sunshine would spear through the brooding clouds; as Southerners say, the devil was beating his wife.

Several hours of speeches commenced—labor speeches and political speeches, some dry and some fiery, but all exhorting the city to do the right thing and settle the strike so that King's death could be redeemed in some way and the fatigued nation could get back to its business.

The whole program was really directed at Henry Loeb, but the mayor wasn't showing his face to this hostile crowd. In fact, he probably wasn't even inside city hall. He had been up all night, negotiating with strike representatives, prodded along by Undersecretary of Labor James Reynolds, whom President Johnson had personally dispatched from Washington to serve as an envoy. The talks had dragged on until 6:00 a.m., but the city still had not reached a resolution. The sour garbage would keep piling up on the curbsides, filling the streets with rank odors, growing happy rats.

King's death in defense of garbage workers made a certain kind of metaphorical sense, especially to the clergymen in the audience, several of whom pointed out a deep biblical irony: Jesus Christ was crucified between two thieves, *upon a mound of trash.*

Now labor leaders, one after another, came to the stage and fulminated. The Memphis strike had clearly become a cause célèbre not just for municipal workers but indeed for all labor organizations around the country: the AFL-CIO, the UAW, the UFWA, the USWA, the IUE— all had representatives on the stage. The whole scene was a white Southern businessman's worst nightmare: Reds encamped at city hall!

AFSCME's Jerry Wurf, who'd been up all night with Loeb in the negotiations, vowed: "Until we have justice and decency and morality, we will not go back to work." But it was the legendary Walter Reuther of the United Auto Workers who got lathered up into a fever pitch. "Mayor Loeb," he said, "will somehow be dragged into the 20th Century!"

All this feisty union talk resonated with many in the audience, but Memphis was not a labor town—neither by tradition nor by style—so much of it soon fell on deaf ears. Besides, the person the crowds had really come to see was Coretta Scott King. Finally, after several hours, she obliged them. Introduced by Belafonte, she rose and addressed the crowd in a calm and level voice, keeping her remarks personal. She spoke of her love for her husband, and of his love for their children. She spoke of the brevity of life. "It's not the quantity of time that's important, but the quality," she said. She sounded only one bitter note when she raised the question: "How many men must die before we can have a free and true and peaceful society? How long will it take?"

Her composure was almost otherworldly. Out in the audience, people were weeping uncontrollably, but her voice never cracked. "If Mrs. King had cried a single tear," said one woman in the crowd, "this whole city would have give way."

Her time in Memphis had inspired her, Coretta King declared. The movement would go on; she had not lost faith. "When Good Friday comes, these are the moments in life when we feel there's no hope." She looked over at her children and said with a faint smile: "But then, Easter comes."

■

THAT EVENING, WHILE Coretta King was returning to Atlanta, the FBI agents Neil Shanahan and William Saucier pulled up to 2608 Highland Avenue in Birmingham. "Economy Rooms," the little sign said out front. The two agents rapped on the door of the large pale gray two-story stucco rooming house located in the foothills of Birmingham, not far from the famed colossus of Vulcan, whose deformed physique lorded over the steel city of the South. Peter Cherpes, the Greek-American who ran Economy Rooms, came to the door. Shanahan and Saucier explained that they were with the FBI and that they were looking for a man named Eric Galt who was supposed to be living there. The Birmingham field office had gotten both the name and the Highland address from an urgent report that the Memphis agents Darlington and Bauer had filed earlier in the day.

"Eric Galt," Cherpes repeated. His mind sifted and turned. Yes, he remembered an Eric Galt. He had been a tenant at the Economy Rooms for about six weeks last year. The seventy-two-year-old Cherpes shuffled back to retrieve his three-by-five index registration cards, but they were in disarray, and he was unable to locate Galt's information.

Still, Cherpes was happy to tell the agents what he knew. Galt had stayed in room 14. He'd shown up sometime in the summer of last year—a quiet sort of guy, neatly dressed, usually wore a suit and tie. He said he was "on vacation," cooling it between jobs. He'd previously been down in Pascagoula, Mississippi, working for a company that manufactured big boats. "You couldn't imagine a nicer guy to have around," Cherpes said. "Paid the rent on time. Usually turned in early, didn't go out much. He never had telephone calls or visitors." Cherpes didn't remember Galt befriending any of the other roomers. He had a way of keeping off to himself, aloof. Another boarder at Cherpes's establishment, a twenty-six-year-old man named Charles Jack Davis, had this to say about Galt: "I don't guess there's any such thing as a 'typical person,' but my memory of him is so dim."

In the mornings, Cherpes recalled, Galt would show up right at the end of the breakfast hour, when all the other guests had left. At night, Galt spent a lot of time in the rooming house lounge, watching television.

Did he have a car? Agent Saucier asked.

Cherpes thought for a second. Yes, matter of fact, Galt *did* drive a car. He couldn't remember the make, but Cherpes recalled with some conviction that it was a white car of some kind. Galt checked out sometime in November, and he'd never returned. "I've gotten a couple pieces of mail for him since he left," Cherpes said. "I just sent them all back to the postman."

Did Galt say where he was going?

"Down to Mobile, or someplace like that. Said he'd gotten a job on a boat."

FOR THREE AND A HALF miles, the mourners crept through the azalea-bright streets of Atlanta. Under cloudless skies, a crowd of more than 150,000 tromped from Ebenezer Baptist Church toward Morehouse College, past Auburn Avenue, past downtown, past the gold-domed capitol, where Governor Lester Maddox, an ardent segregationist, was holed up with phalanxes of helmeted state troopers. Occasionally, the governor, who a few days earlier had suggested that King arranged his own murder, would part the blinds and stare disgustedly at the passing parade.

At the head of the procession, a cross of white chrysanthemums was carried along, and just behind it a team of Georgia farm mules pulled an old wooden wagon bearing the casket of polished African mahogany. King's lieutenants walked with the mule skinners—Abernathy and Lee, Bevel and Orange, Williams and Young—wearing blue denim to symbolize the hard rural folk at the heart of the coming Poor People's Campaign. It was April 9, 1968—Tuesday morning, one day after the silent march in Memphis and five days after the assassination.

Spectators watched from curbsides, from rooftops, from front porches, from the plate-glass windows of small businesses along the route. The best view, however, was probably on national television. All three networks were covering the funeral live, and more than 120 million people were said to be watching around the world. Half of America had taken leave from work; not just government offices and schools and unions and banks, but even the New York Stock Exchange had called the day off, the first time in history that Wall Street had so recognized a private citizen's death. Roulette wheels in Las Vegas would take a two-hour rest.

"Black Tuesday," people all over the country were calling this day of lamentations. April 9 was already a date etched into the national consciousness, a date fraught with racial overtones; it was, after all, the anniversary of Appomattox. A movement was now building to declare a permanent national holiday in King's name, and other ideas were floated to rename parks, office buildings, highways, and whole neighborhoods after the martyred leader. (California politicians, for example, proposed rechristening the riot-scarred Watts section of Los Angeles as "Kingtown.")

In many senses, the ceremony in Atlanta was the equivalent of a head-of-state funeral. Scores of chartered planes, and hundreds of chartered buses, had come to Georgia—disgorging every kind of commoner and every kind of royal. Several hundred garbage workers from Memphis were on hand, but also Rockefellers and Kennedys. Among the dignitaries in the swarming crowds were six presidential contenders, forty-seven U.S. congressmen, twenty-three U.S. senators, a Supreme Court justice, and official delegations from scores of foreign countries. Hollywood turned out in full force as well—Marlon Brando was there, and Paul Newman, and Charlton Heston, and any number of directors and producers. One could also spot a fair cross section from the upper registers of black sports and entertainment—Aretha Franklin, Jackie Robinson, Mahalia Jackson, Sammy Davis Jr., Jim Brown, Stevie Wonder, Floyd Patterson, Dizzy Gillespie, Diana Ross, Ray Charles, Belafonte, Poitier. Towering a foot or more above everyone else, wearing dark black shades that did nothing to camouflage his well-known visage, was Wilt "the Stilt" Chamberlain.

It was a day of odd juxtapositions, to be sure—at one point Richard Nixon was reportedly seen mingling with the actress Eartha Kitt, then playing the role of Catwoman on the popular television series *Batman*—but for anyone who had any connection to black America, or who wanted black America's vote, the funeral of Martin Luther King could not be missed. Stokely Carmichael, long a critic of King, drew stares from conservative church folk as he slipped into the church, wearing a dignified black Nehru jacket.

Jackie Kennedy was probably the most sensational guest in attendance. She had dropped by the King house earlier that morning to pay her respects to Coretta in person. The two national widows took leave of the crowded kitchen and repaired to a bedroom for a few minutes of semi-private conversation—"leaning toward each other," wrote a *Newsweek* reporter, "like parentheses around the tragic half decade." What they said to each other is lost to history, but as one witness who passed by in the hall put it, likely in terrific understatement: "There was a powerful mood in the room."

The most notably absent dignitary, on the other hand, was Lyndon Johnson. Over the preceding few days, the president had hemmed and hawed, he'd sent a dozen mixed signals, he'd listened to Secret Service agents who whispered of threats in the air and implored him to consider that the country couldn't take another assassination. But the truth was, Johnson didn't *want* to go to Martin Luther King's funeral. Although the two figures had made history together, the president could not quite bring himself to honor the man who'd so brazenly undermined him on Vietnam. In his stead, Johnson sent Vice President Hubert Humphrey and stayed in Washington.

That morning at Ebenezer Baptist, the family had held a "small" service of a thousand people. (That was all the modest church could hold, but tens of thousands gathered outside and listened over loudspeakers.) The eulogy was odd and beautiful not so much for what was said as for who was doing the eulogizing—Martin Luther King Jr. himself. The family played a tape recording from one of King's last sermons at Ebenezer, in which he talked poignantly about his own death and how he wanted to be remembered. "If any of you are around when I meet my day, I don't want a long funeral," King said at one point to the audience's soft chuckle—and if that was truly his wish, he most assuredly was not getting it. The service went on and on, and this was only the first part of an all-day extravaganza of mourning. Bored and restless, little Bernice buried herself in Coretta's lap through most of the Ebenezer service, but when she heard her father talking, she perked up.

Confused, she looked over at the open coffin to make sure he was still lying there, unmoving, and then slumped back in her mother's arms until the service let out.

Bernice and the other King children—Martin III, Dexter, and Yolanda—had been smothered with goodwill these past few days. True to his word, Bill Cosby had flown to Atlanta and personally entertained them at the house. The King children had received untold thousands of letters and telegrams from all around the world. "Dear Yolanda," one twelve-year-old girl wrote, "I believed in your father down to the bottom of my soul." Said a grade-schooler named Robert Barocas from Great Neck, New York: "Dear Dexter—if they catch the guy who shot your father, give him a sock in the mouth for me."

Now the four King children slipped out of Ebenezer with their mother, just ahead of the mourners. On Auburn Avenue, most of the flags flew at half-staff, but some flew *upside down,* sending a message not of sorrow but of bitterness and defiance. Along the funeral route, angry mutterings could be heard: Johnson had done it. Hoover had done it. Wallace had done it. The Klan, the White Citizens Council, the Memphis Police Department. The Mafia, the CIA, the National Security Agency, the generals who ran the war King had condemned. In a society already marinated in conspiracy, it was only natural that every form of collusion would be bruited about. Now, with each step the mourners took toward Morehouse, King's death seemed to gather further layers of mystique.

Throughout his civil rights career, King had drawn symbolic meaning and practical power from an Old Testament analogy: he was a black Moses, parting the waters, leading his people on their great exodus out of Egypt. It was an image he consciously and repeatedly invoked, even in his last speech in Memphis—*I may not get there with you but we as a people will get to the Promised Land.* With his assassination, however, the analogy suddenly shifted to the New Testament: King had become a black Jesus, crucified (during the Easter season, no less) for telling society radical truths. If this new analogy was to carry any biblical resonance, then the entire apparatus of the state and culture must be complicit in the Messiah's death—King Herod, Pontius Pilate, the Levites and the Pharisees, the long arm of the Roman Empire.

So as the two mules kept up their doleful clip-clop through Atlanta, the questions multiplied through the ranks of the marchers. The whole power structure, the whole zeitgeist, seemed implicated. As Coretta herself said, "There were many fingers on the rifle."

Even the most alert and conspiracy-tuned observer could not have guessed one irony along the funeral route: late that morning, the cortege passed within a few blocks of the Capitol Homes housing project, where, still sitting locked and abandoned in the parking lot, a white hardtop Mustang with Alabama plates shimmered in the eighty-degree heat.

■

NEARLY A THOUSAND miles due north, Eric Galt was in his room on Ossington Avenue with a growing collection of Toronto newspapers. He was half watching the coverage of the King funeral on the console television while working on a letter to the registrar of births—a letter that he would mail later that day.

The networks sprinkled the funeral coverage with periodic bulletins about the manhunt and also updates on the rioting, which—in most places at least—had finally ended. The statistical tally emerging from the smoldering ruins was staggering: Fires had erupted in nearly 150 American cities, resulting in forty deaths, thousands of injuries, and some twenty-one thousand arrests. In Washington alone, property damages were estimated at more than fifty million dollars. Across the nation, close to five thousand people had become "riot refugees."

The feckless author of all this chaos was sitting quietly in Toronto, Ontario, writing a letter. Mrs. Szpakowski was curious about her new tenant, who was now calling himself Paul Bridgman. There was a sadness about him, a loneliness. Once, when he was away, she went in to clean the room and noticed newsprint crumpled everywhere. Residual piles of frozen-food cartons and pastry crumbs and cellophane wrappers spoke of bad food eaten alone at odd, small hours. Bridgman never brought a visitor into the room. Not once did she hear laughter in there—just the garbled tones of the television.

Galt was starting to get out more at night, making his usual sorts of rounds. He apparently visited a brothel on Condor Avenue and made several appearances at a go-go nightclub called the Silver Dollar, where he watched the dancers and drank Molson Canadian.

Mrs. Szpakowski thought her guest was immersed in a big project of some sort. He seemed serious, rushed, preoccupied to the point of being flustered when interrupted. Sometimes he'd go out to use a pay phone in a booth down the street, always moving at a brisk, businesslike clip. Other times he would walk down to the corner of Dundas Street and hop on a streetcar.

In fact, her new tenant *was* immersed in a project, and a rather complicated one at that, one that would take several weeks to complete. Galt had been working on the ten or so names he'd retrieved the day before from the reading room of the *Telegram*. He looked up their listings in the Toronto phone book and found that two of them, Paul Bridgman and Ramon Sneyd, were both still living in Toronto—and that both resided in a suburb east of the city, not far away, known as Scarborough.

Before going the next step, Galt felt he needed to make sure these unsuspecting candidates of identity theft bore at least a vague resemblance to his own likeness. So it was "time to play detective," as Galt later put it. He went to Scarborough and loitered in the shadows by these two men's houses until he caught glimpses of them. Although on close inspection neither Bridgman (a teacher) nor Sneyd (a cop) especially looked like him, Galt was encouraged to learn that they met his general description—dark hair, fair skin, receding hairline, slender-to-medium build, Caucasian.

That was all he needed: if either one had been obese, or bald, or marked by a pronounced scar, or of another ethnicity altogether, Galt would have to start his search anew. They weren't perfect, but Bridgman and Sneyd passed.

Then Galt did something truly brazen, something that illustrated the extent of his desperation: he called Bridgman and Sneyd on the telephone, probably from the same phone booth Mrs. Szpakowski saw him talking on. One night, Paul Bridgman, who worked as the director of the Toronto Board of Education's Language Study Centre, picked up his home telephone, shortly after finishing his supper.

"Yes, hello," Bridgman later recalled hearing the caller say. "I'm a registrar with the Passport Office in Ottawa. We're checking on some irregularities in our files here and we need to know if you've recently applied for a passport."

Bridgman was naturally a little suspicious. He didn't understand why some bureaucrat in Ottawa would call on official business during the evening. "Are you sure you have the right person?"

"Bridgman," Galt assured him, spelling out the surname. "Paul Edward Bridgman. Born 10 November, 1932. Mother's maiden name—Evelyn Godden."

"Well yes, that's correct," Bridgman replied, deciding the caller must be on the level after all. Soon Bridgman freely told Galt the information he needed to know: Yes, he once had a passport, about ten years ago, but it had expired, and he had not bothered renewing it.

"Thank you very much," Galt said, and hung up.

Galt was concerned that Bridgman might pose a problem—his old passport might still be on file in Ottawa and might set off alarm bells if Galt applied for a new one. So he got back on the phone and reached Ramon Sneyd. Going through the same routine, Galt was relieved to learn from Sneyd that the man had never applied for a passport in his life.

That settled it in Galt's mind: while he might develop the Bridgman alias for sideline purposes, he would *become* Ramon George Sneyd.

■

THE SAME MORNING of the King funeral, the FBI agents Neil Shanahan and Robert Barrett were 150 miles away in Birmingham, trying to learn what they could about a man named Eric S. Galt.

Galt was in no way a suspect yet—his only crime was having checked in to the New Rebel Motel in Memphis the night before King's murder and having driven a car similar to the getaway car (which just so happened to be one of the most popular cars on the American road). The address he'd listed on the New Rebel registration card was correct (if lapsed), and the interview that Agents Saucier and Shanahan had conducted the previous night with Galt's former landlord, Peter Cherpes, hadn't particularly set off any alarm bells. The man that Cherpes had described was a drifter—an itinerant seaman and shipyard laborer with ties to the Gulf Coast—but that was surely no crime. In fact, state police failed to turn up anyone named Eric Galt with an arrest record in Alabama.

Yet the FBI was duty-bound to follow every lead—and the Galt name was just one of innumerable leads to be followed. Inquiries around Mobile and the Gulf Coast turned up no Eric Galt, as did phone calls to Seafarers International and other maritime unions. A quick check with the motor vehicle division in Montgomery did reveal that Eric S. Galt had applied for an Alabama driver's license in September 1967, noting on his application that he was a "merchant seaman, unemployed." Further checks with vehicle registration records showed that an Eric Galt did indeed have a currently titled, licensed, and registered white two-door 1966 Mustang, bearing the same license plate number he provided on the New Rebel registration form—1-38993.

Working off the VIN, the FBI quickly traced the car back to its previous owner, a Birmingham man named William D. Paisley who was a sales manager for a Birmingham lumber company.

Shanahan and Barrett showed up at Paisley's place of work and asked him some questions—never mentioning that they were investigating the assassination of Martin Luther King. Paisley only vaguely recalled the man, but yes, he had sold a pale yellow 1966 Mustang to an Eric Galt some eight months earlier, back in August 1967. Paisley had offered the car for sale in the classified ads in the *Birmingham News* for $1,995. He recalled that Galt, after phoning the house and making arrangements to meet, then came to the Paisley residence by taxi on the early evening of August 28. The man carefully examined the Mustang and seemed to like it. It had whitewall tires, a push-button radio, and a remote-control outside mirror. The tires had had a bit too much wear—they were clearly bald in places—but the body was in near-perfect shape. "This is one of the cleanest ones I've seen," Galt enthused.

"You want to take her for a spin?" Paisley asked.

Galt said no, he didn't have a current driver's license. His previous license, he said, was issued back in Louisiana—and anyway, it had expired, and he didn't want to risk getting stopped by the police. So Paisley got behind the wheel and cranked up the V-8 engine, and Galt hopped in the passenger seat. They tooled around the neighborhood for a quarter hour, while Galt fiddled with the knobs and dials and played with the push-button radio.

Galt told Paisley he liked the red leather interior but wasn't so sure about the pale yellow paint color, which was so light it was almost white. (Galt didn't tell Paisley the real reason for his distaste, but as Galt later put it, "If you are going to do something illegal, I'd rather not have a white car to do it in.") When they got back to the house, Galt thought about the car a few more minutes and then, without even looking under the hood or attempting to negotiate the price, told Paisley, "I'll take it off your hands."

Shaking on the deal and agreeing to meet the next morning to complete the transaction, they talked a bit while standing outside Paisley's house. Galt said that he worked on a Mississippi River barge and that he had a lot of money saved up. He said he'd recently been through an ugly divorce—his ex-wife was an Alabama woman, he said, from the mountain country up around Homewood.

When Paisley offered his sympathies, Galt replied, "Yeah, that's the way it goes."

They met the next morning outside the Birmingham Trust National Bank—"that's where I keep my money," Galt had told Paisley. Galt, who was wearing a sport jacket and an open-collared shirt, said he had $1,995 in cash, fresh from the bank. From his shirt pocket, he removed a prodigious wad of bills—mostly twenties, but a few hundreds as well—and started counting the money out in the open. "*Man*, let's be careful with this kind of money," Paisley said, and they moved into the foyer of the bank to finish the transaction.

Paisley gave Galt the title and a bill of sale and then fished in his pocket for the keys. They shook hands and that was it—Paisley never saw the man again.

■

IN THE HISTORIC quadrangle at Morehouse College, the mule-drawn wagon wound its way to the steps of Harkness Hall, and the large public requiem began. Some 150,000 people crammed onto the campus green and stood for hours in the oppressive heat beneath jumbled canopies of parasols. Mahalia Jackson sang "Take My Hand, Precious Lord," the spiritual King had asked Ben Branch to play "real pretty" moments before he was shot on the Lorraine balcony. So many old ladies fainted in the crowd that the lengthy schedule of eulogies had to be radically truncated. The final speaker, and the marquee attraction, was Dr. Benjamin Elijah Mays, the president emeritus of Morehouse, a distinguished lion of an orator and King's most beloved mentor. The grizzled theologian, whose parents had been former slaves, spoke plainly, with a measured indignation in his voice.

"I make bold to assert," Mays said, "that it took more courage for King to practice nonviolence than it took his assassin to fire the fatal shot. The assassin is a coward; he committed his foul act, and fled. But make no mistake, the American people are in part responsible. The assassin heard enough condemnation of King and of Negroes to feel that he had public support. He knew that millions hated King."

Mays went on to deliver a majestic eulogy in the black Baptist tradition, leaving bitterness behind and building toward a triumphant crescendo. "He believed especially that he was sent to champion the cause of the man furthest down. He would probably say that if death had to come, there was no greater cause to die for than fighting to get a just wage for garbage collectors. He was supra-race, supra-nation, supra-class, supra-culture. He belonged to the world and to mankind. Now he belongs to posterity."

The great funeral broke up, and a smaller crowd of family and friends followed the hearse in a slow motorcade to South View Cemetery, a grand old place that had been created in the 1860s when Atlanta's blacks grew weary of burying their dead through the rear entrance of the city graveyard. This would not be King's final resting place—he was to be only temporarily buried here with his maternal grandparents until a permanent memorial could be built beside Ebenezer Church. Beneath flowering dogwoods, Ralph Abernathy rose to address the winnowed crowd. Drawn and weak, Abernathy had not eaten since the assassination. Like the old days when he and King went to jail together, he was fasting, to purify himself for the trials ahead.

"The grave is too narrow for his soul," Abernathy said, tears streaming down his face. "But we commit his body to the ground. We thank God for giving us a leader who was willing to die, but not willing to kill." Then a retinue of attendants rolled the mahogany casket into a crypt of white Georgia marble that was inscribed:

MARTIN LUTHER KING JR.

JANUARY 15, 1929–APRIL 4, 1968

"FREE AT LAST, FREE AT LAST, THANK GOD ALMIGHTY I'M FREE AT LAST"

As the last of the crowds fell away, Martin Luther King Sr. laid his head on the cool stone of his son's mausoleum and openly wept.

By April 10, the day after King's funeral, the hunt for the man in 5B had begun to take on a momentum of its own. Working around the clock, Ramsey Clark had set up a situation room on the fifth floor of the Justice Department. Cots were placed in various corners of the office, and food was brought in to sustain the teams of bureaucrats working on the legal aspects of the case. "It was a huge operation," Clark later recalled. "I didn't go home, I just stayed there all the time, I had a little place in my office where I'd sleep. It was the biggest investigation ever conducted, for a single crime, in U.S. history."

Several times a day, Clark met with Deke DeLoach over at the FBI nerve center and demanded to hear the latest from the bureau. DeLoach hated these briefings, of course, but he knew he had no choice but to work with the attorney general—while doing his best to keep Clark and Hoover at arm's length. Sadly, on April 10, there wasn't much to report. After an initial flurry of activity, the manhunt had seemingly ground to a halt. Now the case was fraying into multiple slender strands. Over the past few days, the FBI offices had been flooded with crazy leads, sensational rumors, and tantalizing tips that the bureau agents dutifully followed but that never seemed to pan out.

The case now had an official name at least. On all memos and enci-phered Teletype messages, in all FBI and Justice Department correspon-dence, the investigation was to be called MURKIN, a bit of bureaucratic shorthand that simply stood for "Murder, King." Some three thousand agents were now working the case, which was now termed a "special in-vestigation." Although the main activity was still to be found in Robert Jensen's office in Memphis, and in Birmingham, already the investigation had spread out to every field office in the country. In hopes of hunting down biographical traces of Eric Galt, or Harvey Lowmeyer, or John Willard, FBI investigators were now combing through every known repository of names—voter registration lists, parole board lists, telephone directories, utility company records. They were checking with rental car agencies, airlines, credit card companies, motor vehicle divisions, the IRS, and the Selective Service. So far, nothing very promising had turned up.

J. Edgar Hoover, meanwhile, had been frantically sending out Tele-type messages to all the FBI "territories," underscoring the urgency of the investigation. "We are continuing with all possible diligence and dis-patch," Hoover wrote to all special agents in charge on April 9. "The in-vestigation is nationwide in scope as countless suspects are being processed and physical evidence is being traced. You may be completely assured that this investigation will continue on an expedited basis until the matter has been finally resolved. Leads are to be afforded immediate, thorough, imaginative attention. You must exhaust all possibilities from such leads as any one lead could result in the solution of this most im-portant investigation. SAC will be held personally responsible for any failure to promptly and thoroughly handle investigations in this matter."

Attorney General Clark was satisfied that the FBI, despite its his-tory of dirty tricks with respect to King and his organization, was turning over every stone and working in all haste to find the assassin. But he had no shortage of questions for DeLoach. At this juncture, Clark asked, what is your view of the killer?

"A racist," DeLoach replied. "Maybe a member of a hate group. Well groomed, but somebody who would feel at home in a flophouse. And not too bright. Obviously he hadn't planned the crime very well."

"What are the possibilities of a conspiracy?" Clark wanted to know.

"So far, there's no real evidence he had help, either in planning or execution. If he had, his escape would have been better and he would have left fewer witnesses."

The bureau, DeLoach informed Clark, was now exhausting an inordinate amount of time and energy tracking down what seemed to be wild leads. A combination of two factors—the posting of a reward for finding the killer, and the release of an artist's composite sketch to the media—had rapidly accelerated the inflow of these sorts of calls. While the portrait of the assassin published in newspapers and magazines from coast to coast did catch the aquiline sharpness of Galt's nose, it was otherwise so bland and generic-looking it could have been anyone. Still, people swore they saw the assassin in Rock Hill, South Carolina; in Mountain View, California; in Joplin, Missouri; at LaGuardia Airport.

"Tips" arrived from all points of the compass. From the Denver area came a rumor that the killer was an Italian-American associated with a racist outfit called the Minutemen. From North Carolina came a lead that Bobby Ray Graves, the Exalted Cyclops of the Klan in Boiling Springs, was behind the assassination. Out of Baltimore, a local tavern owner reported to police that he overheard "a Cuban" saying that he'd recently been in Memphis and that he knew King was going to be killed five days before it happened. A respected black grocer and civil rights activist from west Tennessee came forward with a chilling story that, only a few hours before the assassination, he'd overheard a Memphis meat market owner, an Italian with possible Mafia ties in New Orleans, yelling into the telephone, "Shoot the son-of-a-bitch on the balcony and then you'll get paid."

Most of the tips were clearly from well-meaning people, but others bore a rascally quality. The Miami field office received an anonymous note scribbled on a scrap of paper that said, cryptically, "Go to La-Grange, Georgia, and you will have King's killer." The writer claimed he'd met the assassin, whom he described as "weird and funny talking," at a recent gun show in Memphis and that the man had bought a .30-06 "much like the gun that killed King."

■

FOR A TIME, it seemed that every psychotic street person, every muttering hobo and colorful transient, was picked up for questioning. A surprising number of tips came from people seeking to implicate their own family members. A Louisiana caller said her ne'er-do-well son drove a 1967 white Mustang and hadn't been heard from since the day of the assassination. A woman from Chicago said the killer looked "an awful lot like my ex-husband."

God help anyone whose last name was Galt, Willard, or Lowmeyer— or any spelling variation thereof. John Willards were found in Los Angeles, Des Moines, and Spokane. Another John Willard, located in Oxford, Mississippi, was interrogated long enough to establish that he had been mowing his own lawn at the time of the assassination. A Reverend Ralph Galt in Birmingham was questioned repeatedly. "We don't know a thing about this person," his wife told the press. "We've checked all the relatives we can think of—and we wonder if it's not a fictitious name."

For a short time, the FBI entertained the possibility that the killer may have been the jealous husband of one of King's lovers—or, more likely, that a jealous husband may have paid someone else to carry off a hit. In Los Angeles, agents interviewed a prominent black dentist who was the husband of King's longtime mistress there, but the questioning went nowhere. In Memphis, meanwhile, Jensen's agents briefly investigated the possibility that the Invaders—having fallen into a bitter argument with King's staff the very day of the assassination—may have been behind King's death, but again, this line of inquiry proved barren.

Then a woman in Memphis called Holloman's office with a tip that raised an eerie possibility: The night after the assassination she had watched a local TV special on Dr. King that, for the first time, aired extensive footage of his final "Mountaintop" speech. When the camera panned the audience at Mason Temple, the woman spotted a mysterious white male who looked a good bit like the artist rendering. To her, the man briefly caught in the bright lights looked uncomfortable and out of place. Police detectives went to the local NBC affiliate and reviewed the footage. Soon they found the frames the caller was referring to, and sure enough an unknown and awkward-looking white male momentarily flashed on the screen—an odd man out "whose actions did not coincide with the male coloreds and female coloreds at the rally." The grainy image was too blurred and brief to make out very much, but the question inevitably arose: Was King's killer present at his final talk? Was the assassin watching as King looked out over the audience and talked about threats from "some of our sick white brothers"?

Another call came from the Mexican consulate in Memphis. Rolando Veloz, the acting consul, told local police that on April 3, he issued a visitor's permit to a suspicious-looking young man who bore a "striking resemblance" to the broadcast description of King's assassin. Veloz said the man gave the name John Scott Candrian with what proved to be a phony address and telephone number in Chicago. "He came here the day before the slaying," said Veloz. "I asked him what was the purpose of his trip. He hesitated for a moment, then answered, 'I'm just going to Mexico.'" On the application, the man said he would enter Mexico on or about April 13 and that he planned to visit the Pacific seaport of Mazatlán.

This tip was considered strong enough that the FBI immediately expanded the MURKIN investigation to Mexico and enlisted the support of the *federales* while keeping a close eye on all crossing points along the border. Mexican authorities soon made a potentially astonishing discovery: the bullet-riddled body of what appeared to be a white male American tourist washed up on the beach in Puerto Vallarta. The unidentified corpse vaguely resembled the man in 5B, but the hands were so shrunken and decomposed that experts, hoping to compare the dead man's fingerprints with the prints on file at the crime lab in Washington, couldn't get an accurate impression, even after injecting the fingers with fluid to puff them up. This investigatory cul-de-sac raised a possibility that was voiced with increasing dread throughout the ranks of the FBI: that the object of their massive search may already be dead—an assassinated assassin, killed off by the very conspirators who had hired him.

■

THROUGHOUT THE WEEK, Mrs. John Riley had been thinking about the Mustang parked outside her window at the Capitol Homes housing project in Atlanta. What was it doing there, untouched for five long days? Why hadn't anyone come to retrieve it? She worried and stewed over what to do. She talked with her neighbors about it. She even consulted with the preacher at her church. But it was her thirteen-year-old son, Johnny, who convinced her to pick up the phone.

On the afternoon of April 10, the day after the King funeral, Johnny heard a report on the television. A newscaster said the authorities were monitoring the border with Mexico, looking for the man who had applied for a tourist permit in Memphis a day before the assassination. Though that report was based on information that would soon prove to be specious, it sparked his adolescent imagination.

"Mom," Johnny said. "That car has stickers on the window. They say, 'Turista.' Whoever drove it has been to Mexico."

Mrs. Riley was sufficiently convinced that she found the number for the local FBI office and put in a call. Whoever picked up the phone wasn't particularly impressed by what this demure housewife had to say. Over the past five days, the overworked and under-rested agents in the Atlanta field office had ventured on every kind of snipe hunt and fool's errand. This sounded like another one.

"I suggest you call the Atlanta police," the man told her, and furnished a number for the stolen-auto division.

She dialed the number and again met with a tepid response. Roy Lee Davis, with the auto theft division, ploddingly took down the information and hung up. He checked with the stolen-auto files and found nothing reported for a 1966 white Mustang with Alabama plates, and nearly filed the information away as extraneous and unremarkable. Then something told Davis to share this piece of information with some Atlanta detectives down the hall who'd been following the King assassination case—and their curiosity was piqued.

Later that night, a cruiser from the Atlanta Police Department slipped into the Capitol Homes parking lot and drove up to the Mustang. Many of the apartment windows were bathed in the blue murk of television sets—the postponed Academy Awards were on. (*In the Heat of the Night* edged out *Bonnie and Clyde* and *The Graduate* for Best Picture, and Katharine Hepburn claimed her second Best Actress Oscar, this time for her role in *Guess Who's Coming to Dinner*, a controversial movie, also starring Poitier, about an interracial marriage.)

Mrs. Riley peeked out her window and spotted the cruiser. She naturally assumed that the police had come in response to her call, but was surprised and a little deflated that after only a cursory inspection, they quickly pulled away from the Mustang and drove off the lot, seemingly uninterested. Figuring the Mustang must have "checked out" after all, Mrs. Riley went back to watching the Academy Awards—and didn't give it another thought.

■

THE FOLLOWING MORNING, while parts of Washington were digging out from the ashen ruins of the riots, Lyndon Johnson presided over a ceremony in the East Room of the White House. On this day, Thursday, April 11, the president was signing into law the Civil Rights Act of 1968, perhaps the last great bill of the movement. The act—whose brisk passage in the House the previous day had largely been in response to the King assassination—made it a federal crime to discriminate in the sale, rental, and financing of some 80 percent of the nation's dwellings. It also gave federal prosecutors increased powers to go after murderers of civil rights figures.

With a mixed throng of white and black leaders looking on, the president now sat at a desk and took up his fountain pen. Calling the act's passage "a victory for all Americans," Johnson declared: "With this bill, the voice of justice speaks again."

It was, some pundits said, the dying gasp of the civil rights era.

■

IN TORONTO THAT same morning, Eric Galt was walking down Yonge Street, intent on an errand of disguise. He turned in to Brown's Theatrical Supply Company and bought a makeup kit. Playing with the cosmetics later that day, he applied a little foundation and powder and eyebrow liner. He parted his hair in a different way and was a bit more conservative with his hair cream. Then he donned a dark suit, a narrow tie with a discreet waffle weave, and his best white dress shirt. As a final touch, he put on a recently purchased pair of dark horn-rimmed glasses, which, sitting on his surgery-sharpened nose, gave him a vaguely professorial cast.

Looking in a mirror, Galt was happy with the transformation: Ramon Sneyd was now ready for his close-up.

Sometime in the afternoon of April 11, he walked into the Arcade Photo Studio, also on Yonge Street, and met the manager, Mrs. Mabel Agnew. He told her he needed some passport photos.

Mrs. Agnew was happy to oblige. She led him to the rear of the studio, which was decorated with a vanity mirror and travel poster of Holland, and sat him on a revolving piano stool before a gray-white screen. Galt doubtless hated the whole ritual, as always, but this time he peered just off camera and kept his eyes wide open, throwing everything he had into playacting his new role. Mrs. Agnew couldn't get her subject to smile, but she finally managed to snap off a decent shot. He left while the pictures developed and returned a few hours later. For two dollars, he retrieved three passport-sized prints.

The image turned out well. His countenance bore a discerning quality, a certain cosmopolitan panache. He could pass for a lawyer, or an engineer, or an international businessman. He almost looked handsome.

■

AT EXACTLY THE same hour that Galt's passport photos were ripening in a darkroom vat, FBI agents in Atlanta were about to enjoy the week's greatest breakthrough. At four minutes past four o'clock that afternoon, a convoy of bureau sedans converged on the Capitol Homes project. In a ruckus of slamming doors and squawking radios, a dozen FBI agents crawled from the cars and swarmed around the abandoned vehicle.

It was no mistake—this was without a doubt Eric S. Galt's car: a white two-door V-8 1966 Mustang hardtop with whitewall tires and a red interior, VIN 6TO7C190647, bearing Alabama license plate number 1-38993.

While some agents inspected the vehicle, taking measurements, notes, and photographs, others soon fanned out and began interviewing Capitol Homes tenants. *Did you see the individual who parked this car? Can you give a physical description? Had you ever seen the man before?* Kids teetered on bicycles, spellbound by all the commotion, but it was more excitement than most of the tenants had bargained for. "There must have been a billion of 'em out here," one lady said. Complained another: "I had to go to bed. It made me sick, so many of them asking me the same thing over and over and over."

Soon a tow truck appeared in the parking lot. Guarded by a police escort, the wrecker hauled the Mustang off to a federal building at the corner of Peachtree and Baker streets. There, deep inside a large locked garage, a detail of agents in latex gloves worked the car over, systematically emptying all its contents and dusting its surfaces for fingerprints.

Every inch of the impounded car was examined. Agents took soil samples from the tire wells, fluid samples from the engine, sweepings from the carpets, seats, and trunk. Fibers, hairs, and several high-quality latent palm prints were teased from the Mustang's recesses and contours. From the glove compartment, inspectors found a pair of sunglasses and a case. From the trunk, they retrieved, among other objects, a pair of men's shorts, a pillow, a fitted sheet, various tools, a container for a Polaroid camera, and a small contraption that appeared to be an air-release cable for a camera shutter. On the right window, a prominent sticker said, "Dirección General de Registro Federal de Automóviles, 1967 Octubre Turista, Aduana de Nuevo Laredo, Tam."

All these contents and samplings were inventoried, wrapped in plastic, and boxed up to be personally sent by air courier to the crime lab in Washington. But one item found on the Mustang urgently spoke for itself and required not a second of lab analysis. Affixed to the inside of its left door, a small sticker showed that Eric Galt had had the oil changed in his Mustang at 34,289 miles. The sticker said, "Cort Fox Ford, 4531 Hollywood Boulevard."

■

WITHIN AN HOUR of the Mustang's discovery in Atlanta, Special Agent Theodore A'Hearn of the FBI's Los Angeles field office arrived at the service desk of the Cort Fox Ford dealership in Hollywood, California, and met a man named Budd Cook Jr. One of the garage's service specialists, Cook dug into his records and soon found the work order, which he himself had taken down only a month and a half earlier. The paperwork was made out to Eric S. Galt and dated February 22, 1968.

He brought the car in at 8:00 that morning, Cook noted. It was a 1966 Mustang.

Do you remember what Galt looked like? A'Hearn asked.

Cook searched his memory and came up short. Hundreds, possibly thousands, of customers had passed through this garage over the previous months. Regrettably, he could not furnish a description of any sort.

"But," Cook said, "Galt's address is right here on the work order."

■

THE NEXT MORNING, April 12, Agent Thomas Mansfield made his way to the large and slightly down-at-the-heels St. Francis Hotel at 5533 Hollywood Boulevard. He asked to speak with the proprietor, and presently a man named Allan Thompson appeared at the front desk. As the resident manager, Thompson had lived at the St. Francis for nearly two years and knew the history of the place, all its various denizens and comings and goings.

Yes, Thompson said. He recalled a man named Eric Galt. Thompson found a registration card that showed Galt had lived at the St. Francis for about two months, checking out on March 17. He resided in room 403 and paid eighty-five dollars a month in rent. "He had dark hair, combed back," Thompson remembered. "Slender to medium build. Quiet, wore conservative business suits. Kept irregular hours. Far as I could tell, he was not employed." Thompson said another tenant now occupied 403, and that Galt had not left any belongings in the room.

"Did he give any indication where he was going next?" Agent Mansfield asked.

"Well, yes," Thompson said, producing a change-of-address card that said, "General Delivery, Main Post Office, Atlanta, Georgia." The card was dated March 17, 1968, and signed "Eric S. Galt."

■

THAT SAME DAY, April 12, two other FBI agents, Lloyd Johnson and Francis Kahl, were only a few blocks away, speaking to a woman named Lucy Pinela. Ms. Pinela was the manager of the Home Service Laundry and Dry Cleaning. Over the past week, the FBI had searched all over the country for laundries that used the Thermo-Seal marking machine—the same identification machine that had produced the tiny laundry tag found on the pair of undershorts left with the bundle now in FBI possession in Washington. The FBI's exhaustive search had led them, most promisingly, to Southern California, where numerous laundries were using the Thermo-Seal system. One of those laundries was Home Service.

Yes, Ms. Pinela told the agents, her shop had been using the

Thermo-Seal machine for a while now. At their request, she stepped back into the workroom and showed them the apparatus and even stamped out a few samples on articles of clothing to demonstrate how the machine worked and what the resulting tags looked like.

Agents Johnson and Kahl then showed her a photograph of the undershorts found in Memphis, with the tag plainly visible: 02B-6. Ms. Pinela recognized the sequence immediately. On closer inspection, another employee who regularly used the marker said she was positive the tag in question had been stamped at Home Service because the 0 was partially cut off—a defect peculiar to their Thermo-Seal machine.

The owner of Home Service, a man named Louis Puterman, then produced some documents from his office files. After a little rummaging, he came up with something that fairly screamed off the page: laundry ticket number 3065, bearing Thermo-Seal tag number 02B-6. The ticket was made out to "E. Galt."

Once she saw the name, Lucy Pinela recalled the customer. Galt never left an address or a phone number, but he was a regular, she said; he'd been bringing his clothes to Home Service for months. He was about thirty-five years old, brown haired, and had a narrow nose. "He usually brought in button-down dress shirts," she said. "Never work clothes."

He was very regular in his habits, she said. He would bring in his dirty clothes every Saturday afternoon and, at the same time, pick up the previous week's clothes. Then, for some reason, he stopped coming in. She hadn't seen him for about a month.

■

WHILE THIS INTERVIEW was taking place, other FBI agents in Los Angeles learned that Eric Galt had briefly secured a telephone service in his room. Although the line had been disconnected in late January, the Pacific Telephone and Telegraph Company was able to supply the FBI with records of every outgoing and incoming call related to that number—469-8096. This led the agents on an interesting series of goose chases.

One of the numbers turned out to be that of a woman who had sold Galt a console Montgomery Ward TV set through a newspaper classified ad. Another number was listed in the name of Elizabeth Pitt, a woman who had placed a singles ad in a lonely hearts club broadsheet: "Tall skinny auburn haired divorcee, 41, seeks prospective husband with patience," the ad read. Galt had apparently called Pitt with the idea of getting her to appear in a pornographic film, but the phone conversation went nowhere, and they never even went out on a date. A third number turned out to be the Wallace campaign headquarters in Century City—which, for the time being, meant nothing to investigating agents. Probably the most productive find in the bank of numbers Galt had called was that of the National Dance Studio in Long Beach, California.

Special Agent George Aiken promptly drove down to the studio, which was located at 2026 Pacific Avenue in Long Beach, in a low-slung building with palm trees out front. There he met the owner, Mr. Rodney Arvidson, who had a vivid memory of his former student. In a large room with a record player and blocking-tape marks on the parquet floor, Galt had taken cha-cha, fox-trot, and swing lessons for several months. "He told me he'd been down in Mexico, sometime in 1967, and that he owned a restaurant," Arvidson said. "He said he was fluent in Spanish, but when I would speak to him in Spanish, he wouldn't say anything back, which led me to believe he wasn't actually conversant."

"How did Galt dress?" Agent Aiken asked.

"Always wore a shirt and tie. He had a pair of shiny black alligator loafers." Arvidson remembered thinking that Galt's appearance didn't jibe with his personality—that he dressed like a businessman, but talked and carried himself like an uneducated and socially awkward person from a decidedly rural, working-class background. "He couldn't seem to relax," Arvidson said. "He didn't smile easily. He was pleasant but evasive—he would never talk about himself and he wouldn't look you in the eye. He had a crooked smile. He said he was a merchant seaman and wanted to return to the sea."

Though Galt seemed to be unemployed, he had plenty of money. Every time Arvidson informed him that another payment was due, Galt would reach into his trousers and happily peel off some twenties from a large roll of bills. All told, he paid more than four hundred dollars for dance lessons and never seemed to balk at the fees.

Arvidson found a card in his office files showing that Galt had previously taken fox-trot and cha-cha dancing lessons while living in

Alabama. "Leaving in a couple of months to work on a ship," the card said. "Wants to travel." A box marked *S* was checked—indicating that Galt was single.

Cathryn Norton, a dance instructor at the studio, told Agent Aiken she had frequently given Galt lessons. "He was a fair dancer," she allowed. "But he wasn't friendly with anyone. He always wore a suit, kept his fingernails clean and neatly trimmed." Norton recalled that he sometimes smoked filter cigarettes and that he had "a nervous habit of pulling on his earlobes with his fingers."

One night someone connected with the dance school hosted a private party at his house, and about twenty people showed up. "Galt came and left alone," Norton recalled. "He had some punch and stayed pretty much to himself. He was like a clam."

Galt's last lesson was on February 12. "When he quit," Arvidson recalled, "all he said was that he wanted to open his own bar and restaurant. He said he was going to enroll in some school to learn how to be a bartender."

■

"YES," TOMAS LAU said, "Eric Galt was a student here." A suave man with a trim mustache, Lau was director of the International School of Bartending at 2125 Sunset Boulevard in Los Angeles. The FBI agents Theodore A'Hearn and Richard Raysa, after canvassing all the bartending schools in Southern California, had quickly found Lau's establishment.

Lau believed Galt was "diligent and well-coordinated" and had the potential to become a fine bartender. Lau thought so much of Galt that he even went to the trouble of finding him a job. "But he declined," Lau recalled. "He said he was going to visit his brother somewhere and didn't want a job. He said he'd call me if he still needed a job when he got back."

Another pupil at the school, a man named Donald Jacobs, recalled that Galt said he'd been a cook in the merchant marine and worked on riverboats and barges on the Mississippi. Jacobs doubted this was true, because he noticed that Galt's hands "didn't appear calloused or used to hard work."

Beyond the fact that Galt had "thin lips and a slight Southern accent," Lau had trouble recalling what his former pupil looked like. Then he remembered graduation day. "I've got a picture of him somewhere," he volunteered.

"How's that?" Agent A'Hearn couldn't believe what he'd just heard.

"All our graduates get their picture taken with me and the diploma," Lau explained. "It's something we've always done around here."

Lau scoured his scrapbooks and soon found the photograph, which was snapped at the school on March 2. For the first time, an FBI agent was peering at the image of the man now being hunted by three thousand bureau colleagues across the country.

There stood Lau, proudly posing with his student—a slender, narrow-nosed, dark-haired, fair-skinned man wearing a tuxedo and a bow tie. The portrait looked pretty much like all the other graduation photos gracing Lau's scrapbooks, though Agent A'Hearn did notice one peculiarity: Galt's eyes were shut.

ARMED AT LAST with a photograph of the manhunt's prime suspect, the FBI began to assert its true institutional might—pressing with renewed focus and multi-tentacled determination all across the country. In Los Angeles, agents canvassed the banks in the vicinity of the St. Francis Hotel in search of any monetary trails left by Eric Galt. This proved a hugely successful tack: Although Galt had kept no savings or checking accounts and had failed to establish any credit history, at the Bank of America in Hollywood the agents found that an Eric Galt, in fact, had purchased a series of modest money orders in late 1967 and early 1968. Several of the orders were made out to an establishment in Little Falls, New Jersey, called the Locksmithing Institute.

Within an hour, agents in New Jersey visited the "institute" and learned that it offered correspondence courses in key cutting, lock picking, safecracking, alarm wiring, and other skills of the trade to students all over the world. Before enrolling in the course, Galt had signed an oath swearing that he'd never been convicted of burglary, adding: "I shall never use my knowledge to aid or commit a crime." According to the Locksmithing Institute's records, Galt's last lesson had been mailed to him, only a week earlier, at 113 Fourteenth Street Northeast in Atlanta.

This lead was immediately flashed to the Atlanta field office, and in minutes a team of agents, driving an unmarked car, pulled up to Jimmie Garner's rooming house on Fourteenth Street. Believing there was a strong possibility that Galt was still hiding inside, the agents stayed in the shadows and kept the building under close surveillance; for the first day, the FBI refrained from asking any questions for fear of exposing themselves—or prematurely tipping off the media.

Two other agents, meanwhile, disguised themselves as hippies—bell-bottom jeans, beads, the whole shtick—and rented a room next to Galt's. Inside, they discovered that the two rooms shared a connecting door; by placing their ears on wood panels, they were able to determine to their satisfaction that Galt's room was vacant. They tried to open the door but found it was locked. A call was then placed to Deke DeLoach in Washington, who said, "Take the door off its hinges if you have to, but get in there!"

The tie-dyed agents did as they were told, and with a little handiwork they were soon inside Galt's room. The dark and sparsely furnished space hardly seemed lived-in, but after poking around in dressers and under tables, they spotted a few telltale artifacts. They found a booklet titled "Your Opportunities in Locksmithing" and a portable Zenith TV. Behind a desk they found a pamphlet, "What Is the John Birch Society?" They noted a small stash of grocery supplies, residue from the budget repasts of a man who appeared to be both a hermit and a pack rat—Nabisco saltines, Kraft Catalina French dressing, Carnation evaporated milk, Maxwell House instant coffee, French's mustard, a package of lima beans.

Also scattered about the room were a number of road maps—the kind usually handed out for free at gas stations—maps that, taken together, seemed to offer a succinct chart of Galt's travels. There were maps of Los Angeles, Mexico, California, Arizona, Texas and Oklahoma, Louisiana, Birmingham, and the southeastern United States.

Finally the agents located a map of Atlanta, which was marked up in pencil. Inscribed on the map were four little circles that, upon closer inspection, seemed to have a chilling import: one circle was near Martin Luther King's home; one indicated Ebenezer Baptist Church and the SCLC office; another designated the approximate location of Jimmie

Garner's rooming house; and a final circle marked the Capitol Homes public housing project, where the Mustang had been abandoned. It seemed clear evidence of an organized plot; not only had Galt charted King's world—and likely stalked him—but he had staked out, well ahead of time, a safe and inconspicuous place where he could ditch his car.

The agents left everything as they'd found it, and after installing the door back on its hinges, they retreated to their "room." They'd learned enough from their surreptitious, albeit legally tenuous, reconnaissance to give DeLoach what he needed. Galt was not living there; there were no clothes, no suitcases, no signs of tenancy other than those old groceries. Now it was time to come out of the shadows—to question Jimmie Garner, issue a search warrant, and confiscate all the assorted belongings in Galt's room.

■

OVER THE PAST few days, FBI agents in Los Angeles had been developing their own series of intriguing leads. While they were conducting follow-up interviews at the bartending school, Tomas Lau had found in his files a sheet of paper on which Galt had listed three local "references," with addresses. They were Charlie Stein, Rita Stein, and Marie Tomaso.

Special Agents William John Slicks and Richard Ross found Charlie Stein at his apartment at 5666 Franklin Avenue, just around the corner from the St. Francis. From the start it was clear that Stein was one odd duck—by turns cagey, rambling, and cosmic—but he was cooperative enough. He told the agents the story of how he met Galt; how his sister Rita needed someone to pick up her distressed twin girls in Louisiana; how she'd managed to convince Stein to accompany Galt in his Mustang on a cross-continental drive to New Orleans around Christmastime; and how Galt, before going on the trip, had insisted on the bizarre precondition that Stein, Rita, and their cousin Marie Tomaso first lend their signatures to George Wallace's California primary effort.

"He said he'd been in the Army," Stein recalled. "He said he was from Alabama, and that he planned to go *back* to Alabama one day. He said that if the Negro wanted to live free, he should move to the North or the West. But if the Negro wants to be a slave, he should remain in the South."

Stein's memories of the drive to New Orleans were vague at first, but when he was reinterviewed the next day, he began to open up. "Galt had money to spend—he said he was part owner of a bar down in Mexico but that he'd sold his interest. He stopped a few times to make long-distance calls at phone booths. He liked hamburgers with everything on them, and liked to sip a beer while he drove. He was always playing country and western music on the car radio."

What did he look like? the agents asked him. *How did he dress?*

"He wore a brown suit and a watch. I'll tell you this, the guy put on an excessive amount of hair cream."

Agents Ross and Slicks found that Stein's cousin Marie Tomaso had sharp recollections of her own. As a cocktail waitress at the Sultan Room and as a fellow tenant in the St. Francis Hotel, Tomaso had seen Galt on more than thirty occasions, she guessed. "He usually drank vodka, or beer," she remembered. "He liked to eat beef jerky. His hands were clean, no calluses. He always had a solemn expression. He was real pale, as if he stayed indoors all the time."

Once Tomaso and Galt shot some billiards together. "He wasn't very good, but you could tell he'd played some pool." Although he was mostly quiet and shy, he had a temper. She recalled the time when Galt turned on her and Rita, furious at their suggestion that Charlie, not Rita, would accompany him to New Orleans. "I got a gun," he'd said. "If this is a setup, I'll kill him."

Sometime around late February, she and Galt arranged to swap televisions. He wanted to exchange his clunky Montgomery Ward console TV, which he'd purchased a few months earlier through a classified ad, for her little Zenith. The trade didn't make much sense to her, because her Zenith really wasn't as good a set, but he explained: "I need a portable—I'm doing some traveling the next few months."

She was happy to take delivery of the big console and went up to Galt's room to help him carry it down. On the back of the television set was a handwritten sign that said: MARTIN LUTHER COON.

■

WHEN SPECIAL AGENTS John Ogden and Roger Kaas knocked on Jimmie Garner's door that Easter Sunday, April 14, the Atlanta landlord was deeply confused—and quite possibly a little drunk. His office records were in shambles, and at first he mixed up Galt with another tenant, a worker from North Carolina who had checked in only a few days earlier. But at the agents' steady prompting, memories of Eric Galt slowly came flooding back to his befogged mind.

Galt had moved in on March 24—"he wore a suit and looked for all the world like a preacher," Garner said. He paid ten bucks a week in rent and stayed in room 2. On March 31, Galt paid a second week's rent, and that was the last time Garner had seen him. On the afternoon of April 5, Garner entered Galt's room to change the linen and found on the bed a scrap of cardboard on which Galt had scrawled in ballpoint pen: "Had to go to Birmingham—left TV. Will return to pick up soon." But Galt *hadn't* returned, and Garner had all but given up on his tenant—in fact, he was beginning to covet that abandoned Zenith for himself.

That night FBI agents kept an eye on the rooming house in case Galt did try to circle back for his things. The next morning, Monday, April 15, Agents Kaas and Ogden showed up again for another round of questioning. *Can we see Galt's room?* they wanted to know.

"Sure," Garner said. Hoisting a big ring of jangling keys, the landlord opened up room 2 and gladly showed them the space. Garner apparently had no idea that FBI agents had already snuck in and cased the joint, but he was beginning to guess what the investigation was all about. "How you guys coming along on the King case?" he asked at one point.

While Garner looked on, the agents donned gloves and collected all of Galt's belongings. (To Garner's chagrin, they took away the TV set, too.) The evidence was soon boxed up at the FBI field office and then entrusted to Agent John Sullivan, who drove straightaway to the Atlanta airport, hopped a Delta flight for Washington, and personally transported the latest trove to the FBI Crime Lab.

Jimmie Garner, meanwhile, was whisked away to the FBI Atlanta office for more questioning. An agent laid out six photographs of six different white males and asked Garner, "Was your roomer any one of these guys?"

Garner didn't hesitate in picking a photograph of Eric Galt—the portrait that had been taken with Tomas Lau at the bartending school. "If this isn't the guy," Garner said, "it's his twin brother."

■

THE NEXT MORNING, in Memphis, the sanitation strike that had lured King to his death was finally drawing to a close. Nearly every day since the assassination, while garbage continued to pile up on the streets and citizens began to suspect King's killer would never be found, negotiators had exhausted long hours at the Hotel Claridge downtown, desperately trying to hammer out an agreement. Several times the discussions had devolved into shouting matches, finger wagging, fist shaking—"we were numb, played out emotionally," said one of the mediators—and the parties representing the city and the union nearly walked away.

It was President Johnson's personal emissary, Undersecretary of Labor James Reynolds, who kept things on track. "Whether you realize it or not," he told the negotiators, "the eyes of the world are on this table."

It was Reynolds, too, who devised an elegant solution to the stalemate: politely ignore Mayor Henry Loeb and negotiate directly with the city council. This allowed the mayor to save face; he could continue to hold on to his intransigent position—*the union is illegal and thus cannot be recognized!*—and then blame any settlement on the council.

Reynolds also helped resolve the other major sticking point—the question of "dues checkoff"—by arranging for an independent, employee-run federal credit union to automatically deduct the sanitation workers' union dues. The final hurdle was a modest pay raise for the garbage workers—a pressing problem, it turned out, as the city had no extra funds in its current budget. This impasse was resolved by a spontaneous act of philanthropy from a Memphis industrialist named Abe Plough, the founder of a large pharmaceutical concern that made such products as Coppertone suntan lotion, Maybelline cosmetics, and St. Joseph aspirin. Insisting on anonymity at the time, Plough put up sixty thousand dollars of his own money, which was enough to answer the city council's immediate needs.

In the end, the strikers got more or less everything they'd been picketing for these past sixty-five days: union recognition, dues checkoff, a more straightforward grievance procedure, and a wage hike. If the symbolic could be reduced to the strictly monetary, the reparations for King's death, as well as the deaths of the two garbage workers whose crushing accident had ignited the strike, came down to a thin dime: the garbage workers, duly represented by AFSCME Local 1733 of the AFL-CIO, would receive a raise of exactly ten cents per hour.

The negotiators finally shook hands and the memorandum of understanding—no one dared call it a contract—was ratified by the city council. Even Mayor Loeb privately conceded that it was good for the city. "After Dr. King was killed," he later said, "we simply had to get this thing behind us." Memphis was reeling from the assassination in every possible way, rethinking itself, questioning its identity. The Cotton Carnival had been completely canceled—and in fact the party would never be quite the same again. Even *Hambone's Meditations,* the regular cartoon in the *Commercial Appeal,* was on its deathbed. That same month, the paper would decide that the beloved Forrest Gump–like Negro had finally outlived his usefulness.

Undersecretary of Labor Reynolds was ecstatic and couldn't wait to report back to President Johnson. " 'I am a man'—they meant it," Reynolds said. "Even though they picked up garbage and threw it into trucks, they wanted somebody to say, 'You are a man!' It was the real thing."

That night, April 16, the garbage workers gathered inside Clayborn Temple, where the walls were still streaked with tear-gas stains from the March 28 siege, and unanimously voted to approve the agreement. People danced in the aisles, they cried, they flashed V-for-victory signs. The local union leader, T. O. Jones, had tears streaming down his face when he mounted the podium. "We have been aggrieved many times," he shouted. "But we have got the victory!"

The good cheer in the room was undercut by a painful recognition of the price that had been paid. One garbage worker, visibly excited by the possibility of returning to work the following morning, put it this way: "We won, but we lost a good man along the way."

■

EARLIER THAT DAY, in Toronto, Eric Galt was undergoing a metamorphosis. He was slowly emerging from the chrysalis of a spent and useless identity and turning into Ramon George Sneyd. In the morning, he found a new apartment for "Sneyd" to live in, this one a few blocks away from the Szpakowski rooming house on Ossington. It was located at 962 Dundas Street West and was run by a Chinese landlady named Sun Fung

Loo. Then he wrote to the registrar of births in Ottawa, requesting a birth certificate for Ramon Sneyd. In his application, he asked the authorities to send the certificate to his new Dundas address.

A few hours later, Sneyd walked into the Kennedy Travel Bureau, a respected travel agency on Bloor Street West, to investigate airline tickets. For the first time, he was calling himself Sneyd in public, and wearing the professorial-looking tortoiseshell glasses that graced the photo he planned to use for his passport application. The travel agency's manager, Lillian Spencer, sat down with Sneyd and gladly helped him with his travel plans. "He just sort of appeared out of nowhere," she recalled. "He was a nebulous person, not the sort of man one notices or remembers. He blended right into the wallpaper."

His unusual name was the only thing that adhered to Spencer's memory: "I thought it was an odd name because Ramon is Spanish and doesn't usually go with George."

Sneyd first inquired about tickets to Johannesburg, South Africa, but recoiled at the price—$820 Canadian round-trip. Instead, he asked Spencer to look into the cheapest available fares to London. She soon found a flight on British Overseas Airways that departed Toronto on May 6. It was a twenty-one-day economy excursion, the cheapest flight available, and came with a fare of only $345 Canadian. Sneyd liked the sound of it and asked her to go ahead and make a reservation.

Do you have your passport with you? she asked.

He didn't have one yet, he said, but he was working on it. Here Spencer must have sensed his hesitation, his awkward uncertainty over how to proceed. Sneyd was under the mistaken impression that to secure a passport, he would have to provide a "guarantor"—a Canadian citizen in good standing who could vouchsafe that he'd known the applicant for more than two years. Meeting this requirement was the main reason he'd been developing *two* identities and *two* addresses; according to his rather convoluted and risky plan, the bespectacled Sneyd would be the traveler, and Bridgman (wearing an altogether different getup and possibly a toupee) would be the guarantor.

Sneyd wasn't going to explain any of this to her, of course, but Spencer graciously intervened before he had to conjure up a story. "*I* can get you a passport," she said. "Do you have a birth certificate?"

"Well, no," he said.

She told him that was okay, he didn't need a birth certificate.

What about the guarantor? he asked. "I don't know anyone who could serve as my guarantor."

"Not necessary, either," Spencer replied. There was a loophole in the passport rules, she said. From her files, she fished out a government form called "Statutory Declaration in Lieu of Guarantor." Sneyd was simply required to sign the form in the presence of a notary. "As it happens," she said sunnily, "we have a notary right here in the office."

Sneyd couldn't believe his good fortune. He'd had no idea how easy it was in wholesome, trusting Canada to acquire travel papers and inhabit another person's identity: no birth certificate required, no proof of residence, no character witnesses. He'd wasted his time fabricating a web of interlocking aliases, disguises, and residences, when all he had to do was swear before a notary that he was who he said he was. *Welcome to Canada*, the expression went, *we believe you.*

Sneyd made quick work of the application forms. Listing his occupation as "car salesman," he provided the real Ramon Sneyd's birth date with his new address at Mrs. Loo's place on Dundas Street West. The application asked, "Person to Notify in Canada in Case of Emergency," to which, predictably, he furnished the name of his doppelgänger, "Paul Bridgman, 102 Ossington Avenue, Toronto." It was all terrifically easy, but in his haste he made one critical mistake—he scribbled the last name "Sneyd" in a way that was barely legible.

From his jacket, he retrieved an envelope containing the passport photos he'd sat for at the Arcade Studio a few days before. Sneyd paid Lillian Spencer five dollars for the application and another three dollars for her processing fee. She said the passport would be ready within two weeks—and should arrive in her office about the same time the British Overseas Airways ticket came in. She bade him farewell, and as he ambled out the door, she affixed to his application a note whose frantic truth she could not have guessed. "Please expedite," she wrote, "as our client wishes to leave the country as soon as possible."

AT THE FBI headquarters in Washington, the MURKIN investigation had been steadily building throughout the week, steadily swelling toward an evidentiary crescendo. Individually, the thousands of isolated puzzle pieces that agents had thus far accumulated meant little and proved nothing; taken as a whole, however, they were starting to paint a single portrait and point toward a single man. The mounting evidence kept landing on the same individual, over and over and over again—the same shadowy figure, nervous, fidgety, wearing a suit, living in flophouses, and driving a white Mustang.

In quite a literal sense, the puzzle pieces *were* coming together: they were now arrayed on a single large table in a harshly lit FBI examination room. Since April 4, the FBI had compiled a staggering amount of stuff—hundreds and hundreds of miscellaneous objects that seemed to bear no relation to one another, like the scattered debris at an airplane crash. A Schlitz beer can. A package of lima beans. A bullet housing. A strand of hair. A scrap of paper. A pocket radio. A receipt with handwriting on it. A shutter-release cable for a camera. A coffee cup immersion heater. A marked-up map. A pair of undershorts. A twenty-dollar bill. A portable television. A set of binoculars. A bottle of French salad dressing. A toothbrush. A rifle.

Cartha DeLoach had the bureau's best minds poring over this mass of evidence—not just fingerprint people, but handwriting people, fiber-analysis people, photographic specialists, ultraviolet light technicians, ballistics experts. The connections these professionals began to discern were dizzying, the links intriguing, the microscopic matches too numerous to count. What they saw was a thousand little arrows, each one seemingly pointing to some other arrow.

Fibers found in the trunk of the impounded Mustang matched fibers taken from the bundle's herringbone bedspread. Eric Galt's signature on the registration card at the New Rebel Motel in Memphis matched handwriting samples obtained all along the investigatory trail. Hairs in Galt's comb matched hairs found in the Mustang sweepings. The physical, the circumstantial, and the purely anecdotal seemed increasingly interwoven: The "Turista" stickers affixed to the car jibed with Stein's recollections that Galt said he'd once owned a bar in Mexico. When buying the gun in Birmingham, Lowmeyer had mentioned going hunting "with my brother," while people at both the bartending and the dancing schools also recalled that Galt mentioned a forthcoming trip to visit a brother. The story about Galt pressuring Charlie and Rita Stein, and their cousin Marie Tomaso, to lend their signatures to the George Wallace campaign seemed somehow connected to Galt's Alabama license plates, his former Alabama residence, and other emerging ties to George Wallace's home state.

Every imaginable detail—the Thermo-Seal laundry tags, the auto service sticker, the change-of-address form, the maps, the fingerprint-laden Afta aftershave lotion, the money orders, Marie Tomaso's Zenith television found abandoned two thousand miles away in Atlanta—seemed to link Galt's movements together. The car was connected to the bundle, was connected to the gun, was connected to the binoculars. Atlanta was connected to Memphis, was connected to Mexico, was connected to Los Angeles and Birmingham and back to Atlanta again. It was all a single web.

Two pieces of late-breaking evidence clinched the FBI's confidence that they were onto the right man. The first came on April 16, when agents in Atlanta found the laundry service Eric Galt had used on Peachtree Street. Annie Estelle Peters, the desk clerk at Piedmont Laundry, checked her records and noted that Galt had picked up his clothes on the morning of April 5, the day after the assassination—the same day he'd parked the Mustang at Capitol Homes and vacated his rooming house, leaving a note on his bed. Galt's inculpatory movements seemed now almost perfectly clear: staying in Memphis at the New Rebel Motel on the night of April 3, he had raced back to Atlanta after the assassination, whereupon he'd abandoned his car, picked up his laundry, cleared out of his room—and apparently left town for good.

Then, from George Bonebrake and his fingerprint experts, came the coup de grâce: a fingerprint raised from a map of Mexico in Galt's Atlanta room matched a fingerprint found on the .30-06 Gamemaster rifle.

"Our net was beginning to close," said DeLoach. "It was all becoming obvious—Galt and Lowmeyer and Willard were one and the same man." What *kind* of man was the subject of ongoing speculation, but DeLoach boiled the suspect down this way: "Poorly educated, without scruples, and with a touch of animal cunning. But we knew he had one weakness—he liked to dance."

■

UNTIL THIS POINT in the investigation, the FBI had been working in almost total secrecy. Hoover and DeLoach had repeatedly admonished all the SACs in all the field offices across the country that the word was mum—nothing, apart from that one artist's composite sketch of the killer, was to be leaked to the media or to any local law-enforcement agencies. This nearly complete lockdown on information served a strategic purpose, of course—to keep the assassin and any accomplices forever guessing—but it also made fertile ground for the sprouting of conspiracy theories.

The longer the investigation crept along without resolution, the more it looked to a doubting public as though the agents of Hoover's famously King-hating bureau either were deliberately dragging their feet or were themselves involved in the assassination. DeLoach felt that arousing public suspicion was a risk the bureau would simply have to take. A case like this could only be solved behind the scenes—through methodical detective work, careful lab analysis, and a relentless pursuit of every plausible lead.

The media were emphatically shut out. For nearly two weeks, even the most enterprising crime reporters, journalists who previously enjoyed an "in" with the FBI, now found themselves rebuffed and stonewalled. The special agent in charge in Atlanta told one such reporter: "All I can say is 'No comment.' We could talk all night and still all I could say is, 'No comment.' "

Wednesday, April 17, would be a very different day for the MURKIN case. It was the day the FBI would finally, briefly go public.

At the Justice Department that morning, the FBI announced that it was issuing a warrant for a thirty-six-year-old fugitive named Eric Starvo Galt. The warrant stated that Galt—alias Harvey Lowmeyer, alias John Willard—along with a person "whom he alleged to be his brother," had entered into a conspiracy "to injure, oppress, threaten, or intimidate Martin Luther King, Junior." The Justice Department had to invoke this slightly garbled legalese because murder is a state and local, not a federal, crime; the FBI could arrest Galt for conspiring to violate King's civil rights, but not for murdering him.

The warrant went on to describe Galt's personal idiosyncrasies in some detail: "He probably does not have a high degree of education . . . is said to drink alcoholic beverages with a preference for vodka and beer . . . has a nervous habit of pulling at an earlobe with his hand . . . an avid dancer . . . left ear protrudes farther from his head than his right." Noting that Galt was a neat dresser and a devotee of country-and-western music, the warrant concluded: "He should be considered armed and dangerous."

The FBI also released to the media two photographs—the bartending school picture of Galt in his bow tie with his eyes closed, and then the same picture, with the eyes filled in by an FBI sketch artist. Perhaps it's true that the outward markers of human identity abide uniquely in the eyes, but neither one of the images looked much like the real fugitive—*especially* the one doctored by the artist. In that image, Galt looked like a wax figure, a mannequin, a freakish fake. Though it was hard to pinpoint just what was "off" about them, the drawn-in eyes gave Galt a creepy cartoon quality that, in terms of helping the public find the killer, would probably do more harm than good. His ruse before the camera seemed to have accomplished what he'd hoped.

The Eric Galt warrant, with its accompanying photos, represented the full extent of the FBI's offerings for the day. Justice Department officials in the room announced that they would take no questions. When one reporter tested an official by asking a question anyway—what was the provenance of the photos?—he brusquely replied: "No comment."

■

WHILE WASHINGTON REPORTERS were scrambling for the phones, the fugitive was walking down a street in Toronto not far from his rooming house, where he very nearly blundered into a disaster. Ramon Sneyd was out of sorts that day, flustered, anxious about the passport application he had submitted, through the Kennedy travel agency, the day before. With some trepidation, he realized he had two weeks to do nothing, two weeks for something to go wrong. What if the paperwork didn't go through? What if the photo set off alarm bells? What if the passport officials contacted the *real* Ramon Sneyd?

Perhaps it was this nagging jumble of worries that caused him not to pay attention to what he was doing that afternoon, leading him to make a stupid mistake: he jaywalked across a busy street.

Immediately, a policeman approached him. Excuse me, sir, the cop said, do you realize you have broken the law?

Sneyd's heart sank. For a brief moment, he thought the jig was up. You must cross at the intersection, the cop said. "I'm afraid I must issue you a ticket. The fine is three dollars."

Sneyd was surprised, amused, relieved, and elated—all at the same time. But when the cop inquired, "Name and address, please," Sneyd realized he had a problem. He wasn't sure what to tell him. He knew that the real Ramon Sneyd was a Toronto policeman—who knew, maybe even a friend of this very traffic cop?—and so he recognized using that name was too risky. In his wallet, stupidly, he still had his Alabama driver's license, made out to Eric Galt—who, although Sneyd didn't know it yet, was the most wanted man in North America.

He had to think on his feet. He gave some other phony name that surfaced from his imagination, then provided an address, 6 Condor

Avenue, which happened to be the real address of a brothel that he had apparently visited in Toronto.

He worried the cop might smell something fishy and feared that he might ask for an ID. But this was wholesome Canada, trusting Canada. The cop believed him. He wrote up the ticket, took Sneyd's three dollars, and went along his way.

Sneyd was disgusted with his obtuseness—not only for jaywalking, but also for still having his Galt ID on his person. As soon as he could, he shredded his driver's license and tossed it in his trash. For a brief time, while awaiting the arrival of his birth certificate and a passport, he was without identity, dwelling in a document-less purgatory, a man without a name.

THE FOLLOWING MORNING, newspapers all across North America and the world carried page-one photos of Eric Starvo Galt. He was the talk of the nation, the subject of party chatter, the name on the lips of every radio voice along the dial. But the queer-looking pictures, together with the bizarre train of facts that the FBI had assembled, seemed to raise more questions than they answered. What kind of name was Eric Starvo Galt? What kind of assassin was this—this avid dancer who listens to hillbilly music? What was the story behind those eyes?

Papers all over the country were full of inflamed speculation. Crime reporters out-purpled each other with nicknames for the wanted man. He was "the man without a past." He was "the man who never was." He was "the sharp-nosed stranger," "the will-o'-the-wisp," "the mystery man," "the phantom fugitive."

Those fake-looking ovoid eyes in the photographs raised doubts across the country. Though both Jimmie Garner and the gun salesman at Aeromarine claimed to recognize the man in the photo, other key witnesses along the trail began to voice their concerns that the FBI had the wrong man. Peter Cherpes, Galt's Greek-American landlord in Birmingham, said: "No, that's not him, I don't think so." Charlie Stephens, the tubercular alcoholic in Memphis who'd glimpsed John Willard in the rooming house hallway, said the FBI portrait "doesn't register." Bessie Brewer shared her roomer's doubts. "I just don't know," she told reporters. "I just don't know if it's him."

Some journalists injected notes of profound skepticism. Galt, said a *Newsweek* writer a few days later, "was a two-dimensional cutout, with a name that could have been pasted together out of paperback novels." Galt, like Willard and Lowmeyer, must be an alias, for the "deepest catacombs of a record-happy society—from the IRS to the Selective Service—yielded nothing under his name." A reporter for Memphis's *Commercial Appeal* thought the character the FBI had presented to the world bore all the hallmarks of bad crime noir. "Fiction wouldn't touch it," the reporter wrote. "The worst detective story writers in the world know how far they can stretch things before the reader throws down the magazine and says, 'Oh, let's not be ridiculous.' "

The sheer oddness of the name Eric Starvo Galt already had people guessing. Journalists and commentators began to ransack the bins of pop culture for clues, and a kind of spirited scavenger hunt of the zeitgeist got under way.

It was widely noted that John Galt was the elusive protagonist of Ayn Rand's controversial 1957 novel, *Atlas Shrugged*. Rand's thousand-page anvil of prose begins with the question "Who is John Galt?"—and as her libertarian saga unfolds, Galt emerges as a savior-like figure who exposes the evils of the welfare state and then brings American civilization to its knees with a top-down strike of the nation's leading innovators, entrepreneurs, scientists, and captains of industry, who decamp to a secret city lofted high in the Rocky Mountains. *Atlas Shrugged* laid out, in fictional form, Ayn Rand's personal philosophy of objectivism, which held that altruism toward society's unfortunates was not only misguided and ineffectual but also evil; that rational self-interest was the only moral principle that could guide a person to happiness; and that government should keep out of the great clashings of human affairs. "I swear by my life and my love of it," Galt declares in the novel's most famous line, "that I will never live for the sake of another man, nor ask another man to live for mine."

Could there be a connection here? Could Eric Galt be a literary allusion, a planted clue, that harked back to the granite-hard philosophies embedded in *Atlas Shrugged*? Could the killer be a radical Ayn Randian? Or some hit man hired by a wacko libertarian industrialist? A reporter for the *Atlanta Constitution* noted that in the novel, John Galt "destroyed the production plants of civilization because he hated the 'welfare state' that took from the producers and gave to the weak"—and then went on to observe that Martin Luther King, with his cries for the redistribution of wealth that lay at the heart of his coming Poor People's Campaign, was "perhaps the world's most outspoken proponent of those things the fictional John Galt hated."

Other commentator-sleuths went in a different direction. Could the name Eric Starvo Galt be a glancing reference to the most famous super-villain then populating the pages of international spy fiction? In several Ian Fleming novels, including *On Her Majesty's Secret Service*, James Bond's arch nemesis is Ernst Stavro Blofeld, an evil genius who leads a criminal organization called SPECTRE that's bent on "a most diabolical plot for murder on a mass scale." In the 007 films, Ernst Stavro Blofeld—a.k.a. Number 1—was depicted as a bald man in a Nehru getup; he had a hideous facial scar and was usually seen stroking a white Persian cat.

True crime growing from the pages of fiction? It didn't make much sense, but its pull was irresistible. All over the country, people began to comb through Bond thrillers and Ayn Rand books, underlining key phrases, hunting for esoteric clues. FBI agents even got in on the research. If nothing else, the allusions to James Bond and John Galt cemented early on the notion that the killer was part of a shadowy and well-oiled international conspiracy—a SPECTRE-like syndicate—that made him seem all the more exotic and mysterious.

■

In Toronto, Eric Galt's photograph was plastered on page one of the morning *Star*. The large headline read: FBI SAYS THERE WAS A CONSPIRACY—MYSTERIOUS SEAMAN SOUGHT IN KING DEATH. When Mrs. Szpakowski saw the picture that morning, April 18, she instantly thought of her roomer. She stared and stared at the photograph with the weird eyes, studying it from all angles. She thought about the man who called himself Paul Bridgman, his odd habits, his nervousness, his seeming addiction to newspapers. All morning she fretted over what to do. She showed a copy of the *Star* to her husband, Adam. Pointing toward the ceiling, she said, "He is the man who killed Martin Luther King."

Who is the man? What are you talking about?

"Paul Bridgman," she said. "The man upstairs. He's the killer they've been looking for."

"You're crazy in the head," Adam told his wife.

"But he looks just like him. We should call the police," she insisted.

"Fela, you're crazy. You'll only make a fool of yourself."

Mrs. Szpakowski relented. She never picked up the phone. Burying her suspicions, she went about her chores for the day. Then, while making the rounds the following morning, she learned that Paul Bridgman, without any notice, had vacated his room. He'd left his key on the table in the foyer. When she cleaned his room, Mrs. Szpakowski found an edition of the Toronto *Star* sitting on the bed, with the same picture of King's accused assassin. The image gave her a chill.

■

THE FBI REMAINED confident that the warrant they'd issued the previous day was correct, that Eric S. Galt was indeed their man. What they weren't sure about was whether Eric Galt was really Eric Galt. The suspect clearly had a penchant for using multiple aliases, and Galt could very well be just another one. As Cartha DeLoach well knew, isolating a suspect was one thing; positively identifying him was something else again.

To that end, the fingerprint expert George Bonebrake and his men at the crime lab had been methodically poring over the fingerprints found on various objects in the bundle, in the Mustang, and in the Atlanta rooming house and comparing them with select batches of prints on file at FBI headquarters. Bonebrake had considerably narrowed the search by concentrating on men under fifty and over twenty-one, but that still left some three million sets of prints to examine—an aneurysm-inducing chore that could take many months and still turn up nothing.

Hoover and DeLoach realized they had to figure out some other way to narrow the search. DeLoach hunkered down with other high-ranking officials and sifted through all the evidence gathered thus far. As they did, a clear pattern began to emerge: Galt, even *before* the assassination, seemed to be acting like a man on the run. "All the signs were there," DeLoach said. "The aliases, the movement from one place to another, the reluctance to make friends, the caution, the restraint. Galt was behaving like an escaped convict trying to avoid detection."

Thus an idea was born. DeLoach picked up the phone and called Bonebrake's boss, Les Trotter, director of the FBI's Identification Division for fingerprints. DeLoach later recalled the conversation in his memoirs. "Les, we have pretty good evidence that Galt is an escapee," DeLoach said. "How many 'Wanted' notices do we currently have in our files?"

"About 53,000," Trotter said.

DeLoach grimaced. "Well," he said, "at least that's better than three million."

The task before them was clear: DeLoach wanted Bonebrake's men to compare the "Galt" prints with the prints of all fifty-three thousand wanted fugitives. "You've got to put *all* your people on this," DeLoach said.

"When do you want us to begin?" Trotter asked.

"How about *today?*"

The examiners began working in the late afternoon of April 18, exactly two weeks after the assassination. Additional experts from Philadelphia, Baltimore, New York, and Richmond hastened to Washington to assist in the round-the-clock effort. DeLoach said he didn't need to remind them that "we're under tremendous pressure, and that our cities are powder kegs."

Bonebrake zeroed in on Galt's left thumbprint found on both the rifle and the binoculars. It was their highest-quality print, the one that manifested a clear loop pattern with twelve ridge counts. To his pleasant surprise, Bonebrake learned that the FBI files of known fugitives held only nineteen hundred thumbprints with loops of between ten and fourteen ridge counts. This was encouraging: suddenly the monumentality of Bonebrake's project had shrunk by several orders of magnitude. The teams of experts ranged around a table, facing a blowup poster of Galt's thumbprint. They got out their magnifying glasses and went to work.

At 9:15 the next morning, April 19, Les Trotter called DeLoach.

"We're getting there," Trotter said, noting that Bonebrake and his team hadn't slept a wink and that they'd already plowed through more than five hundred sets of cards. "Give us just a little more time."

"OK," DeLoach said, and then ducked into a weekly meeting of FBI muckety-mucks led by Clyde Tolson, Hoover's right-hand man. DeLoach was reluctant to tell Tolson the truth—that although countless specialists were hard at work and making progress, the investigation seemed to be momentarily stymied.

Several hours later, as the meeting was adjourning and DeLoach was gathering up his papers, the phone rang. It was Les Trotter on the line. "Deke," he said, and already DeLoach thought he could detect a "note of triumph" in Trotter's voice. There was a long pause, and then Trotter gloatingly said: "Tell the Director. We've got your man!"

"Are you *sure*?"

"No doubt about it. Bonebrake's experts found an exact match just a few minutes ago, on the 702nd card."

"I take it he's not really Eric Galt. Or Lowmeyer. Or Willard."

"Nope," Trotter said. "His card number is 405,942G. The guy's a habitual offender. Escaped last year from the state pen at Jeff City, Missouri. His name is James Earl Ray."

Roman George Doyle

BOOK THREE

THE HOTTEST MAN IN THE COUNTRY

. . . .

Thy chase had a beast in view;
Thy wars brought nothing about;
Thy lovers were all untrue.
'Tis well an old age is out,
And time to begin a new.

JOHN DRYDEN, "THE SECULAR MASQUE"

As the FBI prepared to break the news around the world, Ramon George Sneyd kept a low profile in his digs on Toronto's Dundas Street West. For nearly a week, he refused to venture from his room. Sun Fung Loo, the Chinese lady who ran the place with a lax eye and a wide, gummy smile—and who usually had a small child strapped to her back—hardly ever saw her tenant. "He came with a suit on and a newspaper in his hand," she said. "He never spoke to anybody."

Luckily for Sneyd, Mrs. Loo could neither speak nor read English and, unlike Mrs. Szpakowski, exhibited no interest in the careers and backgrounds of her roomers. She took his rent and left him alone.

Paranoid, exhausted from worry, running out of money, Sneyd knew he must stay in a nerve-racking holding pattern for nearly two weeks while he waited for his passport, birth certificate, and airline ticket to arrive. At some point he bought a new cheap transistor radio to re-place his trusty Channel Master, and from Dundas Street West he con-stantly monitored the airwaves for any news on the manhunt.

On Sunday night, April 21, he did emerge from his room. The Loo rooming house had no television, and that night there was a particular show he wanted to watch—ABC's wildly popular series *The FBI*, which presented semi-fictionalized dramas spun from the FBI's actual case files. Sneyd visited several bars in the neighborhood and found to his dismay that they were all tuned to watch *The Ed Sullivan Show*, but eventually he found a tavern where the barkeep was willing to switch the tube to ABC, which came in over the rabbit ears from an affiliate station across Lake Ontario, in Buffalo, New York. Wearing his horn-rimmed glasses, Sneyd sat at the crowded bar, ordered a drink, and endeavored to stay in the shadows. He watched the one-hour show, which starred Efrem Zimbalist Jr. in the role of Inspector Lewis Erskine. But what Sneyd had really come for was the little kicker that famously ended the program each week—in which the FBI presented the current list of the ten most wanted public enemies in America.

Sure enough, Zimbalist's voice suddenly broke in over the airwaves—*wanted in connection with the fatal shooting of Dr. Martin Luther King Jr.*—and there was Sneyd's photograph, flashing across the screen. Only Zimbalist didn't say Sneyd's name. He didn't say Eric Galt's name, either, or Harvey Lowmeyer's, or John Willard's. Enunciating in his most orotund and officious-sounding baritone, Zimbalist named the name for all the world to hear: *James Earl Ray.*

Sneyd must have felt a stab of terror that was sharpened by the fact that he could not show the slightest flinch of discomfort, in the loud and boisterous bar, lest he draw unwelcome attention to himself. *"An escapee from the Missouri State Penitentiary, he is forty years old, five feet ten inches tall, 174 pounds. The FBI is engaged in a nationwide search but Ray may have fled to Mexico or Canada."* Sneyd sat there during the awkward bulletin, nervously fidgeting with his vodka and orange juice. *"Memphis has offered a reward of $100,000 to anyone with information leading to Ray's capture."* Sneyd later confessed that he was astounded that a Southern city where King had stirred up so much trouble would put up so much money. More and more photographs flashed on the screen, images from a shabby criminal past that Sneyd found all too familiar. *"Consider him armed and extremely dangerous. If you have seen Ray, notify the FBI immediately."*

■

THE "AMERICA'S MOST WANTED" bulletin had hit the airwaves as the result of a three-day spasm of activity in FBI offices around the

United States. At frantic speed, agents had learned much about the life and times of James Earl Ray; they'd followed every lead, digested every stray scrap, tied up every loose end. Hoover, DeLoach, and Clark had no doubts—they had the right man.

Yet they realized they needed to enlist the public to help with the search. So the FBI prepared a series of public service announcements to air on radio stations from coast to coast. The bureau also printed more than 200,000 "Wanted" notices and distributed them around the nation, while another 30,000, printed in Spanish, were plastered all over Mexico. The hunt was entering its most relentless phase.

If there is such a thing as a "typical" assassin, the forty-year-old James Earl Ray didn't seem to meet the description—at least not on the surface. He was not a young male burning with religious fervor, and his racial politics, though smoldering and reactionary, had never led him to join the Klan or any other overtly violent organization. While his rap sheet was long, he had never been convicted of murder or manslaughter— or any crime that involved discharging a gun. While serving in the Army in Bremerhaven, Germany, just after World War II, he had learned to shoot an M1—earning the basic medal as a marksman—but certainly this was no professional hit man.

Ray, above all, was a man who loved the chase, and who seemed almost subconsciously to *want* to get caught in order to break free again and thus initiate another chase. There was a bumbling picaresque quality to many of his escapades; in one of his heists, he fell out of his own swerving getaway car because he forgot to pull the door shut. A high-school dropout, Ray was discharged from the Army for "ineptness and lack of adaptability for military service." Most of his crimes—burglary, forgery, armed robbery—ranged from the petty to the merely pathetic. His criminal career was marked by moments of rash stupidity, yet Ray was not stupid, and he had a reputation in prison as a keen reader and a patient plotter with a perversely creative intelligence, especially when it came to confounding any sort of authority. Anyone who could break from a maximum-security prison and stay on the lam for more than a year possessed a certain kind of street cunning that was not to be dismissed.

At various points in his life, Ray had tried to go straight. He'd been, among other things, a color matcher at a shoe company, a laborer at a tannery, an assembly line worker at a company that manufactured compressors, and a dishwasher at a diner. But he kept slipping deeper into a life of recidivism—it was the only world he knew. "He was a dirty little neck," recalled William Peterson, police chief in the blue-collar town of Alton, Illinois, where Ray was born in 1928 and where he lived off and on between his jail terms. "He was a thief who slept all day and stole all night."

FBI agents arrived at Jefferson City, Missouri, and began to piece together a thumbnail sketch of James Earl Ray's years in prison there and the story of his escape from the bakery a year earlier. Ray, investigators learned, was widely thought to have been using and selling amphetamines inside Jeff City—his role as a narcotics "merchant" was a likely source of funds that had sustained him during his year on the run. (By one close accounting made much later, Ray over the years may have sent out as much as seven thousand dollars he'd made in the narcotics trade—most likely salting it away with members of his family.) But mainly Ray was known as someone obsessed with the notion of escape. Nicknamed the Mole, Ray had tried to break out of Jeff City on several earlier occasions and, as punishment, was forced to serve many hard months in solitary. Though his several escape attempts should have permanently caught the attention of the prison staff, something about his style made him oddly forgettable, innocuous, generic. Most guards just called him by his prison number: 416-J.

To the investigating agents, the vandalized numerals found on the Channel Master radio suddenly made sense. Specialists at the crime lab had successfully used an ultraviolet scanner to "raise" the numerals that Ray had so diligently scratched out. The number: 00416. Jeff City records showed that James Earl Ray had bought the radio from the prison canteen two days before his escape and that, as required by prison regulations, the number had been etched on the radio's housing.

■

OTHER FBI MEN branched out across Missouri and Illinois, tracking down members of Ray's family. Both of Ray's parents were said to be dead, but agents soon found a brother, John Ray, at the bar he ran on Arsenal Street in a rough neighborhood of South St. Louis. The Grapevine Tavern was just a block away from the George Wallace for

President headquarters, and was a frequent gathering place for campaign organizers. John Ray, it turned out, was a die-hard Wallace fan himself and freely used his bar to distribute American Independent Party literature. Because of its proximity to the Wallace office, the Grapevine had become known around town as a watering hole for John Birchers, White Citizens Council members, and other ardent segregationists. Much like his brother James Earl in Los Angeles, John Ray had a habit of personally escorting prospective AIP registrants to the local campaign headquarters to enlist them in the Wallace cause.

John Ray seemed a beefier, ruddier version of the fugitive, with a fast-receding hairline that exposed the bony facades of his forehead. He had a criminal record of his own, having served seven years in an Illinois penitentiary for robbery. His tavern's name, in fact, was an allusion to the "prison grapevine," the mill of intrigue and scuttlebutt that had enlivened his days behind bars. It was a small irony that, as a felon, he couldn't vote at all, much less for Wallace.

At first, John Ray seemed drunk and was not cooperative, especially when FBI agents reminded him that he had visited his brother Jimmy in Jeff City the day before he escaped in a bread box. John claimed he'd had no contact with his brother since the breakout and had no idea of his whereabouts.

The skeptical FBI agents asked John why he smiled when he gave his answers—he constantly flashed a curling smirk that was nearly identical to that of his brother Jimmy. John said it was just "a nervous reaction" that didn't mean anything, but he did concede that this unfortunate tic had sometimes gotten him in trouble with the law.

"Jimmy was never the same after he got out of the Army," John said. "He went crazy, and got mixed up with drugs." If he did kill Martin Luther King, Jimmy was probably dead now—his conspirators would have tried to "seal his lips forever." But if Jimmy was still alive, he was certainly out of the country by now.

Which country would he flee to? the agents wanted to know.

John declined to speculate, but he did recall visiting Jimmy in prison once and getting an earful about Ian Smith and the good job he was doing down in Rhodesia. John Ray characterized himself as "a mild segregationist" and soon confided his frustration to the FBI agents. "What's all the excitement about?" he wondered aloud. "He only killed a nigger. If he'd killed a white man, you wouldn't be here."

Reporters who ended up on John Ray's doorstep similarly found that he was not bashful about sharing his views on King. "He was not a saint as they try to picture him," John would later write the author George McMillan. "King was not only a rat but with his beaded eyes and pin ears, he looked like one, too."

Initially considering John Ray a possible suspect in a conspiracy, FBI agents interrogated him about his whereabouts on April 4 but were unable, either then or in subsequent interviews, to pin anything definitive on him. (Years later, however, John Ray would boast in a co-authored book that he drove from St. Louis and visited his brother Jimmy at a tavern in West Memphis, Arkansas—just across the Mississippi River from the city—on the afternoon before the assassination.)

Meanwhile, a second team of agents soon found Ray's younger brother Jerry Ray at a country club in the Chicago suburbs, where he was a golf course greenskeeper. A clownish man who seemed to take the FBI's manhunt as a thrilling game, Jerry was determined to tell the agents only enough to keep them off his back. His brother Jimmy was now the "hottest man in the country," Jerry reckoned, "the most wanted man there ever was."

Jerry, who was also a felon, said he had no idea where Jimmy went to, or even if he was still alive. He doubted his brother had it in him to kill anyone, though. If Jimmy murdered King, it had to be for money. "He sure didn't have any love for colored people," Jerry conceded. "But he wouldn't have put himself in a spot like this unless there was something in it for him."

Whatever Jimmy Ray did or did not do, Jerry said, he would never tell a soul about it. "Jimmy would never snitch on anyone, I know that. He'll go to his grave with his secrets."

■

FEELING THE STARE of the world boring at his back, Ramon Sneyd skulked through Toronto's darkened streets the night the bulletin ran on *The FBI*, and slipped into Mrs. Loo's place. He locked himself in his room for twenty-four hours and tried to figure out what to do next.

The following morning, April 23, he paid a visit to Loblaws, a grocery store only a few blocks away. Probably packing his .38 Liberty Chief revolver, Sneyd gave serious thought to robbing the joint. "A supermarket—that's really a corporation's money and they're probably gougin' it out of somebody else, anyway," he later rationalized. "Better to rob them than an individual." Samuel Marshall, the assistant manager, found him in the rear of the store in an area off-limits to customers, snooping around near the office safe. Marshall demanded to know what he was doing there.

"Oh I, um, I'm looking for *a job*," the intruder stammered, boasting that he had some experience working in a grocery down in Mexico. When the store manager, Emerson Benns, approached, Sneyd edged toward the door, sprinted down the sidewalk, and hopped on a streetcar. The following day Marshall saw James Earl Ray's photograph in *Newsweek* and alerted police, saying, "That's the man."

Sneyd, prudently deciding he should keep himself scarce from the Dundas neighborhood for a while, headed for the bus station a few hours after his contretemps at Loblaws supermarket and boarded a coach for Montreal. He feared that the Sneyd passport application might fall through, or worse, that it might trip some internal bureaucratic alarm in Ottawa; in any case, he recognized that it was far too risky for him to stick around Toronto for two weeks until his airplane ticket and passport arrived.

In Montreal, he stayed in a rooming house under the name of Walters and wandered the shipyards for several days hunting in vain for a freighter that might take him to southern Africa. Sneyd did find a Scandinavian ship bound for Mozambique with a fare of six hundred dollars, but was disappointed to learn that the line's regulations required all passengers to carry a valid passport.

In desperation, Sneyd returned to Toronto and kept to his room at Mrs. Loo's place for a week. His Sneyd birth certificate arrived in due course, but in his agitated state he made another potentially critical mistake: while placing a call at a nearby phone booth, he absentmindedly left the Bureau of Vital Statistics envelope, holding his Sneyd birth certificate, on the little ledge by the phone. Later that day, Mrs. Loo opened the door and beheld a rotund man clutching an envelope. She hollered up to Mr. Sneyd to tell him he had a caller, but her skittish tenant wouldn't budge from his room. When she bounded up the stairs and coaxed Sneyd to come out, Mrs. Loo thought he looked nervous and "white as a sheet." Sneyd feared the worst: it must be a government official, a plainclothes cop, or a detective. In the foyer, Sneyd awkwardly spoke to the fat stranger, who turned out to be a paint company salesman named Robert McNaulton who'd spotted the official-looking document in the phone booth and, trying to do the right thing, had hand-delivered it to the Dundas address clearly typed on the outside of the envelope.

On May 2, Sneyd called the Kennedy Travel Bureau and to his profound relief learned from Lillian Spencer that his airline ticket and passport had finally arrived. But when he went over to the travel agency to pick up the documents, he fell into a mild panic: his surname was misspelled on the passport. It said "Sneya" instead of "Sneyd"—the result, no doubt, of his poor handwriting in his haste to fill out the application. It was too late to fix the error—his flight was scheduled to leave in a few days. He paid for the ticket, $345 Canadian, in cash.

On May 6, Sneyd quit Mrs. Loo's establishment, giving no advance notice, saying only that he was leaving because the children who constantly played outside his room were too noisy. While cleaning up the room, Mrs. Loo found a small suitcase that only contained a few odd things—some Band-Aids, a couple of sex magazines, maps of Toronto and Montreal, and six rolls of unopened Super 8 movie film. Loo stashed the bag in her storeroom, guessing that Mr. Sneyd might eventually return for it.

Checking in at Toronto International Airport later that afternoon as Ramon George *Sneya*, the world's most wanted fugitive boarded British Overseas Airways Flight 600. The jet took off without incident at 6:00 p.m., and Sneyd breathed a sigh of relief. But as the plane cruised out over the North Atlantic, his mind churned with worries, mainly having to do with his thinning reserve of cash. "I should have pulled a holdup in Canada," he later said, regretfully. "That's where I made my mistake. I let myself get on that plane to London without enough money to get where I intended to go."

At 6:40 the next morning, May 7, Sneyd's flight touched down at London Heathrow, the next stop in his long, strange journey toward Rhodesia.

IN THE FIRST week of May, J. Edgar Hoover and Cartha DeLoach became distracted by another development, one that was separate from, but not entirely unrelated to, the hunt for James Earl Ray. When King was assassinated in Memphis, he had regarded the garbage strike as a miniature of the larger fight he was planning to wage in Washington—the Poor People's Campaign.

The POCAM, as the FBI called it, had been one of Hoover's dreads all along, and the mayhem caused by the assassination riots in Washington only seemed to validate his warnings that a mass convergence of angry indigents on the nation's capital would be a formula for certain violence.

King's death had momentarily taken the wind out of the SCLC's plans; deprived of his charismatic oratory and his judicious leadership, such an ambitious enterprise as the Poor People's Campaign seemed unlikely to happen. But by late April, Ralph Abernathy announced that his organization was going ahead with King's grand protest. Through deft negotiations, the SCLC secured a monthlong permit from the National Park Service to build a sprawling shantytown encampment on sixteen acres of the Mall, in West Potomac Park, between the Washington Monument and the Lincoln Memorial. Thousands, perhaps hundreds of thousands, of the poor were planning to converge on Washington in what Andy Young predicted would be "the greatest nonviolent demonstration since Gandhi's salt march." In honor of King, the shantytown would be called Resurrection City—a name that would symbolize, Young said, "the idea of rebirth from the depths of despair."

Now, it seemed, Hoover's nightmare was about to begin.

All across the country, masses of the destitute—the Poor People's Army—were forming caravans and aiming toward Washington. Just as King had originally envisioned it, they were not only African-Americans but also poor whites from Appalachia, Hispanics from Los Angeles, Puerto Ricans from New York, and Native Americans from all over the country—Seneca, Hopi, Flatheads, Yakama, Sioux.

The eight great caravans got their symbolic kickoff in Memphis on May 2. Returning to the site of her husband's assassination, Coretta King stood outside room 306 at the Lorraine, which was now glassed in and adorned with wreaths. A gold cross had been cemented into the balcony floor, and a plaque nearby bore a passage from Genesis. "Behold," it said, "here cometh the dreamer . . . let us slay the dreamer and we shall see what will become of his dreams." At Mason Temple later that day, Coretta and Ralph Abernathy blessed the marchers, and they took off toward Marks, Mississippi, the tiny town deep in the Delta where King had seen so much despair on the faces of sharecroppers.

From Marks, the pilgrims transformed themselves into a mule caravan, with teams of farm animals pulling wooden carts of the sort widely used, until very recently, by sharecroppers in the South. Facetiously, Abernathy gave all the mules nicknames like Eastland and Stennis—in honor of staunch segregationist senators and congressmen in Washington. The mule-team marchers gathered more and more followers as they inched east on back roads toward Alabama, where state troopers vowed to arrest the caravan for endangering public safety.

Much of Alabama—or at least *white* Alabama—was in a period of mourning: on May 7, Governor Lurleen Wallace had finally succumbed to colon cancer at the age of forty-one. George Wallace, who'd been riding a tidal wave of support across the country, was now so distraught that many assumed he would drop out of the presidential race. Lurleen Wallace's body lay in the rotunda of the state capitol in Montgomery—the same spot where Jefferson Davis, president of the Confederacy, had lain in state. The Poor People's Army rolled past the surreal sight of Confederate flags flying at half-staff and beefy highway patrolmen in tears over the loss of their lady governor. In Birmingham, the mule teams would be put on trailers to be trucked the rest of the way to D.C.

As the caravans drew ever closer, planners in Washington began to build the great tent city. Hundreds of A-frame structures, made of canvas and plywood, began to go up in sight of the Reflecting Pool. There would be electric lines, water lines, sewage lines, phone lines, and a central structure called City Hall for "Mayor" Ralph Abernathy. Resurrection City would even have its own ZIP code.

Hoover, meanwhile, girded his FBI for the imminent "assault on Washington," as he called it. He had informers embedded in all the different caravans and agents bird-dogging every militant group. He urged all the SACs around the country to consider Project POCAM "one of the bigger tasks facing the bureau at the present time."

Pentagon generals were prepared to deploy twenty thousand troops to put down any possible insurrection. President Johnson was personally offended by the Poor People's Campaign; it seemed a direct indictment of his vaunted Great Society programs, which had foundered as the war in Vietnam had escalated. Ramsey Clark said the notion of a shantytown going up beside the White House "hurt the president—*deeply* hurt him."

On Capitol Hill, many senators were apoplectic at the prospect of this invasion of "welfare brood mares," as some conservatives called the Poor People's Army. Senator John McClellan of Arkansas led the charge, saying that Washington was about to be transformed into a "Mecca for migrants" and claiming to possess inside knowledge that black militants had a secret "master plan" for the violent overthrow of the national government.

As the tattered army of pilgrims and mules drew near, the mood in Washington, Clark said, had become "one of paranoia—literally. There were predictions of holocaust, and absurdly improbable testimony on the Hill about clandestine meetings and planned violence. The nation was led to expect horrible crimes."

■

At FBI HEADQUARTERS during the first week of May, the search for James Earl Ray appeared to be going nowhere but backward—back into the creases of Ray's biography, back into the mix of stunting environments and stifling influences, back into the genesis stories of a lifelong criminal. By relentlessly interviewing and reinterviewing Ray's family and acquaintances, the FBI had hoped that some stray piece of information would break loose, some random fact that would lead agents to Ray's hiding place. But the strategy didn't work. Instead, the FBI men, with journalists following close on their heels, began to assemble something altogether different: an exceedingly strange and sad portrait of a man who'd grown up in a cluster of depressed towns along the Mississippi River, in the heart of Twain country. It was a severe story, a heartbreaking story—but one that was thoroughly American.

The Ray clan had a hundred-year history of crime and squalor and hard luck. Ray's great-grandfather was an all-around thug who sold liquor to Indians off the back of a wagon and was hanged after gunning down six men. Ray's beloved uncle Earl was a traveling carnival boxer and convicted rapist who served a six-year prison sentence for throwing carbolic acid in his wife's face.

Throughout James Earl Ray's life, the despair was panoramic. The family suffered from exactly the sort of bleak, multigenerational poverty that King's Poor People's Campaign was designed to address. Living on a farm near tiny Ewing, Missouri, the Rays were reportedly forced to cannibalize their own house for firewood to get through the winter—ripping it apart, piece by piece, until the sorry edifice fell in on itself and they had to move on, to a succession of equally shabby dwellings up and down the Mississippi.

The Ray children, predictably, were a mess. John, Jimmy, and Jerry were all felons, but that was just the start of the family's disappointments. In the spring of 1937, Ray's six-year-old sister, Marjorie, burned herself to death while playing with matches. The two youngest Ray siblings, Max (who was mentally disabled) and Susie, were given up for adoption after Ray's father abandoned the family in 1951. A decade later, Ray's kind-hearted but overwhelmed mother, Lucille, then fifty-one, died in St. Louis from cirrhosis of the liver. Two years after that, Ray's eighteen-year-old brother, Buzzy, missed the bridge in Quincy, Illinois, and plunged his car into a slough of the Mississippi River, drowning himself and his girlfriend.

Then there was Melba—perhaps the saddest and most disheveled of the Ray children. An emotionally disturbed woman who shouted obscenities at strangers and spent much of her time in mental hospitals, Melba made local news a year before, in 1967, when she was found dragging a painted, seven-foot cross down a major street in Quincy. "I made it to keep my sanity," she said, by way of explanation. "After what happened to President Kennedy and the war and all, I had to turn to Jesus."

Melba, when interviewed, said she hardly knew her older brother James Earl. "He liked being clean," she dimly recalled. "He always kept his hair combed."

As the FBI agents took note of the misery that pervaded the Ray family history, the biggest question mark was Ray's father. Who was the patriarch of all this pathos? Whatever happened to the man? On prison forms at both Leavenworth and Jeff City, James Earl Ray had consistently declared his father "deceased," noting that he'd died of a heart attack in 1947. But soon the FBI learned that, on the contrary, Ray's sixty-nine-year-old father was alive and well and living as a recluse on a little farm in Center, Missouri, not far from Twain's childhood home of Hannibal.

Special Agents William Duncan and James Duffey showed up at Old Man Ray's tiny clapboard house, located on a plot of pasture just beyond the town dump, and conducted a series of highly unusual interviews. Ray was a tough and watchful little bantam rooster, quick to warn of guns lying about; despite his advanced years, he was proud of his physique, which had been honed to hardness from years of weight lifting and calisthenics. At first he denied that his name was Ray—it was Jerry *Raynes*, he insisted. He also denied that the fugitive was his son. "*Step-son*," he claimed. "Anyways, I haven't seen Jimmy in seventeen years."

After a while, though, especially when Agent Duffey reminded him of the harsh provisions of the "harboring statute," the old man opened up a little. When a succession of reporters came knocking on his door in the weeks and months ahead, he opened up a little more. Raynes turned out to be the sort of guy who, once he got started, wouldn't shut up. He spoke so slowly that people thought he had a speech impediment. When he was a kid, his languorous drawl earned him what became his lifelong nickname: Speedy.

Yes, it was true, Speedy said, he'd been born George "Jerry" Ray back in 1899, but over the years he'd changed his name to Ryan, Raines, Raynes, Rayns, and assorted other spellings. As he dabbled in petty crimes (breaking and entering, forgery, bootlegging), and as he drifted from job to job (railroad brakeman, farmer, junk hauler), he'd kept his identity deliberately fungible, the better to confuse the tax man and escape the clutches of creditors and landlords and the law. His policy of existential vagueness had confused the kids, too—so much so that some of them were adults before they knew their true names.

And yes, James Earl Ray was his son. Old Man Ray seemed proud of the boy. Of all his kids, he said, Jimmy was the smart and ambitious one, the one destined for big things. "He was thinking all the time," Speedy told a reporter. "Jimmy wanted to be a detective. He'd pick up anything right now and learn it. He had a hell of a lot of drive. He'd tell you he was going right to the top, you know." Yet there was something odd about the boy, too, Speedy admitted. "Jimmy had funny ways about him. Like, he used to walk on his hands. Hell, he could even *run* on his hands."

Speedy Raynes was a muddle of superstitions and rants—tenaciously held ideas that he pummeled into Jimmy's adolescent head while they drove around Ewing together, shooting pool in taverns, hauling junk up and down the Fabius River valley. Speedy wouldn't eat Chinese food, he said, because "those people will poison you." He believed all baseball games were fixed, that doctors were determined to kill you, that pretty much everything in life was a racket. "All politicians are thieves and gangsters," he said. "Well, maybe not Wallace. But when the government gets after anybody, they don't have a chance."

He wanted to make it clear that he wasn't a racist—and didn't raise his kids to think that way. "I don't hate niggers," he said, noting that around Ewing there *weren't* any black folks anyway. On the other hand, he pointed out, "They aren't the same as us. They just lay around and fuck all the time."

As he thought about his son's present troubles, he was convinced that where Jimmy went wrong was in failing to heed his childhood lesson, the one Speedy ingrained in him over and over again—that the little guy can't win, that the cards are stacked against him, that the best course is to keep your identity murky and aim low. "People try to get too much out of life," he told the journalist George McMillan. "Sometimes I think Jimmy outsmarted himself. I can't figure out why he tried to compete with all them bigshots. Life don't amount to a shit anyway. Jimmy had too much nerve for his own good. He tried to go too far too fast."

■

WHILE THE FBI dug ever deeper into the disturbing muck of James Earl Ray's past, Ramon Sneyd was hiding five thousand miles across the ocean, in Portugal.

Balmy Lisbon, the salt-bleached capital of Moorish palaces and Romanesque castles perched on the westernmost edge of Europe, afforded Sneyd a refreshing change from gray Toronto. His hotel was not far from the waterfront and the swirling chaos of Rossio Square, where the acres of marble reverberated night and day with the fat thunk of soccer balls and the longing strains of fado music. The city was crawling with sailors, fishermen, and merchant mariners; huge freighters could often be seen clanking in from the ocean, taking refuge in the estuary of the Tagus River, which formed one of the world's greatest ports.

It was the port, in fact, that had attracted Ramon Sneyd to Lisbon. Knowing that the Portuguese capital was an international recruitment center for mercenaries, he'd come straight from London hoping to catch a cheap ship to Africa. Sneyd had simply exchanged the return portion of his excursion fare for a ticket to Lisbon and then hopped on a flight the same day, May 7. For a week now he'd been prowling the wharves, just as he had in Montreal a few weeks earlier. He found a promising ship bound for Angola, the war-torn Portuguese colony in Africa. The passage would only cost him 3,777 escudos, or about $130. But again Sneyd was stymied by paperwork; entry into Angola, he discovered, required a visa, which would take over a week to obtain. The ship was leaving in three days.

Sneyd thought Lisbon would be a safe place to hide out and cool

off for a while, until he could find passage to Africa or figure out something else to do. He was aware that Portugal's extradition laws were
strict—always favoring the fugitive—and that Portugal, which had abol-
ished capital punishment back in 1867, would not extradite him to the
United States if prosecutors there vowed to seek the death penalty.

Sneyd was staying on the second floor of the Hotel Portugal, a
sternly appointed establishment in a bustling precinct that smelled of
smoked fish and spitted chickens. His rent was 50 escudos—about $1.80 a
night. Gentil Soares, the main desk clerk at the hotel, thought Sneyd was
an "unfriendly tourist." The day clerk, João, said he was a "bashful fellow,
always walked around with his face down." He never tipped, never ordered
room service, never talked with anyone. Soares noticed that Sneyd wore
eyeglasses in his Canadian passport photo, and also when he was checking
in, but that he never wore the glasses again. Once Sneyd tried to bring a
prostitute up to his room, but the hotel management refused; the couple
left and evidently stayed the night together somewhere else, as Sneyd was
not seen again at the hotel until the following afternoon.

Sneyd spent his daytimes at the docks, or at places like the South
African embassy, where he pointedly inquired about immigration procedures. He told someone at the embassy's front office that he was hoping
to travel to southern Africa to search for his long-lost brother; Sneyd
said he had reason to believe that his brother, last seen in the Belgian
Congo, was now a mercenary fighting in Angola. Did the embassy have
any information on how he might sign up to become a soldier of fortune
down there? (On this question, the understandably suspicious embassy
officials proved to be of no help, but Sneyd did eventually learn about
several mercenary groups operating in Angola—he jotted down contact
information on a piece of paper that he then folded and wedged into the
power compartment of his new transistor radio, to ensure a tight battery
connection.) Sneyd also visited, to no avail, the Rhodesian mission and
the unofficial legation for Biafra, then stopped by the offices of South
African Airways and gathered information on flights to Salisbury and
Johannesburg.

Nighttimes Sneyd kept to a fairly regular circuit of sailors' bars—the
Bolero, the Galo, the Bohemia, the Fontoria, Maxine's Nightclub. Usually
he sat off by himself, drinking beer in the shadows, but some nights he tried

to make conversation with women. One evening at the Texas Bar, he met a hooker named Maria Irene Dos Santos and managed to negotiate a bargain rate of three hundred escudos—about eleven dollars—for her favors. At Maxine's, he grew particularly friendly with a prostitute named Gloria Sausa Ribeiro and spent several nights with her. She was a tall, willowy woman with blond hair clipped in a stylish poodle cut. She noticed that Sneyd was obsessed with the news and bought every American and British paper he could get his hands on. For her services, Sneyd insisted on paying not in cash but in gifts—a dress and a pair of stockings. "He did not know any Portuguese," Gloria later told Portuguese police detectives, "and I spoke no English, so we conversed only in the international language of love."

While Sneyd was freely sampling the Iberian nightlife, he knew his time in Lisbon was short. He was desperate over his finances—which, after eight days, had dwindled to about five hundred dollars. He'd had no luck finding a ship, and feared that his complete unfamiliarity with both the Portuguese tongue and the Portuguese currency made it impractical for him to consider pulling a heist or robbing a store. Lisbon was too strange and exotic. He couldn't see a way to fall back into his usual pattern of melting into the crowd.

He decided he had to rethink his options in an English-speaking city. He dropped by the Canadian consulate and had a new passport issued, this time with the surname spelled correctly. On Friday, May 17, Sneyd took a taxi to Lisbon's Portela Airport and boarded a flight on Transportes Aéreos, bound for London.

IN WASHINGTON, DeLoach's men were slowly piecing together field reports that hinted at the answer to perhaps the most salient question about James Earl Ray: his motive for killing King.

It was becoming more apparent to the FBI, and to investigative reporters burrowing into the case, that although Ray had not exactly lived at the forefront of racial politics, he had long been a virulent racist. When he was sixteen, he carried a picture of Hitler in his wallet, and while serving an Army stint in Germany just after World War II, he'd continued his adolescent fascination with Nazis. "What appealed to Jimmy about Hitler," his brother Jerry Ray told the journalist George McMillan, "was that he would make the U.S. an all-white country, no Jews or Negroes. He would be a strong leader who would just do what was right and that was it. Not try to please everybody like Roosevelt. Jimmy thought Hitler was going to succeed, and still thinks he would have succeeded if the Japs hadn't attacked Pearl Harbor."

A number of Ray's acquaintances told FBI agents that Ray couldn't stand black people. Walter Rife, an old drinking buddy who pulled off a postal service money order heist with Ray in the 1950s, said that Ray "was unreasonable in his hatred for niggers. He hated to see them breathe. If you pressed it, he'd get violent in a conversation about it. He hated them! I never did know why." When Ray was in Leavenworth for the money order heist, he turned down a chance to work on the coveted honor farm because the dorms were integrated.

While serving his armed robbery sentence at Jefferson City, Ray allegedly told a number of inmates that he planned to kill King. Investigators had to take such stories with a grain of salt, of course—prisoners were notorious for telling authorities just about anything—but agents found a consistency to the story that was hard to ignore. One Jeff City inmate, a not always reliable man named Raymond Curtis, said Ray would become incensed whenever King appeared on the cell-block TV. "Somebody's got to get him," Ray would say. Curtis said an inmate from Arkansas claimed he knew a "bunch of Mississippi businessmen" who were willing to pay a hundred thousand dollars to anyone who killed King. This got Ray thinking. According to Curtis, Ray liked to analyze the mistakes Oswald had made in killing Kennedy, and talked about what *he* would have done differently. Ray once said that "Martin Luther Coon" was his "retirement plan—if I ever get to the streets, I'm going to kill him."

■

THE FBI, MEANWHILE, had already begun to look for avenues by which Ray might have been paid to kill King—or at least avenues by which Ray might reasonably have *hoped* to get paid. The bureau was well aware of the existence of bounties on King's head. The talk was out there. Throughout 1967 and early 1968, FBI informers across the country got wind of new threats nearly every week. It was loose talk, mostly, whispered among liquored-up hotheads in bars and pool halls. The bureau understood that death threats, though they provided a certain barometer of the culture, weren't the real concern; the people who *didn't* threaten were usually the ones to worry about.

But some of the rumors about bounties seemed to have a basis in fact. The White Knights of the KKK, it was said, had offered a hundred thousand dollars to anyone who killed the Nobel laureate. Other groups, such as the Minutemen and various neo-Nazi cells, had also floated assassination proposals that involved a considerable financial reward.

Perhaps the most serious bounty of all, and the one that, years later, the FBI would deem the most credible, originated in Ray's hometown of St. Louis, where a wealthy patent attorney named John Sutherland had offered a bounty of fifty thousand dollars. Sutherland had a portfolio of stocks and other securities worth nearly a half-million dollars—investments that included sizable holdings in Rhodesia. One of St. Louis's most ardent segregationists, he was founder of the St. Louis White Citizens Council and an active member of the John Birch Society (he was a personal friend of its founder, Robert Welch). In recent years, he had become immersed in a right-wing business organization called the Southern States Industrial Council.

For years Sutherland had been venting his peculiar strain of racial rage. "Like Khrushchev, the collectivists will settle for nothing less than total integration of every residential area, every social gathering, and every privately owned business enterprise," he once wrote, on letterhead stationery that featured entwined Confederate and American flags emblazoned with the motto STATES RIGHTS–RACIAL INTEGRITY. "The white majority must act before state coercion prevents us from doing so!" Sutherland lamented that "we are deep in the throes of minority rule" and insisted that "we forgotten men got that way by failing to heed the admonition of the great seal of Missouri—'United We Stand, Divided We Fall.'"

Throughout 1968, Sutherland spent much of his time organizing for George Wallace. He sometimes could be found down at the Wallace headquarters in South St. Louis, where organizers frequently met at John Ray's tavern, the Grapevine.

Earlier in the year, Sutherland tried to persuade at least one man—Russell Byers, a forty-six-year-old auto parts dealer and sometime car thief—to accept his bounty offer and assassinate King. Byers claimed he met Sutherland in the den of his house, which was conspicuously Confederate themed: swords, bugles, flags. Sutherland wore the hat of a Confederate cavalry colonel, with crossed sabers on the front.

As Byers recalled the encounter to the FBI, Sutherland told him he'd like to pay fifty grand to contract for the killing of a well-known figure.

And who would that be? Byers asked.

"King," Sutherland answered. "Kill Martin Luther King. Or arrange to have him killed."

Byers had long dwelled in a criminal netherworld and was used to having exotic business ventures floated his way, but the whole situation struck him as strange. "Where's the money coming from?" he asked.

Sutherland replied that he belonged to "a secret Southern organization" that could easily raise the bounty.

Byers declined the offer. Though he was a small-time crook, a thief, and a con man, he was no murderer. But Byers could tell that this shadowy wheeler-dealer, this colonel *manqué* in the Confederate cap, was serious about his project. If he was a wacko, he was a well-connected one, someone who could leverage the underworld of St. Louis and get things done.

The bureau never found definitive proof that Ray was ever paid a cent by Sutherland, or even that Ray knew about the bounty. But Sutherland's connections to the Wallace campaign, and to John Ray's Grapevine Tavern, would intrigue investigators for years. Russell Byers did not immediately come forward to the FBI, and it would not be until 1977 that agents were able to piece together the story. Investigators with the House Select Committee on Assassinations found Byers's story "credible" and singled out the Sutherland bounty as one scenario that likely could have motivated James Earl Ray to kill King. But by that point, John Sutherland was beyond the reach of prosecution. He died in 1970.

ALONG THE MALL in Washington, the caravans of the Poor People's Army had all arrived, and on May 13, Resurrection City was declared open for business. Much as Martin Luther King had hoped for, more than two thousand people of all colors and backgrounds were now encamped in a sprawling tabernacle city set among the cherry trees of West Potomac Park. Abernathy was sworn in as "mayor," and Jesse Jackson, having more or less patched up his relationship with King's successor, was named the shantytown's "city manager."

The SCLC began this epic demonstration with high energy and fervent hope and even good humor. Abernathy envisioned a "City on a Hill," a great experiment in protest politics that would last at least a month. It would be a kind of American Soweto perched on the back doorstep of Capitol Hill, a deliberate eyesore meant to force the government to pay attention to the problem of systemic poverty. Protesters vowed to disrupt if not paralyze the business of government, and they planned to go to jail en masse. Abernathy threatened to sic "plague after plague upon the pharaohs of Congress until we get our demands"—which included an economic bill of rights guaranteeing a minimum yearly income, a campaign to end hunger in America, and a multi-point plan to rebuild the nation's worst inner-city ghettos. The price tag on all of Abernathy's antipoverty measures came to nearly thirty billion dollars.

During its first week, Resurrection City made front-page news and enjoyed a sort of honeymoon period in the media. Reporters feasted on the spectacle of this latter-day Hooverville erected in the shadow of the Mall's cold marble monuments. Congressional delegations walked the grounds—among the visitors was a U.S. representative from Texas named George Herbert Walker Bush. There were marches, parades, press conferences, and sit-ins; there was live music, dancing, even an Indian powwow. Peter, Paul, and Mary came, as did Pete Seeger and a host of black entertainers. Abernathy proudly baptized the first child born in the camp. Resurrection City had the feel and pulse of a freewheeling countercultural festival, a full year before Woodstock.

But by the second week, things had started to unravel. It became apparent that the Poor People's Campaign was short on ideas—and even shorter on organizational strategy. The SCLC knew how to run a march, but it had no experience running a functioning city. Ralph Abernathy was no Martin Luther King—he had neither the shrewdness nor the charisma nor the rhetorical discipline to bring off such an ambitious campaign. Even Abernathy recognized it. "Resurrection City was flawed from the beginning," he later conceded. "I realized more every day the loss I had suffered and the burden I had inherited."

Veterans and friends of the movement began to impugn Abernathy's leadership. Stanley Levison, King's old confidant, saw signs of "megalomania—Abernathy is thrill-happy and running around everywhere." As far as Levison was concerned, the campaign was fast becoming "a fiasco." Bayard Rustin, meeting with reporters, shared a similar disdain for Abernathy's abilities. Resurrection City was "just another fish-fry," he said. Instead of engaging government officials and building allies, Rustin argued, the SCLC leader was alienating nearly everyone who could aid the cause, leaving Congress feeling "trapped by Abernathy's nameless demands for an instant millennium."

As Andy Young saw it, Abernathy simply didn't have what it took to hold the already-disintegrating movement together, and he couldn't keep his headstrong young staff under control. Bickering between James Bevel, Hosea Williams, and Jesse Jackson nearly descended to the level of fistfights. "Ralph was frustrated with his inability to be Martin Luther King," Young later wrote. "The team of wild horses was now really running wild."

Most of the SCLC higher-ups didn't even stay in Resurrection City—they decamped to a Howard Johnson across from the Watergate. In the absence of strong and present leadership, Resurrection City fell apart. Teenage gang members, who served as "marshals" along the encampment's tattered thoroughfares, harassed and even beat up reporters. Thugs worked the long rows of tents, shaking down residents for protection money. The camp was treated to a steady drumbeat of weird and troubling anecdotes: An obese man wielding an ax stormed about the camp, hacking down several A-frame structures. Two psychiatric patients, recently released from St. Elizabeths mental hospital, set a phone booth on fire. A band of rowdies threw bottles at cars along Independence Avenue and fell into a protracted tear-gas war with the police at the east end of the Reflecting Pool. Camp officials began to receive threats on Abernathy's life. Then a rumor went out that vandals from Chicago were planning to scale the Lincoln Memorial and spray-paint it *black*.

Just when it seemed as though the news reports emanating from Resurrection City couldn't get any worse, they did. On May 23, the rains came, and the deluge didn't stop for two weeks. As Abernathy put it, "The gray skies poured water, huge sheets that swept across the Mall like the monsoons of India," leaving people "ankle deep in cold, brown slush." It rained so much that people suspected the government had seeded the clouds. Resurrection City became, literally, a quagmire. Hosea Williams, who replaced Jesse Jackson as "city manager" after the internecine feuding became intolerable, called the campsite "that mudhole." Pathways had to be covered in sheets of plywood. Tents collapsed. Hygiene deteriorated. Worried health department officials warned that outbreaks of dysentery and typhoid were imminent. The National Park Service would soon be presenting the SCLC with a bill of seventy-two thousand dollars for damages to the grounds of the Mall. Meanwhile, some twenty-two broken-down mules abandoned after the long trek to Washington were given over to the care of the Society for the Prevention of Cruelty to Animals or placed in perpetuity on a Virginia farm.

No one could have been more pleased by all this bad news than J. Edgar Hoover. Ever since the first caravans had pulled in to Washington a few weeks earlier, he'd been keeping close tabs on Project POCAM. Hoover had dozens of agents, paid informers, and undercover spies milling about the camp. One of his many sources of intelligence came from the Pentagon, which had assigned a unit of signal corpsmen to observe and photograph the encampment, night and day, from the top of the Washington Monument. Once it became obvious to Hoover that the SCLC's internal problems prevented it from becoming the organized subversive force he had feared, he pressed his agents and informers to take a slightly different tack. In a memo, he told them to "document such things as immorality, indecency, dishonesty, and hypocrisy" among the campaign's leadership.

But by this time, the Poor People's Army was running out of steam, out of creativity, out of cash. People were referring to the campaign as the Little Bighorn of the civil rights movement. Now Abernathy was desperately trying to pull out of Washington with his dignity intact.

At some moment during that long, wet, turbulent month, an era had reached its denouement. The battle-fatigued nation had just about had its fill of protest politics, of marching and rioting, of scattershot airings of grievance. As Gerald McKnight put it in his classic study, *The Last Crusade*, most of Washington had come to regard Resurrection City as "some grotesque soap opera whose run could not end soon enough."

The civil rights movement was feeling the final impact of King's assassination, the final measure of his loss. By carrying out their slain leader's wishes in Washington, the SCLC staff had shown the world just how indispensable he was. Though the event still had several weeks to play itself out, Resurrection City had become, in McKnight's words, "almost a perfect failure."

Yet there was also something fiercely apt about Resurrection City and its inability to move the nation. Ramsey Clark, perhaps alone among high-ranking Johnson administration officials, responded to the pathos embedded in King's final flawed experiment on the Mall. "Lincoln smiled kindly, but the American people saw too much of the truth," Clark wrote a few years later. "For poverty is miserable. It is ugly, disorganized, rowdy, sick, uneducated, violent, afflicted with crime. Poverty demeans human dignity. The demanding tone, the inarticulateness, the implied violence deeply offended us. We didn't want to see it on our sacred monumental grounds. We wanted it out of sight and out of mind."

DURING THE MIDDLE of May, the focal point in the hunt for James Earl Ray shifted north to Canada. The FBI learned that Ray had spent time in Toronto and Montreal shortly after his escape from the Missouri penitentiary—that, in fact, he had developed his Eric Galt alias in Canada, stealing identification details from a *real* Eric S. Galt, who lived in a Toronto suburb. On the theory that he might have returned to Canada after the assassination, the FBI asked the Royal Canadian Mounted Police to pursue a variety of labor-intensive leads. Foremost among these, the bureau wanted Canadian authorities to examine all passport applications dating back to April 1967, the month of Ray's escape from Jeff City, and then single out any photos that bore a resemblance to Ray.

It was an immense undertaking: during that time, Canada had issued some 218,000 passports and had renewed 46,000 more. Reviewing this mountain of paperwork would require staggering man-hours—all the document and photo comparisons would have to be done by hand and by eyeball. But the Mounties took up the task with urgency and zest.

Superintendent Charles J. Sweeney, commander of the RCMP criminal investigating squad in eastern Ontario, assumed command of the task force in Ottawa. Sweeney selected twelve uniformed constables and equipped them with magnifying glasses. Night after night, working high up in a government building one block from Parliament, the Mounties painstakingly went through the applications, one by one.

■

THAT SAME WEEK, Ramon Sneyd was staying in a cheap hotel called the Heathfield House, on Cromwell Road, a major thoroughfare that cuts through West London. The Heathfield House was in Earls Court, a low-rent neighborhood then known as Kangaroo Valley because it was especially popular among Australian workers. Sneyd had been here for ten days, holed up in his room, reading newspapers and magazines— and desperately trying to hatch a new plan. He still had *Psycho-Cybernetics* and other self-help books to help him while away the hours, as well as a book on Rhodesia and a detective novel, *The Ninth Directive*. Lying low from dawn until late at night, reading in his small wallpapered room, he could hear the frequent roar of the big Heathrow jumbo jets as they banked over the Thames, offering the promise of freedom in the extremities of the faded empire.

Doris Catherine Westwood, the proprietress of the Heathfield House, hardly ever saw her tenant and wasn't quite sure of his name. "Owing to his bad writing," she later told Scotland Yard, "I thought his name was 'Snezel.'"

May 1968 was a vibrant time to be in groovy, bell-bottom London. The musical *Hair* was about to open at the Shaftesbury Theatre— though censors vowed to ban the show's frontal nudity. In the history of rock 'n' roll super-bands, it was a month of ferment. The same week that Sneyd arrived in London, the Beatles, having returned from a Transcendental Meditation sojourn in Rishikesh, India, buried themselves in Abbey Road Studios to begin recording what would become known as *The White Album*. Elsewhere the Rolling Stones were just wrapping up one of their greatest contributions to vinyl, *Beggars Banquet*, and The Who's Pete Townshend had begun writing the first strains of a rock opera about a deaf, dumb, and blind kid named Tommy.

Trapped in his room, racked with stomach pains and headaches, Sneyd had neither time nor inclination to enjoy the city, and he caught little of London's vibe. Since arriving here, Sneyd had become a lizard-like creature, keeping to the cracks and shadows. He was extremely reluctant to show his face in public during the day. American newspapers and magazines on sale at London newsstands were carrying his photo with some regularity. *Life* magazine had come out with a long cover story on Ray's childhood and criminal career. Sneyd bought a copy of it—"The Accused Killer: Ray, Alias Galt, the Revealing Story of a Mean Kid," the cover said—and he read the story with a feeling of deepening dread that Hoover's men would soon follow his trail across the Atlantic.

Luckily for Sneyd, Great Britain had recently passed the Criminal Justice Act, which, among other things, virtually prohibited British publications from printing anything but the most rudimentary facts about a suspect before trial. Consequently, the London papers had not yet published photographs of Ray, and scarcely anyone in London other than a few Scotland Yard officers knew of the FBI warrant for his arrest. And in truth, although King's assassination had made huge headlines in Great Britain, most English citizens referred to the slain civil rights leader as "Luther King" and had only a vague idea of what, besides winning a Nobel Peace Prize for civil rights, he had actually done. Unlike in the United States, King's death, and the manhunt for his killer, had largely receded into the background.

For all these reasons, Sneyd remained under the radar screen, well hidden among the warrens of London's more than five thousand inns and bed-and-breakfast establishments.

But his troubles were mounting. He'd had no luck finding a cheap passage to Africa. Since his arrival here on May 17, Sneyd's money woes had become truly acute. He now had less than fifty pounds on his person. On May 27, when Mrs. Westwood told him it would soon be time to pay the rent, Sneyd knew he would have to do something desperate, something rash. "I'll go to my bank," he promised her, "and make a withdrawal."

■

A FEW HOURS later, sixty-two-year-old Maurice Isaacs and his wife, Billie, were getting ready to close up their small jewelry store in Paddington. The shop, which had been operating since the end of World War II, was located at 131 Praed Street, only a few blocks from Paddington Station, in a neighborhood bustling with commuters, transients, and tourists.

The gray-haired husband and wife were showing diamond rings to a customer when Ramon Sneyd walked in. In his pocket was his loaded snub-nosed Liberty Chief .38 revolver. He lingered by the glass cases in the front, pretending to be shopping for something. Eventually, the customer left, and Sneyd made his move. He grabbed Maurice Isaacs, brandished the revolver, and stuck it in the side of the jeweler's neck.

"This is a stickup!" Sneyd said. "Now both of you get on back there!" He gestured manically toward the darkened rear of the store, where the couple kept their office.

Over the years, the Isaacses' shop had been burglarized, but they'd never been held up at gunpoint. The couple kept no weapons in their store, nor had they ever rehearsed a plan for how to handle such a situation. Neither of them moved an inch toward the back as Sneyd had commanded—they were determined to take their chances out in the open, where someone on the busy street might see them through the plate-glass window. They knew there was a crowded pub just down the street—the Fountains Abbey—and the sidewalks outside were thronged with rush-hour foot traffic.

Instinct took over. Billie Isaacs, a sweet and matronly woman in her late fifties, leaped onto Sneyd's back. When she did, Maurice wrestled free from Sneyd's grip. He turned and struck the would-be robber several times, then set off the alarm.

Realizing he'd seriously underestimated the tenacity of these shop owners, Sneyd turned and darted from the store. In the early evening light, he raced down busy Praed Street, past St. Mary's Hospital—frustrated that, after his sorry performance, he was none the richer.

■

IN OTTAWA, AFTER a week of exacting work, the team of twelve constables had plowed their way through more than a hundred thousand passport applications—and had singled out eleven as "possibles." But each of these "possibles" led detectives to the valid passports of legitimate

Canadian citizens. As everyone feared, this was shaping up to be a pointless fishing expedition.

But on June 1, a twenty-one-year-old constable named Robert Wood lingered over a certain photograph. He eyed it with his magnifying glass, saw the dimple in the chin, the touch of gray at the temples, the slightly protruding left ear. He compared it carefully with the numerous Ray photos he had as a reference. "This could be him," Wood said out loud, "if he wore glasses." The name on the passport was Ramon George Sneya.

Now Constable Wood's colleagues set aside their work and gathered round to examine the photo. Some saw the likeness; others weren't so sure. The horn-rimmed eyeglasses threw them off, as did the nose, which was sharper at the tip than that in the old Ray photos. This man looked considerably more dignified in his sport coat and tie, almost like an academic.

Wood held the application in his hand for a while. Not knowing what else to do with it, he laid it in the "possibles" pile—and got back to his monotonous work.

■

ON THE AFTERNOON of June 4, Ian Colvin, a foreign-desk journalist and editorial writer for London's *Daily Telegraph*, was sitting in his office when the phone rang. "Hello, this is Ramon Sneyd," the caller nervously said, in a garbled American accent Colvin couldn't quite place. "I got a brother lost somewhere down in Angola, and I've heard you've written about the mercenary situation down there."

"Yes."

"Well," Sneyd continued, "I think my brother's with the mercenaries. Can you put me in touch with someone who can help me find him?"

Colvin was not particularly surprised by the call; it was true, he *had* written a book about the colonial wars and mercenary armies in Africa and had developed an extensive circle of contacts in that world. To his credit, this man Sneyd appeared to have done some homework. "Do you have a telephone number of Major Alastair Wicks?" he asked Colvin.

A British-born Rhodesian mercenary with a swashbuckling reputation, Wicks had been involved with armed conflicts in Biafra and was a

high-ranking officer in an outfit called the Five Commando Unit down in
the Belgian Congo. Though Colvin knew Wicks well, he was reluctant to
give out a phone number. "But give me *your* name and a phone number,"
Colvin offered, "and I'll forward it on to Major Wicks."

At this point, Colvin could hear an electronic chirping on the line—
Sneyd was clearly calling from a pay telephone, and the shrill beep-beep-
beep indicated that he needed to shove another sixpence into the slot. "Uh,
wait a minute," Sneyd said, "I got to put in more money." But he evidently
couldn't dig out his coins fast enough—the phone connection cut off.

Colvin's phone rang a few minutes later. "This is Sneyd," a voice
said, sounding somewhat flustered. "I was just talking to you." Listening
as Sneyd repeated his shaggy-dog story about a long-lost brother, Colvin
began to think that his caller was "odd" and "almost unbalanced." Sneyd
was adamant to the point of desperation about getting himself to Africa,
and seemed to think that if he could only get in touch with the right person, his airfare would be paid for in exchange for his promise to serve a
stint as a soldier.

"Again," Colvin reassured him, "I will be delighted to forward your
contact information on to Major Wicks."

"OK," the caller said. "That's Ramon Sneyd. I'm staying here at the
New Earls Court Hotel."

Right, Colvin said, and Sneyd hung up.

■

SNEYD HAD MOVED from the Heathfield House to the New Earls
Court Hotel only a few days before. Though the little hotel was just
around the corner, on Penywern Road, the weekly rent was cheaper and
the accommodations a little nicer. Besides, Sneyd thought it prudent not
to linger too long in any one place—especially after his aborted jewelry
store stickup in Paddington.

The hotel was a four-story walk-up, with Doric columns and a blue
awning covering a cramped vestibule; it was near the Earls Court tube stop
and Earls Court Stadium, where Billy Graham had recently conducted a
series of wildly successful crusades. For another week, Sneyd remained
faithful to his usual nocturnal schedule, keeping to his brown-wallpapered
room all day, receiving no calls, and taking no visitors. "He was nervous,

pathetically shy, and unsure of himself," the young hotel receptionist, Janet Nassau, later said. Feeling sorry for him, Nassau tried to make conversation and help him out with a few currency questions. "But he was so incoherent," she said, "that nobody seemed able to help him. I thought he was a bit thick. I tried to talk to him, but then I stopped myself, I was afraid he might think I was too forward—trying to chat him up."

For Sneyd, a far bigger worry than the peculiarities of British money was the fact that he scarcely had any money at all; his funds had dwindled to about ten pounds. But on June 4, the same day he called the *Daily Telegraph* journalist Ian Colvin, Sneyd worked up his courage and resolved to finally dig himself out of his financial straits.

That afternoon he put on a blue suit and pair of sunglasses. Then, at 2:13 p.m., he walked into the Trustee Savings Bank in Fulham and stood in the queue until, a few minutes later, he approached the till of a clerk named Edward Viney. Through the slot, Sneyd slid a paper bag toward the teller. At first, Viney didn't know what to do with the rumpled pink bag. Then, on closer inspection, he saw writing scrawled across it.

"Put all £5 notes in this bag," the message demanded. Viney caught a faint glimpse of the man's eyes through his shades and realized he was serious. Glancing down, he saw the glinting nose of a revolver, pointed at him.

Viney quickly emptied his till of all small denominations—in total, only ninety-five pounds. Sneyd was displeased with his slim pickings, and he leaned over the counter and craned his neck toward the adjacent till. "Give me all your small notes!" he yelled, shoving his pistol toward the teller, Llewellyn Heath. In panic, Heath backpedaled and kicked a large tin box, which produced a concussive sound similar to a gunshot. The noise startled everyone, including Sneyd, who leaped away from the counter and sprinted down the street. Two tellers took off after him, but he lost them, ducking into a tailor's shop, where for five minutes he feigned interest in buying a pair of slacks.

At Trustee Savings Bank, Edward Viney surveyed the premises and realized that the robber had left his note behind, scrawled on the pink paper bag. When the bobbies arrived, Viney handed them the bag—upon which, it was soon discovered in the crime lab of New Scotland Yard, the robber had left a high-quality latent thumbprint.

■

IN TORONTO, an investigator with the Royal Canadian Mounted Police, Detective Sergeant R. Marsh, was given a copy of the latest passport application that Constable Wood had placed in the "possibles" pile. Working off the details in the application, Detective Marsh quickly deduced that "Sneya" was merely a clerical error, and then tracked down the *real* Ramon George Sneyd.

Even though Sneyd was a Toronto policeman, Detective Marsh initially had to regard him as a possible suspect in the King assassination—or at least a possible co-conspirator—and he began the interrogation in a distinctly adversarial posture. "Mr. Sneyd," Marsh said, "on April 4, a killing took place in Memphis, Tennessee. The American authorities are seeking a suspect. That suspect later took up residence here, in Toronto, under the name Ramon George Sneyd. What, if anything, can you tell us about this?"

Constable Sneyd was flummoxed, to say the least. He searched his memory for any incident, any stray encounter in which someone might have filched his identity. Then he remembered.

"About a month ago," he replied, "I received a telephone call from a stranger who asked me, 'Is this Mr. Sneyd?' He wanted to know if I'd lost my passport—he said he was with the passport division and was making a routine check. I said, 'You've got the wrong Mr. Sneyd.' But then he asked me again, wasn't I Ramon George Sneyd, born in Toronto on October 8, 1932? I said, 'Yes, but there must be some mistake. I've never had a passport. I've never applied for a passport in my whole life.' The man apologized for the mistake, and hung up."

Sneyd's story was convincing enough that Marsh soon let this very confused policeman go. The passport that had been issued to "Sneya" was obviously phony.

Meanwhile, other RCMP detectives began to investigate the various addresses noted in the passport application. They visited Mrs. Loo's place on Dundas Street, Mrs. Szpakowski's place on Ossington Avenue, and the Arcade Photo Studio, where they confiscated the original negative of the passport photo. They discovered that "Sneyd" had also been using the alias "Paul Bridgman"—and that the real Bridgman, like the real Sneyd, had recently been telephoned by a stranger claiming to be from the passport office in Ottawa.

Their curiosity more than piqued, RCMP detectives then visited the Kennedy Travel Bureau, the Toronto travel agency from which the notarized passport application had originated. There they interviewed Lillian Spencer, the travel agent who had worked with Sneyd. Consulting her files, Spencer told the detectives that Sneyd had presumably traveled to London Heathrow on May 6 aboard British Overseas Flight 600. She hadn't heard from him since.

Airline records at the Toronto International Airport indicated that "Sneya" had indeed kept to his itinerary: on the flight list to London was the name detectives were looking for—Ramon G. Sneyd.

Copies of the passport application were forwarded posthaste to the FBI Crime Lab, where handwriting experts soon ascertained that Sneyd's handwriting matched that of Eric S. Galt and James Earl Ray. The train of evidence was thus indisputable: the fugitive, after acquiring a new identity in Canada, had escaped to England. It was time to notify Scotland Yard.

■

THE DAY AFTER his bank robbery in Fulham, Ramon Sneyd decided he needed to move again, and quickly cleared out of the New Earls Court Hotel. He wended his way through the rainy streets to Pimlico and inquired at a YMCA. It was full, but the YMCA receptionist referred him to a little place a few doors down called the Pax, where a VACANCY sign winked through the fog. Dressed in a beige raincoat with a bundle of papers under his arm, Sneyd asked the hotel's Swedish-born owner, Anna Thomas, for aspirin to soothe his throbbing headache— then went up to his room, which was small but clean, its walls decorated in a cheerful pattern of blue peacocks. "He seemed ill and very, very nervous," Thomas said. "He stayed in bed all day. I asked him several times to sign the register, but he refused."

In truth, Sneyd was in a state of growing panic. He was running out of ideas. He'd heard nothing from Ian Colvin or Major Alastair Wicks, and he still had no notion how he was going to get to southern Africa. His robbery had fetched the paltry equivalent of only $240—not enough to purchase an airline ticket to Salisbury. He'd already spent some of his takings on the street, buying a syringe and drugs—possibly speed or heroin—to shoot up. Mrs. Thomas soon picked up on his narcotized state. "He never smelled of liquor," she said, "but he kept acting sort of dazed."

Something else was on Sneyd's mind: News reports on June 5 carried the sensational story that Senator Robert Kennedy had been shot in the head at the Ambassador Hotel in Los Angeles, not far from where Sneyd, as Eric Galt, had been living a few months earlier. Senator Kennedy was still clinging to life in a hospital, his prognosis grim. Sneyd was no admirer of Senator Kennedy, but he feared that the outrage over another major U.S. assassination would only spur the FBI to redouble its efforts at finding King's murderer. He didn't know how, but he was convinced that the fallout from the Kennedy shooting would pursue him across the ocean.

"That's terrible news—about Senator Kennedy," a hotel staff member later recalled saying to Sneyd.

He replied with what the employee took to be sarcasm dripping from his voice: "It's terrible all right."

■

THE SAME DAY, Andrew Young and Coretta Scott King, along with several other SCLC staff members, were numbly watching the television news in a suite at Washington's Willard Hotel. They had withdrawn from the noise and mud and confusion of Resurrection City, only a few blocks away, to join the national vigil for Robert Kennedy. As the depressing news reports flickered over the screen, both Young and Mrs. King felt a horrible déjà vu. "I was in a daze, functioning on autopilot," Young said. "I had never been so despondent."

Coretta could never forget Senator Kennedy's kindnesses after her husband's death—providing a plane for her to fly to Memphis, delivering that calming off-the-cuff speech in Indianapolis, touring the riot-scarred cities, and offering a vision for how to rewire the inner cities of America. Kennedy was the only presidential candidate who had openly supported the Poor People's Campaign.

Now the bulletins made it increasingly clear that Kennedy was not going to make it. The news was almost too much for Resurrection City to bear; it was the crushing blow to an already weather-beaten and hopelessly disorganized event at the frayed end of the civil rights movement. "We were all still trying to pretend that Martin's death had not devastated us," Young wrote. But with Kennedy's shooting, "I couldn't pretend anymore. I sank into a depression so deep it was impossible to go on."

■

THE FOLLOWING DAY in London, Anna Thomas, the Pax Hotel's owner, went in to clean Sneyd's room and saw a newspaper on the bed opened to news about the RFK assassination. The senator had died overnight, a young Palestinian Arab firebrand named Sirhan Sirhan had been charged, and a stupefied nation was preparing to mourn another Kennedy. The senator's body was to be flown to New York, for a requiem mass at St. Patrick's Cathedral, then taken by a slow train to Washington for burial at Arlington National Cemetery beside his brother's grave.

Thomas found that Sneyd's room was already tidy, the bed made, the blue spread pulled tight. He'd washed his own shirts, and now they were hung up to drip-dry over the small sink beside the window.

Sneyd, it turned out, was at a telephone call box around the corner, ringing Ian Colvin at the *Daily Telegraph*. "I haven't heard from Major Wicks and now I've had to change hotels—did you call him?" Sneyd demanded to know. To Colvin, Sneyd sounded "overwrought and somewhat incoherent."

Colvin told Sneyd that he had phoned Major Wicks (and, in fact, Colvin *had*), but Wicks had said the name Sneyd meant nothing to him. Wicks checked around and found no one who knew Sneyd's brother. "How long has he been missing down there?" Colvin asked.

"Well," Sneyd admitted. "The truth is, he's not really missing. It's just that we haven't heard from him in a few months."

"Are you worried for his safety?" Colvin asked.

"It's not so much that," Sneyd said, hesitating. "You see, I'd really like to become a mercenary *myself*."

All this dissembling was trying Colvin's patience. He told Sneyd that now was a bad time to try to enlist with the mercenaries—in most African countries, the fight was fading, the movement drying up, the soldiers of fortune gradually heading home.

"In any case," he added, trying to make this importunate man go away, "London's not the best place to get information on the mercenaries."

This seemed to catch Sneyd's attention. "Where would you suggest I go?" he asked.

"Well," Colvin replied. "If I were you, I'd get myself over to Brussels." He explained that they had some sort of information center there that kept track of all the mercenaries.

"Where's that again?"

Brussels, Colvin said—Brussels, Belgium.

■

ABOUT A MILE away, at Scotland Yard, one of Great Britain's leading sleuths had taken command of the Ray-Galt-Sneyd fugitive case. His name was Detective Chief Superintendent Thomas Butler, the head of the famed Flying Squad that had recently solved one of England's most notorious heists—the so-called Great Train Robbery of 1963. Blunt, stolid, and balding, the fifty-five-year-old Tommy Butler was a bachelor who lived with his mother in Barnes, near the Thames. He didn't smoke, rarely drank, and was given to wearing natty houndstooth blazers.

Detective Butler had a reputation for methodical relentlessness. Writing of Butler, a London *Times* reporter said that "many criminals seeking refuge abroad later confessed that they knew no peace, even at the other side of the world, when they heard Mr. Butler was actively engaged in their recapture."

Butler's men quickly learned that Ramon "Sneya" had stayed only a few hours at Heathrow and then taken a plane straightaway to Lisbon. Portuguese police, working with the FBI and Interpol, traced Sneyd's movements in Lisbon. They found his hotel, his drinking haunts, his whores. They found that he'd obtained a corrected passport at the Canadian embassy in Lisbon. They found he'd returned to London on May 17.

So the brunt of the investigation, having been briefly tossed to Portugal, was back in Butler's court. The detective chief superintendent wasted no time. Detectives fanned out and began questioning the managers of every cheap hotel and bed-and-breakfast in London. Every airline, train line, bus line, and rental car agency was checked, as were luggage lockers, safe-deposit boxes, and nightclubs. A photo with a description of Sneyd was printed in the *Police Gazette*, a sheet circulated among every police and immigration officer in the British Isles. "Wanted in connection with a serious immigration matter," the caption under Sneyd's photo announced. "Do not interrogate but detain for questioning."

Finally, on June 6, the name Ramon George Sneyd was placed on the "All Ports Warning," which meant that immigration officials at every harbor and air terminal in the British Isles were alerted to halt anyone traveling under that name.

Butler reported back to the FBI in Washington—his men were on the case, he said, and he felt confident that something would turn up soon. Cartha DeLoach was cautiously optimistic: "We knew that the fugitive was hiding somewhere in England, Scotland, or Wales—an area smaller than the United States, but still a haystack in which a needle could disappear for weeks or months or years."

ON THE MORNING of June 8, Anna Thomas knocked on Ramon Sneyd's room and found that her tenant had packed up and taken off. The room was clean, except for the newspapers sprawled everywhere. He'd left behind a Cold War spy thriller, *Tangier Assignment*, whose lurid yellow cover promised a story "seething with international intrigue, Mafia villainy, and freebooting contrabandists." In the sink, crammed down the drain, Thomas found a plastic syringe.

She was quite glad to see her tenant go. "He was so neurotic, such a strange fellow," Thomas recalled. "I felt sorry for him, but he was so obviously a troubled man that he gave me the creeps."

▪

As THOMAS CLEANED the room, Sneyd was sitting in a taxicab, making his way to Heathrow Airport, where he planned to take British European Airways Flight 466 to Brussels, Belgium. The plane was scheduled to leave at 11:50 a.m.

On the strength of Ian Colvin's suggestion, Sneyd had bought a one-way economy ticket the day before. Now, at Heathrow's Terminal 2, he presented the voucher to a clerk at the departures desk and then checked in his one bag. He turned and walked toward customs and immigration. He wore a sport jacket, gray pants, and a long beige raincoat. Under his raincoat, in his right trouser pocket, he could feel the cool metal mass of his loaded pistol.

"Passport please," a young immigration officer named Kenneth Human said when Sneyd approached the window.

Sneyd fished his wallet out of a coat pocket. From an inside fold, he retrieved a dark blue Canadian passport, which the officer opened and studied. Officer Human glanced at Sneyd, and then back at the passport photo. Nothing seemed untoward: the same man, the same glasses, everything matched.

Then Human saw another passport, peeking from Sneyd's billfold. "May I see that other one?" he asked.

Sneyd handed the officer the second passport, which was clearly stamped "Canceled."

"Why are the names different?" Human asked, noting that one said "Sneyd" and the other said "Sneya."

Sneyd explained that his original passport, issued in Ottawa, had contained the misspelling—simply a clerical error—but that he'd had it corrected as soon as possible while in Portugal.

Officer Human appeared to be buying Sneyd's explanation. But at this point, a Scotland Yard detective materialized—a slender, fastidious man with blue eyes and a trim mustache named Philip Birch. While Sneyd and the customs officer continued talking about the passport, Birch studied the Canadian's face and movements. He had an "absentminded professorial air" about him, Birch thought, but something about the traveler looked familiar. He seemed to recall seeing the man's photograph in the pages of the *Police Gazette*.

Birch ran his finger down a list of names typed on an official Scotland Yard document that was labeled "Watch For and Detain." Under the heading "All Ports Warning," the Canadian's name jumped off the page: Ramon George Sneyd.

Detective Birch tapped Sneyd on the shoulder. "I say, old fellow," he later recalled telling the subject. "Would you mind stepping over here for a moment? I'd like to have a word with you."

Seemingly more annoyed than alarmed, Sneyd glanced at his watch. "But my plane's leaving soon."

"Oh, this will only take a moment," Birch assured him in a chipper tone. "May I see those passports, please?"

Two policemen joined Birch, and the three men escorted Sneyd across the busy terminal toward a police administrative office. Sneyd believed this was all just a routine passport mix-up, and so he remained grudgingly cooperative. Should things turn dicey, there was always the loaded revolver in his pocket. As far as he could see, this friendly trio of officers did not carry weapons.

When they arrived at the office, Birch turned and faced Sneyd. "Would you mind if I searched you?" he asked. Sneyd raised his arms and offered no protest.

Carefully patting him down, Birch quickly discovered the revolver: a Japanese-made .38-caliber Liberty Chief—its checkered walnut stock wrapped with black electrical tape. Birch spun the revolver and found five rounds of ammunition.

"Why are you carrying this gun?" Birch asked in an even tone.

"Well," Sneyd replied. "I'm going to Africa. I thought I might need it. You know how things are there." For the first time, a note of alarm had edged into his voice.

Birch handed the revolver to one of the other policemen and continued frisking the suspect. In Sneyd's pockets, Birch found a little booklet on rifle silencers and a blank key, of the sort that a locksmith might carry. Sneyd had a small amount of money—less than sixty pounds—on his person.

"I have reason to believe you have committed an arrestable offense," Birch said, and told Sneyd he was being detained. Now he *would* be missing his flight. Sneyd slumped in his chair.

The officer got on the phone and tried to have Sneyd's bag pulled from the plane—but it was too late, the jet was already easing back from the gate. Then Birch called Scotland Yard headquarters and informed his superiors that just two days after being placed on the "All Ports Warning," Ramon George Sneyd was now in police custody.

■

An hour later, Detective Chief Superintendent Thomas Butler arrived at Heathrow, accompanied by Chief Inspector Kenneth Thompson of the Interpol office. After briefly conferring with Philip Birch in an anteroom, Butler stepped into the office with the suspect and assumed command of the questioning. The poker-faced Butler was known throughout Scotland Yard as a master interrogator, adept at modulating his voice so that a suspect had no idea what he was thinking. Inspector Thompson sat in, but Butler did all the talking.

"We are police officers," Butler began, in a formal, courteous tone. "I understand you had in your possession two passports."

Sneyd seemed glad to see a fresh face to whom he could register his indignation. "I can't understand why I'm here," he said.

Butler would not dignify Sneyd's concern with a reply. "What is your name, sir?"

"Sneyd—my name is *Sneyd*!"

Butler produced the two passports and shuffled them in his hands like a deck of cards. He tapped them, opened them, and shuffled them again. He screwed up his face into a pained expression. "Both of these passports show that you are a Canadian citizen born in Toronto on October 8, 1932. Are these details correct?"

"Of *course* they're correct." Sneyd's frustration was palpable.

Then Butler produced the Liberty Chief pistol and held it in his palm. His pained expression returned. "This .38 revolver with five rounds of ammunition in its chambers was found in your hip pocket when you were first questioned. Is this your gun?"

"Yes."

"Would you like to tell us, Mr. Sneyd, why you are carrying a gun at all?"

"I was going to Brussels."

"Why should you want to take a gun to Brussels?"

Sneyd stammered. "Uh, well. I'm really thinking of going on to Rhodesia and things aren't too good there just now."

Butler traded glances with Inspector Thompson, then studied the revolver some more, knitting his eyebrows for effect. He was deliberately drawing things out, trying to make the suspect sweat. "In this country," he said, "one has to have a firearms certificate to own a gun—even to have ammunition in one's possession. Have you a firearms certificate issued by the competent authority?"

Sneyd shook his head. "No," he said, "I haven't got a certificate."

More pregnant pauses, more scowls and grimaces. "Then I must inform you, Mr. Sneyd, that you are under arrest for possession of a gun without a permit. I must also caution you that anything you say may be held against you."

■

SHORTLY THEREAFTER, SNEYD was transported to Cannon Row jail, a redbrick and granite cell block inside Scotland Yard, less than a hundred yards from the Houses of Parliament. There he was placed inside a large empty cell and detained until Butler and his Yard men could scramble together more information. The iron gates of the compound were guarded by a pair of tall London bobbies. With each passing quarter hour, immured in this gray dungeon, Sneyd could hear, could almost *feel*, the resonant chime of Big Ben, reminding him that he had not made it to the empire's extremities—only to the empire's central police station. Nearby, an armed guard stood vigil.

Scotland Yard detectives at Heathrow had succeeded in retrieving Sneyd's bag from the returning Brussels flight, and around 3:00 p.m. Chief Inspector Kenneth Thompson brought the suitcase to Sneyd's cell. "Is this your luggage?" he asked.

Yes, Sneyd said, it was.

The contents of the suitcase were quickly inventoried—and, in the words of one Scotland Yard official, "proved most enlightening." Among other items, investigators found a map of Portugal, a guidebook to Rhodesia, two books on hypnotism, and a well-marked paperback titled *Psycho-Cybernetics*. There was also a jacket with a label bearing the name Mr. Eric Galt. Wedged inside the battery housing of his transistor radio was a folded sheet of paper scribbled with the names of several mercenary groups in Angola.

A policeman appeared and told Sneyd to remove his clothes; he was to put on prison garb and turn in his present attire to Scotland Yard. Sneyd balked at this indignity—"I don't know what you're doing this for. It's no good for the lab boys, if that's what you think"—but then he did as he was told. The clothes were placed in a cellophane bag and entered into evidence.

A few minutes later Detective Chief Superintendent Thomas Butler entered Sneyd's cell and sat across from the prisoner, now in his jailbird uniform. Butler wasted no time in picking up where he'd left off at Heathrow. "As a result of inquiries made since you were detained," he said, "we have very good reason to believe that you are *not* a Canadian citizen, but an American."

Sneyd averted his eyes and seemed to be struggling with the implications of what he'd just heard. Then he nodded and mumbled, "Oh well, yes I am."

Sensing vulnerability, Butler aggressively pressed his case. "I believe your name is not Sneyd," he said, "but James Earl Ray, also known as Eric Starvo Galt and other names." Butler let that sink in, and then continued. "And that you are wanted at present in the United States for serious criminal offenses, including murder in which a firearm was used."

Sneyd was devastated. He collapsed onto a nearby bench and cradled his head in his hands. "Oh God," he said. "I feel so trapped."

Despite all the dire things Butler had just said about the detainee, the two charges Scotland Yard was now filing against Sneyd alias Galt alias Ray seemed puny indeed: traveling on a forged passport and carrying a firearm without a permit. But that was enough to stop the world's most wanted man and end his sixty-five-day flight from Memphis. He would soon be sent off to London's storied Brixton prison, to await extradition hearings.

"I should caution you again," Butler said, "that anything you say may be held against you."

Sneyd stared at the floor, his blanched face a mask of worry. "Yes, I shouldn't say anything more now. I can't think right."

IN THE SUBURBS of Washington, D.C., Cartha DeLoach was making late Saturday morning pancakes for his kids when the phone rang. It was an operator at FBI headquarters, patching through an international call from London.

"Deke—they've got your man." DeLoach heard a delayed and echoey voice from across the ocean. It was John Minnich, an FBI agent serving as the legal attaché at the American embassy in London.

"They *what?*"

"Scotland Yard," Minnich said. "They've got Sneyd. He was caught at Heathrow a few hours ago."

DeLoach couldn't contain his joy. "Really? Where was he going?"

"On his way to Brussels, apparently," Minnich replied. "He told them he was heading to Rhodesia after that."

DeLoach breathed a sigh of relief that was audible over the international phone lines. "Every muscle in my body relaxed," DeLoach recalled in his memoirs. "I hadn't realized how tense I'd been over the past two months. Light flooded into every corner of the room."

"But, Deke," Minnich said, snatching DeLoach from his reverie. "There's a small problem. We don't have a positive ID on him."

"What do you mean?"

"I mean we're not absolutely sure it's Ray."

"Well, that's easy," DeLoach barked. "Just get his fingerprints."

"Can't," Minnich replied. "It's not allowed here in Great Britain. Not unless the subject voluntarily agrees."

DeLoach almost hurled the phone at the wall in disgust—he had no patience for the Brits and their misplaced courtesies. The bureau had too much riding on this case, too many agents still slaving in the field, following too many costly leads; he *had* to get a positive identification—immediately.

"Dammit, man, give this guy Sneyd a glass of water. Then take the glass and lift the latents."

"But . . ."

"Do it!" DeLoach demanded, and hung up. He was too nervous to cook pancakes, too anxious to do anything but pace the floor.

An hour later, Minnich called back and began with a single word: "Positive!"

The ruse had evidently worked. Sneyd had gripped his glass of water and drunk his fill. Investigators whisked the glass away and submitted it to a Scotland Yard crime lab. The latent prints lifted from the glass were instantly familiar to the FBI—they included a left thumbprint with an ulnar loop of twelve ridge counts. The prints not only matched Ray's fingerprints; they were identical to the ones Scotland Yard experts had found on the scribbled-over paper bag left at Fulham's Trustee Savings Bank.

"Good man!" DeLoach told Minnich. He hung up and then tried to reach Hoover.

He found the director at his usual weekend haunt in New York, the Waldorf-Astoria. Hoover was taciturn and seemed on the verge of grumpiness for being troubled on an off day. When DeLoach broke the good news—that the largest manhunt in the FBI's history was over—all the Old Man said was, "Fine—prepare the press release."

■

AT ST. PATRICK'S CATHEDRAL in Manhattan, the requiem mass let out, and Robert Kennedy's body was shuttled to Penn Station to be placed on a memorial train for Washington. A stream of mourners began to flow from the dim Gothic cavern into the glare of the June day. Lyndon Johnson and Lady Bird stepped into a limousine and took off for Central Park, where the presidential helicopter awaited. Along Fifth Avenue, the dignitaries were too numerous to count, but the energy of the crowds coalesced around a triad of women, the three national widows—Jackie, Coretta, and Ethel.

An FBI agent, waiting on the steps beneath the eaves, buttonholed Ramsey Clark as he emerged from the cathedral. The agent whispered in Clark's ear. The attorney general nodded his understanding. The long chase was over. A press release had already been offered to the media.

For a brief moment, the nation's highest law-enforcement official savored the news. He got on a mobile phone and had a word with DeLoach, then called Assistant Attorney General Fred Vinson and told him to get on a plane to London to oversee extradition proceedings.

But as Clark thought about the timing of the FBI's news flash, he began to suspect that Hoover was deliberately trying to upstage the senator's funeral. If there was one man the director loathed as much as King, it was Bobby Kennedy. How delicious it must have seemed to the Old Man, Clark thought, to trumpet the bureau's triumph here and now, just as the great bronze doors swung open and the chancel organist pulled out all the stops. It would have been in good taste to wait—even just an hour or two—but Hoover couldn't help himself.

Within a few minutes, word had spread through the crowds milling beneath the cathedral's enormous rose window. A pack of journalists approached Coretta Scott King. "They've caught your husband's killer in London—what is your reaction?" one of them asked insistently.

This was news to Coretta. Without saying a word, she turned to the reporter, smiled the sad, wise smile she had perfected through two months of widowhood, and gave a barely perceptible bow. Then she turned and melted into the throngs along Fifth Avenue.

■

LATER IN THE day, as the Kennedy memorial train crept down the Eastern Seaboard past tearful crowds lined along the tracks—killing several spectators in the process—word of Ray's capture reached Resurrection City. An announcer's voice boomed the sensational news over a public address system, and the shantytown crowds spontaneously erupted in a prolonged cheer that was soon undercut with grumbles of skepticism. Was Ray the right man? Was he the *only* man? How could he have gotten all the way to London without help?

Since Abernathy was in New York for the funeral, Hosea Williams, the "city manager," became the encampment's de facto spokesman. "We're happy he's been caught—if he is the man," Williams told reporters. "But I'm not near as worried by that one man as about the system that produced him—the system that killed President Kennedy, Malcolm X, Martin Luther King, and Robert Kennedy. We are concerned with a sick and evil society."

A few hours later, at dusk, the Kennedy train pulled in to Washington's Union Station, and the funeral motorcade eased through the city toward Arlington National Cemetery for a candlelight burial. The cortege passed by the Justice Department building on Constitution Avenue, where Kennedy had served as attorney general, and where the FBI was now contending with the world's response to the Ray capture while prosecutors began to assemble the case for his extradition hearings. As the motorcade rolled by the Lincoln Memorial, a choral group sang "The Battle Hymn of the Republic." Along Constitution Avenue, thousands emerged from the hovels of the Poor People's Campaign and gave the senator a final mournful salute before his hearse passed onto the Memorial Bridge and crossed over the blue-black Potomac toward Arlington Cemetery.

■

IN WASHINGTON the following day, agents in the hallways of the FBI allowed themselves to bask for a moment in the glory of the capture. Although some newspaper editorials injected notes of doubt—*was there a conspiracy? was Ray a patsy?*—most papers and television accounts were full of praise, and on Capitol Hill politicians offered fulsome kudos to Hoover and his men.

Perhaps the loudest praise came from Senator Robert Byrd of West Virginia, a longtime Hoover stalwart. "Some felt this case was impossible," Byrd said. "Others have asserted their belief that Ray would never be captured, implying that the FBI did not really *want* to catch Ray. But in the end, Ray could not have run afoul of three finer law enforcement agencies in the world, even if he had tried—for his final capture resulted from the cooperation of the FBI, the Royal Canadian Mounted Police, and New Scotland Yard."

Hoover's critics saw the bureau in a new light; they found it refreshing to see the FBI *not* spying on citizens, *not* smearing reputations or pulling dirty tricks, but rather doing the close, hard work it was created for—solving major crimes important to the nation. The nine-week investigation was bold, relentless, methodical, creative, multidimensional. It had cost nearly two million dollars and had tied down more than half of Hoover's six thousand agents across the country. In many ways, it was one of the FBI's finest hours. All the advances the young Hoover had pushed for during the bureau's infancy—centralized fingerprint analysis, a state-of-the-art crime lab, a ballistics unit, a continental force of agents working in lockstep—had come fully into play in capturing Ray. For a single fugitive accused of a single crime, it was by far the most ambitious dragnet the FBI ever conducted. Ray had led them on a chase of more than twenty-five thousand miles.

In truth, the bureau had done a much better job of finding Ray than of ascertaining exactly why and how he had committed the crime. There were many unanswered questions—particularly having to do with Ray's motive, his sources of money, and his possible ties to the Sutherland bounty or to other floated plots on King's life. Ray's long flight was full of mysterious gaps, seeming contradictions, and stray facts that were difficult to reconcile. What were his connections to New Orleans, for example? What exactly did he do there and whom did he meet after he dropped off Charlie Stein? What possible role did his brothers play in the assassination, and in aiding Ray while he was on the lam? What help, if any, did he have in gathering his multiple aliases in Toronto? The trail that Ray had left was long, tortuous, and sketchy.

Ray's source of money was perhaps the biggest mystery. The FBI did not have it all sorted out, but it was clear that Ray must have pulled off several robberies while he was in flight. The bureau was intrigued to learn that on July 13, 1967, two men held up a bank in Ray's old hometown of Alton, Illinois. The robbery, which took place a little more than two months after Ray's escape from Jeff City, netted $27,234 in cash.

The case was never solved, but the FBI strongly suspected that the Ray brothers were involved.

Hoover intuitively understood how unusual Ray was. He was cryptic, difficult to pigeonhole; he refused to fit the assassin profile. "We are dealing with a man who is not an ordinary criminal, but a man capable of doing any kind of sly act," Hoover told Ramsey Clark in a meeting on June 20. "Ray is not a fanatic [like] Sirhan Sirhan. But he is a racist and detests Negroes, and Martin Luther King. He had information about King speaking in other towns and then picked out Memphis. I think he acted entirely alone, but we are not closing our minds that others might be associated with him. We have to run down every lead."

Clark had no doubts that Ray had killed King, and that any conspiracy that existed was merely a crude and poorly funded one. The case against Ray was "one of the strongest you're likely to see," Clark said years later. "The evidence is vast. And you can see the ways in which his environment—his history of unhappiness, his tragically sad circumstances—had forged a character who would do it." Despite the profusion of evidence against Ray, Clark predicted the case would be forever awash in conspiracy theories. "Some Americans," he said, "don't want to believe that one miserable person can bring such tragedy on our country and impact so powerfully on the destiny of us all."

None of the papers or newsmagazines mentioned just how close Ray had come to getting away with his crime—or that if he'd made it to Rhodesia, extraditing him would have been nearly impossible. And few accounts gave the Canadian, Mexican, Portuguese, and British authorities their due; catching Ray had been, in every sense, an international effort. Indeed, Hoover seemed a bit embarrassed that it was Scotland Yard, not the FBI, that finally caught his quarry.

For Cartha DeLoach, the hunt for James Earl Ray was the most satisfying case he ever worked on, and he could not have been prouder of his field agents who'd labored in obscurity all across the country—in Memphis, in Atlanta, in Birmingham, in St. Louis, in Los Angeles, and all points in between. "Nothing Ray did threw us off the path," DeLoach boasted. "From the time we found that photograph at the bartender's school, his fate was sealed."

Like Clark, DeLoach entertained no doubts that the FBI had the right man. Ray, he said, "was a loner, an egotist, a bigot, a man who in prison had said he was going to kill Dr. King, a man who wanted to be known, a man who *stalked* Dr. King: The evidence was overwhelming." For years to come, however, DeLoach would have to grapple with the public's understandable suspicion that Hoover's deep hatred of King must have influenced the case in some substantial way.

Yet paradoxically, DeLoach thought Hoover's contempt for King only *intensified* the manhunt. "Truth be told," DeLoach later wrote, "the old feud did have an impact—it drove us to prove, at every moment, that we were doing all we humanly could do to catch King's killer. That may have made our job harder—or at least more pressure-packed—but as I look back on the case, I still feel the same sense of satisfaction. The FBI had never pursued a fugitive with greater patience and imagination."

ON JUNE 10, two days after his arrest, in a chamber deep inside London's Brixton prison, Ramon Sneyd met for the first time with his British solicitor, a diligent young man named Michael Eugene. Sneyd was mild mannered and pleasant at first, but he soon fell into a rant. "Look," he said, "they got me mixed up with some guy called James Earl Ray. My name is Sneyd—Ramon George Sneyd. Never met this Ray guy in my life. I don't know anything about this. They're just trying to pin something on me that I didn't do."

Eugene tried to calm his client and explain to him that he was not concerned with the crimes Sneyd had been accused of in the United States. His concern, properly speaking, was only with the coming extradition hearings. Eugene asked Sneyd whether, in the meantime, he could do anything to make him more comfortable. Eugene later recalled the conversation.

"Yes," Sneyd replied. "I'd like you to call my brother."

"Certainly," Eugene agreed. "How do I reach him? What is his name?"

"Oh, he lives in Chicago," Sneyd said. "His name is Jerry Ray."

Eugene blinked in disbelief. Was this man a blithering idiot? Did he realize what he'd just said? He took down Jerry Ray's contact information and didn't say a word. For days and weeks, the prisoner would continue to insist his name was Sneyd. Eugene happily went along with the fiction.

"And another thing," Sneyd said. "I'm going to need to hire a lawyer in the States—in case we lose the extradition trial. Could you make contact with a few lawyers for me?"

Again, Eugene cheerfully agreed. "Any ones in particular?"

Sneyd was aiming for the stars. First, he said he wanted F. Lee Bailey, the famous Boston trial attorney. If Bailey said no, then he wanted Melvin Belli, out of San Francisco.

What little Eugene knew about American lawyering told him that retaining either of these two celebrity attorneys would cost a king's ransom. "Oh," Sneyd said dismissively. "I'm not worried about their fees. Even if it takes a hundred thousand dollars, I can raise it. They'll be taken care of."

Although Eugene seriously doubted Sneyd's assertion, there was a good deal of truth to the notion that he could quickly build a war chest of funds. In fact, the United Klans of America was already in the process of raising ten thousand dollars to defend Sneyd. Another group, the Patriotic Legal Fund, out of Savannah, Georgia, had pledged to pay *all* of Sneyd's attorney fees, court expenses, the cost of any appeals—as well as his bond. The Patriotic Legal Fund was affiliated with the National States Rights Party, whose chairman and legal adviser, the bow-tie-wearing J. B. Stoner, had already written a letter offering to defend the accused free of charge. Sneyd, Stoner told the media, was a "national hero" who had done America a favor and "should be given a Congressional Medal of Honor."

Sneyd knew about Stoner through reading his neo-Nazi rag the *Thunderbolt.* He was intrigued and flattered by Stoner's overtures, and would soon pursue a correspondence with the racist attorney. For now, though, Sneyd thought he should try to hold out for the biggest name he could get.

■

WHILE SNEYD WAS waiting for his extradition hearings to begin, he had several weeks to kill inside Brixton—and later, another large London prison known as Wandsworth, to which he was eventually transferred.

He knew no one and was kept completely isolated from the rest of the inmate population, living in what the authorities referred to as a "condemned cell." He was a "Category A Prisoner," to whom the highest security precautions applied. The wardens, fearing their celebrity inmate might attempt suicide, would not allow Sneyd to eat his food with utensils. Then, one morning, when he was handed a pile of slimy eggs and greasy sausage, he made a stink. *How was he supposed to eat this mess with his hands?*

His specially assigned guard, a veteran Scotland Yard detective sergeant named Alexander Eist, came to his aid and tried to get him a spoon and fork. For this small favor, Sneyd was extremely grateful, and the two men became, in a manner of speaking, friends. Eist not only guarded Sneyd in prison but also accompanied him to his appearances in court—the two men handcuffed to each other at all times. Along the way, Eist performed other small favors for Sneyd—procuring him American magazines and newspapers, and even bars of chocolate, which were forbidden by the wardens. "He began to look at me," Eist later told the FBI, "as the only friend he had in the country. With my constant contact with him, he began to look on me as somebody he could talk to."

Sneyd carefully studied the papers Eist brought each day. He must have noticed the national reports that George Wallace, having faltered in his presidential bid after Lurleen's death, had resoundingly returned to the fray. On June 11, after a month of mourning, the widower made his first comeback appearance, raising more than a hundred thousand dollars at a luncheon rally that attracted thirteen thousand die-hard fans. He chose to hold the rally in, of all places, Memphis.

Mostly, though, Sneyd was curious about how his own case was playing out in the media. "He seemed absolutely mad about publicity," Eist recalled. "He was continually asking me how he would hit the headlines, and he kept wanting news of publicity."

"Has anything else appeared in the papers this morning?" Sneyd asked Eist one day.

"No, that's it," Eist replied.

"Well, just wait," Sneyd said confidently. "You haven't seen anything yet."

As he got to know the prisoner better, Eist began to worry about the state of Sneyd's mental health. "I formed an opinion that this man was possibly psychiatric," Eist said. "Sometimes he would go into a shell and just look at me. Through it all was coming a clear pathological pattern. It was quite eerie. I had visions of him going berserk any minute when he was in these funny moods."

Over time, Eist earned the prisoner's trust. The two men got to talking about Sneyd's past in America and the King assassination in Memphis. He was clearly replaying the shooting in his head, trying to pinpoint his errors. "When I was coming out of there, I saw a police car," he told Eist one day. "That's where I made my mistake. I panicked and threw the gun away. All I know is, they must've got my fingerprints on it."

Sneyd was still not reconciled to his capture at Heathrow. He kept reliving it in his mind. If he'd only made it onto that plane to Brussels, he was confident that he could have found a cheap way to reach Rhodesia, or Angola. He came within a hairbreadth of making it.

Once he was there in the wilds of southern Africa, he was looking forward to the life of a mercenary soldier. "He just hated black people," Eist recalled. "He said so on many occasions. He called them 'niggers.' In fact, he said he was going to Africa to shoot some more. He mentioned the Foreign Legion. He seemed to have some sort of wild fantasy that he was going to do something of this nature."

Now that he was captured, Sneyd didn't seem at all worried about this future; he had what the Brits call a "Bob's your uncle" air about him. He believed that at most, he would face charges of conspiracy, which would carry a sentence of no more than a dozen years. Neither F. Lee Bailey nor Melvin Belli had agreed to represent him in the United States; instead, he had hired Arthur Hanes, the former mayor of Birmingham, Alabama, who had successfully defended Klansmen in high-profile murder cases. "There's no way they can pin the murder on me," Sneyd told Eist, because "they can't prove I fired the gun." Along the way, he would have no trouble profiting from the notoriety of the case. "I can make a half-million dollars," he boasted to Eist. "I can raise a lot of money, write books, go on television. In parts of America, I'm a national hero."

■

THE IDLING JET engines of the big C-135 whined in the night air as a convoy of Scotland Yard vehicles pulled up on the tarmac. Detective

Chief Superintendent Tommy Butler emerged from one of the police cars, as did Ramon Sneyd, his hands cuffed. Butler and a gaggle of other Scotland Yard officials boarded the plane with their prisoner.

It was just before midnight on July 18 at the U.S. Air Force Base in Lakenheath, Suffolk. Throughout the hour-long ride from London, Butler had been sitting with Sneyd, trying to engage the prisoner in conversation and, though it would have little or no value in court, to draw out a confession of the sort Sneyd had already given, in so many words, to his jailhouse guard, Alexander Eist. But Sneyd proved impervious to Butler's probings, providing only grunts and monosyllabic answers while staring out the window.

On the big, mostly empty plane, Sneyd was met by four FBI agents and an Air Force physician. There in the aisle, Tommy Butler officially remanded the prisoner to the custody of the United States. While Butler and the other Yard men exited the plane, the physician quickly took Sneyd's vital signs to ensure he was in good health. Ordinarily, a C-135 carried 125 passengers or more. On this journey, the Air Force jet would carry only six, plus a small crew. Within a half hour, the big plane taxied down the runway and climbed into the sky, turning west toward North America. The secret transfer of America's most wanted prisoner—officially dubbed Operation Landing—had begun.

Sneyd sat harnessed and locked in his seat, saying nothing, refusing all offers of food and drink. A week earlier, he had lost his extradition hearing; at the famed Bow Street Magistrates' Court in London, Ramsey Clark's team of prosecutors had presented a case utterly convincing to the British authorities, and Sneyd had not bothered to appeal. In a letter to his brother Jerry Ray, he wrote that he would forgo the appeals process because he was "getting tired of listening to these liars." He still stubbornly insisted that he was indeed Ramon Sneyd. He even attempted to have some fun with his character. He facetiously told people he was *Lord* R. G. Sneyd, and claimed no familiarity with anyone named James Earl Ray.

During the long flight, Sneyd got up only once, to use the bathroom. Two FBI agents accompanied him and watched him do his business, with the lavatory door open. He was cinched back in his seat and didn't rise again for the rest of the journey. Once, he complained of a headache and was given aspirin. The agents guarding him noticed that he would pretend to fall asleep—only to cock one eye open, stare at them for a few long moments, and then close it again. It was a little game of peekaboo that went on through the night as the plane arced over the Atlantic.

■

A FEW HOURS before dawn, at the Millington naval air base seventeen miles north of Memphis, Shelby County's sheriff, William Morris, Fire and Police Director Frank Holloman, and the FBI special agent in charge Robert Jensen anxiously waited for the prisoner's arrival. An armored personnel carrier sat squatly on the tarmac, surrounded by a convoy of police cars. Outside stood federal marshals, FBI agents, and guards carrying submachine guns. The night was moonless, and the runway was puddled with water from thunderstorms that had just passed through western Tennessee.

At 3:48 a.m., the sound of a plane bored through the humid darkness, and the C-135 touched down. Sheriff Morris trundled up the steps, where he greeted the FBI agents and made his way toward the prisoner. With a sheriff's deputy recording everything on a video camera, Morris looked into Ray's face and said, in his deepest baritone: "James Earl Ray, alias Harvey Lowmeyer, alias John Willard, alias Eric Starvo Galt, alias Paul Bridgman, alias Ramon George Sneyd, will you please step forward three paces?"

Ray did so.

A Memphis physician, Dr. McCarthy DeMere, approached Ray and asked him to remove his clothes. A few minutes later, Ray stood stark naked and shivering in the aisle, his fish-belly skin shining brightly in the video camera lights. Dr. DeMere took Ray's blood pressure and other vital signs, then nodded to Morris: "He's all yours."

One of the FBI agents handed a receipt to Sheriff Morris and said: "I now give the person and property of James Earl Ray into the custody of Shelby County, State of Tennessee."

While the sheriff read the prisoner his Miranda rights, a deputy opened up a suitcase and produced a plaid flannel shirt, a pair of dark green pants, a pair of sandals, and a bulletproof vest. The deputy helped Ray put on the whole ensemble, and then Ray's hands were manacled to a leather harness.

Morris and his deputy practically lifted the prisoner off his feet and shepherded him down the steps into the open air. For the first time since April 4, the prisoner's feet touched Tennessee soil. Robert Jensen and his agents stood impassively in the shadows, watching. One of Jensen's men was on a mobile phone, narrating the proceedings to Cartha DeLoach in Washington: "They're getting out of the plane . . . Now they're taking the prisoner." DeLoach wanted to hear the blow-by-blow, so that he would know the exact moment James Earl Ray ceased to be *his* problem.

DeLoach had made sure that the federal security around the plane amounted to a "ring of steel." Two lines of armed guards formed a long corridor extending from the plane to the waiting armored vehicle. As he awkwardly walked the gauntlet, Ray kept his head down, his eyes fixed on his sandaled feet.

Sheriff Morris ushered the prisoner into the rear of the personnel carrier, whose multiple armored plates were said to be strong enough to withstand a rocket attack and whose windshield was made of inch-thick bulletproof glass. Within a minute, the motorcade took off. The armored car, with its spinning dome light, made a heavy rumbling sound as it lumbered down the tarmac. The convoy turned onto the main road and aimed for downtown Memphis, the city lights glowing through the haze to the south.

Working with the FBI, Morris had arranged every detail of this choreographed show. The transfer of James Earl Ray was to be carried out in complete secrecy, under cover of night. To throw off the media, Morris had arranged a "decoy convoy" to head simultaneously for the Memphis airport, where most journalists expected Ray's plane would touch down. Sheriff Morris, who was ultimately responsible for keeping Ray safe, feared a reprise of Dallas; Jack Ruby's murder of Lee Harvey Oswald was still fresh in the national memory. No one would be permitted a second's access to Morris's prisoner; no one would even get close.

Morris didn't have to be paranoid to believe that any number of people might want to ambush these proceedings. It was possible, he feared, that black militants might try to kill Ray, or that Klansmen might try to stage a commando-style rescue raid. And if there *was* a larger plot behind the assassination, then the conspirators themselves might try to assassinate Ray—or kidnap him—before he could spill any secrets.

At about 4:30 a.m., the convoy roared up to the Criminal Courts Building in downtown Memphis. Armed guards stood on roofs, while riot-control cops, wielding sawed-off shotguns, lined the street. A city bus pulled up to serve as a screen in case any long-distance snipers were out there. The rear door of the armored car swung open and Ray stepped out. Morris hustled him into the building and into an elevator that whisked them to the third floor. The elevator door opened, and as the prisoner emerged, a sheriff's department photographer snapped a few pictures. Averting his eyes, Ray tried to kick him in the head, screaming, "*You son of a bitch!*"

Morris led Ray down the hall toward his cell, which was really a fortified cell *within* a cell, specially prepared for him at a cost of more than a hundred thousand dollars. All the windows were covered with quarter-inch steel plates, reportedly strong enough to resist small-arms artillery. Bright fluorescent lights were set to burn twenty-four hours a day. Multidirectional microphones dangled from the ceiling, and closed-circuit television cameras trolled the cell block. At least two sets of eyes would be on him at all times—until the day he stood trial.

It was all Ray's tailor-made hoosegow, the entire third floor of what had become a citadel within the county courts complex. He would be the most heavily guarded, and most vigilantly watched, man in the United States.

Morris handed the prisoner over to the guards, who escorted him into his cell and removed his bulletproof vest, his handcuffs, and his leather harness. Then he was given corrections department garb to put on. Though it was impossible to tell through the steel skin that covered the windows, the sun was just beginning to rise over Memphis when James Earl Ray's cell door clanked shut.

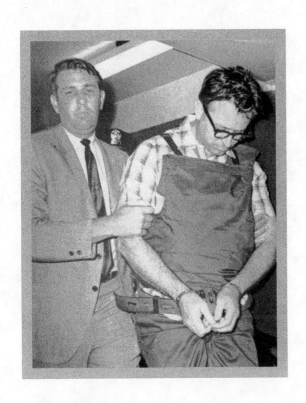

EPILOGUE

#65477

. . . .

June 10, 1977
Petros, Tennessee

AN HOUR BEFORE dusk, as Tammy Wynette's "Stand By Your Man" crackled over the prison radio, two hundred inmates streamed into the recreation yard. They took in the mountain air for a while and then fell into their usual games—horseshoes, basketball, volleyball. The prison walls were thirteen feet tall and strung along the top with high-tension razor ribbon wires humming with twenty-three hundred volts of electricity. Armed guards watched from the seven towers that were set at regular intervals along the wall. An eighth tower, near the yard's northeast corner, was unmanned.

It was a cool spring night, a Friday, the start of another weekend at Brushy Mountain State Penitentiary. "Brushy," as the inmates called their home, was one of Tennessee's tightest maximum-security prisons, a turreted fortress carved from a hillside deep in the Cumberland coal country, in the wrinkled eastern part of the state. It was a small prison, filled with criminals as hard as the surrounding terrain—murderers, rapists, armed robbers, and other violent offenders. The facility's multiple layers of security, combined with the rattlesnakey wilderness in which it was set, long ago prompted corrections experts to confidently declare Brushy Mountain "escape-proof."

As the surrounding thickets of oak and hickory darkened in the approaching twilight, the games played on across the nine-acre yard. The hillsides reverberated with lazy volleyball thwacks and gleeful shouts and the occasional metallic clang of a ringer. If the night's atmosphere seemed languorous, maybe even a bit lax, it was because everyone knew that the prison's no-nonsense warden, Stonney Lane, was on holiday down in Texas—his first vacation in five years. It seemed as though *everyone* was on vacation.

Then, down on the basketball court, an argument erupted. Some of the inmates got into a fistfight. More joined in. A prisoner clutched his ankle and screamed that he'd broken it. Guards stormed into the yard and tried to break up the melee.

It was almost certainly not a real fight but a well-planned ruse. For at this exact moment, near the yard's northeast corner, in the shadow of the unmanned tower, a smaller group of men took advantage of the chaos. Seven prisoners stooped over an assortment of half-inch water pipes that they'd smuggled out to the yard under their clothes. Working frantically with wrenches, they screwed the pipes together. In a few minutes, they constructed a strange, stalky-looking contraption, about nine feet long, that had little rungs and was curved at one end with something that looked like a grappling arm.

Then, just like that, they hooked their jerry-built ladder over the thick stone wall—and started climbing. Within a few seconds, the first man reached the top. He was a forty-nine-year-old man with a slight paunch, wearing a navy blue sweatshirt, dungarees, and black track shoes. He crawled under the high-voltage wire and jumped into a ravine. Then another prisoner went up and over, and another.

In all, six men bolted over the wall before a guard in one of the towers finally turned from the fake fight and spied the ladder. Someone tripped the alarm, and a shrill steam whistle sang down the hollow, all the way to the town of Petros. Corrections officers found that, inexplicably, the power had flickered out through much of the prison and the phone lines were down.

Now marksmen in the various towers replied with shotgun blasts and a fusillade of rifle fire. Inmates scattered from the base of the ladder. The seventh and last man clambering up the wall, a bank robber named

Jerry Ward, was struck in the arm and face with buckshot. He jumped over the edge, smarting and bleeding, but not badly hurt.

The Brushy Mountain guards had no idea how many prisoners might have disappeared over the wall—nor did they know the identities of the escapees. Within a few minutes, lawmen easily caught Ward in the brambles just outside the prison. When they hauled him off to the infirmary to treat his wounds, the prisoner had a curious reaction to the failed escapade: he seemed almost beside himself with joy.

"Ray got out!" Ward cried in delicious disbelief. "Jimmy Ray got away!"

■

A LINEUP OUT in the yard quickly confirmed it: Brushy Mountain's most famous prisoner was indeed one of the six men who'd bolted over the wall. In fact, he'd masterminded the plot. James Earl Ray, #65477, had been planning his breakout for months. He'd been saving pipe, figuring sight lines, measuring distances, patiently waiting through the early spring for the greening forests to sprout sufficient camouflage. He'd conditioned his body by playing volleyball and lifting weights. He apparently designed the queer-looking pipe ladder himself, and he was the first one over the wall. Ray had even dropped hints to the media that an escape was imminent. "They wouldn't have me in a maximum security prison if I wasn't interested in getting out," he told a Nashville reporter only two weeks earlier.

Yet the Brushy Mountain guards didn't see it coming, even though everyone knew Ray had a penchant for disappearing from prisons. The deputy warden Herman Davis said it was "the most daring escape I ever heard of." Scrambling under that high-voltage wire, he said, was all but suicidal. "If you get yourself grounded, you're a cinder." Davis also wondered why the phone lines and power lines had gone out—were some of the prison guards colluding with Ray? "It sure makes you think, don't it?"

It wasn't clear to Davis whether all the escapees had conspired together. Some might have seen the ladder and decided to join in the fun. But the five men who were out there with Ray were all hard-core offenders: two murderers, a rapist, and two armed robbers. C. Murray Henderson, the Tennessee commissioner of corrections, figured that at some point the other fugitives would break away from Ray, because, as he put it, "Ray's hot, hotter than any of them. They'd want him to split off."

Within minutes of the breakout, authorities set in motion the largest fugitive search in Tennessee history. A posse of more than 150 men, armed with shotguns and miner's lamps, fanned out across the mountains. K9 police shepherds barked in the tenebrous woods, and highway patrolmen set up roadblocks within a twenty-mile radius. The families of guards who lived nearby packed up their things and took off.

As soon as the phones were working again, the word was shot to officials in Nashville, and then to Washington. At President Jimmy Carter's behest, a reportedly "terrified" attorney general, Griffin Bell, had the FBI send in a team of agents. The FBI director, Clarence M. Kelley (Hoover had died in office in 1972), immediately gave the case the highest priority. Ray made the bureau's Ten Most Wanted list for the second time in his life. Forty thousand flyers were printed and would soon be circulated around the nation.

After nearly a decade of incarceration, James Earl Ray was again where he most loved to be—on the outside, giving lawmen a good chase.

■

THE LEGAL ROAD he'd traveled from his Memphis holding cell to this dramatic night in the mountains of East Tennessee was long and convoluted. In June 1969, after hiring a succession of lawyers, Ray had pleaded guilty in a Memphis courtroom to the murder of Martin Luther King Jr. and received a ninety-nine-year sentence. Three days later, however, he disavowed parts of his confession and claimed that though he *had* bought the rifle that killed King and *had* checked in to the flophouse only hours before the assassination, a criminal associate of his named Raoul had actually pulled the trigger. Ray's frustratingly vague tales about "Raoul" opened up an eternal cataract of conspiracy theories and captivated many within King's inner circle and family. Yet Ray couldn't offer a consistent description of his mysterious partner in crime, or give his nationality, or provide a phone number or an address. He couldn't produce a single witness who'd ever met "Raoul" or who'd ever seen him in the same place with Ray.

Some people close to the case sensed that "Raoul" might be a cover for Ray's brother Jerry, whom the FBI still suspected as an accomplice in the assassination. But to most people, "Raoul" smelled distinctly like a figment of Ray's imagination—another a.k.a. in a life spent developing aliases and making shit up.

What an enigmatic piece of work James Earl Ray had turned out to be, far stranger than anyone could have imagined. Lawyers, prosecutors, wardens, guards, prison shrinks, journalists—no one could figure him out. Through all his mumbled mixed signals, he seemed to have what psychiatrists call the "duping delight." He loved to launch people on crazy searches, even people who were trying to *help* him. It meant nothing to him for his own attorneys to waste months or even years burrowing in mazy rabbit holes, running down leads that he knew had no basis in fact. He took pleasure in other people's bafflement. Behind his clouds of squid ink, he seemed to be grinning. One of Ray's many lawyers had an expression: the only time you can tell if Ray's lying is when his lips are moving.

Yet he craved something, maybe some brand of fame but maybe something else entirely. His lies seemed to have design, reaching for an endgame known only to him. Percy Foreman, the celebrity Houston lawyer who ended up representing him during his plea bargain in Memphis, put it this way: "Ray is smart like a rat. He has a strongly developed, fundamental instinct to be somebody. He would rather be a name than a number."

■

SINCE HIS CONVICTION in Memphis, James Earl Ray had served his first few years in a Nashville prison, most of the time in solitary confinement—an ordeal that, he thought, may have made him "funny in the head." He hired J. B. Stoner, the neo-Nazi firebrand, as his lawyer. Jerry Ray quit his job as a Chicago golf course greenskeeper and moved south to become Stoner's bodyguard and driver.

Ray was released from solitary in early 1971. Shortly thereafter, the Tennessee Corrections Department transferred him to Brushy Mountain, where almost immediately he set about trying to escape. One night in May 1971, he left a dummy of pillows in his cell room bed, squeezed through a ventilation duct, and pried open a manhole cover leading to a steam shaft. He might have made it to freedom had he not been repelled by the four-hundred-degree temperatures lurking deeper inside the tunnel.

A year later, in May of 1972, Ray's beloved George Wallace, campaigning again for president but renouncing his old segregationist policies, was paralyzed from the waist down by an assassin's bullet.

For a time, during the mid-1970s, Ray's interest turned from escaping to legal stratagems designed to win a new trial. Constantly reading law books, he burned through another string of lawyers, but his legal efforts foundered. In December 1976, his attempt to withdraw his guilty plea was rejected by the U.S. Court of Appeals for the Sixth Circuit—as well as by the U.S. Supreme Court. Two months later, in February 1977, his case received another blow. The Justice Department, which had been leading an inquiry into the King assassination, concluded in its final report that the FBI's investigation was "thoroughly, honestly and successfully conducted . . . The sum of all the evidence of Ray's guilt points to him exclusively."

On the eve of his escape, Ray's only hope was the House Select Committee on Assassinations, which the U.S. House of Representatives had recently impaneled to investigate the JFK and MLK murders. In the late winter, the House's chief counsel, Richard Sprague, had come to Brushy Mountain and led several long cell-block interviews with Ray. The talks got off to a shaky start, but in recent weeks the prisoner finally seemed to be opening up. Ray was even beginning to come clean, hinting that "Raoul" might be fictitious after all. Upon his final interview with Ray, Sprague was moved to declare with complete confidence: "Raoul does not and did not exist."

While these interviews were being conducted, a curious development was taking place just outside Brushy Mountain's walls. Jerry Ray had come to the Petros area to *live* for several months that spring and was seen casing the wooded terrain outside the prison. Then he visited Jimmy one week before the escape—much as their brother John had visited Ray just before his breakout from Missouri's Jeff City prison ten years earlier. (John could not lend his help this time around; he was in prison, serving an eighteen-year federal sentence for robbing a bank.)

The timing of Ray's breakout was beginning to make sense. His legal prospects had dimmed. He'd grown weary of maneuvering. He figured he had nothing left to lose. His brother had scoped out the country around the prison and had probably given him a recon report. So his thoughts returned, fully and passionately, to escape.

"You always have it in the back of your mind," he told an interviewer from *Playboy* only days before he went over the wall. "When you come to the penitentiary, you check out various escape routes. You file them away, and, if the opportunity arises, well, you can go ahead. I suspect that everyone in here has it in the back of his mind. The only thing is whether they have the fortitude to go through with it."

■

By Saturday afternoon, two of the runaways had been captured—but James Earl Ray was still out there. Authorities stepped up the manhunt. Governor Ray Blanton called out the National Guard, and soon the skies shuddered with helicopters that were equipped with infrared heat-sensing scopes much like the ones that American servicemen had used to hunt Vietcong in the jungles of Southeast Asia.

Predictably, a hue and cry rose up in the national media. Reporters were calling it "the escape of the century." The ease with which Ray had broken out from a maximum-security prison, some said, was further proof of the massive conspiracy that was behind the death of Martin Luther King. The people who had killed King now wanted Ray to disappear (or die) before he could testify in Washington in front of the House Select Committee on Assassinations. Ray's escape wasn't an escape at all, some said; it was an abduction.

Ralph Abernathy, who had stepped down from the SCLC, said he was "convinced beyond a shadow of a doubt" that "authorities in very high places have planned the escape. I would say Ray is going to be destroyed." Abernathy's worries were echoed by Representative Louis Stokes, the Ohio Democrat who was serving as chairman of the House Select Committee on Assassinations. Stokes speculated that the escape was "engineered to see that Ray is permanently lost and never heard from again. There are people out there who would not want him to talk."

An even more horrifying conspiracy theory rose up from the depths of the newspapers. As it happened, Martin Luther King's father, Daddy King, was only forty miles away from Brushy Mountain on that particular weekend. He was scheduled to preach in a Baptist church in Knoxville on Sunday. People began to speculate that this was not a coincidence at all, that the escape was somehow tied to King's appearance in Knoxville: people literally feared that King's life was in danger.

It wasn't as crazy as it sounded, given the tragedies that had befallen Daddy King since his son's assassination. In 1969, his other son, A. D. King, was found dead at the age of thirty-eight, floating in his swimming pool in Atlanta. Then, in 1974, the matriarch of the family, Daddy King's beloved wife, Alberta, was gunned down by a deranged black man while she was playing the organ during a service at Ebenezer Baptist Church.

How much pain could one man bear? How much bad fortune could be directed at a single family? On Saturday, reporters reached Daddy King in Knoxville and asked him about the manhunt for his son's assassin that was going on in the mountains just to the west. "I hope they don't kill him," King said. "Let's hope he doesn't get killed. You're looking at the face of a black man who hates nobody." But King wasn't taking any chances, either, especially with a posse of known murderers on the loose. He had a bodyguard with him at all times, he said, and he'd "stopped checking into hotels in my own name a long time ago. I go nowhere without someone traveling with me, without security at both ends. I've gotten used to it."

The hysteria that Ray's escape had generated was understandable, as were the public suspicions that something much larger was afoot. Nonetheless, prison officials insisted that—so far, at least—they'd found absolutely no evidence that anyone had aided the runaways, and no evidence of a wider conspiracy either inside or outside the prison walls. Warden Stonney Lane, somewhat irritable from having to return prematurely from his vacation to deal with the crisis, promised a full investigation. For now, all he could report was that the phone lines had gone out because the prison had received too many calls all at once from people down in Petros who'd heard the steam whistle shrieking. The power lines had temporarily fizzled as a result of what he rather opaquely called a "panic button overload on the penitentiary circuits."

Mostly, though, Lane was focused on finding Ray and the others.

He vowed that the search would venture into "every hollow and back road where a man could hide."

Governor Ray Blanton, meanwhile, tried to reassure the nation that, whatever else happened, his National Guardsmen and corrections department officers would not shoot James Earl Ray. They were, he said, "under orders to use all possible restraint." He conceded that the breakout might have been avoided, that there was possibly "a failure and a laxity" on the part of the Brushy Mountain guards. But, he added, this James Earl Ray character was something else, a fish too big and slippery for any state pen to keep.

"It's not a matter of we can't handle him," the governor said. "It's a matter of we can't *contain* him. The breakout was concocted, designed, and planned in such a manner that he could be in Guatemala now."

■

BY SUNDAY MORNING, officials were fairly boiling with frustration. Although three of the prisoners had been caught, Ray remained at large. The full might of the state and the nation could not bring the prime fugitive to bay—not the planes and helicopters with their heat-sensing machines, not the National Guardsmen with their night-vision goggles, not the FBI with its topo maps and roving surveillance cameras. So the search would have to come down to the man hunter's oldest technology, the surest technology of all. It would have to come down to the dogs.

Sammy Joe Chapman was the captain of the bloodhound team at Brushy Mountain. He was a big, pale guy with a miner's lamp blazing from his forehead and an impressive Civil War mustache that crimped and tweezed when he smiled. People around the prison called him a "sniffer" and a "dog boy." He'd spent his life tracking coons and hunting for ginseng root in the Cumberland woods, learning what he called "the tricks of the mountains." He knew all the landmarks around the New River valley—Flag Pole, Chimney Top, Twin Forks, Frozen Head. He knew where the burned-out cabins were, and the abandoned mine shafts, and the naked faces of the mountains where the strip miners had done their crude scrapings.

Chapman had grown impatient with the feds and all their instruments and all their worrying. He knew that his bloodhounds would find

Ray in due course. All they needed was a good drenching rainstorm. That was the funny thing about bloodhounds: their extraordinary snouts didn't work well in dry weather. When the forest was in want of moisture, all the wild odors mingled into olfactory confusion, and the dogs couldn't pick out a man's clear scent.

Then, on Sunday afternoon, the weather turned. For hours and hours it rained strong and steady, flushing out the forest, driving the stale airborne smells to the ground. Chapman looked at the gray skies and smiled.

Around nightfall he put a harness to his two best hounds, a pair of fourteen-month-old bitches named Sandy and Little Red. He'd personally trained them, teaching them to hunt in perfect silence—none of the usual yelping and singing normally associated with hounds. Late that night, along the New River about eight miles north of the prison, the dogs picked up something strong. The wet ground quickened their senses, just as Chapman knew it would. Tugged by Sandy and Little Red, Chapman followed the river toward the Cumberland strip mine. After a few miles, they crossed over to the other side, then started up the steep flanks of Usher Top Mountain. An hour into the chase, the hounds remained keen.

Now Chapman radioed back to the prison: "We've got a hot trail!" He crossed a set of railroad tracks and a logging road and a clearing strewn with coal. In his headlamp, Chapman could see a rusty conveyor belt and other industrial machinery of the West Coal Company. It was nearly midnight, but the dogs kept leading him uphill, toward Usher Top. For two hours, he strained and struggled up the face of the ridge, his dogs never letting up. At one point he halted them and heard thrashing in the blackberry bushes, not more than fifty yards up the mountain.

In another ten minutes, Chapman and the dogs had nearly reached the mountain's summit. Halting his dogs again, he heard silence—nothing but the crickets and a slight breeze whispering through the oaks and the rush of the river down in the moonlit valley, hundreds of feet below. It was ten minutes past two on Monday morning. Sandy and Little Red yanked Chapman a few feet farther. They snuffled and sniffed in the wet leaves. Their bodies went rigid, but still they didn't bark or bay—they only wagged their tails.

Chapman shined his lamp at a bulge in the forest floor. From his shoulder holster, he produced a Smith & Wesson .38 Chiefs Special. "Don't move or I'll shoot!"

Then, like a ghoul, a pale white man rose lurchingly from the leaves. He was wet and haggard and smeared in mud. His scratched arms were crusted with poison ivy. He wore a navy blue sweatshirt and dungarees and black track shoes. James Earl Ray's fifty-four hours of freedom had come to an end.

Chapman slapped some cuffs over the fugitive's wrists and frisked him. Ray had a map of East Tennessee and $290—a stash he'd apparently saved up from his $35-per-month job in the prison laundry. Aside from the map, he had nothing on his person that appeared to have come from outside the prison, nothing that indicated he'd had any help.

"Ray, how do you feel?"

"Good," he mumbled, averting his eyes in the lamp glare.

"Had anything to eat?"

"Naw," Ray said. "Only a little wheat germ, is all."

Chapman got on the radio to share the good news—and in the process learned that other bloodhounds had found another fugitive down on the New River several hours earlier (the sixth and final runaway wouldn't be caught until Tuesday). Chapman congratulated Sandy and Little Red, tugging at their slobbery dewlaps. But he had to hand it to Ray, too. "For a 49-year-old man who didn't know the mountains," he said later, "Ray really didn't do bad."

Inmate #65477 headed down the mountain, back to a prison term that would last, unbroken by any more escapes, until his death in 1998 from hepatitis C (probably contracted through a tainted blood transfusion he would receive after several black inmates repeatedly stabbed him). Now, tromping in manacles through the soggy Cumberland woods, Ray didn't say a word. He only thought about his mistakes and what he'd do differently next time, if he ever got another chance.

"It's disappointing being caught," he told an interviewer back at the prison. "I wasn't happy being run down. I'd rather be . . . *out there*. But it's not the end of the world. There's tomorrow."

ACKNOWLEDGMENTS

In order to trace the final days of Martin Luther King, and to follow in James Earl Ray's fugitive footsteps, I had to go on a round-the-world odyssey, one that required many road trips and many flights over many years—and one that now taxes my memory of all the good folks I need to thank.

But let me try: In Puerto Vallarta, Lori Delgado was most generous in guiding me to Ray's haunts. In the early going, the prizewinning King scholar David Garrow proved extremely helpful during a visit to Cambridge University. Pedro and Isabel Branco were nice enough to show me Lisbon and introduce me to the melancholy joys of fado—Portugal's answer to the Delta blues. In Austin, Doug and Anne Brinkley nursed me back to health after a hard fluish stint at the LBJ Presidential Library. My researches in London were a success thanks in no small part to Ben and Sarah Fortna, to Robert McCrum, and to Sarah Lyall of the *New York Times*. In Toronto, I must thank Mike Fuhr and the CBC's John Nicol for their expert help. In North Carolina, a big thanks to Sir Newton Stevens for his hospitality during my research junket to the UNC archives. In Birmingham, Arthur Hanes Jr., one of Ray's first lawyers, graciously shared his view of the case over a sumptuous pile of Jim 'n Nick's BBQ. In Boston,

I thank Jon Haber and Carolyn Goldstein for their hospitality, as well as Tony Decaneas at the Panopticon Gallery and the archivist Alex Rankin at BU's Gotlieb Center.

I'm enormously grateful to the Hoover Institution's Edwards Media Fellows Program at Stanford University, which provided a generous research grant. Also at Stanford, a hearty thanks to Clayborne Carson and Clarence Jones at the King Papers Project. I also thank the MacDowell Colony for recharging my fizzled batteries in the mountains of New Hampshire, and the Bunburys in Ireland.

Several researchers proved indispensable in helping me track down key sources and exhume old newspaper and magazine accounts. I must especially thank Scott Reid in Atlanta, Jean Hannah Edelstein in London, Ciara Neill in Memphis, and Shay Brown in Santa Fe.

I logged a lot of quality time in my old hometown of Memphis, and my list of people to thank there is long and wide-ranging. First, my appreciation to Beverly Robertson and the staff of the National Civil Rights Museum, which organized a fascinating symposium in April 2008 to commemorate the fortieth anniversary of the MLK assassination. I thank also John Campbell with the Shelby County District Attorney's Office, the retired pathologist Jerry Francisco, and the attorneys Mike Cody and Charlie Newman at Burch, Porter & Johnson.

Others who generously gave their time include Martha Huie, Louis Donelson, Charles Crump, John T. Fisher, and Marc Perrusquia. A special thanks to the whole crew at *Memphis* magazine, especially Ken Neill, Mary Helen Randall, and Michael Finger. Hope Brooks, at Cargill Cotton, helped me understand the world of "white gold," as did the fine folks at the Cotton Museum downtown.

I doff my hat to Edwin Frank, curator of the amazing Mississippi Valley Collection at the University of Memphis, and to Wayne Dowdy, over at the Memphis Room. I sincerely appreciate the forbearing souls at Quetzal on Union, my well-caffeinated research bunker during all my Memphis stays. Thanks also to Robin and Ann Smithwick, Billy Withers, John Harris, Jim McCarter, and everyone at the *Drake and Zeke* show. My gratitude to John Ruskey—a.k.a. River Jesus—for showing me the *real* Mississippi during a fabulous spring canoe trip, and to Mary Turner, at *Outside*, for making it possible.

Profound thanks (!) to my family in Memphis for all their love and support—Dot and Walker Wilkerson, Link Sides, Mona Smith, and Lynn and Jack Gayden. Thanks also to Mike Deaderick, my high-school history teacher: you inspired me more than you'll ever know.

I inflicted early versions of my manuscript on a number of friends who generously lent their sharp eyes and sound judgment. Special thanks to Kevin Fedarko, Laura Hohnhold, Tom Carroll, Ken Neill, James Conaway, and Ken DeCell. Thanks also to Mark Bowden for his early encouragement, to Ron Bernstein at ICM in Los Angeles, and to Jay Stowe and Hal Espen for their candid insights. To ReBecca and everyone at the Tart's Treats, my home away from home: you saved my hide.

I enjoyed a fruitful collaboration with the folks at Insignia Films in New York as they put together their provocative documentary *Roads to Memphis* for the PBS series *American Experience*. I thank everyone on the Insignia crew, especially Steve Ives, Amanda Pollak, Lindsey Megrue, and Dan Amigone. Likewise, Susan Bellows and Mark Samels at Boston's WGBH were a delight to work with.

In a category all by himself is the estimable Vince Hughes, whose first-class digital archive on the King assassination is perhaps the planet's greatest compendium on the subject. As both a colleague and a friend— and as a former police officer who was on duty that fateful April night— Vince has consistently been my ace in the hole. I can't thank him enough. Likewise, my friend Pallas Pidgeon, a fellow traveler in the mysteries of Memphis, helped me keep this project on track.

I'm blessed to have the finest editor, Bill Thomas, and the finest agent, Sloan Harris, in the business. Fancy praise would do no justice: they're simply the best. At Doubleday, I thank Melissa Ann Danaczko, who has stayed unwaveringly on the case, as well as the wizardly Todd Doughty. Thanks also to Kristyn Keene at ICM, always a source of good cheer.

And finally, a massive, blubbery thanks to Anne and the boys, who time and time again rescued me from the shadows of this book: I love you with all my heart and soul.

A NOTE ON SOURCES

The literature of the King murder, much like that of the Kennedy assassinations, is vast and dizzying, characterized by tendentious works that are often filled with bizarre assertions, anonymous sources, and grainy photographs purporting to prove that every organization this side of the Boy Scouts of America was involved in King's death. However, there are many excellent works on the King assassination, and three of them proved especially valuable in my research. The late William Bradford Huie, the first journalist to investigate Ray's claims, did an enormous amount of legwork and imaginative sleuthing; I relied not only on Huie's book *He Slew the Dreamer* (1970) but also on his personal papers archived at Ohio State—as well as documents provided by his widow, Martha Huie. The late George McMillan, author of *The Making of an Assassin* (1976), was the only journalist who spent serious time digging into Ray's early biography, family, and psychological profile. I made considerable use of McMillan's mountainous Ray archives housed at the University of North Carolina. Finally, when it comes to isolating and then ferociously dismantling conspiracy theories arising from the case, no one has come close to the formidable Gerald Posner and his first-rate *Killing the Dream* (1998).

My rendering of the ever-potent (and ever-bizarre) figure of J. Edgar Hoover was particularly enriched by three fine biographies: Curt Gentry's highly readable *J. Edgar Hoover: The Man and the Secrets*; Richard Gid Powers's exhaustively researched *Secrecy and Power: The Life of J. Edgar Hoover*; and Burton Hersh's provocative dual biography, *Bobby and J. Edgar: The Historic Face-Off Between the Kennedys and J. Edgar Hoover That Transformed America*. In helping me understand Hoover's intense antipathy toward King, I am greatly indebted to the Johnson administration's attorney general Ramsey Clark, who sat for an interview, as well as to David Garrow for his groundbreaking work *The FBI and Martin Luther King Jr.: From "Solo" to Memphis*. Also of great utility was the revealing compendium *Martin Luther King Jr.: The FBI File*, painstakingly assembled by Michael Friedly and David Gallen.

My account of the international manhunt for James Earl Ray is drawn from multiple sources—including personal interviews, memoirs, and official documents. Chief among these are the FBI's MURKIN files, including a wealth of largely unpublished FD-302 reports assembled by FBI agents in field offices across the nation. I also relied heavily on the thirteen-volume King assassination *Appendix Reports* compiled by the House Select Committee on Assassinations. Three books, by three official participants in various aspects of the manhunt, were extremely useful to my research: Cartha DeLoach's revealing memoir, *Hoover's FBI*; the Justice Department official Roger Wilkins's searching autobiography, *A Man's Life*; and Ramsey Clark's *Crime in America*.

Anyone interested in knowing more about the George Wallace movement has three excellent biographies to choose from—authoritative works on which I relied in my several passages concerning the 1968 Wallace campaign. Foremost among these is Dan Carter's absorbing work, *The Politics of Rage*. Also of great interest are Stephan Lesher's *George Wallace: American Populist* and Marshall Frady's engagingly well-written *Wallace: The Classic Portrait of Alabama Governor George Wallace*.

In describing the tragic swirl of events in Memphis that led up to the King assassination, I found two books especially helpful. Joan Turner Beifuss's engrossing and highly readable *At the River I Stand* was the first work to make use of a treasure trove of oral histories taken by the Memphis Search for Meaning Committee. Michael Honey's definitive *Going*

Down Jericho Road elucidates the sanitation strike and shows how events in Memphis fit into larger movements of U.S. labor history. The best work on the riots that consumed the nation after King's assassination is undoubtedly *A Nation on Fire* by Clay Risen.

I drew from a wealth of memoirs written by the King family and the SCLC inner circle. Among the most helpful were works by King's widow (Coretta Scott King, *My Life with Martin Luther King Jr.*); by his father (Martin Luther King Sr., *Daddy King*); by his son (Dexter Scott King, *Growing Up King*); by his second-in-command (Ralph Abernathy, *And the Walls Came Tumbling Down*); by his legal adviser (Clarence Jones, *What Would Martin Say?*); and by his most loyal lieutenant (Andrew Young, *An Easy Burden*). I must also convey my admiration for the two preeminent, broad-canvas works on King and the movement—David Garrow's Pulitzer Prize–winning *Bearing the Cross* and Taylor Branch's remarkable three-volume achievement, *America in the King Years*.

My account of James Earl Ray's travels is drawn principally from his own words found in a rich and sometimes bewildering range of documents. These include Ray's "20,000 Words" (a handwritten account of his movements while on the lam); Ray's testimony before the House Select Committee on Assassinations, including eight official interviews conducted while he was incarcerated at Brushy Mountain State Penitentiary; lengthy interviews Ray gave to such media outlets as *Playboy*, CBS News, and the Nashville *Tennessean*; handwritten letters he sent to his brothers while serving at Brushy Mountain; and his own two books, *Tennessee Waltz* and *Who Killed Martin Luther King?* Ray's ever-changing accounts over the years, like his ever-changing aliases, make for a record that's sometimes maddening and sometimes mystifying but also, at times, quite revealing. As they say, a busted watch tells the truth twice a day.

NOTES

PROLOGUE:
#416-J

4   "bloodiest forty-seven acres in America": This and other details relating to Jeff City prison are adapted from Patrick J. Buchanan, "Jefferson City: The Pen That Just Grew," *Nation*, Nov. 6, 1964.

4   "He was just a *nothing* here": McMillan, *Making of an Assassin*, p. 173, from his personal interview with Missouri corrections commissioner Fred Wilkinson.

4   "an interesting and rather complicated individual": Dr. Henry V. Guhleman (prison psychiatrist) to the Missouri Board of Promotion and Parole, Dec. 20, 1966, Hughes Collection.

4   Librium for his nerves: Ibid.

4   "in need of psychiatric help": Ibid.

5   applying a walnut dye: See the FBI's MURKIN Files, 4441, sec. 56, pp. 4–6.

5   considerable quantities of mineral oil: McMillan, *Making of an Assassin*, p. 181.

5   "When he was using": George McMillan, interview with the inmate Raymond Curtis, box 1, interview notes, McMillan Papers.

5   visitor was his brother: Huie, *He Slew the Dreamer*, p. 40. See also Ray and Barsten, *Truth at Last*, p. 72, in which John Ray acknowledges he visited his brother at Jeff City the day before the escape and agreed to assist in his brother's flight (facts that he had denied for years, including while under oath before the House Select Committee on Assassinations).

6   **rather astonishing quantity of eggs:** This and other descriptions of the escape come from James Earl Ray's own account in *Tennessee Waltz*, p. 42.

6   **two wads of cash:** Ray, *Who Killed Martin Luther King?*, p. 57.

7   **he could strut while sitting:** James J. Kilpatrick, "What Makes Wallace Run?" *National Review*, April 18, 1967.

7   **"backlash against anybody of color":** Wallace on *Meet the Press*, April 23, 1967, quoted in Lesher, *George Wallace*, p. 389.

7   **"This is a movement of the people":** Ibid., p. 390.

7   **"If the politicians get in the way":** Ibid.

8   **gave it all to the chickens:** FBI, MURKIN Files, 3503, sec. 39, p. 9.

8   **"I looked at the stars a lot":** This quotation and other first-person depictions of Ray's flight from prison are drawn from James Earl Ray's "20,000 Words," House Select Committee on Assassinations, *Appendix Reports*, vol. 12.

9   **called his brother:** Ray and Barsten, *Truth at Last*, p. 73. John Ray admits that his brother called him and that he picked up the fugitive at a tavern in central Missouri and then drove him back to St. Louis.

9   **hopped an eastbound freight train:** Ray, *Tennessee Waltz*, p. 45.

CHAPTER I
CITY OF WHITE GOLD

13   **all the secret krewes:** The 1967 Cotton Carnival details here are drawn from Magness, *Party with a Purpose*, p. 242. The description of the 1967 Royal Barge and other carnival atmospherics is drawn from newspaper coverage in the *Memphis Commercial Appeal* and *Memphis Press-Scimitar*, April and May 1967.

14   **Memphis was built on the spot:** For details on the early history of Memphis, see Capers, *Biography of a River Town;* Roper, *Founding of Memphis;* Magness, *Past Times;* and Harkins, *Metropolis of the American Nile.*

15   **Front Street, cotton's main drag:** Details here on the business of cotton are drawn from Bearden, *Cotton,* and Yafa, *Big Cotton.* I also relied on collections displayed at the Cotton Museum in Memphis.

16   **a yellow fever epidemic:** For a vivid account of the 1878 yellow fever epidemic, see Crosby, *American Plague.*

16   **"was built on a bluff":** Wills, "Martin Luther King Is Still on the Case."

17   **Marcus Brutus Winchester:** Weeks, *Memphis*, pp. 25–34.

17   **Ida B. Wells:** For anyone curious about the courageous life of this civil rights matriarch, I recommend her excellent memoir, *Crusade for Justice.*

17   **renouncing the Klan:** Jack Hurst's fine biography, *Nathan Bedford Forrest*, deftly traces Forrest's evolution, in his later years, toward racial moderation. See esp. pp. 359–67.

18   **masked green jesters:** See Magness, *Party with a Purpose*, pp. 205–10.

CHAPTER 2
GOING FOR BROKE

21   **"For years, I labored with reforming"**: King interview with David Halberstam, quoted in Dyson, *I May Not Get There with You,* p. 39.

21   **"My own government"**: *Autobiography of Martin Luther King Jr.,* p. 338.

21   **"The good and just society"**: Washington, *Testament of Hope,* p. 630.

22   **"It didn't cost the nation"**: Kotz, *Judgment Days,* p. 382.

22   **"I'm on fire"**: Branch, *At Canaan's Edge,* p. 652.

23   **go on a brief sabbatical:** Garrow, *Bearing the Cross,* p. 602.

24   **"I'm tired of all this traveling"**: Ibid., p. 572.

24   **"I feel discouraged"**: Ibid., p. 592.

24   **"The Southern Christian Leadership Conference"**: Branch, *At Canaan's Edge,* p. 656.

24   **"represents moral irresponsibility"**: Garrow, *Bearing the Cross,* p. 583.

24   **"This is a kind of last, desperate demand"**: Ibid.

CHAPTER 3
THE MONTH OF THE IGUANA

25   **On an empty beach:** This scene is primarily drawn from interviews with Manuela Medrano, in House Select Committee on Assassinations (hereafter HSCA), *Appendix Reports,* vol. 4, pp. 157–58.

26   **bought a Kodak Super 8:** McMillan, *Making of an Assassin,* p. 263.

26   **Visibly upset:** HSCA, *Appendix Reports,* vol. 4, pp. 157–58.

27   **modest but respectable enough place:** On a research trip to Puerto Vallarta, I visited the Rio, still a popular downtown hotel, and viewed archival photographs from the 1960s.

27   **"publisher's assistant"**: See Huie, *He Slew the Dreamer,* p. 94, and McMillan, *Making of an Assassin,* p. 266.

27   **"idyllic"**: Ray, *Who Killed Martin Luther King?* p. 78.

27   **"everybody there wanted"**: Ray, "20,000 Words," HSCA, *Appendix Reports,* vol. 12, p. 69.

28   **erotic feedback loop:** William Bradford Huie visited this whorehouse in 1968 and describes it in some detail in his book *He Slew the Dreamer,* pp. 95–96.

28   **Galt began frequenting:** My description of Ray's favorite bordello is drawn from the summary of the time he spent in Mexico in HSCA, *Appendix Reports,* vol. 4, as well as in Huie, *He Slew the Dreamer,* pp. 94–95.

30   **He complained of headaches:** McMillan, *Making of an Assassin,* p. 270.

30   **He rarely tipped:** Huie, *He Slew the Dreamer,* p. 97.

30   which he called his "equalizer": Ray, *Tennessee Waltz*, p. 66.

30   trips into the hills: HSCA, *Appendix Reports*, vol. 4, p. 159.

30   keen on learning . . . local Mexican dances: Ibid.

30   "I seriously considered the trade": Ray, *Tennessee Waltz*, p. 61.

31   "He said many insulting things": A good overview of the incident at Casa Susana is in HSCA, *Final Assassinations Report*, pp. 328–29.

31   "I'm going to kill them": This and other details of the confrontation with the black sailors are in an official interview with Medrano, HSCA, *Appendix Reports*, vol. 4, p. 158. Also p. 174.

32   he straddled Elisa: McMillan, *Making of an Assassin*, p. 269.

32   He had a mirror: Huie, *He Slew the Dreamer*, p. 97.

32   "I couldn't accomplish anything": Ray, *Tennessee Waltz*, p. 61.

32   "I don't believe you can live in Mexico": Ray interview, HSCA, *Appendix Reports*, vol. 9, p. 488.

33   in the direction of Tijuana: Ray, *Tennessee Waltz*, p. 62.

CHAPTER 4
ANATHEMA TO EVIL MEN

35   Burrhead—that was one of his many names: Garrow, *FBI and Martin Luther King Jr.*, p. 106.

35   "Based on King's recent activities": Ibid., p. 182.

35   weird phobias: Gentry, *J. Edgar Hoover*, p. 280.

35   "mental halitosis": DeLoach, *Hoover's FBI*, p. 67.

35   "a mythical person": Buchwald, quoted in Richard Gid Powers, *Secrecy and Power*, p. 395.

36   "Are you familiar": Capote, quoted in Hersh, *Bobby and J. Edgar*, p. 464.

36   "You must understand": Gentry, *J. Edgar Hoover*, p. 501.

36   "Watch the borders": DeLoach, *Hoover's FBI*, p. 95.

36   Helen Gandy: Ibid., p. 109.

37   "high and distant and quiet": Hugh Sidey, *Life*, May 12, 1972.

37   "transformed the FBI": Jack Anderson, *Washington Post*, May 3, 1972.

37   "dangerous and rather a psycho": Robert Kennedy, quoted in Richard Gid Powers, *Secrecy and Power*, p. 397.

37   "I'd rather have him": Ibid., p. 393.

38   "J. Edgar Hoover is a hero": President Johnson, Executive Order 11154, May 8, 1965, quoted in Ralph de Toledano, *J. Edgar Hoover: The Man in His Time* (New Rochelle, N.Y.: Arlington House, 1973), p. 301.

38   "is a pillar of strength": Johnson, quoted in Gentry, *J. Edgar Hoover*, p. 611.

38   "the most notorious liar": *Newsweek*, Nov. 30, 1964.

38   "They had to dig deep": Richard Gid Powers, *Secrecy and Power*, p. 416.

38   "top alley cat": Garrow, *FBI and Martin Luther King Jr.*, p. 121.

38   "I am amazed": Ibid., p. 121.

39   "There are as many Communists": King 1965 interview in *Playboy*, quoted in Dyson, *I May Not Get There with You*, p. 231.

39   "a tom cat": Richard Gid Powers, *Secrecy and Power*, p. 417.

39   "narrow his eyes": DeLoach, *Hoover's FBI*, p. 203.

39   "saw extramarital sex": Ibid.

39   "if the country knew": Hersh, *Bobby and J. Edgar*, p. 386.

39   "I don't understand": Ibid., p. 379.

40   "King, look into your heart": Richard Gid Powers, *Secrecy and Power*, p. 420.

40   "They are out to break me": Garrow, *FBI and Martin Luther King Jr.*, p. 134.

40   "Hoover is old": Ibid., p. 124.

CHAPTER 5
DIXIE WEST

41   the Cicero of the Cabdriver: The reporter James Dickenson, quoted in Lesher, *George Wallace*, p. 395.

41   "bit himself": Ibid., p. 401.

41   "the surly orphan": Frady, *Wallace*, p. 253.

42   "pointy-headed intellectuals": Carter, *Politics of Rage*, p. 313.

42   "the nigra would still be in Africa": Ibid., p. 161.

42   "Let 'em call me a racist": Frady, *Wallace*, p. 9.

43   "a fraud, marching and going to jail": Lesher, *George Wallace*, p. 184.

43   "who could go to bed": Ibid., p. 199.

43   "the blood of our little children": *New York Times*, Sept. 17, 1963, pp. 1, 25.

43   "how costly Wallace": Abernathy, *And the Walls Came Tumbling Down*, p. 357.

44   "He has just four [speeches]": King to Dan Rather, quoted in Carter, *Politics of Rage*, p. 156.

44   "In both the North and South": *Life*, Aug. 2, 1968, pp. 17–21.

45   "The capital of Alabama": *Wall Street Journal*, Dec. 7, 1967.

45   "political ventriloquism": Carter, *Politics of Rage*, p. 294.

CHAPTER 6
THE GRADUATE

46   "A nice fellow": This "graduation" scene is primarily drawn from FBI interviews with Tomas Lau and former students at the bartending school. See "Investigation of International School of Bartending, Los Angeles, Attended by Galt from January 19, 1968, to March 2, 1968," FBI, MURKIN Files, 2325, sec. 22, pp. 135–36. I have also relied here on Huie, *He Slew the Dreamer*, p. 117; Posner, *Killing the Dream*, p. 214; and Ray, "20,000 Words," in House Select Committee on Assassinations, *Appendix Reports*, vol. 12.

47   St. Francis Hotel: My description of the St. Francis Hotel is drawn from Huie, *He Slew the Dreamer*, p. 99, and my own visit to the former hotel—now an apartment house—on Hollywood Boulevard in Los Angeles.

48   he had amphetamines: There are several telltale signs that Ray continued his amphetamine use after escaping from Jeff City, including the discovery, several months later, of a syringe in his bed-and-breakfast room in London. Charles Stein, an acquaintance of Ray's in Los Angeles, told the FBI that Ray may have been "a pillhead." See FBI interview with Stein, May 5, 1968, MURKIN Files, 2751–2925.

48   fizzly neon sign: The large orange neon sign outside the St. Francis is mentioned in multiple documents and books, including Posner's *Killing the Dream*, p. 210.

49   recently bought himself a set of barbells: Frank, *American Death*, p. 168.

51   "I don't think that a man": McKinley, "Interview with James Earl Ray," p. 174.

51   "to get his knob polished": McMillan, *Making of an Assassin*, p. 267.

51   "I find myself attracted": McKinley, "Interview with James Earl Ray," p. 76.

52   "He was the withdrawn type": My rendering of Galt's lessons at the National Dance Studio is largely drawn from the FBI report "Investigation at National Dance Studio, Long Beach, California, Where Galt Attended Classes, December 1967 to February 1968." Also, FBI interview with Arvidson, National Dance Studio, April 13, 1968, MURKIN Files, 1051–1175, sec. 9, pp. 276–77.

52   "overcome his shyness": My account of Ray's visits with Freeman is primarily drawn from the journalist George McMillan's transcription of his interviews with Freeman, box 9, McMillan Papers.

53   "He had the old power idea": Frank, *American Death*, p. 308. Also, Posner, *Killing the Dream*, p. 196.

53   "He was a good pupil": McMillan, *Making of an Assassin*, p. 275. See also FBI interview with Freeman, April 19, 1968, Los Angeles field office.

CHAPTER 7
SURREPTITIOUSNESS IS CONTAGIOUS

54   "a moral crusader": Clark, *Crime in America*, p. 151.

55   "Here we all were biting our nails": Author interview with Clark, Oct. 9, 2008, New York City.

55   "We must create a reverence": Clark, *Crime in America*, p. 95.

55   "a humane and generous concern": Ibid., p. 8.

55   "the Jellyfish": Hersh, *Bobby and J. Edgar*, p. 486.

55   "What kind of person is *that*?": See Gentry, *J. Edgar Hoover*, p. 599.

56   "I describe our relationship": Ibid., p. 601.

56   "by the excessive domination": Clark, *Crime in America*, p. 65.

56   "Surreptitiousness is contagious": Ibid., p. 271.

56   "more than a mere dirty business": Ibid., p. 276.

56   "Hoover had three": Gentry, *J. Edgar Hoover*, p. 500.

57   "a man of monstrous ego": DeLoach, *Hoover's FBI*, p. 11.

57   "crotchety, dictatorial": Ibid., p. 111.

57   "you were not so much": Ibid., p. 24.

58   "Such behavior": Ibid., pp. 202–3.

58   "like the biblical mustard seed": Ibid., p. 200.

58   "We need this installation": Garrow, *FBI and Martin Luther King Jr.*, p. 184.

58   "A.G. will not approve": Ibid.

59   "There has not been an adequate": Ibid.

CHAPTER 8
A BUGLE VOICE OF VENOM

60   Galt told a representative: Posner, *Killing the Dream*, p. 194.

61   "Several recruits": Carter, *Politics of Rage*, p. 310.

61   "The Rockefeller interests": Ibid., p. 311.

61   stock car track: My description of the Burbank rally for Wallace is primarily drawn from Carter, *Politics of Rage*, pp. 314–15.

62   "He has a bugle voice of venom": *New Republic*, Nov. 9, 1968.

62   "the heat, the rebel yells": Lesher, *George Wallace*, p. 410.

62   he wrote to the American–Southern Africa Council: Ray's correspondence is reprinted in House Select Committee on Assassinations (hereafter HSCA), *Appendix Reports*, vol. 13, p. 252.

62   the Friends of Rhodesia: Ray's letter is reproduced in ibid., vol. 4, p. 116.

63   reader of the *Thunderbolt*: Ray is thought to have read the *Thunderbolt* while in prison; after his arrest for King's assassination, he eventually hired J. B. Stoner as his attorney, and his brother Jerry Ray served as Stoner's personal bodyguard.

63   "Invariably the bastard": See Carter, *Politics of Rage*, p. 165.

63   archly effeminate organizer: Ibid., p. 166.

64   "the last chance": Lesher, *George Wallace*, p. 301.

64   **pasted the racist sobriquet:** McMillan, *Making of an Assassin,* p. 285.

64   **"a murky, jukebox-riven hole in the wall":** Huie, *He Slew the Dreamer,* p. 99.

64   **"a moody fellow from Alabama":** Ibid., p. 110.

64   **Pat Goodsell:** My account of the incident inside the Rabbit's Foot is mainly drawn from interviews with eyewitnesses in bureau reports, especially the FBI interview with Bo Del Monte, April 22, 1968, MLK Exhibit F-168, in HSCA, *Appendix Reports,* vol. 4, p. 122. Also see Posner, *Killing the Dream,* pp. 215–17, and Huie, *He Slew the Dreamer,* pp. 109–12. Ray himself discusses the incident, giving slightly varying versions, in his two books, *Tennessee Waltz* and *Who Killed Martin Luther King?*

CHAPTER 9
RED CARNATIONS

66   **"Did you get the flowers?":** My account of King's gift of artificial carnations comes from Coretta Scott King's memoir, *My Life with Martin Luther King Jr.,* p. 308.

66   **"a guilt-ridden man":** Garrow, *Bearing the Cross,* p. 588.

67   **"Tonight I have taken a vow":** Branch, *At Canaan's Edge,* p. 653.

67   **confessed to her:** Ibid., p. 678.

67   **"Each of us is two selves":** Dyson, *I May Not Get There with You,* p. 162.

67   **"That poor man":** William Rutherford, quoted in Garrow, *Bearing the Cross,* p. 617.

67   **"Martin had . . . an ambivalent attitude":** Dyson, *I May Not Get There with You,* pp. 212–13.

68   **"There was nothing fashionable":** Ibid., p. 210.

68   **"I won't have any money":** Ibid., p. 276.

68   **"We had a sense of fate":** Coretta Scott King, *My Life with Martin Luther King Jr.,* p. 303.

68   **"This is what will happen to me":** Dyson, *I May Not Get There with You,* p. 214.

CHAPTER 10
AN ORANGE CHRISTMAS

69   **Marie Tomaso:** FBI FD-302 interview with Marie Martin (Tomaso), conducted on April 13, 1968, by Special Agents William Slicks and Richard Ross.

69   **"like he didn't get out too often":** Ibid.

70   **a deeply eccentric man:** My depiction of Charles Stein and his relationship with Galt is primarily drawn from the initial FBI interview with Stein on April 13, 1968, conducted by Special Agents Slicks and Ross out of the Los Angeles field office, as well as a follow-up interview on April 15, 1968. The FBI also interviewed Rita Stein on April 13, 1968 (MURKIN Files, 1051–1175, sec. 9, p. 270), and Stein's mother on April 27, 1968 (MURKIN Files, 3762, sec. 45, p. 43).

70   "I got a gun": FBI FD-302 follow-up interview with Marie Martin, April 14, 1968.

70   Galt had one stipulation: Galt's requirement that Charles Stein, his sister, and his cousin stop by the Wallace headquarters and sign their names is found in FBI interviews with Rita Stein, Charles Stein, and Marie Martin.

71   "I figured he was getting paid": McMillan, *Making of an Assassin*, p. 280.

71   "What's God got to do with it?": Frank, *American Death*, p. 165.

71   They rode all night: My account of Ray's cross-country journey to New Orleans is largely adapted from "Analysis of James Earl Ray's Trip to New Orleans, December 15–December 21, 1967," House Select Committee on Assassinations, *Appendix Reports*, vol. 13, pp. 268–69.

71   "Charlie would nudge me": Ray, *Tennessee Waltz*, p. 65.

72   "It's Galt": Frank, *American Death*, p. 166.

72   "a train whistle": Posner, *Killing the Dream*, p. 206.

73   "You ought to know that Christmas": Ray, "20,000 Words," quoted in Huie, *He Slew the Dreamer*, p. 105.

73   "I didn't do any gambling": Ibid.

73   "a nearly impossible feat": Lesher, *George Wallace*, p. 400.

74   "All persons": William Bradford Huie interview with Koss, in Huie's *He Slew the Dreamer*, pp. 114–16.

74   "You must complete your course": Ibid.

74   "I lost him": Ibid.

CHAPTER 11
WALKING BUZZARDS

75   At the wheel of the big truck: My account of the deaths of Robert Walker and Echol Cole is largely drawn from the news story in the *Memphis Commercial Appeal*, Feb. 2, 1968. See also Honey, *Going Down Jericho Road*, pp. 1–2; Beifuss, *At the River I Stand*, p. 30; and Branch, *At Canaan's Edge*, pp. 684–85.

76   in 1964, two garbage workers were killed: Honey, *Going Down Jericho Road*, p. 2.

77   "He was standing there": *Memphis Commercial Appeal*, Feb. 2, 1968.

78   Earline Walker: Branch, *At Canaan's Edge*, p. 685.

78   Elvis Presley—whose wife, Priscilla, had given birth: Guralnick, *Careless Love*, p. 288. See also Branch, *At Canaan's Edge*, p. 685.

78   "I am so lucky": Goldman, *Elvis*, p. 404.

79   "This you can't do": Beifuss, *At the River I Stand*, p. 40.

79   Henry Loeb III was a garrulous: My sketch of Loeb relies on biographical details

adapted from "Profile: Henry Loeb," a comprehensive, two-part article that ran in *Memphis* magazine in January and February 1980.

79   **he called them "nigras":** The *Memphis Commercial Appeal* reporter Joe Sweat, quoted in Honey, *Going Down Jericho Road*, p. 119.

80   **"the world's least likely revolutionaries":** Wills, "Martin Luther King Is Still on the Case," reprinted in *The New Journalism*, ed. Tom Wolfe, p. 392.

80   **"This is not New York":** Honey, *Going Down Jericho Road*, p. 117.

81   **Lawson had studied the tenets:** For a good biographical sketch of Lawson's earlier days in the civil rights movement, see Halberstam, *The Children*.

81   **"You are human beings":** Lawson, quoted in Honey, *Going Down Jericho Road*, p. 211.

CHAPTER 12
ON THE BALCONY

82   **King fell into an argument:** Frank, *American Death*, p. 90.

83   **"I don't play with them anymore":** Ibid., p. 91.

83   **Abernathy woke up in the dead of night:** This anecdote from King and Abernathy's trip to Acapulco is adapted from ibid., pp. 91–92, and also Abernathy's testimony in House Select Committee on Assassinations, *Appendix Reports*, vol. 1, pp. 33–34.

84   **"a team":** Abernathy, *And the Walls Came Tumbling Down*, p. 478.

84   **another letter from the FBI:** See Branch, *At Canaan's Edge*, p. 708.

84   **"You see that rock out there?":** Frank, *American Death*, p. 92.

CHAPTER 13
FACES ARE MY BUSINESS

86   **"Your brain and nervous system":** Maltz, *Psycho-Cybernetics*, p. 17.

86   **"The automatic creative mechanism":** Ibid., p. 37.

87   **"Don't think before you act":** Ibid., p. 169.

87   **"When you change a man's face":** Ibid., pp. vii–viii.

87   **Galt visited a prominent plastic surgeon:** My account of Galt's visits to Hadley's office is drawn from the FBI's initial interview with Hadley, conducted on October 2, 1968, out of the Los Angeles field office. See also Huie, *He Slew the Dreamer*, pp. 119–21; McMillan, *Making of an Assassin*, pp. 285–86; Frank, *American Death*, p. 311; and Ray's own version in *Tennessee Waltz*.

87   **"I casually told him":** Ray, *Tennessee Waltz*, p. 68.

88   **"The ears":** Ibid.

88   **"in a position":** Ibid.

89   **"I'm a fairly observant person":** Hadley, quoted in Huie, *He Slew the Dreamer*, p. 121.

89 **"The government is emotionally committed"**: Branch, *At Canaan's Edge*, p. 717.

89 **"I've seen hatred"**: King's comments were reported in the *Los Angeles Times*, March 18, 1968, and also reproduced in Huie, *He Slew the Dreamer*, p. 123.

90 **official postal service card**: "Investigation at St. Francis Hotel, Hollywood, California," compiled by the FBI's Los Angeles field office. Here I relied on the FD-302 report of an FBI interview with the St. Francis Hotel manager, Allan O. Thompson, conducted on April 12, 1968, by Special Agent Thomas G. Mansfield.

CHAPTER 14
SOMETHING IN THE AIR

92 **"You are demonstrating"**: My account of King's March 18 speech in Memphis is drawn from the Memphis Commercial Appeal; from news footage of the speech captured in the PBS documentary *At the River I Stand*; and from secondary accounts in Honey, *Going Down Jericho Road*, pp. 296–303, and Beifuss, *At the River I Stand*, pp. 193–96.

94 **The Lorraine had long been popular**: My sketch of the Lorraine's history largely comes from the National Civil Rights Museum Web site, clippings in the *Memphis Commercial Appeal*, and Honey, *Going Down Jericho Road*, p. 442.

94 **The old part of the lodge**: Wills, "Martin Luther King Is Still on the Case," reprinted in *The New Journalism*, ed. Tom Wolfe, p. 395.

94 **"the King-Abernathy suite"**: See Abernathy's testimony concerning the Lorraine Motel in House Select Committee on Assassinations, *Appendix Reports*, vol. 1, p. 32.

95 **"seeming so modern"**: Young, *Easy Burden*, p. 460.

96 **Flamingo Motel**: My account of Galt's stay at the Flamingo Motel comes from the following sources: Huie, *He Slew the Dreamer*, pp. 130–31; Posner, *Killing the Dream*, p. 219; McMillan, *Making of an Assassin*, p. 289; Ray, *Tennessee Waltz*, p. 70; and my own visit to the motel in Selma.

98 **Nature . . . had gone on strike**: Honey, *Going Down Jericho Road*, p. 323.

98 **"We've got a perfect work stoppage"**: Beifuss, *At the River I Stand*, p. 205.

98 **"Well, the Lord has done it again"**: Ibid., p. 203.

98 **"It had never snowed"**: Honey, *Going Down Jericho Road*, p. 309.

98 **He located a rooming house**: My description of Galt's Atlanta rooming house is based on several accounts in the *Atlanta Constitution* and on FBI FD-302 reports of interviews with his landlord, Jimmie Garner, conducted on April 14 and 15, 1968, by Special Agents John Ogden and Roger Kaas. See also Huie, *He Slew the Dreamer*, p. 132.

99 **"Every time I look at Atlanta"**: Reed, quoted in Horwitz, *Confederates in the Attic*, p. 283.

99 **"wouldn't have to answer"**: Ray, *Who Killed Martin Luther King?* p. 89.

100 **"this place was just *infested* with hippies"**: FD-302 report of the Ogden and Kaas interviews with Garner, the FBI Atlanta field office.

100 **looked "like a preacher"**: Blair, *Strange Case of James Earl Ray*, p. 139.

NOTES

100   "to bone up": Ray, *Who Killed Martin Luther King?* p. 90.

100   **One of his circles** A description of the markings found on Ray's Atlanta map are in the FBI summary report of Ray chronology, MURKIN Files, 4143, sec. 52, p. 34. See also Frank, *American Death,* p. 172, and Posner, *Killing the Dream,* p. 220.

CHAPTER 15
"MARTIN LUTHER KING IS FINISHED"

101   "losing hold" of his faculties: Garrow, *Bearing the Cross,* p. 609.

102   "just wrong": McKnight, *Last Crusade,* p. 66.

103   "All the police would have to do": Beifuss, *At the River I Stand,* p. 220.

103   "Make the crowds stop pushing!": *Memphis Press-Scimitar,* March 29, 1968, p. 15.

104   "If you were black": Thomas, quoted in Bond and Sherman, *Memphis in Black and White,* p. 123.

105   "Turn around!": Honey, *Going Down Jericho Road,* p. 349.

105   "Take Dr. King out of the way": Beifuss, *At the River I Stand,* p. 225.

106   "never had trouble": Ibid., p. 227.

107   "the march was abandoned": Honey, *Going Down Jericho Road,* p. 366.

107   "We have a war": Holloman, quoted in the *Memphis Commercial Appeal,* March 29, 1968.

108   "Until then, King really didn't have any idea": Garrow, *Bearing the Cross,* p. 611.

108   "Get your ass out of Memphis": Honey, *Going Down Jericho Road,* p. 367.

108   " 'Martin Luther King is dead' ": Garrow, *Bearing the Cross,* p. 614.

109   "Ralph, we live in a sick nation": Abernathy, *And the Walls Came Tumbling Down,* p. 420. Also see Garrow, *Bearing the Cross,* p. 612, and Taylor Branch, *At Canaan's Edge,* p. 734.

CHAPTER 16
THE GAMEMASTER

110   **He made his way over to a salesman:** My account of Galt's visit to the Long-Lewis hardware store is based on the initial FBI interview with the salesclerk Mike Kopp, April 8, 1968, FBI, MURKIN Files, 2323, sec. 21, pp. 143–44.

111   "Mr. Sullivan requested": Halter, quoted in Garrow, *The FBI and Martin Luther King Jr.,* p. 196.

111   "Did Martin Luther King do anything": Sullivan to Halter, memorandum, March 28, 1968, FBI files on the Memphis sanitation strike, doc. 167.

112   "The fine Hotel Lorraine": G. C. Moore to Sullivan, blind memorandum, March 29, 1968, quoted in Friedly and Gallen, *Martin Luther King Jr.,* pp. 575–76.

112   "could end in great violence": Sullivan to DeLoach, memorandum, March 20, 1968, quoted in ibid., p. 570.

113   "Chicken à la King": *Memphis Commercial Appeal,* March 31, 1968.

113   "The headline-hunting high priest": *Dallas Morning News* article reprinted in the *Memphis Commercial Appeal,* April 2, 1968, p. 6.

113   "A Judas goat": *St. Louis Globe-Democrat* article cited in Honey, *Going Down Jericho Road,* p. 364.

113   "a man who gets other people into trouble": Senator Robert Byrd news footage reproduced in the Insignia Films documentary *Roads to Memphis,* produced for the PBS program *American Experience,* WGBH, Boston.

113   "a powerful embarrassment": *New York Times,* March 31, 1968, p. 46.

113   "like striking a match": *Memphis Commercial Appeal,* March 30, 1968, p. 1.

113   took a shower and pulled on some clothes . . . just buttoning his shirt: In Beifuss, *At the River I Stand,* p. 253, the Invader Calvin Taylor is quoted as saying, "Dr. King came in. He had gotten out of the shower." In *At Canaan's Edge,* p. 737, Branch says, "King emerged just then buttoning his shirt."

113   warned him of a plot: Honey, *Going Down Jericho Road,* p. 373.

114   "What can I do to have a peaceful march?": My description of the conversation in the Rivermont suite between King and the young Invaders is primarily drawn from oral histories recorded in Beifuss, *At the River I Stand,* p. 254.

114   "He wasn't raising his voice": Ibid.

114   large sporting goods store: My depiction of Galt's visit to the Aeromarine sporting goods store is primarily drawn from the initial FBI interviews conducted on April 5, 1968, by Special Agent Neil Shanahan and other agents working out of the Birmingham field office. Among those interviewed were the salesclerks U. L. Baker and Don Wood, as well as the Aeromarine customer John DeShazo.

116   "I did *not* run away": King's quotation from the Rivermont press conference are taken from newsreels housed in the Sanitation Strike Collection, Memphis Multi-Media Archival Project, March 29, 1968, reels 35–37.

117   "It was perhaps his finest performance": Abernathy, *And the Walls Came Tumbling Down,* p. 422.

117   "must be called": Lee, quoted in Coretta Scott King, *My Life with Martin Luther King Jr.,* p. 311.

117   "Can you get me out of Memphis?": Abernathy, *And the Walls Came Tumbling Down,* p. 422.

117   dropped King off at the Butler Street YMCA: Ibid.

118   somber dinner at the Abernathy house: The dinner is described in detail in Abernathy, *And the Walls Came Tumbling Down,* pp. 423–24. Also in Raines's interview with Abernathy in *My Soul Is Rested,* pp. 466–67. See also Garrow, *Bearing the Cross,* p. 615, and Branch, *At Canaan's Edge,* p. 741.

118   Galt returned to Aeromarine: My description of Galt's second trip to Aeromarine

is adapted from the aforementioned FBI interviews, conducted in Birmingham on April 5, 1968, with store employees.

119   **"The pump-action aids"**: Remington company literature describing the Gamemaster 760's attributes is quoted in Huie, *He Slew the Dreamer,* p. 138.

119   **"wide enough field of view"**: Specifications and special features of the Redfield scope come from company literature reproduced in McMillan, *Making of an Assassin,* pp. 292–93.

CHAPTER 17
TO LIVE OR DIE IN MEMPHIS

121   "was a set up": James Orange, quoted in Honey, *Going Down Jericho Road,* p. 381.

122   "We are in serious trouble": Branch, *At Canaan's Edge,* p. 742.

122   "Memphis is the Washington campaign in miniature": Ibid.

122   "You guys come up": Garrow, *Bearing the Cross,* p. 616.

123   "Ralph, give me my car keys": My description of the argument and King's abrupt exit from the SCLC meeting primarily derives from Abernathy, *And the Walls Came Tumbling Down,* pp. 425–27.

123   "Everything's *not* going to be all right": Ibid. See also Branch, *At Canaan's Edge,* p. 743.

123   "The leader is confused": Abernathy, *And the Walls Came Tumbling Down,* p. 426.

123   "We had never seen Martin": Young, *Easy Burden,* p. 459.

124   war whoops and hallelujahs: Branch, *At Canaan's Edge,* p. 744.

124   one of his mistresses: Ibid. See also Garrow, *Bearing the Cross,* p. 617.

124   "one of the most unjust wars": My depiction of King's sermon comes from the *Washington Post,* April 1, 1968. See also Garrow, *Bearing the Cross,* p. 618; Branch, *At Canaan's Edge,* p. 745; and Kotz, *Judgment Days,* p. 409.

125   "I see an alternative": Kotz, *Judgment Days,* p. 409.

126   "I would be glad": Garrow, *Bearing the Cross,* p. 618.

126   "I felt that I was being chased": Goodwin, *Lyndon Johnson and the American Dream,* p. 343.

127   "With the world's hopes": Kotz, *Judgment Days,* p. 411.

127   "His air was that of a prisoner let free": Dallek, *Flawed Giant,* pp. 529–30.

127   "I never felt so right": Branch, *At Canaan's Edge,* p. 749.

CHAPTER 18
TARGET PRACTICE AT SHILOH

128   "You must have a goal": Maltz, *Psycho-Cybernetics,* p. 37.

129   **dropped off a bundle of dirty clothes:** FBI interview with Annie Estelle Peters, manager of the Piedmont Laundry, conducted on April 16, 1968, by Special Agents Charles Rose and Robert Kane. The Piedmont Laundry's ledger and receipts were taken into evidence.

129   **hide his snub-nosed .38 revolver:** Ray claimed he buried the revolver in the rooming house basement, which had a dirt floor. Ray, *Who Killed Martin Luther King?* p. 91.

130   **found a secluded place:** Ray told his first lawyers, as well as the journalist William Bradford Huie, that he pulled off the road near Corinth, Mississippi, and test-fired the new rifle. See Huie, *He Slew the Dreamer,* p. 140, and McMillan, *Making of an Assassin,* pp. 297–98. Years later, before the House Select Committee on Assassinations, Ray changed his story and said that although he indeed drove through Corinth, Mississippi, he never test-fired the rifle.

130   **"smoking jungle":** Bierce, quoted in Horwitz, *Confederates in the Attic,* pp. 166, 170.

CHAPTER 19
TORNADO WARNINGS

131   **"It was an ordinary goodbye":** Coretta Scott King, *My Life with Martin Luther King, Jr.,* p. 314.

131   **"We have a celebrity":** Abernathy, *And the Walls Came Tumbling Down,* p. 428.

132   **"Nobody's going to kill you":** Ibid.

132   **"We have not fully made up our minds":** Honey, *Going Down Jericho Road,* p. 403.

132   **"If I were a man":** Ibid., p. 402.

133   **"We are fearful":** *Memphis Commercial Appeal,* April 4, 1968, p. 1.

134   **"Martin fell silent":** Abernathy, *And the Walls Came Tumbling Down,* p. 429.

134   **"Well, we are not going to be stopped":** Beifuss, *At the River I Stand,* p. 269.

134   **Lucius Burch:** For a good overview of Burch's multifaceted career, see the fine anthology *Lucius: Writings of Lucius Burch.*

134   **"Dr. King":** Beifuss, *At the River I Stand,* p. 271.

135   **"I had no second thoughts":** Ibid., p. 272.

135   **holding up binoculars:** Memphis Police Department official statements, "Edward E. Redditt, MC, 37, Detective with the Memphis Police Department" and "Ptm. W. B. Richmond, MC, 27, Inspectional Bureau," box 5, Posner Papers, Gotlieb Center.

136   **"This is the wrong place for you":** Ibid.

136   **"People started looking at us":** Ibid.

CHAPTER 20
NOT FEARING ANY MAN

137   **Galt coasted into the parking lot:** FBI interview with New Rebel Motel desk clerk

Henrietta Hagermaster, conducted on April 11, 1968, by Special Agent John Bauer, out of the FBI's Memphis field office.

137   **He got a haircut:** Ray told the journalist William Bradford Huie that on April 3 he got a haircut and bought a shaving kit at a Rexall drugstore in Memphis. Stickers from the Rexall drugstore were later found on several of his abandoned items. See Huie, *He Slew the Dreamer*, p. 142.

137   **a six-pack of Schlitz:** Several unopened Schlitz beers were later found among Ray's abandoned belongings and, on the basis of Mississippi state liquor tags affixed to the cans, were traced to a bait shop in Southaven, Mississippi, near the city limits of Memphis.

138   **"the kind of place where more or less legitimate people's around":** "Staff Report: Compilation of the Statements of James Earl Ray," in House Select Committee on Assassinations, *Appendix Reports*, vol. 3, p. 226.

138   **Galt put his money down:** FBI interview with Hagermaster, conducted on April 11, 1968, by Special Agent Bauer.

139   **"Ralph, I want you to go speak for me tonight":** Abernathy, *And the Walls Came Tumbling Down*, p. 430.

139   **"Something is happening in Memphis":** My depiction of King's "Mountaintop" speech at Mason Temple is drawn from Memphis television newsreels, newspaper accounts, and the documentary film *At the River I Stand*. I've also leaned on accounts in Abernathy, *And the Walls Came Tumbling Down*, p. 433; Branch, *At Canaan's Edge*, pp. 757–58; Honey, *Going Down Jericho Road*, pp. 415–24; and Beifuss, *At the River I Stand*, pp. 277–80.

141   **"it seemed like he was just saying":** Honey, *Going Down Jericho Road*, p. 424.

141   **"It seemed like he reached down":** Interviews with striking sanitation workers present at Mason Temple, from the documentary *Roads to Memphis*, Insignia Films, for the PBS program *American Experience*, WGBH, Boston.

141   **"I was full of joy":** Honey, *Going Down Jericho Road*, p. 425.

142   **Ivan Webb:** FBI interview with Webb, conducted on April 11, 1968, by Special Agent Bauer, out of the FBI's Memphis field office.

142   **"He was like a kid again":** Interview with Kyles, *Roads to Memphis*.

142   **"Senator!":** Author interview with Georgia Davis Powers, May 7, 2008, Louisville.

143   **"I didn't idolize him":** Ibid.

143   **"Senator, our time together":** Georgia Davis Powers, *I Shared the Dream*, p. 227.

CHAPTER 21
A ROOM WITH A VIEW

144   **"Oh, I'll come back later":** FBI interview with the New Rebel Motel laundress Sadie McKay, conducted on April 11, 1968, by Special Agent John Bauer, out of the FBI's Memphis field office, Hughes Collection.

144   **"beer house":** James Earl Ray's testimony in House Select Committee on Assassinations (hereafter HSCA), *Appendix Reports*, vol. 1, p. 101.

144 **"Soon it will all be over"**: Interview with James Earl Ray's brother Jerry Ray, in McMillan, *Making of an Assassin,* p. 299.

145 **tumbledown rooming house**: My description of Brewer's flophouse is drawn from multiple sources, including Memphis Police Department crime scene photographs, newspaper and magazine accounts from 1968, and Memphis Police Department and FBI interviews with Brewer and her rooming house guests, as well as my own visits to the rooming house, which is now part of the National Civil Rights Museum.

146 **"Got any vacancies?"**: My account of Galt's checking in to Brewer's rooming house is primarily drawn from FBI interviews with Brewer, especially the initial bureau interview conducted on April 5, 1968, by Special Agent Robert Boyle, Hughes Collection. I also relied on a number of Memphis Police Department statements: "Statement of Mrs. Bessie Ruth Brewer," April 4, 1968; "Statement of Jewell G. Ray, Captain of the Memphis Police Department," April 17, 1968; and "Statement of James Vincent Papia, Lieutenant with the Memphis Police Dept.," April 16, 1968. Finally, I drew from my own interviews with Jewell Ray on February 13, 2009, and with James Papia on March 2, 2009.

147 **Charlie Stephens**: FBI interview with Stephens, conducted on April 4, 1968, by Special Agents John Bauer and Stephen Darlington, Hughes Collection.

148 **Grace Walden**: FBI interview with Grace Stephens, conducted on April 4, 1968, by Special Agents Bauer and Darlington, Hughes Collection.

CHAPTER 22
THE MAN IN 5B

149 **ordered a mess of fried Mississippi River catfish**: My account of King's last meal comes from Abernathy, *And the Walls Came Tumbling Down,* p. 437. See also Abernathy's testimony in HSCA, *Appendix Reports,* vol. 1, p. 32, and Abernathy's oral history in Raines, *My Soul Is Rested,* p. 468.

151 **they demanded ten thousand dollars**: Honey, *Going Down Jericho Road,* p. 432.149

151 **"Hosea, no one will be on our payroll"**: Garrow, *Bearing the Cross,* p. 622.

151 **"I don't negotiate with brothers"**: Branch, *At Canaan's Edge,* p. 760.

151 **Cabbage stormed out**: Honey, *Going Down Jericho Road,* p. 432.

152 **"Got any binoculars?"**: The passage concerning Galt's purchase of binoculars at York Arms sporting goods store is largely drawn from the initial FBI interview with Carpenter, conducted on April 5, 1968, by Special Agents Robert Goodwin and Ralph Liewer. I also relied on the Memphis Police Department statement "Ralph Meredith Carpenter, Salesman, York Arms Company," April 9, 1968, Hughes Collection.

153 **back at their surveillance post**: My account of Redditt and Richmond undertaking surveillance work from inside the fire station is largely drawn from the Memphis Police Department statements "Edward E. Redditt, Detective with the Memphis Police Department," April 10, 1968, and "Ptm. W. B. Richmond, Inspectional Bureau," April 9, 1968, box 5, Posner Papers, Gotlieb Center, as well as my interview with Richmond, December 30, 2009.

154 **They all sat around joking**: Author interview with Georgia Davis Powers, May 7, 2008, Louisville, Ky.

154   **decided to call their mother:** Abernathy, *And the Walls Came Tumbling Down*, p. 438; Garrow, *Bearing the Cross*, p. 622.

154   **"He really sensed":** Author interview with Georgia Davis Powers.

154   **"Senator, you like soul food?":** Ibid.

154   *Where you been all day?:* Young, *Easy Burden*, pp. 463–64.

154   **full-scale pillow fight:** Ibid., p. 464.

155   **Elizabeth Copeland:** Copeland was interviewed by Memphis FBI agents on April 5, 1968, FBI, MURKIN Files, ME, sub. D, sec. 1, p. 18.

155   **Peggy Hurley:** The FBI interviewed Hurley on April 5, 1968, FBI, MURKIN Files, ME, sub. D, sec. 1, p. 3.

155   **Once inside 5B:** Details about what Galt did inside 5B are primarily drawn from the Memphis Police Department and FBI investigations of the room immediately after the assassination. His binocular straps were found on the floor; the dresser had been moved away from the open window; the straight-backed chair was placed in front of the window.

156   **At that moment, King was inside the room with Abernathy:** My account of King's last hour is adapted from multiple sources, including Abernathy, *And the Walls Came Tumbling Down*, pp. 438–39; Garrow, *Bearing the Cross*, p. 623; Branch, *At Canaan's Edge*, p. 765. See also Abernathy's testimony in House Select Committee on Assassinations, *Appendix Reports*, vol. 1, p. 30.

156   **Magic Shaving Powder:** Frank, *American Death*, p. 66.

157   **"Billy, we're not going to get *real* soul food":** Kyles's recollection of the late afternoon he spent with King and Abernathy at the Lorraine is primarily drawn from his interviews for the Insignia Films documentary *Roads to Memphis*, produced for the PBS program *American Experience*.

158   **Richmond, watching through his binoculars:** Memphis Police Department statement, "Ptm. W. B. Richmond, Inspectional Bureau," April 9, 1968, box 5, Posner Papers. I also relied on Richmond's report to the Inspectional Bureau of the Memphis Police Department, dated April 4, 1968, and signed "W. B. Richmond," Hughes Collection.

159   **George Loenneke:** FBI interview with Loenneke, conducted on April 13, 1968, by Special Agents Edward Quinn and Shields Smith, Hughes Collection. I also consulted the Memphis Police Department statement "George Loenneke, Lieutenant at Fire Station #2," box 5, Posner Papers.

160   **could hear the new roomer's footsteps:** FBI interview with Stephens, conducted on April 4, 1968, by Special Agents John Bauer and Stephen Darlington, Hughes Collection.

CHAPTER 23
AT THE RIVER I STAND

161   **"I'd feel like a bird in a cage":** Garrow, *Bearing the Cross*, p. 607.

161   **He wouldn't even let his children carry *toy* guns:** See Dexter King, *Growing Up King*, pp. 34–35.

162   **"He just act so different"**: Bailey, quoted in the *Memphis Commercial Appeal*, April 6, 1968, p. 8.

162   **Willie Anschutz**: FBI interview with Anschutz, conducted on April 4, 1968, by Special Agents John Bauer and Stephen Darlington, Hughes Collection.

163   **"an undue length of time"**: FBI interview with Stephens, conducted on April 4, 1968, by Special Agents John Bauer and Stephen Darlington, Hughes Collection.

163   **"In a second"**: This passage is primarily drawn from Abernathy, *And the Walls Came Tumbling Down*, p. 440. See also Abernathy's testimony in House Select Committee on Assassinations, *Appendix Reports*, vol. 1, p. 20.

163   **"Nothing is gained without sacrifice"**: In December 2008, this scrap of paper found in King's coat pocket after his death was put up for auction at Sotheby's in New York City by King's friend the actor and singer, Harry Belafonte, and was widely reported in the media. Belafonte said proceeds from the sale would go to charity.

163   **"I want you to come to dinner"**: King's last words to members of his staff, uttered from the balcony, have been adapted from a multitude of sources. See Young, *Easy Burden*, p. 464, and Abernathy, *And the Walls Came Tumbling Down*, p. 440. See also Garrow, *Bearing the Cross*, p. 623; Branch, *At Canaan's Edge*, p. 766; Frank, *American Death*, pp. 73–74; and Raines, *My Soul Is Rested*, p. 469. I have also made use of interviews with the Reverend Billy Kyles and Andrew Young taken for the Insignia Films documentary *Roads to Memphis*, produced for the PBS program *American Experience* by WGBH in Boston.

164   **Georgia Davis was down in 201**: Author interview with Georgia Davis Powers, May 7, 2008, Louisville, Ky.

164   **Inside the mildewy bathroom**: My depiction of Galt's actions inside the bathroom is taken from James Earl Ray's own confession (as part of his plea bargain in 1969), as well as Memphis Police Department and FBI investigations of the bathroom immediately following the assassination and interviews conducted with the tenants Charlie Stephens and Willie Anschutz. Among the findings: the bathroom window facing the Lorraine was opened several inches, the screen pried loose and found lying on the ground below; a palm print was left on the wall; and scuff marks were found in the tub.

164   **bathroom was disgustingly dirty**: My detailed description of the flophouse bathroom, including the condition of the toilet and bathtub, is primarily drawn from crime scene photographs taken by homicide detectives of the Memphis Police Department, on April 4 and 5, 1968, Hughes Collection. I also consulted photographs of the bathroom taken by the Memphis photographer Ernest Withers, Withers Collection.

166   **watching the Lorraine**: Memphis Police Department statement "Ptm. W. B. Richmond, Inspectional Bureau," April 9, 1968, box 5, Posner Papers, Gotlieb Center.

166   **"He's been shot!"**: Ibid.

167   **"I know a shot when I hear one"**: FBI interview with Stephens, April 4, 1968.

167   **Charlie Stephens opened the door**: Ibid.

167   **"Hey, that sounded like a *shot*!"**: FBI interview with Anschutz, April 4, 1968.

CHAPTER 24
LIKE A MAN ON A CROSS

169   **"His arms went out"**: Frady, *Martin Luther King Jr.*, p. 205.

169   **"Oh my God, Martin's been shot!"**: My account of the shot and its immediate aftermath is drawn from dozens of sources, including photographs, newspaper accounts, oral histories, and official records. I especially relied on Abernathy's testimony in House Select Committee on Assassinations (hereafter HSCA), *Appendix Reports*, vol. 1, p. 20; Abernathy's memoir, *And the Walls Came Tumbling Down*, pp. 440–42; Young's memoir *Easy Burden*, pp. 464–65; and Memphis Police Department statements and FBI interviews gathered from witnesses at the Lorraine Motel, Hughes Collection. I also consulted "The Last Moments: Memphis, Tenn., April 4, 1968," in HSCA, *Final Assassinations Report*, pp. 282–85.

170   **"It's all right"**: Abernathy, *And the Walls Came Tumbling Down*, p. 441.

171   **made a solid thunk**: FBI interview with Canipe, April 5, 1968, Hughes Collection.

171   **"The understanding"**: Abernathy, *And the Walls Came Tumbling Down*, p. 441.

171   **"crimson molasses"**: Frank, *American Death*, p. 82.

172   **Kyles discreetly slipped it out of his grip**: Interview with Kyles on CNN, Special Investigations Unit, that aired on April 4, 2009. Kyles says, "I took a crushed cigarette out of his hand. He didn't want kids to see him smoke." See also Frady, *Martin Luther King Jr.*, p. 205.

172   **Louw trembled with a manic rage**: The story of how Louw photographed his world-famous image on the balcony is best captured in Frank, *American Death*, pp. 77–80.

172   **"shaking like a leaf"**: Honey, *Going Down Jericho Road*, p. 442.

173   **"We have information"**: Memphis Police Department radio dispatcher recordings from April 4, 1968, Hughes Collection.

173   **"Where's he been hit?"**: Frank, *American Death*, pp. 85–86.

174   **"Murder! Murder!"**: Ibid., p. 83.

CHAPTER 25
THE WEAPON IS NOT TO BE TOUCHED

175   **sitting at his desk**: My account of what transpired at Canipe's Amusement Company is primarily drawn from the initial FBI interview with the shop owner, Guy Canipe, and from FBI interviews with the customers Julius Graham and Bernell Finley, April 5, 1968. I also relied on Memphis Police Department statements taken from Canipe, Graham, and Finley. Additional details came from my own interviews with the retired Memphis police officers James Papia and Jewell Ray, who were among the first on the scene at Canipe's.

177   **"You are not to touch the weapon!"**: Memphis Police Department radio dispatcher recordings from April 4, 1968, Hughes Collection.

177   **"Suspect described as young white male"**: Ibid.

177   **Stephens dashed back to his room**: FBI interview with Stephens, conducted on April 4, 1968, by Special Agents John Bauer and Stephen Darlington, Hughes Collection.

178   **"Georgia, I don't think"**: Author interview with Georgia Davis Powers, May 7, 2008, Louisville, Ky.

178   **"Give me the loop lights!"**: Frank, *An American Death,* p. 85.

179   **"Is he alive?"**: This passage from inside the ambulance is largely adapted from Abernathy, *And the Walls Came Tumbling Down,* p. 442.

179   **Captain Jewell Ray**: My account of Jewell Ray's initial investigation of the crime scene at Canipe's and inside Bessie Brewer's rooming house is primarily drawn from my interview with Ray, on Feb. 13, 2009. I also interviewed the retired police officer James Papia, who investigated the scene with Ray. Additionally, I relied on Memphis Police Department statements taken from Ray, Papia, Canipe, Willie Anschutz, Charlie Stephens, and Bessie Brewer. See also Frank, *An American Death,* pp. 98–103.

CHAPTER 26
A PAUSE THAT WOULD NEVER END

183   **"Coretta, Doc just got shot"**: Coretta Scott King's recollection of Jackson's phone call from Memphis is in her memoir, *My Life with Martin Luther King Jr.,* p. 318.

184   **"Mama? You hear that?"**: Dexter Scott King, *Growing Up King,* p. 48.

184   **"I understand"**: Ibid.

184   **team of nurses and ER orderlies**: My passages concerning the efforts to save King's life inside the St. Joseph's ER are drawn from multiple sources. I especially relied on Memphis Police Department summaries (Hughes Collection) gathered immediately after King's death by homicide detectives who interviewed a number of ER doctors and nurses. Other important sources include the oral history of Dr. Frederick Gioia and other attending physicians in Beifuss, *At the River I Stand,* pp. 297–99; Abernathy's memoirs, *And the Walls Came Tumbling Down,* pp. 443–44; Frank's vivid account in *American Death,* pp. 90, 93, 95–96, 119; and my own interview with Dr. Ted Galyon, December 30, 2009.

185   **"I'm staying"**: Abernathy, *And the Walls Came Tumbling Down,* p. 443.

185   **Gioia stepped into the fray**: For my passage on Dr. Gioia and his efforts to treat King, I'm grateful for the insights of his daughter, Dominique Gioia Skaggs, with whom I spoke and corresponded.

186   **"It would be a blessing"**: Abernathy, *And the Walls Came Tumbling Down,* p. 443. See also Raines, *My Soul Is Rested,* p. 471.

186   **Rufus Bradshaw**: My account of the CB radio "chase" heard by Bradshaw is primarily drawn from the radio dispatcher recording, Hughes Collection. I also relied on Memphis Police Department and the FBI's Memphis field office investigations of the CB radio transmission, Hughes Collection.

189   **In the waiting room, Andy Young sat**: Young, *Easy Burden,* p. 466.

189   **"The *neck*"**: Ibid.

189   **Hanging up the beige receiver**: Dexter King, *Growing Up King,* p. 48.

189   **"Your father—there's been an accident"**: Ibid.

189   "I need to see Dr. King!": Frady, *Jesse*, p. 229.

191   "And I caught his head": Ibid.

191   "You dirty, stinking, lying . . . !": Williams, quoted in Kenneth R. Timmerman, *Shakedown: Exposing the Real Jesse Jackson* (Washington, D.C.: Regnery, 2002), p. 8.

191   "It's a helluva thing": Ibid., p. 7.

191   "This whole thing's": Frady, *Jesse*, p. 229.

191   David Burrington: Timmerman, *Shakedown*, p. 8.

192   "He won't make it": Abernathy, *And the Walls Came Tumbling Down*, p. 443.

192   "nothing more than prolonged shudders": Ibid., p. 443.

193   Father Bergard closed King's eyes: Beifuss, *At the River I Stand*, p. 300.

193   King's parents listened to the radio: Martin Luther King Sr., *Daddy King*, p. 189.

193   "No matter how much protection": Ibid., p. 187.

194   "My first son": Ibid., p. 189.

194   Two agents: This passage is drawn from Arthur L. Murtagh's testimony in House Select Committee on Assassinations, *Appendix Reports*, vol. 6, p. 107; and from James J. Rose's testimony, ibid., vol. 6, pp. 125–27.

CHAPTER 27
A FEW MINUTES AND A FEW MILES

196   "entirely a hoax": My passages concerning the Memphis Police Department's postmortem analysis of the CB car chase hoax are primarily drawn from the sixteen-page report "Dr. Martin Luther King Jr., Homicide #3367, Supplement #85, Re: C.B. Incident," Hughes Collection. The Memphis Police Department investigated the probable culprit behind the hoax, a teenage CB enthusiast named in the report. Also see House Select Committee on Assassinations (hereafter HSCA), *Final Assassinations Report*, pp. 383–85.

197   he headed southeast: Ray's exact route out of Memphis is not absolutely known, but he consistently stated that he drove southeast toward Birmingham; Highway 78 would have been the fastest, most direct, and (having stayed in a motel on that same road the previous night) most familiar route for his exit. See Ray, *Tennessee Waltz*, p. 80, as well as Ray's testimony in HSCA, *Appendix Reports*, vol. 3, p. 240.

198   broadcasters now broke in: In all his accounts, Ray consistently stated that he heard the news about King's death over his car radio. However, the FBI investigation of the abandoned Mustang later determined that the radio was not in good working order at the time of inspection.

198   Coretta King hurried down: My depiction of the scene at the Atlanta airport is adapted from the *Atlanta Constitution*, April 5, 1968, p. 1, and from Coretta Scott King, *My Life with Martin Luther King Jr.*, pp. 319–20.

199   "a tragic setback": Author interview with Clark, Oct. 9, 2008, New York City.

199   "I think the bureau": This conversation between Clark and DeLoach is recalled in DeLoach's, *Hoover's FBI,* p. 224.

200   "a crime of immense importance": DeLoach's testimony, HSCA, *Appendix Reports,* vol. 7, p. 22.

200   "Hoover remained at war": DeLoach, *Hoover's FBI,* p. 222.

201   "He was as anxious": Ibid., p. 226.

201   "The FBI's reputation": Author interview with Clark.

201   "the guy with a thousand opportunities": DeLoach, *Hoover's FBI,* p. 225.

201   Born in Denmark: These biographical details concerning Jensen derive primarily from his obituary in the *Memphis Commercial Appeal,* March 22, 1992, as well as from Jensen's testimony in HSCA, *Appendix Reports,* vol. 6, pp. 586–87.

201   "As you well know": DeLoach, *Hoover's FBI,* p. 225.

202   Now Jensen removed: This passage concerning Jensen's analysis of the evidence is primarily drawn from the FBI FD-302 report filed on April 4 and 5, 1968, by Special Agent in Charge Jensen and Special Agent Robert Fitzpatrick, enumerating and describing all items in the abandoned bundle, Hughes Collection.

CHAPTER 28
THEY'VE TORN IT NOW

205   Johnson sat at his mahogany desk: My account of Johnson's reaction to the King assassination is drawn from a number of sources, including Kotz, *Judgment Days,* p. 415; Dallek, *Flawed Giant,* p. 533; Risen, *Nation on Fire,* pp. 40–42, 53–54; and Califano, *Triumph and Tragedy of Lyndon Johnson,* pp. 273–75. Especially helpful to me was "The President's Appointment File, 4/3/68 to 4/11/68," box 95, Lyndon Baines Johnson Papers, Johnson Presidential Library.

205   "Justice has just advised": This memo is at the Johnson Presidential Library.

205   "A jumble of anxious thoughts": Johnson, quoted in Risen, *Nation on Fire,* p. 42.

206   "Everything we've gained": Dallek, *Flawed Giant,* p. 533.

207   "America is shocked": "Statement by the President on the Assassination of Dr. Martin Luther King Jr.," Johnson Presidential Library.

207   "Don't send your skinny little rookies": Busby, *Thirty-first of March,* p. 236.

207   "They're holed up like generals": Ibid.

207   "*The D.C. Civil Defense*": Situation Room memorandums from the night of April 4, 1968, Johnson Library.

207   "King was the last prince of nonviolence": Floyd McKissick, quoted in the *Washington Post,* April 5, 1968, p. 1.

207   "The next Negro to advocate nonviolence": Risen, *A Nation on Fire,* p. 56.

208   "When white America killed Dr. King": Stokely Carmichael, quoted in Gilbert et al., *Ten Blocks from the White House,* pp. 60–61.

208   **"The nation is steeped in violence"**: Church, quoted in a UPI report on the White House ticker tape on the night of April 4, 1968, Johnson Presidential Library.

209   **"It was one of those frozen moments"**: Mrs. Johnson, quoted in Dallek, *Flawed Giant,* p. 533, and Risen, *Nation on Fire,* p. 54.

210   **"I and all the citizens of Memphis"**: *Memphis Commercial Appeal,* April 5, 1968, p. 1.

210   **"We feel that the assassin crouched"**: *Memphis Press-Scimitar,* April 5, 1968, p. 1.

211   **"damned to hell"**: Blanchard, quoted in Honey, *Going Down Jericho Road,* p. 440.

211   **"I'm so sorry"**: Beifuss, *At the River I Stand,* p. 300.

212   **"Our neighborhood was like a tomb"**: Honey, *Going Down Jericho Road,* p. 444.

212   **"This is the darkest day I've ever seen"**: Beifuss, *At the River I Stand,* p. 283.

212   **"that nigger King"**: Honey, *Going Down Jericho Road,* p. 441.

213   **"The Lord has deserted us"**: Beifuss, *At the River I Stand,* p. 303.

213   **"Just respect the man"**: Ibid.

213   **"rioting and looting is now rampant"**: Fire and Police Director Frank Holloman, quoted in the *Memphis Commercial Appeal,* April 5, 1968, p. 1.

213   **"That's what I thought"**: Honey, *Going Down Jericho Road,* p. 447.

214   **"Stay calm"**: Beifuss, *At the River I Stand,* p. 301.

214   **"I went numb"**: Honey, *Going Down Jericho Road,* p. 437.

215   **"I thought I was going to get away"**: Ray, quoted in Ayton, *Racial Crime,* p. 143. See also Frank, *American Death,* p. 390.

216   **"I had to drive slow"**: James Earl Ray, "20,000 Words," quoted in Huie, *Making of an Assassin,* p. 145.

216   **"I knew that the car could be hot"**: Ray, *Who Killed Martin Luther King?* p. 97.

216   **"I just wanted to get rid"**: Ray, *Tennessee Waltz,* p. 80.

CHAPTER 29
POWER IN THE BLOOD

217   **"King wouldn't make a decision without him"**: Hosea Williams, quoted in McKnight, *The Last Crusade,* p. 108.

217   **"flashbulbs still blinked"**: Wills, "Martin Luther King Is Still on the Case," reprinted in *The New Journalism,* ed. Tom Wolfe, p. 393.

218   **"sleepwalk through the night"**: Young, *Easy Burden,* p. 467.

218   **"had received, through letter or telephone"**: Abernathy's testimony in House Select Committee on Assassination, *Appendix Reports,* vol. 1, p. 19.

218   **"We can't let Martin down"**: Bevel, quoted in Young, *Easy Burden,* p. 468.

219   **"They got him"**: Ibid.

219   **"I touched the pillow"**: Georgia Davis Powers, *I Shared the Dream,* p. 233.

219   "This is Martin's precious blood": Frady, *Jesse*, p. 232.

219   Withers took several shots: Frank, *American Death*, p. 109.

219   wiped them down the front of his shirt: Young, quoted in Frady, *Jesse*, p. 232.

219   "There's nothing that unusual": Ibid.

220   "composed but dazed": *Atlanta Constitution*, April 5, 1968, p. 1.

220   King had not written a will: Kathryn Johnson, "Dr. King Leaves Little—He Gave It All Away," *Atlanta Constitution*, May 13, 1968, p. 1.

220   "If something happens": Honey, *Going Down Jericho Road*, p. 452.

220   "but there was something a little different": *Memphis Commercial Appeal*, April 2, 1978.

220   "just to do any little menial thing": Belafonte, quoted in Coretta Scott King, *My Life with Martin Luther King Jr.*, p. 322.

221   "Mommy, when is Daddy coming home?": Ibid., p. 321.

221   "No, darling": Ibid.

221   Dr. Jerry Francisco: Biographical details and physical descriptions of Francisco are adapted from *Memphis Commercial Appeal* clippings and my interview with Francisco, Jan. 20, 2009.

222   "somehow looked more dead": Abernathy, *And the Walls Came Tumbling Down*, p. 445.

222   "This is the body": Ibid.

223   "It might tell us something": Ibid.

223   "giving the appearance": Memphis Police Department document, "Martin Luther King Homicide No. 3367, Supplement #5, Re: Consent for Autopsy and Autopsy," p. 2, Hughes Collection.

223   "More than any case": Author interview with Francisco.

224   "I felt very safe": Ibid.

224   "This is a well developed": Francisco's autopsy report, Hughes Collection.

225   "Every light in every store": Wills, "Martin Luther King Is Still on the Case," reprinted in *New Journalism*, p. 390.

225   "tens of thousands of Americans": Graham's reaction to King's murder, and the other reactions reproduced in this passage from various international figures, are taken from White House newswires, Situation Room memorandums, and State Department telexes received on April 4 and 5, 1968, Johnson Presidential Library.

CHAPTER 30
A SUMMONS TO MEMPHIS

231   Lockheed Jetstar taxied: My account of the initial trip to Memphis made by Clark and DeLoach on April 5 derives from multiple sources. I especially relied on DeLoach,

Hoover's FBI, pp. 228–30, as well as my own interview with Clark, Oct. 9, 2008, New York City. I also gained valuable insights from Wilkins, *A Man's Life*, pp. 211–12, and Risen, *Nation on Fire*, pp. 95–97. See also DeLoach's testimony in House Select Committee on Assassinations (hereafter HSCA), *Appendix Reports*, vol. 7, pp. 18–117, as well as Clark's testimony, HSCA, *Appendix Reports*, vol. 7, pp. 120–63.

232   **fugitive named John Willard:** DeLoach, *Hoover's FBI*, p. 228.

232   **Now he opened his briefcase:** Wilkins, *A Man's Life*, p. 212. See also Risen, *Nation on Fire*, p. 95.

233   **"At daybreak I stopped for gas":** Ray, *Tennessee Waltz*, p. 80.

233   **location he had scoped out:** FBI agents later discovered that the map Ray left behind in his Atlanta rooming house bore a circle on it, presumably made by Ray, at the location of the Capitol Homes project—which seemed to indicate that he had investigated the location prior to abandoning his car there.

233   **Mary Bridges:** My depiction of Galt's abandoning his Mustang at the Capitol Homes project on the morning of April 5 is adapted from varied sources. I especially relied on a thirty-four-page FBI report titled "Eric Starvo Galt, Bureau File #44–38861" prepared by Special Agent Alan G. Sentinella of the Atlanta field office, filed on April 18, 1968, Hughes Collection. This report contains a detailed description of the Mustang's location and condition (with accompanying photographs) as well as interviews with the various Capitol Homes tenants (including Mary Bridges) who saw the Mustang and its driver. I also made use of "Capitol Homes Stirred Up by That Mustang," *Atlanta Constitution*, April 22, 1968.

234   **United Cab Company driver:** FBI interview with Stephens conducted on April 12, 1968, by Special Agent Thomas J. Barrett, Hughes Collection.

234   **"This is one of the darkest days":** Abernathy's comments at the morning press conference at the Lorraine Motel were reprinted in the *Atlanta Constitution*, April 6, 1968.

235   **had hired a public relations agent:** Kenneth R. Timmerman, *Shakedown: Exposing the Real Jesse Jackson* (Washington, D.C.: Regnery, 2002), pp. 9–10.

235   **"To prostitute and lie":** Bevel, quoted in Frady, *Jesse*, p. 230.

236   **"was somehow in shock":** Abernathy, *And the Walls Came Tumbling Down*, p. 449.

236   **Shanahan walked through the door:** FBI interview with Wood, conducted on April 5, 1968, by Shanahan out of the Birmingham field office. Shanahan's FD-302 report of the interview, along with a copy of the receipt showing the rifle's purchase, is in the Hughes Collection.

237   **"He wasn't drunk":** FBI interview with DeShazo, conducted on April 7, 1968, by Special Agents Robert Barrett and William Saucier out of the Birmingham field office, Hughes Collection.

CHAPTER 31
LOOPS AND WHORLS, LANDS AND GROOVES

238   **At the FBI Crime Lab:** My passages here concerning the FBI lab's initial examination of the bundle from Memphis are primarily drawn from "Report of the FBI Laboratory,

FBI, April 17, 1968, Evidence Recovered in Front of 424 So. Main St. April 4th, 1968," Hughes Collection. I also relied on "Scientific Report on the Subject of Analysis of Fingerprint Evidence Related to the Assassination of Dr. Martin Luther King Jr. by the Fingerprint Panel," House Select Committee on Assassinations (hereafter HSCA), *Appendix Reports*, vol. 8, pp. 109–21.

238   **esoteric profession:** For a good overview of the history, lore, science, and shortcomings of fingerprint analysis, see Michael Specter, "Do Fingerprints Lie?" *New Yorker,* May 27, 2002.

240   **Frazier spent the morning:** "Testimony of the Firearms Panel," HSCA, *Appendix Reports*, vol. 4, pp. 78–111.

242   **Annie Estelle Peters:** This passage on Galt's picking up his laundry in Atlanta on the morning of April 5 is primarily drawn from the FBI's initial interview with Peters, conducted on April 16, 1968, by Special Agents Charles Paul Rose and Robert Kane working out of the bureau's Atlanta field office. The FD-302 report of this interview is in the Hughes Collection. I also relied on Peters's testimony in HSCA, *Appendix Reports*, vol. 3, pp. 302–514.

242   **"satisfied there was no unusual activity":** Ray, *Tennessee Waltz,* p. 80.

243   **wad of bills:** Ray, in his book *Who Killed Martin Luther King?* says, on p. 100, that upon his arrival in Toronto the following day, he was "down to $1,200 or so."

243   **dashed off a short note:** My description of Galt's actions at the rooming house on April 5 are primarily drawn from the FBI's interviews with Garner, conducted on April 14 and 15, 1968, by Special Agent Roger Kaas of the bureau's Atlanta field office. FD-302 reports of these interviews are in the Hughes Collection.

243   **"There was so much to do":** Garry Wills, "Martin Luther King Is Still on the Case," reprinted in *The New Journalism,* ed. Tom Wolfe, p. 393.

243   **"The body appeared unblemished":** Abernathy, *And the Walls Came Tumbling Down,* p. 448.

244   **"We all wanted to be there":** Young, *Easy Burden,* p. 469.

244   **"It will spoil the makeup job":** Wills, "Martin Luther King Is Still on the Case," reprinted in *New Journalism,* p. 394.

244   **"I wish it was Henry Loeb":** Ibid., p. 395.

244   **"Why'd this happen to you":** My description of the public viewing at the R. S. Lewis Funeral Home on the morning of April 5 is drawn from the *Memphis Commercial Appeal,* April 6, 1968, as well as from Beifuss, *At the River I Stand,* pp. 315–16.

CHAPTER 32
ONE MAN ON THE RUN

245   **"I thought it was a provocation":** Author interview with Clark, Oct. 9, 2008, New York City.

245   **"What a message that was":** Ibid.

246   **"To see these men":** Roger Wilkins interview, *Roads to Memphis,* an Insignia Films documentary produced for the PBS program *American Experience,* WGBH, Boston.

246   "gracious in a Southern kind of way": Ibid.

246   "He was just about out on his feet": Beifuss, *At the River I Stand*, p. 325.

247   "I had not a scintilla": Holloman's testimony in House Select Committee on Assassinations, *Appendix Reports*, vol. 4, p. 332.

247   "All of our evidence": Clark's comments from his Memphis press conference were
printed in the *Memphis Press-Scimitar*, April 5, 1968, and the *Memphis Commercial Appeal*,
April 6, 1968.

248   "In view of Mr. Hoover's": DeLoach, *Hoover's FBI*, p. 229.

248   "courageous and calm": Wilkins, *Man's Life*, p. 212.

248   "a bloated and faded version": Ibid.

248   "We'll do everything we can": DeLoach, *Hoover's FBI*, p. 229.

249   "We aren't so much concerned": Andrew Young, in *Roads to Memphis*.

250   "Why, it's sitting right out there": FBI interview with Capitol Homes tenants in
"Eric Starvo Galt, Bureau File #44–38861" prepared by Special Agent Alan G. Sentinella
of the Atlanta field office, filed on April 18, 1968, Hughes Collection. I also adapted material here from "Capitol Homes Stirred Up by That Mustang," *Atlanta Constitution*,
April 22, 1968.

CHAPTER 33
1812 REDUX

251   "Please know that I join you": King senior to Johnson, telegram, quoted in Risen,
Nation on Fire, p. 89.

251   "If I were a kid in Harlem": Busby, *Thirty-first of March*, p. 238.

252   "Help us, Lord": Ibid., p. 239.

252   "take as many white people": Stokely Carmichael, quoted in Risen, *Nation on Fire*,
p. 93.

253   "Gentlemen, I think you better see this": Busby, *Thirty-first of March*, p. 239.

253   Morris S. Clark: Here I consulted the FBI Crime Lab's initial fiber analysis in "Report of the FBI Laboratory, FBI, April 17, 1968, Evidence Recovered in Front of 424 So.
Main St. April 4th, 1968," p. 9, Hughes Collection.

254   quickly dispatched to Rompage: See Frank, *American Death*, p. 142.

254   tiny tag was made of white tape: Here I primarily consulted the eighteen-page FBI
report "Investigation to Trace the Laundry Marks Found on Underwear Abandoned near
the Scene of the Shooting of Dr. King," Hughes Collection.

255   "I thought of the brittle smile": Abernathy, *And the Walls Came Tumbling Down*,
p. 450.

255   "Martin was unworried": Ibid.

256   "Daddy is lying down in the back": Coretta Scott King, *My Life with Martin Luther
King Jr.*, p. 325.

256   "I'd look around": Dexter Scott King, *Growing Up King*, p. 52.

256   "Mother knew I was avoiding": Ibid.

256   "looked so young and smooth": Coretta Scott King, *My Life with Martin Luther King Jr.*, p. 325.

256   "Uncle Andy, this man": Young, *Easy Burden*, p. 470.

257   buying a one-way ticket: My account of Ray's bus trip north is drawn from his statements and testimony in House Select Committee on Assassinations (hereafter HSCA), *Appendix Reports*, vol. 3, p. 245, as well as from his two books, *Tennessee Waltz*, p. 81, and *Who Killed Martin Luther King?* p. 98. I also consulted Ray's own account for his lawyers, "20,000 Words," Hughes Collection.

257   DR. KING SHOT: *Atlanta Constitution*, April 5, 1968, p. 1.

258   checked his suitcase in to a locker: HSCA, *Appendix Reports*, vol. 3, p. 245.

258   boarded a second bus: Ibid.

259   bottle of the finest sherry: Oral history with Ramsey Clark, interview 4, conducted by Harri Baker on April 16, 1969, Johnson Presidential Library.

259   "We had considerably more evidence": Author interview with Clark, Oct. 9, 2008, New York City.

260   "We are virtually unique": Clark, *Crime in America*, p. 95.

260   "to dam the flood": DeLoach, *Hoover's FBI*, p. 230.

260   now occupied by federal troops: My depictions of the D.C. riots here are largely drawn from Risen, *Nation on Fire*, and Gilbert et al., *Ten Blocks from the White House*.

261   "the air of a parliament": The columnist Mary McGrory, quoted in Risen, *Nation on Fire*, p. 127.

261   "In all my life": Author interview with Clark.

CHAPTER 34
HOME SWEET HOME IN TORONTO

262   coach reached the Motor City: See James Earl Ray's testimony in House Select Committee on Assassinations, *Appendix Reports*, vol. 3, p. 245, as well as his two books, *Tennessee Waltz*, p. 81, and *Who Killed Martin Luther King?* p. 98, and Ray's own account for his lawyers, "20,000 Words," Hughes Collection.

262   "It is better to overreact": Cavanaugh, quoted in Risen, *Nation on Fire*, p. 141.

263   Galt later claimed that he stashed his suitcase: See Huie, *He Slew the Dreamer*, p. 148.

264   Mrs. Szpakowski showed him up to the room: My description of Ray's room on Ossington, and his behavior and actions while staying there as a guest, is largely drawn from O'Neil, "Ray, Sirhan—What Possessed Them?" I also relied on a special report, "King Murder Suspect Held—He Hid 1 Month in Metro," *Toronto Daily Star*, June 8, 1968, p. 1. Finally, I also relied on the Royal Canadian Mounted Police Files, a large body of documents concerning Ray's time in Toronto, Hughes Collection.

265   Sidney Poitier and Harry Belafonte: See Poitier, *This Life*, pp. 319–20.

265   "I didn't want to face Coretta": Georgia Davis Powers, *I Shared the Dream*, p. 233.

265   "Sorry for what?": Ibid., p. 234.

265   didn't leave his room: See Huie, *He Slew the Dreamer*, p. 149, and Posner, *Killing the Dream*, pp. 239–40.

266   He was in Baltimore: See Gentry, *J. Edgar Hoover*, p. 606.

266   "This man, in the full prime": Lawson, quoted in Honey, *Going Down Jericho Road*, pp. 473–74.

266   "I noticed how worried": Huie, *He Slew the Dreamer*, p. 149.

CHAPTER 35
THEN EASTER COMES

267   Coretta Scott King wore a bittersweet smile: My account of the April 8 march in Memphis is adapted primarily from page-one articles in the *Memphis Press-Scimitar*, the *Memphis Commercial Appeal*, the *New York Times*, and the *Atlanta Constitution*. I also relied on newsreels in the Mississippi Valley Collection. See also Beifuss, *At the River I Stand*, pp. 340–43; Honey, *Going Down Jericho Road*, pp. 474–82; Abernathy, *And the Walls Came Tumbling Down*, pp. 458–60; and Coretta Scott King, *My Life with Martin Luther King Jr.*, pp. 327–29.

268   "The people were kind": Dexter Scott King, *Growing Up King*, p. 53.

268   "We gave Dr. King what he came here for": *Memphis Commercial Appeal*, April 9, 1968, p. 1.

268   "Each of you is on trial today": Flyer prepared by Lawson, quoted in Honey, *Going Down Jericho Road*, p. 476.

269   "once you reach Main Street": Ibid., p. 478.

269   "the spilling of one man's blood": Abernathy, *And the Walls Came Tumbling Down*, p. 458.

270   "I guess it was my mother": *Memphis Commercial Appeal*, April 11, 1968. See also Honey, *Going Down Jericho Road*, p. 475, and Beifuss, *At the River I Stand*, p. 341.

270   Now the agents pulled their bureau sedan: This passage about the FBI's initial investigations at the New Rebel Motel is based largely on my own interview with the former FBI agent Stephen Darlington, May 15, 2009. I also relied on FD-302 reports of the interview Agents Darlington and Bauer conducted at the New Rebel on April 8, 1968, Hughes Collection.

271   made his way down to the offices: My depiction of Galt's efforts to gather aliases in the reading room of the *Telegram* is primarily adapted from Ray's own accounts in *Tennessee Waltz*, p. 84, and *Who Killed Martin Luther King?* p. 99. Other accounts suggest he actually visited the newspaper microfilm archives at a public library in Toronto. See also Posner, *Killing the Dream*, p. 240.

272   "I'd read somewhere": Ray, *Who Killed Martin Luther King?* p. 98.

272   "Teenagers are adopting": Royal Canadian Mounted Police Files, a compendium of police investigations into Galt's movements while in Toronto, Hughes Collection.

272   brief expeditionary detour: See Posner, *Killing the Dream,* p. 240.

273   "Until we have justice": *Memphis Commercial Appeal,* April 9, 1968, p. 10.

273   "Mayor Loeb will somehow be dragged": Reuther, quoted in Beifuss, *At the River I Stand,* p. 343.

274   "It's not the quantity": The entire text of Coretta Scott King's speech in Memphis is reprinted in her memoir, *My Life with Martin Luther King Jr.,* pp. 344–47.

274   "If Mrs. King had cried": Honey, *Going Down Jericho Road,* p. 481.

274   "When Good Friday": Coretta Scott King, *My Life with Martin Luther King Jr.,* p. 345.

274   Neil Shanahan and William Saucier: This passage is drawn from the FD-302 report of the April 8, 1968, interview that Shanahan and Saucier conducted with the rooming house proprietor, Peter Cherpes, Hughes Collection.

CHAPTER 36
THE MAN FURTHEST DOWN

276   For three and a half miles: My depiction of King's funeral in Atlanta is drawn primarily from newspaper coverage in the *Atlanta Constitution* and the *New York Times* that appeared on April 10, 1968. I also relied on photographs and other displays at the King Center in Atlanta. Finally, I consulted memoirs of participants, including Young, *Easy Burden,* pp. 477–78; Abernathy, *And the Walls Came Tumbling Down,* pp. 460–65; Coretta Scott King, *My Life with Martin Luther King Jr.,* pp. 329–36; Martin Luther King Sr., *Daddy King,* pp. 190–91; and Wofford, *Of Kennedys and Kings,* p. 203. I benefited from Risen's vivid account in *Nation on Fire,* pp. 205–13.

276   had suggested that King arranged: See Risen, *Nation on Fire,* p. 208.

278   "leaning toward each other": *Newsweek,* April 22, 1968.

278   "There was a powerful mood": Ibid.

279   "I believed in your father": A letter I viewed in January 2009 from a collection of correspondence on exhibit at the King National Historic Site in Atlanta.

279   "if they catch the guy": Ibid.

280   "There were many fingers": *Time,* March 21, 1969.

280   Galt was in his room on Ossington Avenue: My account of what Galt did in his room on April 9 is primarily drawn from newspaper and magazine interviews with the landlady, Mrs. Feliksa Szpakowski. See especially O'Neil, "Ray, Sirhan—What Possessed Them?"

280   nightclub called the Silver Dollar: Ibid.

281   "time to play detective": Ray, *Who Killed Martin Luther King?* p. 99.

281   "Yes, hello": My account of the telephone conversation between Ray and Bridgman

is derived both from Ray's own recollection in his memoirs and from Toronto police interviews with Bridgman in the Royal Canadian Mounted Police Files, Hughes Collection.

283   **Paisley's place of work:** This passage is drawn primarily from the FD-302 report of the interview that Shanahan and Barrett conducted with Paisley on April 9, 1968.

284   **"If you are going to do something illegal":** James Earl Ray statement to investigators, House Select Committee on Assassinations, *Appendix Reports*, vol. 9, p. 430.

285   **"I make bold to assert":** King eulogy by Benjamin Mays, quoted in the *Atlanta Constitution*, April 10, 1968, p. 1.

CHAPTER 37
THE MURKIN FILES

287   **"It was a huge operation":** Author interview with Clark, Oct. 8, 2009, New York City.

288   **"We are continuing":** Memo signed by J. Edgar Hoover, MURKIN Files, sec. 2, which the author viewed on microfilm at Stanford University.

288   **"A racist":** DeLoach, *Hoover's FBI*, p. 233.

289   **"Tips" arrived from all points of the compass:** All these various leads are taken from the opening weeks of the manhunt and are in the MURKIN Files, sec. 2.

289   **"Shoot the son-of-a-bitch":** See Frank, *American Death*, p. 143.

290   **woman in Memphis called Holloman's office:** From a Memphis police report investigating the footage taken by WMC-TV Channel 5, the NBC affiliate in Memphis, dated April 10, 1968, box 5, Posner Papers, Gotlieb Center.

291   **call came from the Mexican consulate:** *Memphis Press-Scimitar*, April 19, 1968.

291   **white male American tourist:** Frank, *American Death*, p. 188.

291   **Mrs. John Riley had been thinking:** This passage is drawn largely from "Capitol Homes Stirred Up by That Mustang," *Atlanta Constitution*, April 22, 1968.

293   **president was signing into law:** See Kotz, *Judgment Days*, p. 421, and Dallek, *Flawed Giant*, p. 534.

293   **Brown's Theatrical Supply Company:** See Huie, *He Slew the Dreamer*, p. 154.

293   **Arcade Photo Studio:** Ibid., p. 152.

294   **convoy of bureau sedans:** Here I relied on a compilation document of FBI interviews with tenants at the housing project titled, "Capitol Homes Interviews," Hughes Collection.

294   **"There must have been a billion of 'em":** "Capitol Homes Stirred Up by That Mustang."

295   **Every inch of the impounded car:** This passage is largely drawn from the FBI analysis of the Mustang, in "Report of the FBI Laboratory, April 19, #44–38861," Hughes Collection.

295   **Theodore A'Hearn:** FD-302 report of A'Hearn's April 11, 1968, interviews at Cort Fox Ford in the compendium document "Los Angeles Investigations," Hughes Collection.

296   **Thomas Mansfield:** FD-302 report of Agent Mansfield's April 12, 1968, interviews at the St. Francis Hotel, in "Los Angeles Investigations," Hughes Collection.

296   **Lloyd Johnson and Francis Kahl:** FD-302 report from the interview conducted by Johnson and Kahl with Pinela at Home Service Laundry, in "Los Angeles Investigations," Hughes Collection.

298   **George Aiken:** FD-302 report from interviews conducted at the National Dance Studio by Aiken, in "Los Angeles Investigations," Hughes Collection.

299   **"Yes, Eric Galt was a student here":** FD-302 report from interviews conducted at the International School of Bartending by A'Hearn and Raysa, in "Los Angeles Investigations," Hughes Collection.

299   **Donald Jacobs:** Ibid.

CHAPTER 38
CANADA BELIEVES YOU

302   **disguised themselves as hippies:** Frank, *American Death,* p. 172.

302   **"Take the door off its hinges":** Ibid.

302   **a few telltale artifacts:** FD-302 report filed on April 17, 1968, by the FBI agents Harry Lee, John Sullivan, Roger Kaas, and John Ogden, which enumerates and describes all the items found inside Galt's room.

303   **William John Slicks and Richard Ross:** This passage is drawn from the FBI's FD-302 report of the April 13, 1968, interview conducted with Stein by Slicks and Ross, in "Los Angeles Investigations," Hughes Collection.

304   **Tomaso had sharp recollections:** FD-302 report of the April 13, 1968, interview conducted with Tomaso (a.k.a. Marie Martin) by Slicks and Ross, in "Los Angeles Investigations," Hughes Collection.

304   **handwritten sign:** McMillan, *Making of an Assassin,* p. 285.

304   **John Ogden and Roger Kaas:** FD-302 report of April 14 and 15, 1968, interviews conducted with Garner by Ogden and Kaas, Hughes Collection.

306   **"we were numb":** Beifuss, *At the River I Stand,* p. 348.

306   **Abe Plough:** See Honey, *Going Down Jericho Road,* p. 489.

307   **"After Dr. King was killed":** Beifuss, *At the River I Stand,* p. 345.

307   **" 'I am a man'—they meant it":** Reynolds, quoted in Beifuss, *At the River I Stand,* pp. 346–47.

307   **"We have been aggrieved":** *Memphis Press-Scimitar,* April 17, 1968, p. 1.

307   **"We won":** *Newsweek,* April 29, 1968, p. 22.

307   **Sun Fung Loo:** The FBI's summary of Ray's activities while in Canada, in the MURKIN Files, 4442–4500, sec. 57, p. 61.

308   **wrote to the registrar of births:** A copy of Galt's request for Ramon Sneyd's birth certificate is in the House Select Committee on Assassinations, *Appendix Reports,* vol. 5, p. 15.

308   **Lillian Spencer:** This passage concerning Spencer at the Kennedy Travel Bureau is drawn from "King Murder Suspect Held—He Hid 1 Month in Metro," *Toronto Daily Star,* June 8, 1968, p. 1. I also relied on RCMP interviews with Spencer in the Royal Canadian Mounted Police Files, Hughes Collection.

308   **"I thought it was an odd name":** Huie, *He Slew the Dreamer,* p. 155.

CHAPTER 39
ARMED AND DANGEROUS

312   **found the laundry service:** FBI interview with Estelle Peters conducted on April 16, 1968, by Special Agents Charles Rose and Robert Kane, FD-302 report, Hughes Collection.

312   **fingerprint raised from a map:** "Scientific Report on the Subject of Analysis of Fingerprint Evidence Related to the Assassination of Dr. Martin Luther King Jr. by the Fingerprint Panel," House Select Committee on Assassinations, *Appendix Reports,* vol. 13, pp. 109–21.

312   **"Our net was beginning to close":** DeLoach, *Hoover's FBI,* pp. 242, 247.

313   **"All I can say":** See Frank, *American Death,* p. 124.

313   **FBI announced that it was issuing a warrant:** A copy of the warrant, with accompanying shots of Galt/Ray adapted from his bartending school photo, is in the Hughes Collection.

314   **jaywalked across a busy street:** Ray discusses the jaywalking incident in both of his books, *Tennessee Waltz,* p. 84, and *Who Killed Martin Luther King?* p. 99. See also Huie, *He Slew the Dreamer,* p. 158.

315   **shredded his driver's license:** Ray, *Tennessee Waltz,* p. 84.

CHAPTER 40
THE PHANTOM FUGITIVE

316   **"the man without a past":** These characterizations are taken from a variety of media sources immediately after Galt was identified—including the *Memphis Commercial Appeal,* the *Washington Post,* the *Atlanta Constitution, Newsweek,* and *Time.*

316   **"No, that's not him":** "Eric Galt, Alleged Brother Conspired to Assassinate Dr. King, FBI Declares," *Atlanta Constitution,* April 18, 1968, pp. 1, 29.

317   **"I just don't know":** Ibid.

317   **"was a two-dimensional cutout":** *Newsweek,* April 29, 1968.

317   **"Fiction wouldn't touch it":** *Memphis Commercial Appeal,* June 16, 1968.

318   **"destroyed the production plants":** "Who Is Phantom Fugitive? Reporters Put Together Facts," a special "Task Force Report" in the *Atlanta Constitution,* April 22, 1968, p. 8.

319   **"He is the man who killed":** Mrs. Szpakowski's conversation with her husband concerning Galt is recounted in Frank, *American Death,* p. 316.

320   **"All the signs were there":** DeLoach, *Hoover's FBI,* pp. 241–42.

320   **"Les, we have pretty good evidence":** The conversation between DeLoach and Les Trotter is recalled in DeLoach, *Hoover's FBI,* p. 245.

320   "we're under tremendous pressure": Ibid., p. 246.

321   "We're getting there": Ibid.

CHAPTER 41
THE TOP TEN

325   "He came with a suit on": Loo, quoted in the *Memphis Commercial Appeal*, June 10, 1968.

326   Sneyd sat at the crowded bar: Posner, *Killing the Dream*, pp. 244–45; Huie, *He Slew the Dreamer*, p. 160.

328   "He was a dirty little neck": Peterson, quoted in *Life*, May 3, 1968.

328   thumbnail sketch: This information concerning Ray's prison history is primarily drawn from FD-302 reports of the FBI's interviews with Ray's former prison inmates at Jefferson City, in the voluminous compendium document St. Louis Files, Hughes Collection.

328   "raise" the numerals: See Shaw, "Are You Sure Who Killed Martin Luther King?"

328   agents soon found a brother, John Ray: My description of the FBI's initial contact with John Ray is primarily based on FD-302 reports of interviews in St. Louis Files, Hughes Collection.

329   "seal his lips forever": Interview with John Ray conducted on May 2, 1968, by Special Agents Jack Williams and Patrick Bradley, FD-302 report, Hughes Collection.

329   "What's all the excitement about?": The FBI's initial interview with John Ray, conducted on April 22, 1968, by Special Agents Harry C. Jun and Robert Hess, FD-302 report, Hughes Collection.

330   John Ray would boast: See Ray and Barsten, *Truth at Last*, p. 109.

330   "hottest man in the country": Jerry Ray, quoted in the *Chicago Sun-Times*, May 3, 1968.

330   "He sure didn't have any love": Jerry Ray, quoted in *Life*, May 3, 1968.

331   "A supermarket": Ray, quoted in McKinley, "Interview with James Earl Ray," p. 134.

331   found him in the rear of the store: For a good account of the incident at Loblaws, see Frank, *American Death*, p. 317.

331   beheld a rotund man: Ibid.

332   "I should have pulled a holdup": Posner, *Killing the Dream*, p. 249.

CHAPTER 42
RESURRECTION CITY

334   "the greatest nonviolent demonstration": Young, quoted in McKnight, *Last Crusade*, p. 84.

334   "the idea of rebirth": Young, *Easy Burden*, p. 481.

335   Lurleen Wallace's body lay in the rotunda: Carter, *Politics of Rage*, pp. 320–21.

335   electric lines, water lines: For plans and preparations for the Poor People's Cam-

paign, see Abernathy, *And the Walls Came Tumbling Down*, pp. 500–506, and Young, *Easy Burden*, pp. 484–85.

335 **"one of the bigger tasks"**: McKnight, *Last Crusade*, p. 85.

335 **"hurt the president—*deeply* hurt him"**: Ramsey Clark, quoted in McKnight, *The Last Crusade*, p. 110.

335 **"Mecca for migrants"**: Ibid., p. 87.

335 **"one of paranoia"**: Clark, *Crime in America*, p. 235.

336 **The Ray clan had a hundred-year history**: For background on the Ray family, I relied largely on McMillan's psychological study, *Making of an Assassin*, and documents in the McMillan Papers.

336 **cannibalize their own house**: Posner, *Killing the Dream*, p. 85.

337 **"I made it to keep my sanity"**: *Life*, May 3, 1968.

337 **"He liked being clean"**: *Newsweek*, April 29, 1968.

337 **William Duncan and James Duffey**: FBI interview with Jerry Raynes conducted in Center, Missouri, by Duncan and Duffey on April 17, 1968, FD-302 report, Hughes Collection.

338 **"He was thinking all the time"**: McMillan interview with Jerry Raynes, March 20, 1969, box 1, McMillan Papers.

338 **"those people will poison you"**: Ibid.

338 **"All politicians are thieves"**: Ibid.

338 **"I don't hate niggers"**: Ibid.

339 **"People try to get too much out of life"**: McMillan interview with Ray's father, Oct. 20, 1969, box 1, McMillan Papers.

339 **ship bound for Angola**: Ray, *Tennessee Waltz*, pp. 86–87.

340 **second floor of the Hotel Portugal**: My descriptions of Sneyd's hotel and its Lisbon environs are drawn from O'Neil, "Ray, Sirhan—What Possessed Them?" and my own visit to the hotel in July 2007.

340 **Gentil Soares**: In this section I chiefly relied on FBI reports prepared in collaboration with the Portuguese International and State Security Police in Lisbon. These reports include interviews (with customs officials, hotel personnel, nightclub employees, and prostitutes who had contact with Sneyd) conducted in Lisbon on June 8–12, 1968, and distilled in a thirteen-page document titled "Lisbon Files," Hughes Collection.

341 **Gloria Sausa Ribeiro**: Ibid.

341 **"He did not know any Portuguese"**: Ibid.

CHAPTER 43
A RETIREMENT PLAN

342 **"What appealed to Jimmy about Hitler"**: George McMillan interview with Jerry Ray on April 1, 1972, box 5, McMillan Papers.

342   **"was unreasonable in his hatred":** Rife, quoted in McMillan, *Making of an Assassin,* p. 147.

343   **"retirement plan":** This passage concerning Curtis is primarily drawn from "Raymond Curtis Interviews, Whitfield County Jail, Dalton, Georgia," box 1, McMillan Papers. See also McMillan, *Making of an Assassin,* pp. 175–85; Frank, *American Death,* p. 183; and Posner, *Killing the Dream,* p. 136.

344   **John Sutherland:** The passage here on Sutherland and the alleged fifty-thousand-dollar bounty to kill King is chiefly drawn from "Evidence of a Conspiracy in St. Louis," House Select Committee on Assassinations (hereafter HSCA), *Final Assassinations Report,* pp. 359–75. I also relied on the testimony of Russell Byers in HSCA, *Appendix Reports,* pp. 177–310.

CHAPTER 44
PLAGUES

346   **declared open for business:** My passage on the Poor People's encampment on the Mall is primarily drawn from daily coverage in the *Washington Post* throughout May and June 1968, as well as from McKnight, *Last Crusade,* pp. 107–39; Risen, *Nation on Fire,* pp. 235–36; Abernathy, *And the Walls Came Tumbling Down,* pp. 494–539; and Young, *Easy Burden,* pp. 477–92.

346   **"plague after plague":** Abernathy, quoted in McKnight, *Last Crusade,* p. 130.

347   **"Resurrection City was flawed":** Abernathy, *And the Walls Came Tumbling Down,* pp. 503, 516.

347   **"megalomania":** McKnight, *Last Crusade,* p. 116.

347   **"just another fish-fry":** Ibid., p. 126.

348   **"Ralph was frustrated":** Young, *Easy Burden,* p. 490.

348   **"The gray skies poured water":** Abernathy, *And the Walls Came Tumbling Down,* p. 517.

349   **"document such things as immorality":** Hoover memo quoted in McKnight, *Last Crusade,* p. 128.

349   **"some grotesque soap opera":** McKnight, *Last Crusade,* p. 134.

349   **"almost a perfect failure":** Ibid., p. 107.

350   **"Lincoln smiled kindly":** Clark, *Crime in America,* p. 236.

CHAPTER 45
A BANK WITHDRAWAL

351   **Charles J. Sweeney:** My depiction of Sweeney's task force is drawn from the Royal Canadian Mounted Police Files, Hughes Collection. See also Posner, *Killing the Dream,* p. 43.

352   **Doris Catherine Westwood:** Westwood statement in the sixty-three-page compendium document Scotland Yard Files, Hughes Collection.

353   **Maurice Isaacs and his wife:** This passage is drawn from various accounts in the London papers—including the *Times* and the *Telegraph*—and my own visit to the jewelry store address near Paddington Station. I also benefited from an interview with the Isaacses' son, Vincent Isaacs, June 27, 2008, London.

355   **Robert Wood:** From Royal Canadian Mounted Police Files, Hughes Collection.

355   **Ian Colvin:** My recounting of Sneyd's calls to Colvin is primarily drawn from Colvin's article "Dr. King Suspect Here 3 Weeks, Mystery Calls to the Daily Telegraph," *London Daily Telegraph*, June 10, 1968, p. 1. See also Frank, *American Death*, p. 320.

356   **"He was nervous":** Nassau, quoted in Huie, *He Slew the Dreamer*, p. 166.

357   **Trustee Savings Bank in Fulham:** My account of Sneyd's robbery is largely drawn from Scotland Yard interviews with the bank employees, in Scotland Yard Files, Hughes Collection. See also Posner, *Killing the Dream*, p. 249; Huie, *He Slew the Dreamer*, p. 166; and Frank, *American Death*, p. 321.

358   **"Mr. Sneyd, on April 4":** My depiction of the Royal Canadian Mounted Police interrogation of Ramon Sneyd is primarily drawn from "Statement of Ramon George Sneyd, Born October 8, 1932, Cautioned by: R. Marsh, Detective Sergeant, Metro Toronto P.D.," Royal Canadian Mounted Police Files 1, Hughes Collection.

359   **"He seemed ill":** My depiction of Sneyd's stay at the Pax Hotel in Pimlico is drawn from "The Man in Locked Room," *Evening Standard*, June 10, 1968. See also Huie, *He Slew the Dreamer*, p. 167.

360   **"I was in a daze":** Young, *Easy Burden*, pp. 486–87.

361   **"We were all still trying":** Ibid.

361   **"I haven't heard from Major Wicks":** Colvin, "Dr. King Suspect Here 3 Weeks," p. 1. See also Posner, *Killing the Dream*, p. 248.

362   **"many criminals seeking refuge":** Butler's obituary, *Times* (London), April 21, 1970.

363   **"We knew that the fugitive":** DeLoach, *Hoover's FBI*, p. 249.

CHAPTER 46
I CAN'T THINK RIGHT

364   **"He was so neurotic":** This passage is chiefly derived from "Statement of Anna Elizabeth Thomas, Hotel Proprietress, Pax Hotel," Flying Squad Office, New Scotland Yard, Hughes Collection. See also Huie, *He Slew the Dreamer*, p. 167.

365   **"Passport please":** My account of the Heathrow Airport encounter between Sneyd and Human is drawn from "Statement of Kenneth Leonard Human, Immigration Officer, London Airport Heathrow Terminal Two," taken on June 10, 1968, at the Flying Squad Office, New Scotland Yard, Hughes Collection.

365   **Philip Birch:** My depiction of Birch's initial questioning of Sneyd is adapted from "Statement of Philip Birch, Detective Sergeant, Special Branch," taken on June 10, 1968, at the Flying Squad Office, New Scotland Yard, Hughes Collection.

366   **Thomas Butler arrived:** This passage concerning Butler's interrogation of Sneyd

comes from "Statement of Thomas Butler, Detective Chief Superintendent, Flying Squad, New Scotland Yard," taken on June 10, 1968, Hughes Collection. I also relied on "Statement of Witness, Kenneth Thompson," Scotland Yard Files, Hughes Collection.

369   **"As a result of inquiries":** "Statement of Thomas Butler," Hughes Collection.

369   **"Yes, I shouldn't say":** Ibid.

CHAPTER 47
THREE WIDOWS

370   **DeLoach was making late Saturday morning pancakes:** This passage is primarily drawn from DeLoach, *Hoover's FBI*, p. 249.

370   **"Every muscle in my body relaxed":** Ibid.

371   **"Dammit, man":** Ibid., p. 250.

371   **"Fine—prepare the press release":** Ibid.

371   **At St. Patrick's Cathedral:** My account of the scene outside St. Patrick's is largely drawn from the coverage of Robert Kennedy's funeral in the *New York Times* and the *Washington Post,* June 9, 1968.

372   **in good taste to wait:** Author interview with Clark, Oct. 9, 2008, New York City. See also Richard Gid Powers, *Secrecy and Power,* p. 422, and Gentry, *J. Edgar Hoover,* pp. 606–7.

373   **"We're happy he's been caught":** Williams, quoted in *Atlanta Constitution,* June 9, 1968, p. 20.

373   **"Some felt this case":** Byrd's comments before the U.S. Senate, in MURKIN Files, sec. 57, p. 71.

374   **two men held up a bank:** For an in-depth discussion of the Alton bank robbery and the possible involvement of the Ray brothers, see House Select Committee on Assassinations (hereafter HSCA), *Final Assassinations Report,* pp. 342–50.

375   **"We are dealing with a man":** Hoover, quoted in HSCA, *Appendix Reports,* vol. 7, p. 7.

375   **"one of the strongest":** Author interview with Clark.

375   **"Some Americans":** Ibid.

375   **"Nothing Ray did":** DeLoach, *Hoover's FBI,* p. 256.

376   **"was a loner":** DeLoach testimony in HSCA, *Appendix Reports,* vol. 7, p. 28.

376   **"Truth be told":** DeLoach, *Hoover's FBI,* p. 257.

CHAPTER 48
RING OF STEEL

377   **"Look, they got me mixed up":** This exchange between Sneyd and Eugene is recounted in Frank, *American Death,* p. 201.

377   "Yes, I'd like you to call my brother": Ibid., p. 203.

378   Patriotic Legal Fund: Huie, *He Slew the Dreamer*, p. 181.

379   Alexander Eist: The passages concerning Eist and his time spent with Sneyd in London are drawn from a lengthy interview with Eist conducted at Cambridge, England, on August 4, 1978, by Edward Evans, chief investigator, House Select Committee on Assassinations, *Appendix Reports*, vol. 3, pp. 264–84.

379   "He seemed absolutely mad about publicity": Ibid.

380   "There's no way": Ibid.

381   Sneyd was met by four FBI agents: Custody Log, James Earl Ray, July 19, 1968, Aboard USAF Plane C135," MURKIN Files, 4901–4982, sec. 66, pp. 178–81. See also Posner, *Killing the Dream*, pp. 55–56.

382   At 3:48 a.m.: My depiction of Ray's arrival in Memphis is largely drawn from the *Memphis Press-Scimitar*, July 19, 1968, and the *Memphis Commercial Appeal*, July 20, 1968. See also Frank, *American Death*, pp. 223–34.

383   "They're getting out of the plane": DeLoach, *Hoover's FBI*, p. 254.

383   "ring of steel": Ibid.

383   Morris had arranged: Frank, *American Death*, pp. 228–34.

EPILOGUE
#65477

387   two hundred inmates: My reenactment of Ray's prison escape is drawn primarily from newspaper and magazine accounts from June 1977—especially the *Atlanta Constitution*, the *New York Times*, the *Memphis Commercial Appeal*, the *Nashville Tennessean*, and the *Washington Post*. In-depth stories in *Time* and *Newsweek*, both appearing on June 20, 1977, proved especially helpful. I also consulted *Building Time at Brushy*, a semi-fictional memoir by the prison's warden, Stonney Lane. Finally, I found James McKinley's interview with Ray (*Playboy*, Sept. 1977) extremely useful.

390   "Ray's hot": *New York Times*, June 12, 1977, p. 1.

391   "Ray is smart like a rat": Foreman, quoted in *Newsweek*, June 20, 1977, p. 25.

391   "funny in the head": McKinley, "Interview with James Earl Ray," p. 176.

392   "Raoul does not and did not exist": *Time*, June 20, 1977, p. 17.

393   "You always have it": McKinley, "Interview with James Earl Ray," p. 86.

393   "convinced beyond a shadow of a doubt": Abernathy, quoted in the *Washington Post*, June 11, 1977, p. A10.

393   "engineered to see that Ray": *Time*, June 20, 1977, p. 14.

394   "I hope they don't kill him": Martin Luther King Sr., quoted in the *Atlanta Constitution*, June 13, 1977, p. 19A.

395   Sammy Joe Chapman: This passage involving the bloodhounds is largely drawn

from my interview with Sammy Joe Chapman, Sept. 2009. I also relied on "How the Mountain Men Did It," *Time,* June 27, 1977, pp. 11–12, and "Back in Cell: Ray Brought to Bay by Two Bloodhounds," *Washington Post,* June 14, 1977, p. 1.

397   **"For a 49-year-old man"**: "How the Mountain Men Did It," p. 11.

397   **"It's disappointing being caught"**: McKinley, "Interview with James Earl Ray," p. 94.

BIBLIOGRAPHY

OFFICIAL DOCUMENTS

City of Memphis v. Martin Luther King Jr. et al., April 3, 1968. Hearing proceedings.

Federal Bureau of Investigation. MURKIN Files. King Assassination Documents, FBI Central Headquarters. Viewed on microfilm at Stanford University's Cecil H. Green Library.

House Select Committee on Assassinations. U.S. Congress. *Investigation of the Assassination of Martin Luther King Jr.: Appendix Reports*, Vols. 1–13. Washington, D.C.: U.S. Government Printing Office, 1979.

————. *Investigation of the Assassination of Martin Luther King Jr.: The Final Assassinations Report*. New York: Bantam, 1979.

State of Tennessee v. James Earl Ray. Shelby County Criminal Court, div. 3, Tenn., 1969. Proceedings.

United States of America v. James Earl Ray. Extradition proceedings.

U.S. Justice Department. "Report of the Department of Justice Task Force to Review the FBI Martin Luther King Jr. Security and Assassination Investigations," Jan. 11, 1977.

ARCHIVES, LIBRARIES, AND MUSEUMS

Hughes, B. Venson Collection on the Assassination of Martin Luther King, Germantown, Tenn. Collection includes unpublished crime scene and evidentiary photos, Memphis Police Department files, police dispatcher audio files, rare and unpublished FBI reports, and other investigation documents.

Birmingham Civil Rights Institute, Birmingham, Ala.

British Library Newspaper Archives, Colindale, U.K.

Howard Gotlieb Archival Research Center, Boston University. Collections consulted include the Gerald Posner Papers, the letters of James Earl Ray, and the Martin Luther King Collection.

Huie, William Bradford. Papers. Rare Books and Manuscripts Library, Ohio State University, Columbus.

King Center Library and Archives, and the Martin Luther King Jr. National Historic Site, Atlanta.

Lyndon Baines Johnson Presidential Library and Museum, University of Texas, Austin.

Martin Luther King Papers Project, Stanford University.

Mary Ferrell Foundation Digital Archive (www.maryferrell.org), Ipswich, Mass. Collections consulted include FBI MURKIN files, HSCA executive sessions, and Church Committee hearings.

McMillan, George. Papers. Southern Historical Collection, Wilson Library, University of North Carolina, Chapel Hill.

Memphis and Shelby County Room, Benjamin L. Hooks Central Library, Memphis. Collections consulted include the Henry Loeb Papers, the Frank Holloman Papers, and news clippings from the *Memphis Commercial Appeal* and the *Memphis Press-Scimitar*.

Memphis Magazine Archives. Contemporary Media, Inc., Memphis.

Mississippi Valley Collection. Ned R. McWherter Library, University of Memphis.

National Civil Rights Museum, Lorraine Motel, Memphis.

Withers, Ernest C. Photographic Collection. Panopticon Gallery of Photography, Boston. Collection houses the work of the legendary Memphis civil rights photographer Ernest Withers.

NEWSPAPERS

Atlanta Constitution

London Daily Mirror

London Daily Telegraph

London Evening Standard

London Observer

Los Angeles Times

Manchester Guardian

Memphis Commercial Appeal

Memphis Press-Scimitar

New York Times

St. Louis Post-Dispatch

Times (London)

Toronto Telegram

Washington Post

BOOKS

Abernathy, Ralph David. *And the Walls Came Tumbling Down*. New York: Harper & Row, 1989.

Ayton, Mel. *A Racial Crime: James Earl Ray and the Murder of Dr. Martin Luther King Jr.* Las Vegas: ArcheBooks, 2005.

Barry, John M. *Rising Tide: The Great Mississippi Flood of 1927 and How It Changed America*. New York: Simon & Schuster, 1997.

Bearden, William. *Cotton: From Southern Fields to the Memphis Market*. Charleston, S.C.: Arcadia, 2005.

———. *Memphis Blues: Birthplace of a Music Tradition*. Charleston, S.C.: Arcadia, 2006.

Beifuss, Joan Turner. *At the River I Stand: Memphis, the 1968 Strike, and Martin Luther King*. Memphis: B & W Books, 1985.

Biles, Roger. *Memphis in the Great Depression*. Knoxville: University of Tennessee Press, 1986.

Bishop, Jim. *The Days of Martin Luther King Jr.* New York: G. P. Putnam's Sons, 1971.

Blair, Clay, Jr. *The Strange Case of James Earl Ray: The Man Who Murdered Martin Luther King*. New York: Bantam Books, 1969.

Bond, Beverly G., and Janann Sherman. *Beale Street*. Charleston, S.C.: Arcadia, 2006.

———. *Memphis in Black and White*. Charleston, S.C.: Arcadia, 2003.

Bowman, Rob. *Soulsville U.S.A.: The Story of Stax Records*. New York: Schirmer Trade Books, 1997.

Branch, Taylor. *At Canaan's Edge: America in the King Years, 1965–68*. New York: Simon & Schuster, 2006.

———. *Parting the Waters: America in the King Years, 1954–63*. New York: Touchstone, 1989.

———. *Pillar of Fire: America in the King Years, 1963–65*. New York: Simon & Schuster, 1998.

Branston, John. *Rowdy Memphis: The South Unscripted*. Nashville: Cold Tree Press, 2004.

Brinkley, Douglas. *Rosa Parks*. New York: Viking, 2000.

Burch, Lucius. *Lucius: Writings of Lucius Burch*. Nashville: Cold Tree Press, 2003.

Burrough, Bryan. *Public Enemies: America's Greatest Crime Wave and the Birth of the FBI, 1933–34*. New York: Penguin, 2004.

Busby, Horace. *The Thirty-first of March: An Intimate Portrait of Lyndon Johnson's Final Days in Office*. New York: Farrar, Straus and Giroux, 2005.

Califano, Joseph A. *The Triumph and Tragedy of Lyndon Johnson*. New York: Simon & Schuster, 1991.

Capers, Gerald M. *The Biography of a River Town: Memphis, Its Heroic Age*. New Orleans: Tulane University Press, 1966.

Carson, Clayborne, ed. *The Autobiography of Martin Luther King*. New York: Time Warner Books, 1998.

Carson, Clayborne, and Peter Holloran, eds. *A Knock at Midnight: Inspiration from the Great Sermons of Martin Luther King Jr.* New York: Warner Books, 1998.

Carson, Clayborne, et al., eds. *The Papers of Martin Luther King Jr.* Vols. 1–6. Berkeley: University of California Press, 1992–2009.

Carter, Dan T. *The Politics of Rage: George Wallace, the Origins of the New Conservatism, and the Transformation of American Politics*. Baton Rouge: Louisiana State University Press, 1995.

Carter, Hodding. *Lower Mississippi*. New York: Farrar & Rinehart, 1942.

Cash, Johnny, with Patrick Carr. *Cash: The Autobiography*. San Francisco: HarperCollins, 1997.

Chapman, C. Stuart. *Shelby Foote: A Writer's Life*. Jackson: University of Mississippi Press, 2003.

Christopher, Warren. *Chances of a Lifetime: A Memoir*. New York: Scribner, 2001.

Church, Annette E., and Roberta Church. *The Robert A. Churches of Memphis*. Ann Arbor, Mich.: Edwards Brothers, 1974.

Clark, Ramsey. *Crime in America: Observations on Its Nature, Causes, Prevention, and Control*. New York: Simon & Schuster, 1970.

Cobb, James C. *The Most Southern Place on Earth: The Mississippi Delta and the Roots of Regional Identity*. New York: Oxford University Press, 1992.

Conaway, James. *Memphis Afternoons: A Memoir*. Boston: Houghton Mifflin, 1993.

Cooper, William J. *Jefferson Davis, American*. New York: Vintage Civil War Library, 2001.

Coppock, Paul R. *Paul Coppock's Mid-South, Volumes I–IV*. Edited by Helen M. Coppock and Charles W. Crawford. Nashville: Williams Printing Company, 1993.

Crosby, Molly Caldwell. *The American Plague: The Untold Story of Yellow Fever, the Epidemic That Shaped Our History*. New York: Berkley Books, 2006.

Cunningham, O. Edward. *Shiloh and the Western Campaign of 1862*. New York: Savas Beatie, 2007.

Dallek, Robert. *Flawed Giant: Lyndon Johnson and His Times, 1961–1973*. New York: Oxford University Press, 1998.

DeLoach, Cartha D. *Hoover's FBI: The Inside Story by Hoover's Trusted Lieutenant*. Washington, D.C.: Regnery, 1997.

Dowdy, G. Wayne. *Mayor Crump Don't Like It: Machine Politics in Memphis*. Jackson: University of Mississippi Press, 2006.

Doyle, William. *An American Insurrection: James Meredith and the Battle of Oxford, Mississippi, 1962*. New York: Anchor Books, 2001.

Dyson, Michael Eric. *April 4, 1968: Martin Luther King Jr.'s Death and How It Changed America*. New York: Basic Civitas Books, 2008.

———. *I May Not Get There with You: The True Martin Luther King Jr.* New York: Free Press, 2000.

Estes, Steve. *"I Am a Man!": Race, Manhood, and the Struggle for Civil Rights*. Chapel Hill: University of North Carolina Press, 2005.

Fager, Charles. *Uncertain Resurrection: The Poor People's Washington Campaign*. Grand Rapids, Mich.: Eerdmans, 1969.

Fairclough, Adam. *Martin Luther King Jr.* Athens: University of Georgia Press, 1995.

Faulkner, William. *Sanctuary*. New York: Jonathan Cape & Harrison Smith, 1931.

Fisher, David. *Hard Evidence: How Detectives Inside the FBI's Sci-Crime Lab Have Helped Solve America's Toughest Cases*. New York: Simon & Schuster, 1995.

Fleming, Ian. *On Her Majesty's Secret Service*. New York: Signet Books, 1963.

Foote, Shelby. *September, September*. New York: Random House, 1978.

Frady, Marshall. *Jesse: The Life and Pilgrimage of Jesse Jackson*. New York: Simon & Schuster, 1996.

———. *Martin Luther King Jr.: A Life*. New York: Viking Penguin, 2002.

———. *Wallace: The Classic Portrait of Alabama Governor George Wallace*. New York: New American Library, 1968.

Frank, Gerold. *An American Death: The True Story of the Assassination of Dr. Martin Luther King Jr.* Garden City, N.Y.: Doubleday, 1972.

Friedly, Michael, and David Gallen. *Martin Luther King Jr.: The FBI File*. New York: Carroll & Graf, 1993.

Gabriel, Michael. *James Earl Ray: The Last Days of Inmate #65477*. Los Angeles: CatYoga, 2004.

Garrow, David J. *Bearing the Cross: Martin Luther King Jr. and the Southern Christian Leadership Conference*. New York: William Morrow, 1986.

———. *The FBI and Martin Luther King Jr.: From "Solo" to Memphis*. New York: W. W. Norton, 1981.

Gentry, Curt. *J. Edgar Hoover: The Man and the Secrets*. New York: W. W. Norton, 1991.

Gilbert, Ben W., et al. *Ten Blocks from the White House: Anatomy of the Washington Riots of 1968*. New York: Frederick A. Praeger, 1968.

Goldman, Albert. *Elvis*. New York: McGraw-Hill, 1981.

Goodwin, Doris Kearns. *Lyndon Johnson and the American Dream*. New York: St. Martin's Press, 1976.

Gordon, Robert. *Can't Be Satisfied: The Life and Times of Muddy Waters*. Boston: Little, Brown, 2002.

———. *It Came from Memphis*. New York: Pocket Books, 1995.

Green, Laurie B. *Battling the Plantation Mentality: Memphis and the Black Freedom Struggle*. Chapel Hill: University of North Carolina Press, 2007.

Guralnick, Peter. *Careless Love: The Unmaking of Elvis Presley*. Boston: Back Bay Books, 1999.

———. *Last Train to Memphis: The Rise of Elvis Presley*. Boston: Little, Brown, 1994.

———. *Searching for Robert Johnson: The Life and Legend of the "King of the Delta Blues Singers."* New York: Plume, 1998.

———. *Sweet Soul Music: Rhythm and Blues and the Southern Dream of Freedom*. New York: HarperCollins, 1986.

Halberstam, David. *The Children*. New York: Random House, 1998.

Handy, W. C. *Father of the Blues: An Autobiography*. New York: Da Capo, 1969.

Harkins, John. *Historic Shelby County: An Illustrated History*. Memphis: West Tennessee Historical Society, 2008.

———. *Metropolis of the American Nile: Memphis and Shelby County*. Memphis: West Tennessee Historical Society, 1982.

Hendrickson, Paul. *Sons of Mississippi*. New York: Alfred A. Knopf, 2003.

Hersh, Burton. *Bobby and J. Edgar: The Historic Face-Off Between the Kennedys and J. Edgar Hoover That Transformed America*. New York: Carroll & Graf, 2007.

Honey, Michael K. *Going Down Jericho Road: The Memphis Strike, Martin Luther King's Last Campaign*. New York: W. W. Norton, 2007.

Horwitz, Tony. *Confederates in the Attic: Dispatches from the Unfinished Civil War*. New York: Vintage Books, 1998.

Huie, William Bradford. *He Slew the Dreamer: My Search, with James Earl Ray, for the Truth About the Murder of Martin Luther King*. New York: Delacorte Press, 1970.

Hurst, Jack. *Nathan Bedford Forrest: A Biography*. New York: Vintage Books, 1994.

Jones, Clarence, and Joel Engel. *What Would Martin Say?* New York: Harper, 2008.

Joyce, Peter. *Anatomy of a Rebel: Smith of Rhodesia, a Biography*. Salisbury, Rhodesia: Graham, 1974.

Kaiser, Charles. *1968 in America: Music, Politics, Chaos, Counterculture, and the Shaping of a Generation*. New York: Weidenfeld & Nicolson, 1988.

Kaiser, Robert Blair. *"R.F.K. Must Die!": Chasing the Mystery of the Robert Kennedy Assassination*. New York: Overlook Press, 2008.

Kelly, John F., and Phillip K. Wearne. *Tainting Evidence: Inside the Scandals of the FBI Crime Lab*. New York: Free Press, 1998.

King, B. B., with David Ritz. *Blues All Around Me: The Autobiography of B. B. King*. New York: Avon Books, 1997.

King, Coretta Scott. *My Life with Martin Luther King Jr.* New York: Holt, Rinehart, and Winston, 1969.

King, Dexter Scott. *Growing Up King: An Intimate Memoir*. New York: Warner Books, 2003.

King, Martin Luther, Jr. *Stride Toward Freedom*. New York: Harper & Row, 1958.

————. *Where Do We Go from Here? Chaos or Community?* New York: Harper & Row, 1967.

King, Martin Luther, Sr. *Daddy King: An Autobiography*. New York: William Morrow, 1980.

Kirwan, Albert D. *Revolt of the Rednecks: Mississippi Politics, 1876–1925*. New York: Harper & Row, 1965.

Kotz, Nick. *Judgment Days: Lyndon Baines Johnson, Martin Luther King Jr., and the Laws That Changed America*. Boston: Houghton Mifflin, 2005.

Lane, Mark, and Dick Gregory. *Code Name "Zorro": The Murder of Martin Luther King Jr.* Englewood Cliffs, N.J.: Prentice-Hall, 1977.

————. *Murder in Memphis: The FBI and the Assassination of Martin Luther King*. New York: Thunder's Mouth Press, 1993.

Lane, Stonney Ray. *Building Time at Brushy*. Bloomington, Ind.: First Books, 2003.

Lemann, Nicholas. *The Promised Land: The Great Black Migration and How It Changed America*. New York: Alfred A. Knopf, 1991.

Lesher, Stephan. *George Wallace: American Populist*. Cambridge, Mass.: Perseus, 1994.

Levine, David. *Bayard Rustin and the Civil Rights Movement*. New Brunswick, N.J.: Rutgers University Press, 2000.

Lewis, David. *King: A Biography*. Champaign: University of Illinois Press, 1978.

Lewis, John, with Michael D'Orso. *Walking with the Wind: A Memoir of the Movement*. New York: Harcourt Brace & Company, 1998.

Lischer, Richard. *The Preacher King: Martin Luther King Jr. and the Word That Moved America*. New York: Oxford University Press, 1995.

Lomax, Louis E. *To Kill a Black Man*. Los Angeles: Holloway House, 1968.

Magness, Perre. *The Party with a Purpose: 75 Years of Carnival in Memphis*. Jonesboro, Ark.: Pinpoint Printing, 2006.

————. *Past Times: Stories of Early Memphis*. Memphis: Parkway Press, 1994.

Maltz, Michael. *Psycho-Cybernetics: A New Technique for Using Your Subconscious Power*. Englewood Cliffs, N.J.: Prentice-Hall, 1960.

McKnight, Gerald D. *The Last Crusade: Martin Luther King Jr., the FBI, and the Poor People's Campaign*. Boulder, Colo.: Westview Press, 1998.

McMillan, George. *The Making of an Assassin: The Life of James Earl Ray*. Boston: Little, Brown, 1976.

McWhorter, Diane. *Carry Me Home: Birmingham, Alabama, the Climactic Battle of the Civil Rights Revolution*. New York: Simon & Schuster, 2001.

Melanson, Philip H. *The Murkin Conspiracy: An Investigation into the Assassination of Dr. Martin Luther King Jr.* New York: Praeger, 1989.

Memphis Commercial Appeal. *I Am a Man: Photographs of the 1968 Memphis Sanitation Strike and Dr. Martin Luther King Jr.* Memphis: Memphis Publishing Co., 1993.

Miller, William D. *Mr. Crump of Memphis.* Memphis: Memphis State University Press, 1957.

Nager, Larry. *Memphis Beat: The Lives and Times of America's Musical Crossroads.* New York: St. Martin's Press, 1998.

O'Reilly, Kenneth. *"Racial Matters": The FBI's Secret File on Black America, 1960–1972.* New York: Free Press, 1989.

Palmer, Robert. *Deep Blues: A Musical and Cultural History.* New York: Viking Penguin, 1981.

Panabaker, James. *Two Gates to the City: Shelby Foote and the Art of History.* Knoxville: University of Tennessee Press, 2004.

Pearson, Hugh. *When Harlem Nearly Killed King: The 1958 Stabbing of Dr. Martin Luther King Jr.* New York: Seven Stories Press, 2002.

Percy, William Alexander. *Lanterns on the Levee: Recollections of a Planter's Son.* New York: Alfred A. Knopf, 1941.

Phillips, Robert L. *Shelby Foote: Novelist and Historian.* Jackson: University of Mississippi Press, 1992.

Poitier, Sidney. *This Life.* New York: Ballantine Books, 1981.

Posner, Gerald. *Killing the Dream: James Earl Ray and the Assassination of Martin Luther King Jr.* New York: Random House, 1998.

Powers, Georgia Davis. *I Shared the Dream: The Pride, Passion, and Politics of the First Black Woman Senator from Kentucky.* Far Hills, N.J.: New Horizon Press, 1995.

Powers, Richard Gid. *Secrecy and Power: The Life of J. Edgar Hoover.* New York: Free Press, 1987.

Raban, Jonathan. *Old Glory: A Voyage Down the Mississippi.* New York: Vintage Books, 1981.

Raichelson, Richard M. *Beale Street Talks: A Walking Tour Down the Home of the Blues.* Memphis: Arcadia Records, 1999.

Raines, Howell. *My Soul Is Rested: Movement Days in the Deep South Remembered.* New York: G. P. Putnam's Sons, 1977.

Rasmussen, Nicolas. *On Speed: The Many Lives of Amphetamine.* New York: New York University Press, 2008.

Ray, James Earl. *Tennessee Waltz: The Making of a Political Prisoner.* St. Andrews, Tenn.: Saint Andrew's Press, 1987.

————. *Who Killed Martin Luther King? The True Story by the Alleged Assassin.* New York: Marlowe, 1992.

Ray, John Larry, with Lyndon Barsten. *Truth at Last: The Untold Story Behind James Earl Ray and the Assassination of Martin Luther King Jr.* Guilford, Conn.: Lyons Press, 2008.

Risen, Clay. *A Nation on Fire: America in the Wake of the King Assassination.* Hoboken, N.J.: John Wiley & Sons, 2009.

Roberts, Gene, and Hank Klibanoff. *The Race Beat: The Press, the Civil Rights Struggle, and the Awakening of a Nation*. New York: Alfred A. Knopf, 2006.

Robertson, David. *W. C. Handy: The Life and Times of the Man Who Made the Blues*. New York: Alfred A. Knopf, 2009.

Roper, James. *The Founding of Memphis, 1818–1820*. Memphis: West Tennessee Historical Society, 1970.

Rowan, Carl T. *Breaking the Barriers: A Memoir*. Boston: Little, Brown, 1991.

Rustin, Bayard. *Down the Line: The Collected Writings of Bayard Rustin*. Chicago: Quadrangle Books, 1971.

Sigafoos, Robert A. *Cotton Row to Beale Street: A Business History of Memphis*. Memphis: Memphis State University Press, 1979.

Sullivan, William C., with Bill Brown. *The Bureau: My Thirty Years in Hoover's FBI*. New York: W. W. Norton, 1979.

Taylor, Peter. *The Old Forest and Other Stories*. New York: Ballantine Books, 1986.

———. *A Summons to Memphis*. New York: Alfred A. Knopf, 1986.

Timmerman, Kenneth R. *Shakedown: Exposing the Real Jesse Jackson*. Washington, D.C.: Regnery Publishing, 2002.

Tolson, Jay, ed. *The Correspondence of Shelby Foote and Walker Percy*. New York: W. W. Norton, 1997.

Tucker, David M. *Memphis Since Crump: Bossism, Blacks, and Civil Reformers, 1948–1968*. Knoxville: University of Tennessee Press, 1980.

Twain, Mark. *Life on the Mississippi*. New York: Signet Classic, 1961.

Vivian, Octavia. *Coretta: The Story of Coretta Scott King*. Minneapolis: Fortress Press, 2006.

Waldron, Lamar, with Thom Hartmann. *Legacy of Secrecy: Robert Kennedy, National Security, the Mafia, and the Assassination of Martin Luther King*. Berkeley, Calif.: Counterpoint, 2008.

Washington, James M., ed. *A Testament of Hope: The Essential Writings of Martin Luther King Jr*. New York: Harper & Row, 1986.

Weeks, Linton. *Memphis: A Folk History*. Little Rock, Ark.: Parkhurst, 1982.

Weisberg, Harold. *Martin Luther King: The Assassination*. New York: Carroll & Graf, 1993.

Wells, Ida B. *Crusade for Justice: The Autobiography of Ida B. Wells*. Edited by Alfreda M. Duster. Chicago: University of Chicago Press, 1970.

Werner, Craig. *A Change Is Gonna Come: Music, Race, and the Soul of America*. Ann Arbor: University of Michigan Press, 2006.

Wilkins, Roger. *A Man's Life: An Autobiography*. Woodbridge, Conn.: Ox Bow Press, 1982.

Williams, Juan. *Eyes on the Prize: America's Civil Rights Years, 1954–1965*. New York: Viking, 1987.

Wills, Garry. *The Second Civil War: Arming for Armageddon*. New York: New American Library, 1968.

Withers, Ernest C., with Jack F. Hurley, Brooks Johnson, and Daniel J. Wolff. *Pictures Tell the Story: Ernest C. Withers, Reflections in History*. Norfolk, Va.: Chrysler Museum of Art, 2000.

Wofford, Harris. *Of Kennedys and Kings: Making Sense of the Sixties*. New York: Farrar, Straus and Giroux, 1980.

Woodruff, Nan. *American Congo: The American Freedom Struggle in the Delta*. Cambridge, Mass.: Harvard University Press, 2003.

Woodward, C. Vann. *The Burden of Southern History*. New York: New American Library, 1969.

———. *The Strange Career of Jim Crow*. New York: Oxford University Press, 1974.

Yafa, Stephen. *Big Cotton: How a Humble Fiber Created Fortunes, Wrecked Civilizations, and Put America on the Map*. New York: Viking, 2005.

Young, Andrew. *An Easy Burden: The Civil Rights Movement and the Transformation of America*. New York: HarperCollins, 1996.

———. *A Way Out of No Way: The Spiritual Memoirs of Andrew Young*. Nashville: Thomas Nelson, 1994.

ORAL HISTORY

I made extensive use of oral histories collected by the Memphis Multi-Media Archival Project housed at the Ned R. McWherter Library at the University of Memphis. This extraordinary research endeavor, undertaken in the late 1960s by the Memphis Search for Meaning Committee under the direction of Carol and David Yellin, includes audiotape, videotape, and oral histories collected from hundreds of eyewitnesses to the 1968 events in Memphis—including the sanitation strike, King's appearances, and the assassination and its aftermath.

My collaboration with the Insignia Films documentary *Roads to Memphis* (produced for the PBS series *The American Experience*) also yielded a substantial body of oral history. Subjects interviewed for the series include Andrew Young, Benjamin Hooks, Harris Wofford, Arthur Hanes Jr., Ramsey Clark, Louis Stokes, Samuel "Billy" Kyles, Dorothy Cotton, Roger Wilkins, John Campbell, Vince Hughes, Joseph Sweat, Dan Rather, and Gerald Posner.

SELECTED MAGAZINE AND JOURNAL ARTICLES

Biles, Roger. "Cotton Fields or Skyscrapers? The Case of Memphis, Tennessee." *Historian: A Journal of History* (Feb. 1988).

Huie, William Bradford. "I Got Involved Gradually, and I Didn't Know Anybody Was to Be Murdered." *Look*, Nov. 22, 1968.

———. "I Had Been in Trouble All My Life, in Jail Most of It." *Look*, Nov. 12, 1968.

———. "The Story of James Earl Ray and the Plot to Assassinate Martin Luther King." *Look*, Nov. 22, 1968.

———. "Why James Earl Ray Murdered Dr. King." *Look*, April 1969.

"I Still Believe We Shall Overcome: The Martin Luther King Jr. Assassination, 40th Anniversary Issue." *Memphis*, April 2008.

King, Coretta Scott. "Tragedy in Memphis." *Life*, Sept. 19, 1969.

McKinley, James. "Interview with James Earl Ray." *Playboy*, Sept. 1977.

McKnight, Gerald D. "The 1968 Memphis Sanitation Strike and the FBI: A Case Study in Urban Surveillance." *South Atlantic Quarterly* 83 (Spring 1984).

O'Neil, Paul. "Ray, Sirhan—What Possessed Them?" *Life*, June 21, 1968.

"Ray's Breakout." *Time*, June 20, 1977.

"Ray's Escape." *Newsweek*, June 20, 1977.

Shaw, Bynum. "Are You Sure Who Killed Martin Luther King?" *Esquire*, March 1972.

Wills, Garry. "Martin Luther King Is Still on the Case." *Esquire*, Aug. 1968, reprinted in *The New Journalism*, edited by Tom Wolfe. London: Picador, 1996.